BRAIN AND MEMORY

Modulation and Mediation of Neuroplasticity

EDITED BY

James L. McGaugh

Norman M. Weinberger

Gary Lynch

New York   Oxford
OXFORD UNIVERSITY PRESS
1995

Oxford University Press

Oxford   New York
Athens Auckland Bangkok Bombay
Calcutta Capetown Dar es Salaam Delhi
Florence Hong Kong Istanbul Karachi
Kuala Lumpur Madras Madrid Melbourne
Mexico City Nairobi Paris Singapore
Taipei Tokyo Toronto

and associated companies in
Berlin Ibadan

Copyright © 1995 by Oxford University Press, Inc.

This work relates to Department of Navy Grant N00014-92-J-1853 issued
by the Office of Naval Research. The United States Government has a royalty-free
license throughout the world in all copyrightable material contained herein.

Published by Oxford University Press, Inc.
200 Madison Avenue, New York, New York 10016

Oxford is a registered trademark of Oxford University Press

Library of Congress Cataloging-in-Publication Data
Brain and memory : modulation and mediation of neuroplasticity /
edited by James L. McGaugh, Norman M. Weinberger, Gary Lynch.
p. cm.
"This work relates to Department of Navy Grant N00014-92-J-1853
issued by the Office of Naval Research"—T.p. verso.
Based on a conference organized by the Center for the Neurobiology
of Learning and Memory at the University of California, Irvine.
Includes bibliographical references and index.
ISBN 0-19-508294-X
1. Memory—Congresses. 2. Neuroplasticity—Congresses.
I. McGaugh, James L. II. Weinberger, Norman M. III. Lynch, Gary.
IV. University of California, Irvine. Center for the Neurobiology
of Learning and Memory.
[DNLM: 1. Memory—physiology—congresses. 2. Neuronal
Plasticity—congresses. 3. Brain—physiology—congresses.
WL 102 B81225 1995]
QP406.B69 1995
612.8′2—dc20
DNLM/DLC 94-4499

9 8 7 6 5 4 3 2 1

Printed in the United States of America
on acid-free paper

Preface

We are approaching the end of the first century of research attempting to discover how the brain enables us to acquire, retain, and use information based on experiences. The first half-century ended with Lashley's progress report (1950) and Hebb's attempt to provide a theory of brain organization and plasticity that was faithful to the facts of behavior (1949). The past several decades have witnessed an ever accelerating pace of research on brain and memory. The increase is, of course, due to the development of new techniques for the analysis of brain and behavior. But, to a greater extent the research efforts have been fueled by some seminal findings and the accumulation of knowledge based on systematic inquiry in many laboratories throughout the world. Simply put, in this last decade of the twentieth century our understanding of the neurobiological bases of learning and memory, as incomplete as it is, is enormously more detailed than that of our research ancestors and includes many unanticipated critical facts and concepts.

Over the century, the "big" questions have remained the central ones: What processes underlie the formation of new memories? What processes determine the strength of memories? Where are the changes underlying memory located? In judging research progress it is important to ask periodically what we have learned about each of these questions. Furthermore, it is equally important to see how these questions are rephrased and refined by new findings, hypotheses, and theories.

The chapters in this book review recent progress in research investigating (1) emotion and memory, (2) aging and memory, (3) plasticity of the cerebral cortex, and (4) synaptic connectivity and memory. James, Pavlov, Lashley, Hebb, and the other pioneers in this field would, of course, find these topics familiar. But they would also find that in recent years these topics have been investigated in unexpected ways and that the findings have greatly expanded the questions that can be asked as well as the experimental techniques that can be employed. And, we believe that they would be delighted, if not astounded, by the progress that has been made in understanding the brain processes underlying learning and memory.

Irvine, Calif.   J. L. McG.
October 1993   N. M. W.
                                                                          G. L.

Acknowledgments

This book, which is the fifth in a series, is based on a conference organized by the Center for the Neurobiology of Learning and Memory at the University of California, Irvine, and held in Irvine from October 22 to 24, 1992. The planning for the conference and the book grew out of extensive and often animated discussions with many of our colleagues in the Center, including Michel Baudry, Ron Frostig, Richard Granger, Mary-Louise Kean, Michael Leon, Rachael Neve, Gordon Shaw, Arthur Shimamura, Larry Squire, Larry Stein, Richard Thompson, and Stuart Zola-Morgan. We are grateful to the National Science Foundation, the Office of Naval Research, and the University of California, Irvine Office of Research and Graduate Studies for their support of the conference. The conference was superbly managed and coordinated by Lynn Brown with the able assistance of Nan Collett, Deanna Sanders, and Lori LaSalle. We also thank Lynn Brown and Nan Collett for editorial assistance.

Contents

Contributors

AILEEN J. ANDERSON
Department of Psychobiology
University of California
Irvine, California

C. A. BARNES
Division of Neural Systems,
    Memory and Aging
University of Arizona
Tucson, Arizona

FRANÇOIS BURETTE
Laboratoire de Neurobiologie de
    l'Apprentissage et de la Mémoire
Centre National de la Recherche
    Scientifique
Université Paris-Sud
Orsay, France

REBECCA D. BURWELL
Department of Psychology
University of North Carolina
Chapel Hill, North Carolina

MICHAEL B. CALFORD
Vision Touch and Hearing Research
    Center
The University of Queensland
Brisbane, Queensland, Australia

SERGE CAMPEAU
Department of Psychiatry
Yale University
Connecticut Mental Health Center
New Haven, Connecticut

CARL W. COTMAN
Department of Psychobiology
University of California
Irvine, California

CORINNA DARIAN-SMITH
Rockefeller University
New York, New York

K. L. DAVIS
Department of Psychiatry
Mt. Sinai School of Medicine
New York, New York

MICHAEL DAVIS
Department of Psychiatry
Yale University
Connecticut Mental Health Center
New Haven, Connecticut

S. DAVIS
Division of Neural Systems,
    Memory and Aging
University of Arizona
Tucson, Arizona

VALÉRIE DOYÈRE
Laboratoire de Neurobiologie de
    l'Apprentissage et de la Mémoire
Centre National de la Recherche
    Scientifique
Université Paris-Sud
Orsay, France

YADIN DUDAI
Department of Neurobiology
Weizmann Institute of Science
Rehovot, Israel

C. A. ERICKSON
Department of Psychology
University of Arizona
Tucson, Arizona

WILLIAM A. FALLS
Department of Psychiatry
Yale University
Connecticut Mental Health Center
New Haven, Connecticut

CALEB E. FINCH
Andrus Gerontology Center
University of Southern California
Los Angeles, California

JOAQUIN M. FUSTER
Neuropsychiatric Institute
University of California
Los Angeles, California

FRED H. GAGE
Department of Neuroscience
University of California, San Diego
La Jolla, California

MICHELA GALLAGHER
Department of Psychology
University of North Carolina
Chapel Hill, North Carolina

C. R. GALLISTEL
Department of Psychology
University of California
Los Angeles, California

CHARLES D. GILBERT
Rockefeller University
New York, New York

PAUL E. GOLD
Department of Psychology
University of Virginia
Charlottesville, Virginia

V. HAROUTUNIAN
Department of Psychiatry
Mt. Sinai School of Medicine
New York, New York

FRIDERIKE HEUER
Lewis and Clark College
Portland, Oregon

JON H. KAAS
Department of Psychology
Vanderbilt University
Nashville, Tennessee

MUNSOO KIM
Department of Psychiatry
Yale University
Connecticut Mental Health Center
New Haven, Connecticut

Y. KOMATSU
Department of Physiology
Kyoto Prefectural School of
    Medicine
Kawaramachi-Hirokoji
Kamikhyoku, Kyoto, Japan

SERGE LAROCHE
Laboratoire de Neurobiologie de
    l'Apprentissage et de la Mémoire
Centre National de la Recherche
    Scientifique
Université Paris-Sud
Orsay, France

B. L. MCNAUGHTON
Division of Neural Systems,
    Memory and Aging
University of Arizona
Tucson, Arizona

ALAN H. NAGAHARA
Anatomy Department
Stritch School of Medicine
Loyola University
Maywood, Illinois

CATHERINE RÉDINI-DEL NEGRO
Laboratoire de Neurobiologie de
l'Apprentissage et de la Mémoire
Centre National de la Recherche
Scientifique
Université Paris-Sud
Orsay, France

SCOTT P. ORR
Harvard Medical School
Psychophysiology Laboratory
V.A. Research Service
Manchester, New Hampshire

ROGER K. PITMAN
Harvard Medical School
Psychophysiology Laboratory
V.A. Research Service
Manchester, New Hampshire

DANIEL REISBERG
Department of Psychology
Reed College
Portland, Oregon

A. C. SANTUCCI
Department of Psychiatry
Mt. Sinai School of Medicine
New York, New York

URSULA V. STAUBLI
Center for Neural Science
New York University
New York, New York

M. TANIFUJI
Department of Physiology
Kyoto Prefectural School of
Medicine
Kawaramachi-Hirokoji
Kamikhyoku, Kyoto, Japan

K. TOYAMA
Department of Physiology
Kyoto Prefectural School of
Medicine
Kawaramachi-Hirokoji
Kamikhyoku, Kyoto, Japan

W. WALLACE
Department of Psychiatry
Mt. Sinai School of Medicine
New York, New York

NORMAN M. WHITE
Department of Psychology
McGill University
Montreal, Quebec, Canada

I

Emotion and Memory

1

Neural Systems of Emotion: The Amygdala's Role in Fear and Anxiety

MICHAEL DAVIS
SERGE CAMPEAU
MUNSOO KIM
WILLIAM A. FALLS

In addition to its role in appetitive and perhaps attentional processes (e.g., Gallagher & Holland, 1992; Kapp, Whalen, Supple, & Pascoe, 1992), converging evidence now indicates that the amygdala, and its many efferent projections, may represent a central fear system involved in both the expression and acquisition of conditioned fear (Davis, 1992; Gloor, 1960; Gray, 1989; Kapp & Pascoe, 1986; Kapp, Pascoe, & Bixler, 1984; Kapp, Wilson, Pascoe, Supple, & Whalen, 1990; LeDoux, 1987; Sarter & Markowitsch, 1985). The amygdala receives highly processed sensory information from all modalities through its lateral and basolateral nuclei (Amaral, 1987; LeDoux, Cicchetti, Xagoraris, & Romanski, 1990a; Ottersen, 1980; Turner, 1981; Van Hoesen, 1981). In turn, these nuclei project to the central amygdaloid nucleus (Aggleton, 1985; Amaral, 1987; Krettek & Price, 1978b; Millhouse & DeOlmos, 1983; Nitecka, Amerski, & Narkiewicz, 1981; Niteka & Frotscher, 1989; Ottersen, 1982; Roberts, Woodhams, Polak, & Crow, 1982; Russchen, 1982; Smith & Millhouse, 1985), which then projects to a variety of hypothalamic and brainstem target areas (Fig. 1.1) that directly mediate specific signs of fear and anxiety (cf. Davis, 1992). Electrical stimulation of the amygdala elicits many of the behaviors used to define a state of fear, whereas stimulation of selected target areas of the amygdala produces more selective effects. Conditioned fear may result when a formerly neutral stimulus now comes to activate the amygdala by virtue of pairing that stimulus with an aversive event. In fact, the amygdala has long been implicated in the evaluation and memory of emotionally significant stimuli (Bennett, Liang, & McGaugh, 1985; Bresnahan & Routtenberg, 1972; Ellis & Kesner, 1983; Gallagher & Kapp, 1978, 1981;

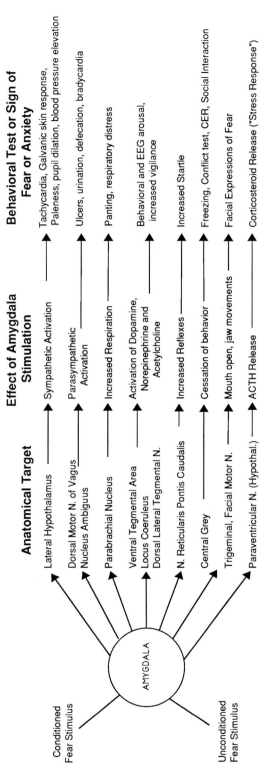

Anatomical Target

- Lateral Hypothalamus
- Dorsal Motor N. of Vagus
  Nucleus Ambiguus
- Parabrachial Nucleus
- Ventral Tegmental Area
  Locus Coeruleus
  Dorsal Lateral Tegmental N.
- N. Reticularis Pontis Caudalis
- Central Grey
- Trigeminal, Facial Motor N.
- Paraventricular N. (Hypothal.)

Effect of Amygdala Stimulation

- Sympathetic Activation
- Parasympathetic Activation
- Increased Respiration
- Activation of Dopamine, Norepinephrine and Acetylcholine
- Increased Reflexes
- Cessation of behavior
- Mouth open, jaw movements
- ACTH Release

Behavioral Test or Sign of Fear or Anxiety

- Tachycardia, Galvanic skin response, Paleness, pupil dilation, blood pressure elevation
- Ulcers, urination, defecation, bradycardia
- Panting, respiratory distress
- Behavioral and EEG arousal, increased vigilance
- Increased Startle
- Freezing, Conflict test, CER, Social Interaction
- Facial Expressions of Fear
- Corticosteroid Release ("Stress Response")

Conditioned Fear Stimulus

AMYGDALA

Unconditioned Fear Stimulus

FIGURE 1.1. Schematic diagram showing direct connections between the central nucleus of the amygdala and a variety of hypothalamic and brainstem target areas that may be involved in different animal tests of fear and anxiety. (From Davis, 1992, with permission from Wiley-Liss, Inc.)

Gallagher, Kapp, Frysinger, & Rapp, 1980; Gold, Hankins, Edwards, Chester, & McGaugh, 1975; Handwerker, Gold & McGaugh, 1974; Kesner, 1982; Liang, Bennett, & McGaugh, 1985; Liang, Bennett, & McGaugh, 1986; McGaugh, Introini-Collision, Nagahara, Cahill, Brioni, & Castellano, 1990; Mishkin & Aggleton, 1981) and may be at least a temporary site of plasticity for aversive conditioning, because treatments that alter amygdala function have profound effects on aversive conditioning (cf. McGaugh et al., 1990).

THE FEAR-POTENTIATED STARTLE PARADIGM

Over the last several years, our laboratory has been studying the role of the amygdala in fear conditioning using the fear-potentiated startle paradigm. This phenomenon was first described by Brown, Kalish, and Farber (1951) who demonstrated that the amplitude of the acoustic startle reflex in the rat can be augmented by presenting the eliciting auditory startle stimulus in the presence of a cue (e.g., a noise or a light) that has previously been paired with a shock. This augmentation of startle has been termed the "fear-potentiated startle effect" and has been replicated using either an auditory or visual conditioned stimulus (cf. Davis, 1986). In this paradigm, rats are first trained to be fearful of a weak neutral stimulus, such as a visual or auditory stimulus (conditioned stimulus [CS]), by consistently pairing it with an aversive stimulus, such as a footshock (Fig. 1.2). Following this training session, the startle reflex is elicited by a loud noise burst in the presence or the absence of the CS. Fear-potentiated startle is said to occur if startle is larger in amplitude when elicited in the presence versus the absence of the CS. Potentiated startle occurs only following paired presentations of the CS and the shock and not following unpaired or "random" presentations, which indicates that it is a valid measure of associative conditioning (Davis & Astrachan, 1978). In rats, increased startle in the presence of the CS still occurs very reliably at least one month after original training, making it appropriate for the study of long-term memory as well (Campeau, Liang, & Davis, 1990; Cassella & Davis, 1985).

THE ROLE OF THE AMYGDALA
IN FEAR-POTENTIATED STARTLE

A major advantage of the potentiated startle paradigm is that fear is measured by a change in a relatively simple reflex. Hence, with potentiated startle, fear is expressed through some neural circuit that is activated by the conditioned stimulus and ultimately impinges on the startle circuit. Figure 1.3 shows a schematic summary diagram of the amygdala and its connection to the startle pathway that we believe is required for fear-potentiated startle. These pathways involve convergence of a CS and an unconditioned shock stimulus (US) at the lateral and baso-

TRAINING: LIGHT and SHOCK PAIRED

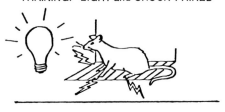

TESTING:

NOISE-ALONE
TRIALS

NORMAL STARTLE (in dark)

LIGHT-NOISE
TRIALS

POTENTIATED STARTLE (in light)

FIGURE 1.2. Cartoon depicting the fear-potentiated startle paradigm. During training, a neutral stimulus (conditioned stimulus) such as a light is consistently paired with a foot-shock. In training, a 3700-msec light is typically paired with a 500-msec, 0.6-mA shock presented 3200 msec after the light onset. During testing, startle is elicited by an auditory stimulus (e.g., a 100-dB burst of white noise) in the presence (Light–Noise trial type) or absence (Noise-Alone trial type) of the conditioned stimulus. In testing, the noise burst is typically presented 3200 msec after light onset (i.e., at the same time as the shock was presented in training). It is important to note that the rat does not startle to light onset, but only to the noise burst presented alone or 3200 msec after light onset. This is simply a cartoon so that the positions and postures that are pictured may not mimic the actual behavior of the animals. (From Davis, Hitchcock, & Rosen, 1987, with permission from Academic Press)

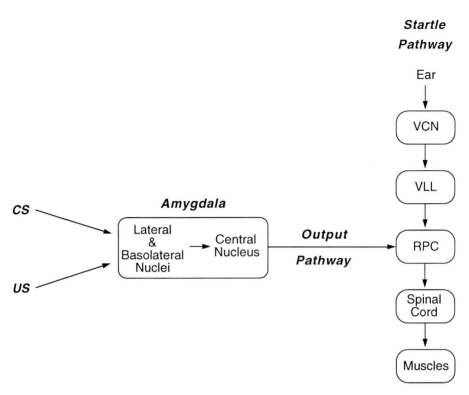

FIGURE 1.3. Proposed neural pathways involved in fear-potentiated startle. Convergence of the conditioned stimulus and the unconditioned stimulus occurs at the lateral and basolateral amygdaloid nuclei which in turn project to the central amygdaloid nucleus. Activation of the central nucleus of the amygdala may be both necessary and sufficient to facilitate startle through a direct connection to the nucleus reticularis pontis caudalis, an obligatory part of the acoustic startle pathway.

lateral amygdaloid nuclei, which then project to the central nucleus of the amygdala, which then projects directly to a particular nucleus in the acoustic startle pathway.

The Acoustic Startle Pathway

In the rat, the latency of acoustic startle is 6 msec recorded electromyographically in the foreleg and 8 msec in the hindleg (Ison, McAdam, & Hammond, 1973). This very short latency indicates that only a few synapses could be involved in mediating acoustic startle. Using a variety of techniques (Davis, Gendelman, Tischler, & Gendelman, 1982; Cassella & Davis, 1986b), we have proposed that the acoustic startle reflex is mediated serially by the ventral cochlear nucleus (VCN), an area just medial and ventral to the ventral nucleus of the lateral lemniscus (VLL) (the paralemniscal zone or the central nucleus of the acoustic tract), an area just dorsal to the superior olives in the nucleus reticularis pontis caudalis

(RPC), and motor neurons in the spinal cord. Bilateral lesions using ibotenic acid in each of these nuclei eliminate startle, whereas lesions in a variety of other auditory or motor areas do not. Startlelike responses can be elicited electrically from each of these nuclei, with progressively shorter latencies as the electrode is moved further along the pathway (Davis et al., 1982).

The Point in the Startle Pathway where Fear Alters Neural Transmission

We have attempted to determine the point within the startle circuit where a fearful stimulus ultimately modulates transmission following conditioning. In these studies, startlelike responses were elicited electrically from various points along the startle pathway before and after presentation of a light that was either paired or not paired with a shock in different groups of rats (Berg & Davis, 1985). Startle elicited electrically from either the ventral cochlear nucleus or from the paralemniscal zone was potentiated by a conditioned fear stimulus, whereas elicitation of startle in the nucleus reticularis pontis caudalis or beyond was not. Based on these and other data (see below), we have concluded that fear ultimately alters transmission at the nucleus reticularis pontis caudalis.

Lesions of the Central Nucleus of the Amygdala Block Fear-Potentiated Startle

Electrolytic lesions of the central nucleus of the amygdala (Hitchcock & Davis, 1986) or ibotenic-acid-induced destruction of cell bodies in the central nucleus (Hitchcock & Davis, unpublished observations) completely block fear-potentiated startle. A visual prepulse test indicated that the blockade of potentiated startle observed in animals with lesions of the amygdala could not be attributed to gross visual impairment. Fear-potentiated startle is also eliminated by electrolytic- (Hitchcock & Davis, 1987) or ibotenic-induced (Campeau & Davis, submitted) lesions of the central nucleus of the amygdala when an auditory conditioned stimulus is used.

Electrical Stimulation of the Amygdala Increases Acoustic Startle

Electrical stimulation of the amygdala has been reported to produce fearlike behaviors in many animals, including humans (cf. Davis, 1992). We have found that startle is an extremely sensitive index of amygdala stimulation because low-level electrical stimulation of the amygdala (e.g., 40–400 μA, 25-msec trains of 0.1-msec square-wave cathodal pulses) markedly increases acoustic startle amplitude (Rosen & Davis, 1988a) with no obvious signs of behavioral activation at the stimulation currents and durations employed. Moreover, the duration of stimulation is well below that used to produce kindling in rats (Handforth, 1984), so that the effects on startle are not associated with convulsions.

With electrical stimulation of the amygdala, the excitatory effect on startle appears to develop very rapidly. By eliciting startle at various times before and after electrical stimulation of the amygdala, we estimate a transit time of about 5 msec from the amygdala to the startle pathway (Rosen & Davis, 1988b), comparable to the very short latency (2–5 msec) of facilitation of trigeminal motoneurons following amygdala stimulation reported by Ohta (1984). This very rapid facilitation means that the increase in startle is not secondary to autonomic or hormonal changes that might be produced by amygdala stimulation, because these would have a much longer latency. In addition, electrical stimulation of the amygdala alone does not elicit startle at these currents. Moreover, electrical stimulation of several other nearby brain areas such as the endopiriform nucleus, fundus striati, internal capsule, or some sites in the basolateral nucleus of the amygdala does not increase startle. Finally, using electrically elicited startle, electrical stimulation of the amygdala appears to modulate startle at the level of the nucleus reticularis pontis caudalis (Rosen & Davis, 1990), like conditioned fear.

The Role of Various Amygdala Projection Areas in Fear-Potentiated Startle

The central nucleus of the amygdala projects to a variety of brain regions via two major efferent pathways, the stria terminalis and the ventral amygdalofugal pathway. The caudal part of the ventral amygdalofugal pathway is known to project directly to the pons, medulla, and spinal cord (Krettek & Price, 1978a; Mizuno, Takahashi, Satoda, & Matsushima, 1985; Post & Mai, 1980; Price & Amaral, 1981; Sandrew, Edwards, Poletti, & Foote, 1986; Schwaber, Kapp, Higgins, & Rapp, 1982). Inagaki, Kawai, Matsuzak, Shiosake & Tohyama (1983) reported direct connections between the central nucleus of the amygdala and the exact part of the nucleus reticularis pontis caudalis that is critical for startle (an area just dorsal to the superior olives). We have confirmed this direct connection using anterograde (Phaseolus vulgaris-leucoagglutinin (PHA-L)) and retrograde (Fluro-Gold) tracing techniques (Rosen, Hitchcock, Sananes, Miserendino, & Davis, 1991). In addition, we have found that electrolytic lesions at various points along the output pathway of the amygdala to the startle circuit completely block fear-potentiated startle (Hitchcock & Davis, 1991). In contrast, lesions of the other major output of the amygdala through the stria terminalis and bed nucleus of the stria terminalis do not block fear-potentiated startle.

A diagram of the output pathways of the central nucleus of the amygdala and the effects of lesions at various points along this pathway is summarized in Figure 1.4. Lesions of the stria terminals itself, or the bed nucleus of the stria terminalis, a major projection area of this pathway, do not block potentiated startle. Knife cuts of the rostral part of the ventral amygdalofugal pathway, which would interrupt its projections to the rostral lateral hypothalamus and substantia innominata, also fail to block potentiated startle. On the other hand, lesions of the caudal part of the ventral amygdalofugal pathway, at the point where it passes through the subthalamic area and cerebral peduncles, completely block potentiated startle.

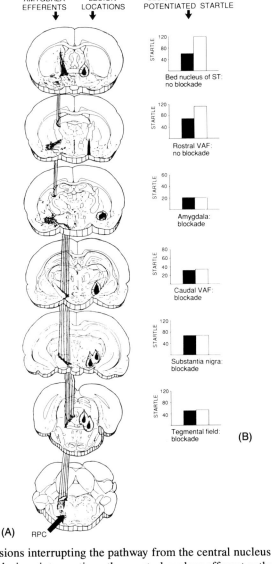

AMYGDALA
EFFERENTS

LESION
LOCATIONS

LESION EFFECTS ON
POTENTIATED STARTLE

Bed nucleus of ST:
no blockade

Rostral VAF:
no blockade

Amygdala:
blockade

Caudal VAF:
blockade

Substantia nigra:
blockade

Tegmental field:
blockade   **(B)**

(A)   RPC

FIGURE 1.4.   Lesions interrupting the pathway from the central nucleus of the amygdala to the RPC, but not lesions interrupting other central nucleus efferent pathways, block fear-potentiated startle. (A) A series of coronal rat brain sections, with the top section being the most rostral. The left sides of the sections show a schematic representation, based on PHA-L tracing studies, of the efferent pathways of the central nucleus of the amygdala. The right sides of the sections show representative lesions that interrupted the central nucleus effer-ent pathways at various levels. The black areas represent the cavities produced by the lesions and the stippled areas represent the surrounding gliosis. (B) Graphs showing the effects of bilateral lesions in each area on fear-potentiated startle. The graphs show the mean amplitude startle response on Noise-Alone trials (black-bars) and Light–Noise trials (white bars) in rats given bilateral lesions in the locations shown in the corresponding brain section to the left of the graph. (Adapted from Hitchcock & Davis, 1991, with permission from the American Psychological Association)

Lesions of the substantia nigra, which receives central amygdaloid nucleus projections as well as fibers of passage from the central nucleus of the amygdala to more caudal brainstem regions, also block potentiated startle. This blockade does not seem to involve dopamine cells in the zona compacta because infusion of the dopamine neurotoxin 6-OHDA into the substantia nigra did not block potentiated startle despite over a 90% depletion of dopamine in the caudate nucleus. Finally, lesions of the lateral tegmental field, caudal to the substantia nigra, also block fear-potentiated startle (Hitchcock & Davis, 1991).

Effects of Lesions of the Lateral and/or Basolateral Amygdaloid Nuclei on Potentiated Startle

Most sensory information enters the amygdala through its lateral and basolateral nuclei (Amaral, 1987; LeDoux et al., 1990; Ottersen, 1980; Turner, 1981; Van Hoesen, 1981). In turn, these nuclei project to the central nucleus (Amaral, 1987; Aggleton, 1985; Krettek & Price, 1978b; Millhouse & DeOlmos, 1983; Niteka & Frotscher, 1989; Nitecka et al., 1981; Ottersen, 1982; Roberts et al., 1982; Russchen, 1982; Smith & Millhouse, 1985), which, as discussed earlier, then projects directly to the acoustic startle pathway. Recent evidence indicates that the lateral nucleus of the amygdala provides a critical link for relaying auditory information to the central nucleus of the amygdala involved in fear conditioning using an auditory conditioned stimulus (LeDoux et al., 1990). Hence, we wondered how lesions of the lateral and basolateral nuclei would affect fear-potentiated startle (Sananes & Davis, 1992). Selective destruction of the lateral and basolateral nuclei was accomplished by local infusion of N-methyl-D-aspartate (NMDA) into the basolateral nucleus (Crooks, Robinson, Hatfield, Graham, & Gallagher, 1989; Lewis et al., 1989), based on extensive work with this technique in Dr. Michela Gallagher's laboratory, which generously supplied the details of the methodology.

Figure 1.5 shows that NMDA lesions of the lateral and basolateral nuclei completely blocked fear-potentiated startle when the lesions were made before training. Histological examination indicated complete, bilateral lesions of the lateral and basolateral nuclei. In addition, in most animals there was also damage to the dorsal endopiriform nucleus. Partial damage of the amygdalostriatal transition zone, medial aspects of the perirhinal cortex, and the ventral endopiriform nucleus was seen in some animals, although this was typically only unilateral. Most animals had sparing of the accessory basolateral nucleus and ventral basolateral nucleus and all animals had sparing of the central nucleus.

In these studies the NMDA lesions were performed before training, so that the blockade of potentiated startle could have resulted from a blockade of acquisition or a blockade of the expression of potentiated startle, or both. In a subsequent study, NMDA lesions of the lateral and basolateral nuclei also caused a complete blockade of fear-potentiated startle when lesioning was performed after training. Hence, these lesions clearly block the expression of fear-potentiated startle, probably because they prevent the conditioned stimulus from activating the amygdala. These animals can clearly see, however, because they still demonstrate

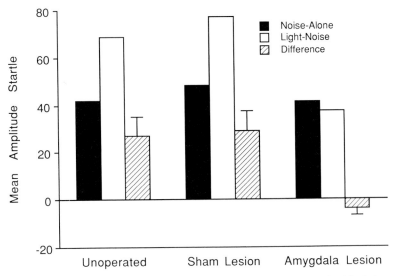

FIGURE 1.5. Mean amplitude startle response on Noise-Alone trials (black bars) and Light–Noise trials (white bars), and the difference between these two trial types (+ standard error of the mean, hatched bars), in rats given bilateral NMDA lesions of the lateral and basolateral nuclei of the amygdala. (From Sananes & Davis, 1992, with permission from the American Psychological Association)

visual prepulse inhibition comparable to that shown by normal rats. Very similar results have now been found using an auditory CS (Campeau & Davis, submitted). These results provide further evidence that the lateral/basolateral amygdaloid nuclei are obligatory relays in fear conditioned to visual or auditory stimuli.

The Visual Pathway Involved in Fear-Potentiated Startle

The data outlined thus far suggest that visual input critical for fear-potentiated startle using a visual conditioned stimulus may enter the amygdala through the lateral and/or basolateral nuclei, which then project to the central nucleus and which in turn projects to the startle pathway. At the present time, however, the visual pathway(s) critical for fear-potentiated startle using a visual conditioned stimulus linking the retina to these basolateral nuclei are still unclear. Recently, we have found that relatively small lesions of the perirhinal cortex completely block fear-potentiated startle, provided the lesion included an area of perirhinal cortex both dorsal and ventral to the rhinal sulcus (Rosen et al., 1992). McDonald and Jackson (1987) find heavy retrograde and anterograde labeling in the basolateral, accessory basolateral and especially the lateral nucleus of the amygdala after HRP–WGA deposits in the perirhinal cortex. Thus, it is possible that visual information is relayed from the perirhinal cortex to the amygdala, forming the last part of the conditioned stimulus pathway to the amygdala. Currently, we are using retrograde tracing techniques to evaluate how subcortical visual information might reach this area of the perirhinal cortex.

THE ROLE OF DIFFERENT AUDITORY AFFERENT
PATHWAYS TO THE AMYGDALA
IN FEAR-POTENTIATED STARTLE

Thus far we have not thoroughly investigated the neural pathways by which a visual CS can come to activate that amygdala, although some information on this question is available (Davis, Hitchcock, & Rosen, 1987). However, given the extensive information from other laboratories concerning the neural substrates of fear conditioning using auditory CSs (Iwata, LeDoux, Meeley, Arneric, & Reis, 1986; Jarrell, Romanski, Gentile, McCabe & Schneiderman, 1986a; Jarrell, Gentile, McCabe, & Schneiderman, 1986b; LeDoux et al., 1990a; LeDoux, Sakaguchi, & Reis, 1984; LeDoux, Sakaguchi, Iwata, & Reis, 1986) we have also been investigating the role of different auditory afferent pathways to the amygdala in fear-potentiated startle. At least three separate neural pathways could relay auditory information to the lateral and/or basolateral nuclei of the amygdala (Fig. 1.6). They all originate in the auditory thalamus, which comprises the medial geniculate nucleus and the immediately adjacent posterior intralaminar nucleus and peripeduncular area (Arnault & Roger, 1987, 1990; LeDoux, Farb, & Ruggiero, 1990; LeDoux, Farb, & Milner, 1991; LeDoux, Ruggiero, & Reis, 1985; LeDoux, Sakaguchi & Reis, 1984; Mehler, 1980; Ottersen, 1981a, 1981b; Ottersen & Ben-Ari, 1979; Roger & Arnault, 1989; Ryugo & Killackey, 1974; Turner & Herkenham, 1981, 1991; Veening, 1978). The first pathway involves direct projections from the medial division of the medial geniculate body (MGM), posterior intralaminar nucleus (PIL), and the peripeduncular area (PPA) to the lateral nucleus of the amygdala. The second pathway involves indirect projections from these same thalamic nuclei to the lateral nucleus of the amygdala via the perirhinal cortex (Guldin & Markowitsch, 1983; LeDoux, Farb, & Romanski, 1991; McDonald & Jackson, 1987; Turner & Zimmer, 1984). The third pathway involves projections from the ventral (MGV) and dorsal (MGD) divisions of the medial geniculate body to the primary and secondary auditory cortices (LeDoux, Ruggiero, & Reis, 1985; Roger & Arnault, 1989; Ryugo & Killackey, 1974), which in turn innervate the perirhinal cortex, itself sending terminals to the lateral/basolateral amygdaloid nuclei.

Lesions of the Entire Auditory Thalamus

Having shown the essential requirement of the lateral/basolateral amygdaloid nuclei in mediating auditory and visual fear conditioning, the role of the various auditory afferents to this complex was evaluated. To study the specificity of the lesion effects using an auditory conditioned stimulus while investigating the role

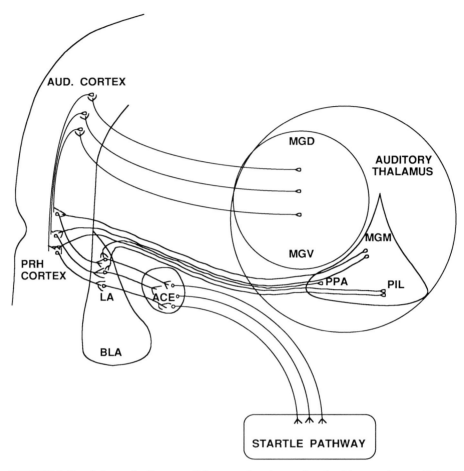

FIGURE 1.6.   Schematic diagram of the neural pathways involved in aversive conditioning using an auditory conditioned stimulus, as measured with the fear-potentiated startle paradigm. (*Abbreviations:* ACE, central amygdaloid nucleus; AUD.CORTEX, auditory cortex; BLA, basolateral amygdaloid nucleus; LA, lateral amygdaloid nucleus; MGD, dorsal division of the thalamic medial geniculate nucleus; MGM, medial division of the thalamic medial geniculate nucleus; MGV, ventral division of the thalamic medial geniculate nucleus; PIL, posterior intralaminar nucleus of the thalamus; PPA, peripeduncular area of the thalamus; PRH CORTEX, perirhinal cortex.)

of the auditory thalamus, a visual CS was also conditioned in the same training session. Thus, the training session in this and all subsequent experiments investigating potentiated startle to an auditory CS, consisted of 10 pairings of a 70 dB, 3.7-sec noise centered at 2 kHz (24 dB/octave attenuation), mixed with 10 pairings of a 3.7-sec bright fluorescent light, each coterminating with a 0.5-sec, 0.5-mA scrambled footshock, presented at a variable intertrial interval of 3.0 min (range: 1.5–4.5 min), on each of two consecutive days, for a total of 20 conditioning trials for each CS modality.

Because the auditory thalamus is the only source of subcortical and cortical auditory projections ultimately reaching the lateral nucleus of the amygdala, lesions of all auditory thalamic subnuclei were expected to specifically disrupt fear-potentiated startle using an auditory, as compared to a visual conditioned stimulus. Figure 1.7 shows that posttraining electrolytic lesions of the auditory thalamus specifically blocked the expression of fear-potentiated startle to the auditory CS,

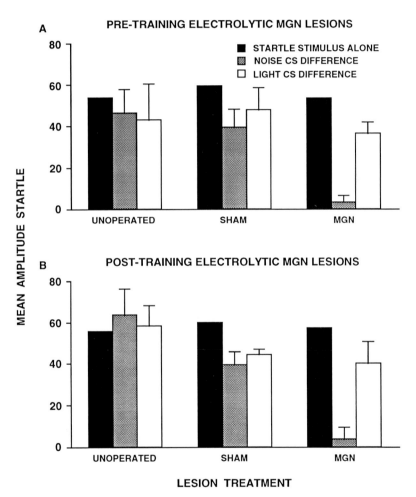

FIGURE 1.7. Fear-potentiated startle to auditory and visual conditioned stimuli in unoperated or sham operated rats, or rats given electrolytic lesions of the entire auditory thalamus (medial geniculate nucleus—MGN). Surgeries were made either before (A) or after (B) training. The black bars indicate mean amplitude startle in the absence of the CSs (startle stimulus alone), and the gray (noise CS difference) and white (visual CS difference) bars indicate the mean difference scores of the auditory and visual CSs, respectively. These difference scores (+ the standard errors of the means) represent the mean change in startle amplitude in the presence vs. the absence of the CSs.

while potentiation of the visual CS was not affected. The same results were obtained when rats were given fiber-sparing ibotenic acid lesions of the auditory thalamus (data not shown). To our knowledge, this is the first demonstration of a specific blockade of auditory fear conditioning by lesions of the auditory thalamus, when animals are tested simultaneously with two different CS modalities and in the same test procedure (see LeDoux, Iwata, Pearl, & Reis, 1986, for auditory-specific impairments using different tasks for auditory and visual learning). These results support the hypothesis that intrinsic neurons of the auditory thalamus are necessary for aversive conditioning using an auditory CS. Importantly, pretraining electrolytic lesions of the entire auditory thalamus blocked acquisition of fear-potentiated startle to the auditory CS but not to the visual CS (Fig. 1.7). These results do not support the hypothesis that the medial division of the medial geniculate and posterior intralaminar nuclei of the thalamus are essential in the mediation of nociceptive information during fear conditioning (Cruikshank, Edeline, & Weinberger, 1992; Romanski, Clugnet, Bordi, & LeDoux, 1990), although it cannot be ruled out that it might be sufficient to mediate transmission of nociceptive activity when these nuclei are intact (Cruikshank, Edeline, & Weinberger, 1992).

Lesions of Specific Auditory Thalamic Nuclei

Because lesions of the entire auditory thalamus selectively blocked fear-potentiated startle using an auditory CS, the role of specific auditory thalamic subnuclei and their terminal fields were investigated, given that the MGM, PIL, and PPA subnuclei project directly to the lateral amygdala, whereas the MGV and MGD subdivisions project only indirectly to the lateral amygdala. Posttraining electrolytic lesions aimed more specifically at the MGV and MGD subnuclei significantly attenuated potentiated startle to the auditory CS as compared to the unoperated and sham rats. However, this was not a complete blockade. Potentiation to the visual CS in these animals was nonsignificantly attenuated. Substantial, but nonsignificant attenuation of potentiated startle to both CS types was obtained in MGM/PIL/PPA lesioned rats. Histological analysis of these lesions indicated more ventrally placed lesions than originally intended. Because the efferent fibers from the central nucleus of the amygdala to the startle pathway course partly through that ventral region (see Fig. 1.4), it is probable that the attenuation of potentiated startle following these MGM/PIL/PPA lesions resulted from damage to these efferent fibers. Fiber-sparing NMDA lesions of the MGM/PIL/PPA versus MGV/MGD subdivisions are currently under way to evaluate this possibility.

These results suggest that the MGV and MGD subdivisions of the thalamus play a significant role in relaying auditory information to the amygdala. However, because lesions of selected auditory thalamic nuclei only partially blocked potentiated startle, compared to a complete blockade with lesions of the entire auditory thalamus, it would appear that efferents from each of the subnuclei may transmit auditory information in parallel to the amygdala, and that each of these pathways can, at least, partially support fear-potentiated startle. This conclusion is consistent with results from Jarrell, Gentile, Romanski, McCabe, and Schneiderman (1987), in which posttraining electrolytic lesions of either the MGM/PIL/PPA or the MGV/MGD thalamic subdivisions did not significantly attenuate bradycardiac CRs to their CS +, suggesting that either region alone is sufficient for the expression of auditory aversive conditioning.

Lesions of Auditory Cortex

To further dissociate the MGV and MGD from the MGM/PIL/PPA thalamic subdivisions, aspirations of the auditory cortex (the terminal fields of the MGV and MGD) were made before or after fear conditioning. Posttraining cortical aspirations tended to attenuate potentiated startle to an auditory CS to a greater extent than to a visual CS, although the decrease in potentiated startle to the auditory CS did not reach statistical significance. Again, this outcome indicates that the primary auditory cortical pathway, originating from the MGV and MGD subdivisions, is partially involved in the transmission of auditory information that ultimately reaches the lateral nucleus of the amygdala.

When the cortical aspirations were made before training, no deficits were observed with either auditory or visual CSs. The lack of effect of pretraining auditory cortical lesions on simple fear conditioning is consistent with prior observations using different species and classical aversive conditioning (LeDoux et al., 1986; Romanski & LeDoux, 1991; Teich et al., 1988) or avoidance procedures (Neff & Diamond, 1975). This indicates that the subcortical projections from the MGM/PIL/PPA nuclei may completely compensate for the deficits produced by auditory cortical damage produced prior to conditioning. The auditory cortex may be partially involved under normal conditions, however, as suggested by the partial loss of potentiated startle when decortication was performed after conditioning.

Lesions of the Perirhinal Cortex

Finally, posttraining electrolytic or NMDA lesions of the perirhinal cortex were performed to evaluate the role of the direct lateral amygdaloid afferents originating from the MGM/PIL/PPA subnuclei as opposed to those from the perirhinal cortex. In addition, such lesions can also help determine the relative contributions of the direct thalamic projections to the perirhinal cortex, as compared to primary and secondary auditory cortical projections to the perirhinal cortex, because in the previous experiment auditory decortication only partially blocked potentiated startle. That is, if lesions of the perirhinal cortex were found to completely block potentiated startle, this would indicate a significant contribution of the direct MGM/PIL/PPA projections to the perirhinal cortex. Consistent with prior results (Rosen et al., 1992), posttraining perirhinal cortex lesions completely disrupted fear-potentiated startle to both auditory and visual CSs (Fig. 1.8). Retraining these lesioned rats, however, led to normal levels of fear-potentiated startle to both stimuli. Moreover, NMDA lesions of the perirhinal cortex carried out in other animals before training did not prevent fear conditioning to either CS (Fig. 1.8).

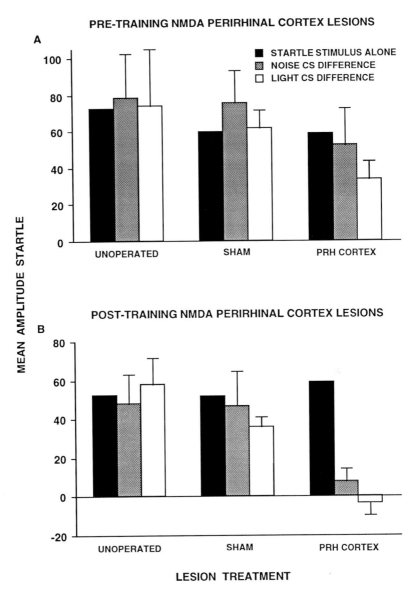

FIGURE 1.8.   Fear-potentiated startle to auditory and visual conditioned stimuli in unoperated, sham operated, or perirhinal cortex (PRH CORTEX) lesioned rats. Lesions were produced by infusion of *N*-methyl-*D*-aspartic acid either before (A) or after (B) training. The black bars indicate mean amplitude startle in the absence of the CSs (startle stimulus alone), and the gray (noise CS difference) and white (light CS difference) bars indicate the mean difference scores of the auditory and visual CSs, respectively. These difference scores (+ the standard errors of the means) represent the mean change in startle amplitude in the presence vs. the absence of the CSs.

Taken together, these data suggest that the perirhinal cortex normally may mediate transmission of both auditory and visual information in fear-potentiated startle. In contrast, the direct projection from the MGM/PIL/PPA to the lateral amygdaloid nucleus may not normally mediate fear-potentiated startle using an auditory CS. In the absence of the perirhinal cortex, however, this direct subcortical pathway can sustain normal levels of conditioning to an auditory CS. In addition, these results indicate that the direct perirhinal projections from the MGM/PIL/PPA subdivisions contribute significantly to the transmission of auditory information to the amygdala in addition to that relayed through the primary and secondary auditory cortical areas in aversive conditioning.

   In conclusion, these experiments indicate that the auditory thalamus is a necessary relay nucleus specifically involved in the mediation of auditory fear-potentiated startle, and auditory fear conditioning in general (Iwata et al., 1986; Jarrell et al., 1986a, 1986b; LeDoux et al., 1986). Furthermore, the pathway from the perirhinal cortex to the lateral amygdaloid nucleus to the central amygdaloid nucleus of the amygdala is essential in mediating the transmission of auditory and visual information necessary for the expression of fear conditioning, as assessed with the fear-potentiated startle paradigm (see Fig. 1.6). The evidence also suggests that auditory information emanating from the auditory thalamus reaches the perirhinal cortex directly from the medial division of the medial geniculate, intralaminar, and peripeduncular nuclei, and indirectly from the ventral and dorsal divisions of the medial geniculate nucleus through the primary and secondary auditory cortices. Moreover, because auditory decortication attenuates, and perirhinal decortication completely disrupts auditory fear expression, it would appear that both pathways convey auditory information to the perirhinal cortex and that it is these pathways that are normally used during aversive conditioning. This conclusion is consistent with a recent study by Romanski & LeDoux (1991), in which either pretraining electrolytic MGM/PIL/PPA or auditory cortex lesions alone did not affect the conditioning of blood pressure or freezing conditioned responses, but the combined lesions totally impaired conditioning as assessed by these measures.

EFFECTS OF EXCITATORY AMINO-ACID RECEPTOR ANTAGONISTS ON FEAR-POTENTIATED STARTLE USING AN AUDITORY CS

Delineation of the auditory pathways mediating fear-potentiated startle now allows an evaluation of the site or sites of neural plasticity along this circuitry and the identity of the neurotransmitters that might be involved in both the acquisition and expression of fear-potentiated startle. One of the most promising models of learning in vertebrates is long-term potentiation (LTP). The finding that NMDA receptor antagonists, such as 2-amino-5-phosphonovalerate (AP5), block the induction of LTP in certain hippocampal synapses, but not the expression of LTP, has lead to very powerful biochemical models of learning in vertebrates (cf. Brown, Chapman, Kairiss, & Keenan, 1988; Collingridge & Bliss, 1987; Nicoll, Kauer, & Malenka, 1988). Moreover, a number of behavioral studies have now shown that competitive as well as noncompetitive NMDA antagonists attenuate or block various measures of learning (cf. Davis, 1992; Morris, 1989; Morris, Halliwell, & Bowery, 1989). Recent studies have shown that LTP can occur in amygdala brain slices (Chapman, Kairiss, Keenan, & Brown, 1990) or in vivo following tetanic stimulation of the part of the medial geniculate nucleus that projects to the lateral nucleus of the amygdala (Clugnet & LeDoux, 1990). If convergence between the CS and shock occurs at the amygdala, and an NMDA-dependent process is involved in the acquisition of conditioned fear, then local infusion of NMDA antagonists into the amygdala should block the acquisition of conditioned fear measured with the fear-potentiated startle effect.

Because the lateral/basolateral complex is a site of multimodal convergence essential for fear-potentiated startle and contains relatively high concentrations of NMDA receptors (Monaghan & Cotman, 1985), it was of interest to test the involvement of lateral/basolateral NMDA receptors in auditory fear-potentiated startle. If fact, we have found that intraamygdala infusion of the NMDA antagonist AP5 caused a dose-dependent blockade of auditory fear-potentiated startle acquisition when AP5 was infused immediately before training (Campeau, Miserendino, & Davis, 1992) (Fig. 1.9A). Observation of the animals during training found no evidence of catalepsy or ataxia (e.g., Leung & Descorough, 1988). The effect did not seem to result from a decrease in sensitivity to footshock, because local infusion of AP5 into the amygdala did not alter overall reactivity to footshock. On the other hand, AP5 did not block the expression of fear-potentiated startle when infused immediately prior to testing in rats previously trained in the absence of the drug (Fig. 1.9B). A dose-dependent blockade of the expression of fear-potentiated startle was obtained, however, by pretesting infusion of the non-NMDA receptor antagonist CNQX (Fig. 1.9C). This suggests that the CS ultimately releases glutamate in the amygdala, which activates non-NMDA receptors. Moreover, this finding makes it more difficult to ascribe the fear acquisition deficit observed with AP5 to nonspecific antagonism of the non-NMDA receptors, because AP5, unlike CNQX, did not block the expression of fear-potentiated startle.

The ability of AP5 to block the acquisition but not the expression of fear-potentiated startle using an auditory CS is consistent with prior work indicating that intra-amygdala AP5 at comparable doses blocks the acquisition of fear to visual or contextual stimuli, as assessed by potentiated startle and other indices of aversive conditioning (Fanselow, Kim, & Landeira-Fernandez, 1991; Kim & McGaugh, 1992; Miserendino, Sananes, Melia, & Davis, 1990).

Together, these results suggest the involvement of NMDA receptors in the lateral/basolateral amygdaloid nuclei in the acquisition of aversive conditioning. It is unlikely that the observed acquisition deficit is mediated by a blockade of NMDA receptors located on central amygdaloid neurons because recent findings indicate that acquisition of conditioned fear is not blocked by direct infusion of AP5 in this nucleus (Fanselow, Kim, & Landeira-Fernandez, 1991). Future investigations of the lateral/basolateral amygdaloid complex will be aimed at determining the sec-

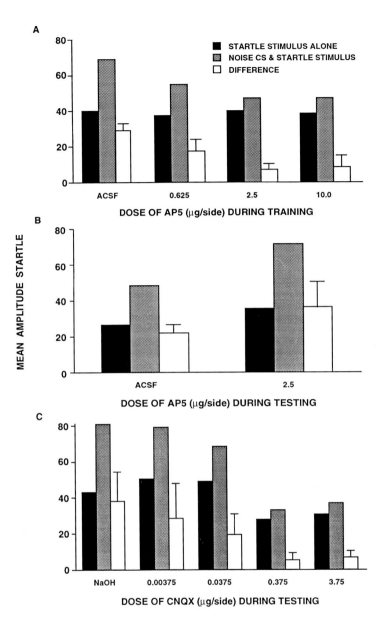

FIGURE 1.9. Mean startle amplitude in the presence (noise CS and startle stimulus) and absence (startle stimulus alone) of the auditory CS, and the difference scores (+ the standard errors of the means). (A) Shows the effects of pretraining intra-amygdala infusion of artificial cerebrospinal fluid (ACSF; $n = 4$), or 0.625 (n = 7), 2.5 (n = 7), or 10.0 μg/ side dl-2-amino-5-phosphonopentanoic acid (AP5; $n = 5$). (B) Shows the effects of pre-testing intra-amygdala infusion of ACSF ($n = 7$), or 2.5 μg/side AP5 ($n = 7$) in rats trained in the absence of drug infusions. (C) Shows the effects of pretesting intra-amygdala infusion of a weakly aqueous base (0.01 N NaOH, $n = 9$), or 0.00375 ($n = 5$), 0.0375 ($n = 9$), 0.375 ($n = 9$), or 3.75 μg/side 6-cyano-7-nitroquinoxaline-2,3-dione (CNQX; $n = 10$). The residual potentiated startle at the highest doses of AP5 given prior to training or CNQX given prior to testing is produced by a moderate unconditioned effect of the auditory CS used. (See Campeau & Davis, 1992.)

21

ond messenger systems and possibly, the long-term changes in gene expression that are ultimately responsible for laying down memories of past aversive events. For instance, we have found an induction in the amygdala of the immediate early-gene *c-fos* in response to unconditioned and conditioned fear (Campeau et al., 1991), suggesting that this class of proto-oncogene might be involved in the initiation of the cellular and genetic changes forming the basis of aversive memories.

IS THE AMYGDALA ABSOLUTELY ESSENTIAL FOR FEAR-POTENTIATED STARTLE?

As outlined so far, the amygdala plays a crucial role in both the acquisition and expression of fear-potentiated startle. There are examples in the literature, however, where some effects of amygdala lesions on aversively motivated conditioning are dependent on the degree of learning achieved before surgery. For example, posttraining lesions of the amygdala impair the retention of an active avoidance response in weakly trained animals, but not in overtrained animals (Brady, Schreiner, Geller, & Kling, 1954; Fonberg, Brutkowski, & Mempel, 1962; Horvath, 1963; Thatcher & Kimble, 1966). Because our animals typically receive only 10–20 training trials prior to amygdala lesions, it is still not known whether more extensive training would prevent or attenuate the effects of amygdala lesions on the expression of fear-potentiated startle. Such information would have important implications for the role of the amygdala versus alternative brain structures in fear-potentiated startle.

Accordingly, we have tested whether overtraining would interact with the effect of amygdala lesions on fear-potentiated startle. To determine the number of training trials required to produce an asymptotic level of fear-potentiated startle, an acquisition curve was obtained by giving rats two training trials (light CS paired with 0.6-mA footshock US) and six fear-potentiated startle test trials per day for 30 days. To prevent the rats from learning that the shocks were only given at a fixed time point in the daily experimental session, the order of presenting the training versus test trials was alternated daily. Figure 1.10 shows the acquisition of fear-potentiated startle using this procedure. The magnitude of fear-potentiated startle gradually increased to reach a significant level on day 6 (after 10 training trials) and an asymptotic level by about day 12 (after 22 training trials).

On days 32–33, the rats were given either sham ($n = 4$) or electrolytic lesions of the amygdala aimed at the central nucleus ($n = 5$). Five to six days later, all animals were retrained and tested for seven more days, as previously described. Figure 1.11 shows that even though the rats were overtrained for roughly 20 days beyond asymptote before surgery, lesions of the amygdala still totally blocked the expression of fear-potentiated startle. These results provide strong evidence that, unlike the findings from active avoidance tasks, overtraining does not alter the ability of amygdala lesions to block the expression of fear-potentiated startle. The fact that lesions of the central amygdaloid nucleus have very similar effects in non-

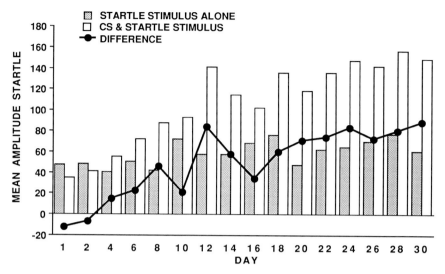

FIGURE 1.10.   Mean amplitude startle response on Noise-Alone trials (grey bars) and Light–Noise trials (white bars), and the difference between these two trial types (black dots) produced by giving two training trials and six test trials per day for 30 days. To prevent the rats from learning that the shocks would only be given at a fixed time point in the daily experimental session, the order of presenting the training vs. test trials was alternated daily. Only the data for the days when the test trials were given before the training trials are presented.

overtrained (Hitchcock & Davis, 1986, 1987) and overtrained rats strongly suggests that the central nucleus of the amygdala is necessary for the expression of fear-potentiated startle, regardless of the degree of learning.

Most surprisingly, however, these lesioned rats quickly reacquired fear-potentiated startle when retrained (Fig. 1.11). This unexpected result suggests that an intact central nucleus of the amygdala is not necessary for reacquisition of potentiated startle, or for its expression following reacquisition. Histological analysis, however, indicated that the central nucleus was not completely destroyed in all animals (range of damage = 65–100%), allowing for the possibility that the efficient reacquisition resulted from residual amygdaloid tissue. Hence, in a subsequent experiment, the effect of complete lesions of the central nucleus on reacquisition was examined by using slightly different lesion parameters. In this experiment, rats received 16 training trials per day for 4 days (i.e., a total of 64 trials) and were tested on day 5. Based on the level of fear-potentiated startle during this first test session, the animals were assigned to either a sham ($n = 7$) or central-nucleus-lesion group ($n = 6$) with both groups having similar preoperative performance. Nine to ten days later, a second test was given to evaluate the effects of the lesions on the expression of potentiated startle. One day later all groups were retrained with 16 trials per day for 4 days, followed by a final test to evaluate the effects of retraining.

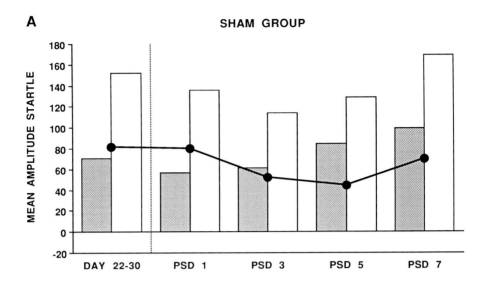

A

SHAM GROUP

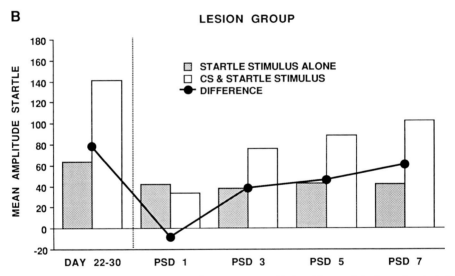

B

LESION GROUP

FIGURE 1.11.   Mean amplitude startle response on Noise-Alone trials (gray bars) and Light–Noise trials (white bars), and the difference between these two trial types (black dots) across the last 5 days before surgery (days 22–30 presented in Fig. 1.10) and at various times after surgery (PSD = post surgery data) in sham operated (A) or amygdala-lesioned (B) animals.

In this case, histological analysis showed 100% damage to the central nucleus of the amygdala in five of the six lesioned rats. As shown in Figure 1.12, the lesioned rats showed a complete blockade of fear-potentiated startle after surgery, but still reacquired significant fear-potentiated startle with retraining. These results thus replicate those of the earlier experiment and clearly indicate that the central

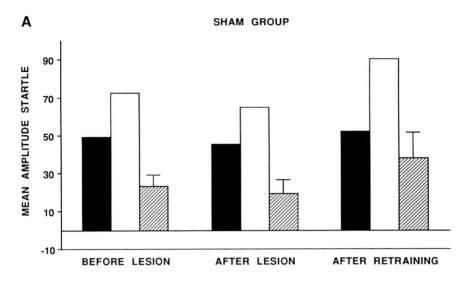

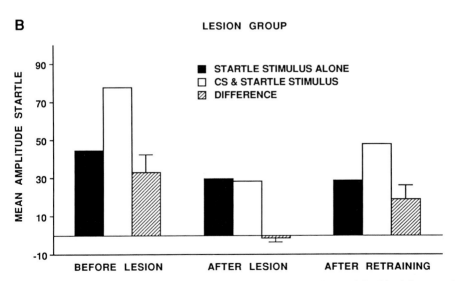

FIGURE 1.12. Mean amplitude startle response on Noise-Alone trials (black bars) and Light–Noise trials (white bars), and the difference between these two trial types (+ standard error of the mean, hatched bars) in sham operated (A) or amygdala-lesioned (B) animals. Training and retraining were given as 16 training trials per day for 4 days.

nucleus is not absolutely essential for the expression of fear-potentiated startle. Hence, there must be another brain system that can compensate for the loss of the central nucleus, project to the startle circuit, and support reacquisition of fear-potentiated startle.

If there is a secondary system that can compensate for the loss of the central nucleus of the amygdala to support reacquisition, it is conceivable that rats without an intact central nucleus might acquire fear-potentiated startle by using this secondary system. Earlier exploratory studies in our laboratory indicated that electrolytic lesions of the central nucleus made before training did block the acquisition of potentiated startle (Hitchcock & Davis, unpublished observations). Only 20 training trials were used in those studies, however, making it necessary to examine the effects of central nucleus lesions on the initial acquisition of fear-potentiated startle using a much larger number of training trials and a procedure where the rate of acquisition of potentiated startle could be measured.

To do this, rats were given either sham lesions ($n = 7$) or lesions of the central nucleus of the amygdala ($n = 7$) and 10 days later presented with two training and six test trials per day, as previously described. As shown in Figure 1.13, rats with the central nucleus lesions did not show any indication of fear-potentiated startle, even with extensive training, whereas the controls showed an acquisition curve similar to that in Figure 1.10. Because the lesioned rats did not acquire fear-potentiated startle, the shock intensity for this group was increased from 0.6 mA to 1.0 mA on day 15. The shock intensity for the controls was kept at 0.6 mA throughout the experiment. The lesioned rats still did not learn, even using this much higher shock intensity. Because it was obvious that these rats could not learn using these parameters, the experiment was terminated on day 24 (i.e., after 46 training trials).

In the three experiments just described, the rats' reactivity to shock was also measured during training. Consistent with earlier results (Hitchcock & Davis, 1986), rats with central nucleus lesions tended to react less to the shock compared to that of the controls. However, this reduction in shock reactivity was only significant on a few of the many test days. In addition, using a single shock intensity in normal animals, we do not find significant correlations between the magnitude of the shock reactivity and the magnitude of fear-potentiated startle, indicating that rats showing higher shock reactivity do not necessarily have higher levels of fear-potentiated startle. Most importantly, however, the somewhat reduced shock reactivity of the lesioned rats cannot account for the finding that the lesions blocked initial acquisition but not reacquisition. That is, if the central-nucleus-lesioned rats did not acquire fear-potentiated startle because their shock sensitivity was impaired by the lesions, it is difficult to understand how rats lesioned after initial acquisition could have so readily reacquired fear-potentiated startle. Thus, we believe that the slight reduction of shock reactivity caused by the central nucleus lesions was not a major factor for the blockade of initial acquisition of fear-potentiated startle. It is still possible, however, that central-nucleus-lesioned rats might learn if shock levels higher than 1.0 mA were used.

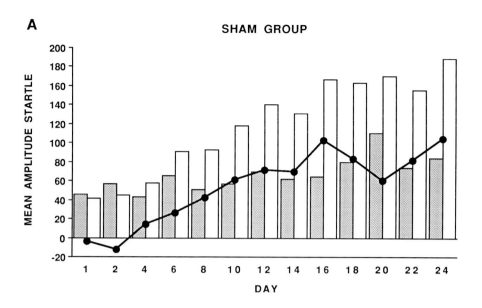

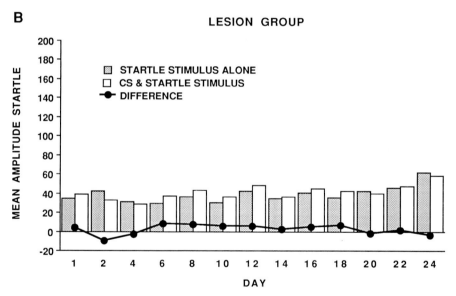

FIGURE 1.13. Mean amplitude startle response on Noise-Alone trials (grey bars) and
Light–Noise trials (white bars), and the difference between these two trial types (black
dots) across 24 days of training in animals given either sham lesions (A) or amygdala
lesions (B) prior to training.

The findings that overtraining did not alter the effects of central nucleus lesions on the expression of fear-potentiated startle and that the central nucleus lesions totally blocked the initial acquisition of fear-potentiated startle are consistent with the proposal that the central nucleus is the essential efferent pathway through which conditioned fear exerts its modulatory effects upon the acoustic startle reflex circuit in the brainstem (Davis, 1992). In spite of the seemingly critical role of the central nucleus in the initial acquisition and expression of fear-potentiated startle, the fact that these same lesions did not prevent reacquisition indicates the presence of a secondary brain system that can compensate for the central nucleus under certain circumstances. The fact that the central nucleus lesions still prevented initial acquisition of potentiated startle indicates, however, that this secondary brain system cannot compensate for the central nucleus in all cases. It would appear that the central nucleus either induces some sort of functional change in this secondary brain system during initial training or plays a permissive role so that this secondary system, alone, can support fear-potentiated startle when the central nucleus is subsequently removed. This idea implies that the central nucleus is not simply an efferent pathway for the expression of fear-potentiated startle, but also plays an important role in acquisition by affecting other brain structures during training.

At the present time, we have no direct information on the identity of a secondary brain structure that could compensate for the central nucleus of the amygdala. Our first assumption is that it is probably a forebrain structure that projects directly to the same part of the startle pathway as the central nucleus does. As mentioned earlier, the central nucleus directly projects to the startle pathway through the caudal division of the ventral amygdalofugal pathway (Rosen, Hitchcock, Sananes, Miserendino, & Davis, 1991) and electrolytic lesions of this pathway at several levels of the brainstem block the expression of fear-potentiated startle (Hitchcock & Davis, 1991). Preliminary data suggest that reacquisition is not observed in rats with lesions of the caudal division of the ventral amygdalofugal pathway performed after 60 training trials, whereas once again, reacquisition is still observed in rats with lesions of the central nucleus (Kim & Davis, in preparation). Thus, the secondary brain system that can compensate for the central nucleus in reacquisition may be one or some of those forebrain structures that project to the brainstem startle reflex circuit through the caudal ventral amygdalofugal pathway.

INHIBITION OF FEAR

Extinction

Although a great deal of progress has thus been made in determining the neural systems involved in the acquisition and expression of fear and anxiety, practically nothing is known about the neural systems that may be involved in the reduction or elimination of conditioned fear. Clinically, the inability to eliminate fear and anxiety ranks as one of the major problems in psychiatry. Hence, it would be important to develop methods to begin to identify brain systems involved in the inhibition of fear.

There are many examples in the behavioral literature of learning-induced changes that involve the reduction or elimination of conditioned fear. Experimental extinction is a primary example. To begin to identify neural systems that might be involved in the reduction of conditioned fear, we asked whether blockade of NMDA receptors at the level of the amygdala would alter the process of experimental extinction (Falls, Miserendino, & Davis, 1992). Rats were implanted with bilateral cannulae aimed at the basolateral nucleus of the amygdala and trained for potentiated startle in the usual way. One week later, all animals were given an initial short test session and subsequently matched into four groups each having equivalent levels of fear-potentiated startle. The next day half the animals were presented with 30 light-alone trials at a 1-min intertrial interval in which shocks were omitted. Five minutes before this extinction session, one group was infused with 50 nmol/side of the selective NMDA receptor antagonist AP5 and one group with artificial CSF vehicle. The two remaining groups were treated identically, except no lights were presented. They were placed into the test cages immediately after receiving either AP5 or artificial CSF. Twenty-four hours later, all rats were tested for fear-potentiated startle.

Figure 1.14 shows that animals infused with AP5 or artificial CSF, but not given light-alone trials, had levels of potentiated startle equivalent to that observed in their initial test. Animals infused with artificial CSF immediately before light-alone trials had very little potentiated startle on their second test, indicating that extinction had occurred. In contrast, animals infused with AP5 immediately before light-alone trials had levels of potentiated startle that did not differ from their initial test or from the groups infused with either artificial CSF or AP5 but not given light-alone trials and significantly higher levels than the group given artificial CSF and light-alone trials. These data indicate, therefore, that AP5 infused into the amygdala blocked extinction of fear-potentiated startle, suggesting that an NMDA-dependent mechanism in the vicinity of the amygdala may be important for extinction of conditioned fear.

Because NMDA antagonists infused into the amygdala prevent extinction, it is possible that an NMDA-dependent form of LTP in the vicinity of the amygdala may underlie extinction of conditioned fear. Given this, the interesting question becomes how an increase in synaptic efficacy (i.e., LTP) can lead to a *reduction* in conditioned fear. One of the first behavioral theories of extinction proposed that extinction resulted from the development of inhibition that acted to oppose the existing excitation (Konorski, 1948). Such functional inhibition could result from an activity-dependent increase in synaptic efficacy (i.e., LTP) of neurons that ultimately inhibit cells that are otherwise responsible for the performance of conditioned fear. Alternatively a decrease in synaptic efficacy may underly extinction of conditioned fear. Long-term depression (LTD) of synaptic responses has been observed in the hippocampus and cortex (Abraham & Goddard, 1983; Artola, Brocher, & Singer, 1990; Bear & Cooper, 1989; Charttari, Stanton, &

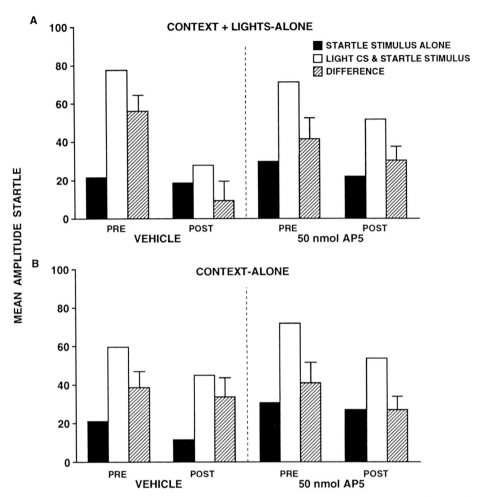

FIGURE 1.14. Mean amplitude startle response on Noise-Alone trials (black bars) and Light–Noise trials (white bars), and the difference between these two trial types (+ standard error of the mean, hatched bars) prior to (Pre) or following (Post) presentation of 60 lights (A) or an equivalent amount of exposure to the experimental context (B) in rats infused with either 50 nmole AP5 or its vehicle. A indicates that rats that received vehicle immediately before Light-Alone presentations showed a significant reduction in fear-potentiated startle (i.e., extinction), whereas rats that received AP5 did not. B shows that exposure to the experimental context alone was not sufficient to produce extinction.

Sejnowski, 1989; Levy & Steward, 1983; Stanton & Sejnowski, 1989) and several authors have proposed that LTD may be the cellular mechanism for weakening behavioral responses (Artola, Brocher, & Singer, 1990; Goldman, Chavez-Noriega, & Stevens, 1990; Teyler & DiScenna, 1984). Recent behavioral experiments suggest, however, that extinction does not result from the erasure of the original associations that led to the conditioned response (Bouton & Bolles, 1985;

Bouton & King, 1983, 1986). Instead, extinction may result from the accrual of new associations that compete with or mask the expression of the original associations. Therefore, rather than a depression of *potentiated synapses* (i.e., reversal of LTP), extinction might result from a depression of nonpotentiated synapses that might normally carry conditioned stimulus information to the same postsynaptic cell that underwent LTP during excitatory conditioning. If the strength of the conditioned response reflected the net result of both depressed and potentiated synaptic inputs to this postsynaptic cell, LTD would compete with LTP to reduce the production of the conditioned response. Importantly, however, the original potentiation would remain intact, even though the overall output of the system would be reduced.

Conditioned Inhibition

Extinction has been considered a special case of the more general phenomenon of conditioned inhibition (cf. Bouton, 1991). In the typical conditioned inhibition procedure, one stimulus, denoted as *A*, predicts shock, while another stimulus, *X*, predicts the absence of shock. The result of this procedure is that *A* comes to elicit a fear reaction when presented alone but not when it is accompanied by *X*, the conditioned inhibitor. Extinction may be analogous to conditioned inhibition in that the experimental context is like *X* in that it predicts the absence of shock (cf. Bouton & Bolles, 1985; Bouton & King, 1983, 1986). The conditioned inhibition procedure, however, offers advantages over the extinction procedure. In the conditioned inhibition procedure, the reduction of fear is under the control of an explicit CS, rather than under the control of contextual cues. Moreover, fear reduction is assessed at the same time as fear production, allowing one to disentangle the inhibition of fear from a more global disruption in fear performance or stimulus processing.

Because of the possible advantages of the conditioned inhibition procedure, we have devised a procedure for obtaining conditioned inhibition of fear-potentiated startle. Rats underwent two days of training in which one stimulus, denoted as *A*+, was repeatedly paired with footshock. Following this, the rats underwent five additional days of training in which a serial compound, denoted as *X**A−, was not paired with shock. *A*+ training was continued during this second phase. Conditioned inhibition was assessed by measuring the amplitude of the startle reflex in the presence or absence of *A* when it was or was not preceded by *X* (i.e., *A* or *X**A).

Figure 1.15A shows substantial fear to *A* as evidenced by greater startle amplitude in the presence of *A* than in its absence. However, the rats showed significantly less fear-potentiated startle to *A* when it was preceded by *X*. This suggests that *X* had acquired the ability to inhibit the fear produced by *A*. This inhibitory effect of *X* was dependent on the rats having been given explicit nonreinforced presentations of the serial *X**A compound, because, in a control experiment, rats given *X* alone trials in the second phase of training did not show inhibition of fear-potentiated startle to *A* when preceded by *X* in testing (Fig. 1.15B). Moreover, the

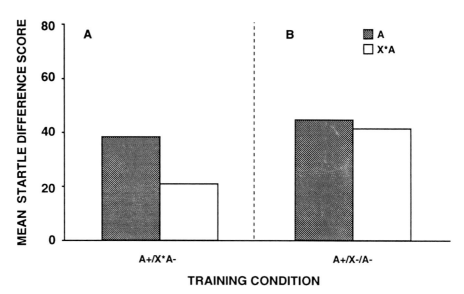

FIGURE 1.15.   (A) Shows the mean change in startle amplitude (i.e., difference in mean startle amplitude in the presence vs. the absence of the conditioned stimulus [A] or a compound stimulus [$X*A$]) in rats where cue A signaled shock during training and compound $X*A$ signaled the absence of shock. (B) Shows comparable data in animals where A and X were not presented in compound to signal the absence of shock. The results show that compound $X*A$ only inhibited fear-potentiated startle when $X*A$ had previously predicted the absence of shock.

lack of potentiated startle on $X*A$ trials cannot be readily attributed to a configural discrimination (i.e., A vs. XA) because in a subsequent experiment, the inhibitory effect of X transferred to another fear-eliciting stimulus, C, such that fear-potentiated startle to $X*C$ was less than that to C alone (data not shown). Taken together, these results suggest that X in a $A+/X*A-$ procedure acquires the ability to inhibit fear-potentiated startle.

Because so much is known about the neural systems mediating the acquisition and performance of fear-potentiated startle, we are now in a position to begin to ask what structures may be responsible for the reduction of conditioned fear. In light of the finding that extinction of conditioned fear-potentiated startle seems to involve an NMDA-dependent mechanism in the vicinity of the amygdala, we are currently investigating whether a similar mechanism underlies conditioned inhibition of fear-potentiated startle. In addition, we have begun to ask whether structures extrinsic to the amygdala are critical for either extinction or conditioned inhibition of fear-potentiated startle.

SUMMARY AND CONCLUSIONS

A great deal of data now indicate that the amygdala and its efferent projections to the hypothalamus and brainstem form a central fear system. We have been evaluating the role of the amygdala in fear conditioning, using the fear-potentiated startle test, in which the amplitude of the acoustic startle reflex is increased when elicited in the presence of a stimulus previously paired with a shock. Reliable fear-potentiated startle can be obtained using either a visual conditioned stimulus or a low-frequency auditory conditioned stimulus. Chemical or electrolytic lesions of either the central nucleus or the lateral and basolateral nuclei of the amygdala block the expression of fear-potentiated startle. These latter amygdaloid nuclei may actually be the site of plasticity for fear conditioning, because local infusion of the NMDA antagonist AP5 blocks the acquisition but not the expression of fear-potentiated startle. Auditory information about the conditioned stimulus seems to be transmitted to the amygdala via three parallel pathways. One involves the dorsal and ventral division of the medial geniculate through the auditory cortex and perirhinal cortex. A second and third pathway involve the medial division of the medial geniculate body, the peripeduncular, and posterior intralaminar nuclei. These structures project either directly to the lateral amygdaloid nucleus or indirectly via the perirhinal cortex. Normally, the auditory pathways involving the perirhinal cortex seem to act in parallel to mediate fear-potentiated startle. The subcortical pathway, however, can fully support potentiated startle if these pathways are destroyed. While the amygdala is critically involved in both the acquisition and expression of fear-potentiated startle, it may not be absolutely necessary under certain circumstances. When animals are given extensive overtraining, lesions of the central nucleus completely block the expression of fear-potentiated startle, yet these same animals can then show reacquisition with retraining. In contrast, animals with lesions of the central nucleus never seem to acquire fear-potentiated startle when the lesions are made before any training has occurred. Thus, other brain regions are capable of supporting fear-potentiated startle, although these areas seem to require an intact amygdala if no prior fear conditioning has occurred. Finally, we have begun to investigate brain systems that might be involved in the inhibition of fear. Local infusion of AP5 into the amygdala was found to block the acquisition of experimental extinction, a prototypical method for reducing fear. We have also established a reliable procedure for producing conditioned inhibition of fear-potentiated startle and hope to eventually understand the neural systems involved in this phenomenon.

ACKNOWLEDGMENTS

Research reported in this chapter was supported by NIMH Grant MH-25642, MH-47840, Research Scientist Development Award MH-00004, a grant from the Air Force Office of Scientific Research, and the State of Connecticut. Our sincere thanks are extended to Lee Schlesinger, who tested many of the animals used for these studies and to Leslie Fields for help in typing the paper.

REFERENCES

Abraham, W. C., & Goddard, G. V. (1983). Asymetrical relationships between homosynaptic long-term potentiation and heterosynaptic long-term depression. *Nature, 305,* 717–719.

Aggleton, J. P. (1985). A description of intra-amygdaloid connections in the old world monkeys. *Experimental Brain Research, 57,* 390–399.

Amaral, D. (1987). Memory: Anatomical organization of candidate brain regions. In F. Plum (Ed.), *Handbook of physiology, Sec. 1: Neurophysiology, Vol. 5: Higher functions of the brain* (pp. 211-294). Bethesda, MD: American Physiological Society.

Arnault, P., & Roger, M. (1987). The connections of the peripeduncular area studied by retrograde and anterograde transport in the rat. *Journal of Comparative Neurology, 258,* 463-476.

Arnault, P., & Roger, M. (1990). Ventral temporal cortex in the rat: Connections of secondary auditory areas Te2 and Te3. *Journal of Comparative Neurology, 302,* 110-123.

Artola, A., Brocher, S., & Singer, W. (1990). Different voltage-dependent thresholds for inducing long-term depression and long-term potentiation in slices of rat visual cortex. *Nature, 347,* 69-72.

Bear, M. F., & Cooper, L. N. (1989). Molecular mechanisms for synaptic modification in the visual cortex: Interactions between theory and experiment. In M. A. Gluck & D. E. Rumelhart (Eds.), *Neuroscience and connectionist theory* (pp. 65-93). Hillsdale, NJ: Erlbaum.

Bennett, C., Liang, K. C., & McGaugh, J. L. (1985). Depletion of adrenal catecholamines alters the amnestic effect of amygdala stimulation. *Behavioral Brain Research, 15,* 83-91.

Berg, W. K., & Davis, M. (1985). Associative learning modifies startle reflexes at the lateral lemniscus. *Behavioral Neuroscience, 99,* 191-199.

Bouton, M. E. (1991). A contextual analysis of fear extinction. In P. R. Martin (Ed.), *Handbook of behavior therapy and psychological science: An integrative approach* (pp. 435-453). New York: Pergamon.

Bouton, M. E., & Bolles, R. C. (1985). Context, event-memories, and extinction. Hillsdale, NJ: Erlbaum.

Bouton, M. E., & King, D. A. (1983). Contextual control of conditioned fear: Tests for the associative value of the context. *Journal of Experimental Psychology: Animal Behavior Processes, 9,* 248-256.

Bouton, M. E., & King, D. A. (1986). Effect of context with mixed histories of reinforcement and nonreinforcement. *Journal of Experimental Psychology: Animal Behavior Processes, 12,* 4-15.

Brady, J. V., Schreiner, L., Geller, I., & Kling, A. (1954). Subcortical mechanisms in emotional behavior: The effect of rhinencephalic injury upon the acquisition and retention of a conditioned avoidance response in cats. *Journal of Comparative Physiology and Psychology, 47,* 179-186.

Bresnahan, E., & Routtenberg, A. (1972). Memory disruption by unilateral low level, sub-seizure stimulation of the medial amygdaloid nucleus. *Physiology & Behavior, 9,* 513-525.

Brown, J. S., Kalish, H. I., & Farber, I. E. (1951). Conditioned fear as revealed by magnitude of startle response to an auditory stimulus. *Journal of Experimental Psychology, 41,* 317-328.

Brown, T. H., Chapman, P. F., Kairiss, E. W., & Keenan, C. L. (1988). Long-term synaptic potentiation. *Science, 242,* 724-728.

Campeau, S., Liang, K. C., & Davis, M. (1990). Long-term retention of fear-potentiated startle following a short training session. *Animal Learning and Behavior, 18,* 462-468.

Campeau, S., Hayward, M. D., Hope, B. T., Rosen, J. B., Nestler, E. J., & Davis, M. (1991). Induction of the c-fos proto-oncogene in rat amygdala during unconditioned and conditioned fear. *Brain Research, 565,* 349-352.

Campeau, S., Miserendino, M. J. D., & Davis, M. (1992). Intra-amygdala infusion of the N-methyl-D-aspartate receptor antagonist AP5 blocks acquisition but not expression of fear-potentiated startle to an auditory conditioned stimulus. *Behavioral Neuroscience, 106,* 569-574.

Cassella, J. V., & Davis, M. (1985). Fear-enhanced acoustic startle is not attenuated by acute or chronic imipramine treatment in rats. *Psychopharmacology (Berlin), 87,* 278-282.

Cassella, J. V., & Davis, M. (1986a). Habituation, prepulse inhibition, fear conditioning, and drug modulation of the acoustically elicited pinna reflex in rats. *Behavioral Neuroscience, 100,* 39-44.

Cassella, J. V., & Davis, M. (1986b). Neural structures mediating acoustic and tactile startle reflexes and the acoustically-elicited pinna response in rats: Electrolytic and ibotenic acid studies. *Society for Neuroscience Abstracts, 12,* 1273.

Chapman, P. F., Kairiss, E. W., Keenan, C. L., & Brown, T. H. (1990). Long-term synaptic potentiation in the amygdala. *Synapse, 6,* 271–278.

Charttari, S., Stanton, P. K., & Sejnowski, T. J. (1989). Commisural synapses, but not mossy fiber synapses, in the hippocampal field CA3 exhibit associative long-term potentiation and depression. *Brain Research, 495,* 145–150.

Clugnet, M. C., & LeDoux, J. E. (1990). Synaptic plasticity in fear conditioning circuits: Induction of LTP in the lateral nucleus of the amygdala by stimulation of the medial geniculate body. *Journal of Neuroscience, 10,* 2818–2824.

Collingridge, G. L., & Bliss, T. V. P. (1987). NMDA receptors—Their role in long-term potentiation. *Trends in Neuroscience, 10,* 288–293.

Crooks, G. B., Jr., Robinson, G. S., Hatfield, T. J., Graham, P. W., & Gallagher, M. (1989). Intraventricular administration of the NMDA antagonist APV disrupts learning of an odor aversion that is potentiated by taste. *Society for Neuroscience Abstracts, 15,* 464.

Cruikshank, S. J., Edeline, J.-M., & Weinberger, N. M. (1992). Stimulation at a site of auditory-somatosensory convergence in the medial geniculate nucleus is an effective unconditioned stimulus for fear conditioning. *Behavioral Neuroscience, 106,* 471–483.

Davis, M. (1986). Pharmacological and anatomical analysis of fear conditioning using the fear-potentiated startle paradigm. *Behavioral Neuroscience, 100,* 814–824.

Davis, M. (1992). The role of the amygdala in conditioned fear. In J. P. Aggleton (Ed.), *The amygdala: Neurobiological aspects of emotion, memory, and mental dysfunction* (pp. 255–305). New York: Wiley–Liss.

Davis, M., & Astrachan, D. I. (1978). Conditioned fear and startle magnitude: Effects of different footshock or backshock intensities used in training. *Journal of Experimental Psychology: Animal Learning Behavior Processes, 4,* 95–103.

Davis, M., Gendelman, D. S., Tischler, M. D., & Gendelman, P. M. (1982). A primary acoustic startle circuit: Lesions and stimulation studies. *Journal of Neuroscience, 6,* 791–805.

Davis, M., Hitchcock, J. M., & Rosen, J. B. (1987). Anxiety and the amygdala: Pharmacological and anatomical analysis of the fear-potentiated startle paradigm. In *The psychology of learning and motivation* (pp. 263–292). New York: Academic Press.

Ellis, M. E., & Kesner, R. P. (1983). The noradrenergic system of the amygdala and aversive information processing. *Behavioral Neuroscience, 97,* 399–415.

Falls, W. A., Miserendino, M. J. D., & Davis, M. (1992). Extinction of fear-potentiated startle: Blockade by infusion of an excitatory amino acid antagonist into the amygdala. *Journal of Neuroscience, 12,* 854–863.

Fanselow, M. S., Kim, J. J., & Landeira-Fernandez, J. (1991). Anatomically selective blockade of Pavlovian fear conditioning by application of an NMDA antagonist to the amygdala and periaqueductal gray. *Society for Neuroscience Abstracts, 17,* 659.

Fonberg, E., Brutkowski, S., & Mempel, E. (1962). Defensive conditioned reflexes and neurotic motor reactions following amygdalectomy in dogs. *Acta Biologiae Experimentalis, 22,* 51–57.

Gallager, M., & Holland, P. C. (1992). Understanding the function of the central nucleus: Is simple conditioning enough? In J. P. Aggleton (Ed.), *The amygdala: Neurobiological aspects of emotion, memory, and mental dysfunction* (pp. 307–322). New York: Wiley–Liss.

Gallagher, M., & Kapp, B. S. (1978). Manipulation of opiate activity in the amygdala alters memory processes. *Life Sciences, 23,* 1973–1978.

Gallagher, M., & Kapp, B. S. (1981). Effect of phentolamine administration into the amygdala complex of rats on time-dependent memory processes. *Behavioral and Neural Biology, 31,* 90–95.

Gallagher, M., Kapp, B. S., Frysinger, R. C., & Rapp, P. R. (1980). Beta-Adrenergic manipulation in amygdala central n. alters rabbit heart rate conditioning. *Pharmacology Biochemistry and Behavior, 12,* 419–426.

Gloor, P. (1960). Amygdala. In J. Field (Ed.) *Handbook of physiology: Sec I. Neurophysiology* (pp. 1395–1420). Washington, DC: American Physiological Society,

Gold, P. E., Hankins, L., Edwards, R. M., Chester, J., & McGaugh, J. L. (1975). Memory inference and facilitation with posttrial amygdala stimulation: Effect varies with footshock level. *Brain Research, 86,* 509–513.

Goldman, R. S., Chavez-Noriega, L. E., & Stevens, C. F. (1990). Failure to reverse long-term potentiation by coupling sustained presynaptic activity and N-methyl-D-aspartate receptor blockade. *Procedures of the National Academy of Science, 87,* 7165–7169.

Gray, T. S. (1989). Autonomic neuropeptide connections of the amygdala. In Y. Tache, J. E. Morley, & M. R. Brown (Eds.), *Hans Selye symposia on neuroendocrinology and stress, Vol. 1: Neuropeptides and stress* (pp. 92–106). Berlin: Springer-Verlag.

Guldin, W. O., & Markowtisch, H. J. (1983). Cortical and thalamic afferent connections of the insular and adjacent cortex of the rat. *Journal of Comparative Neurology, 215,* 135–153.

Handforth, A. (1984). Implication of stimulus factors governing kindled seizure threshold. *Experimental Neurology, 86,* 33–39.

Handwerker, M. J., Gold, P. E., & McGaugh, J. L. (1974). Impairment of active avoidance learning with posttraining amygdala stimulation. *Brain Research, 75,* 324–327.

Hitchcock, J. M., & Davis, M. (1986). Lesions of the amygdala, but not of the cerebellum or red nucleus, block conditioned fear as measured with the potentiated startle paradigm. *Behavioral Neuroscience, 100,* 11–22.

Hitchcock, J. M., & Davis, M. (1987). Fear-potentiated startle using an auditory conditioned stimulus: Effect of lesions of the amygdala. *Physiology & Behavior, 39,* 403–408.

Hitchcock, J. M., & Davis, M. (1991). Efferent pathway of the amygdala involved in conditioned fear as measured with the fear-potentiated startle paradigm. *Behavioral Neuroscience, 105,* 826–842.

Horvath, F. E. (1963). Effects of basolateral amygdalectomy on three types of avoidance behavior in cats. *Journal of Comparative Physiology Psychology, 56,* 380–389.

Inagaki, S., Kawai, Y., Matsuzak, T., Shiosaka, S., & Tohyama, M. (1983). Precise terminal fields of the descending somatostatinergic neuron system from the amygdala complex of the rat. *Journal fur Hirnforsch, 24,* 345–365.

Ison, J. R., McAdam, D. W., & Hammond, G. R. (1973). Latency and amplitude changes in the acoustic startle reflex of the rat produced by variation in auditory prestimulation. *Physiology & Behavior, 10,* 1035–1039.

Iwata, J., LeDoux, J. E., Meeley, M. P., Arneric, S., & Reis, D. J. (1986). Intrinsic neurons in the amygdala field projected to by the medial geniculate body mediate emotional responses conditioned to acoustic stimuli. *Brain Research, 383,* 195–214.

Jarrell, T. W., Romanski, L. M., Gentile, C. G., McCabe, P. M., & Schneiderman, N. (1986a). Ibotenic acid lesions in the medial geniculate region prevent the acquisition of differential Pavlovian conditioning of bradycardia to acoustic stimuli in rabbits. *Brain Research, 382,* 199–203.

Jarrell, T. W., Gentile, C. G., McCabe, P. M., & Schneiderman, N. (1986b). The role of the medial geniculate region in differential Pavlovian conditioning of bradycardia in rabbits. *Brain Research, 374,* 126–136.

Jarrell, T. W., Gentile, C. G., Romanski, L. M., McCabe, P. M., & Schneiderman, N. (1987). Involvement of cortical and thalamic auditory regions in retention of differential bradycardic conditioning to acoustic conditioned stimuli in rabbits. *Brain Research, 412,* 285–294.

Kapp, B. S., & Pascoe, J. P. (1986). Correlation aspects of learning and memory: Vertebrate model systems. In J. L. Martinez & R. P. Kesner (Eds.), *Learning and memory: A Biological view* (pp. 399–440). New York: Academic Press.

Kapp, B. S., Pascoe, J. P., & Bixler, M. A. (1984). The amygdala: A neuroanatomical systems approach to its contribution to aversive conditioning. In N. Butlers & L. S. Squire (Eds.), *The neuropsychology of memory* (pp. 473–488). New York: Guilford.

Kapp, B. S., Wilson, A., Pascoe, J. P., Supple, W. F., & Whalen, P. J. (1990). A neuroanatomical systems analysis of conditioned bradycardia in the rabbit. In M. Gabriel & J. Moore

(Eds.), *Neurocomputation and learning: Foundations of adaptive networks.* New York: Bradford.

Kapp, B. S., Whalen, P. J., Supple, W. F., & Pascoe, J. P. (1992). Amygdalolid contributions to conditioned arousal and sensory information processing. In J. P. Aggleton (Ed.), *The amygdala: Neurobiological aspects of emotion, memory, and mental dysfunction* (pp. 229–245). New York: Wiley-Liss.

Kesner, R. P. (1982). Brain stimulation: Effects on memory. *Behavioral Neural Biology, 36,* 315–367.

Kim, M. & McGaugh, J. L. (1992). Effects of intra-amygdala injections of NMDA receptor antagonists on acquisition and retention of inhibitory avoidance. *Brain Research, 585,* 35–48.

Konorski, J. (1948). *Conditioned reflexes and neuronal organization.* London: Cambridge University Press.

Krettek, J. E., & Price, J. L. (1978a). Amygdaloid projections to subcortical structures within the basal forebrain and brainstem in the rat and cat. *Journal of Comparative Neurology, 178,* 225–254.

Krettek, J. E., & Price, J. L. (1978b). A description of the amygdaloid complex in the rat and cat with observations on intraamygdaloid connections. *Journal of Comparative Neurology, 178,* 255–280.

LeDoux, J. E. (1987). Emotion. In F. Plum & V. Mountcastle (Eds.), *Handbook of physiology: Nervous system* (pp. 419–459). Washington, DC: American Physiological Society.

LeDoux, J. E., Cicchetti, P., Xagoraris, A., & Romanski, L. M. (1990). The lateral amygdaloid nucelus: Sensory interface of the amygdala in fear conditioning. *Journal of Neuroscience, 10,* 1062–1069.

LeDoux, J. E., Farb, C., & Ruggiero, D. A. (1990). Topographic organization of neurons in the acoustic thalamus that project to the amygdala. *Journal of Neuroscience, 10,* 1043–1054.

LeDoux, J. E., Farb, C. R., & Milner, T. A. (1991). Ultrastructure and synaptic associations of auditory thalamo-amygdala projections in the rat. *Experimental Brain Research, 85,* 577–586.

LeDoux, J. E., Farb, C. R., & Romanski, L. M. (1991). Overlapping projections to the amygdala and striatum from auditory processing areas of the thalamus and cortex. *Neuroscience Letters, 134,* 139–144.

LeDoux, J. E., Iwata, J., Pearl, D., & Reis, D. J. (1986). Disruption of auditory but not visual learning by destruction of intrinsic neurons in the medial geniculate body of the rat. *Brain Research, 371,* 395–399.

LeDoux, J. E., Ruggiero, D. A., & Reis, D. J. (1985). Projections to the subcortical forebrain from anatomically defined regions of the medial geniculate body in the rat. *Journal of Comparative Neurology, 242,* 182–213.

LeDoux, J. E., Sakaguchi, A., & Reis, D. J. (1984). Subcortical efferent projections of the medial geniculate nucleus mediate emotional responses conditioned to acoustic stimuli. *Journal of Neuroscience, 4,* 683–698.

LeDoux, J. E., Sakaguchi, A., Iwata, J., & Reis, D. J. (1986). Interruption of projections from the medial geniculate body to an archi-neostriatal field disrupts the classical conditioning of emotional responses to acoustic stimuli. *Neuroscience, 17,* 615–627.

Leung, L. W. S., & Desborough, K. A. (1988). APV, an N-methyl-D-aspartate receptor antagonist, blocks the hippocampal theta rhythm in behaving rats. *Brain Research, 463,* 148–152.

Levy, W. B., & Steward, O. (1983). Temporal contiguity requirements for long-term associative potentiation/depression in the hippocampus. *Neuroscience, 8,* 791–797.

Lewis, S. J., Verberne, A. J. M., Robinson, T. G., Jarrott, B., Louis, W. J., & Beart, P. M. (1989). Excitotoxin-induced lesions of the central but not basolateral nucleus of the amygdala modulate the baroreceptor heart rate reflex in conscious rats. *Brain Research, 494,* 232–240.

Liang, K. C., Bennett, C., McGaugh, J. L. (1985). Peripheral epinephrine modulates the effects of post-training amygdala stimulation on memory. *Behavioral Brain Research, 15,* 93–100.

Liang, K. C., Bennett, C., & McGaugh, J. L. (1986). Modulating effects of posttraining epinephrine on memory: Involvement of the amygdala noradrenergic systems. *Brain Research, 368,* 125–133.

McDonald, A. J. (1984). Neuronal organization of the lateral and basolateral amygdaloid nuclei in the rat. *Journal of Comparative Neurology, 222,* 589–606.

McDonald, A. J., Jackson, T. R. (1987). Amygdaloid connections with posterior insular and temporal cortical areas in the rat. *Journal of Comparative Neurology, 262,* 59–77.

McGaugh, J. L., Introini-Collison, I. B., Nagahara, A. H., Cahill, L., Brioni, J. D., & Castellano, C. (1990). Involvement of the amygdaloid complex in neuromodulatory influences on memory storage. *Neuroscience Biobehavioral Reviews, 14,* 425–432.

Mehler, W. (1980). Subcortical afferent connections of the amygdala in the monkey. *Journal of Comparative Neurology, 190,* 733–762.

Millhouse, O. E., & DeOlmos, J. (1983). Neuronal configurations in lateral and basolateral amygdala. *Neuroscience, 10,* 1269–1300.

Miserendino, M. J. D., Sananes, C. B., Melia, K. R., & Davis, M. (1990). Blocking of acquisition but not expression of conditioned fear-potentiated startle by NMDA antagonists in the amygdala. *Nature, 345,* 716–718.

Mishkin, M., & Aggleton, J. (1981). Multiple functional contributions of the amygdala in the monkey. In Y. Ben-Ari (Ed.), *The amygdaloid complex.* New York: North-Holland.

Mizuno, N., Takahashi, O., Satoda, T., & Matsushima, R. (1985). Amygdalospinal projections in the macaque monkey. *Neuroscience Letters, 53,* 327–330.

Monaghan, D. T., & Cottman, C. W. (1985). Distribution of N-Methyl-D-aspartate-sensitive L-[3H]Glutamate-binding sites in rat brain. *Journal of Neuroscience, 5,* 2909–2919.

Morris, R. G. M. (1989). Synaptic plasticity and learning: Selective impairment of learning in rats and blockade of long-term potentiation in vivo by the N-methyl-D-aspartate receptor antagonist AP5. *Journal of Neuroscience, 9,* 3040–3057.

Morris, R. G. M., Halliwell, R., & Bowery, N. (1989). Synaptic plasticity and learning: II. Do different kinds of plasticity underlie different kinds of learning? *Neuropsychologia, 27,* 41–59.

Neff, W. D., & Diamond, I. T. (1975). Behavioral studies of auditory discrimination: Central nervous system. In W. D. Keidel & W. D. Neff (Eds.), *Handbook of sensory physiology: Vol. 2. Auditory system. Physiology (CNS). Behavioral studies of psychoacoustics* (pp. 307–400). Berlin: Springer-Verlag.

Nicoll, R. A., Kauer, J. A., & Malenka, R. C. (1988). The current excitement in long-term potentiation. *Neuron, 1,* 97–103.

Nitecka, L., Amerski, L., & Narkiewicz, O. (1981). The organization of intraamygdaloid connections—An HRP study. *Journal fur Hirnforsch, 22,* 3–7.

Niteka, L., & Frotscher, M. (1989). Organization and synaptic interconnections of GABAergic and cholinergic elements in the rat amygdaloid nuclei: Single- and double-immunolabeling studies. *Journal of Comparative Neurology, 279,* 470–488.

Ohta, M. (1984). Amygdaloid and cortical facilitation or inhibition of trigeminal motoneurons in the rat. *Brain Research, 291,* 39–48.

Ottersen, O. P. (1980). Afferent connections to the amygdaloid complex of the rat and cat. II. Afferents from the hypothalamus and the basal telencephalon. *Journal of Comparative Neurology, 194,* 267–289.

Ottersen, O. P. (1981a). The afferent connections of the amygdala of the rat as studied with retrograde transport of horseradish peroxidase. In Y. Ben-Ari (Ed.), *The amygdaloid complex* (pp. 91–104). Amsterdam: North-Holland.

Ottersen, O. P. (1981b). Afferent connections to the amygdaloid complex of the rat with some observations in the cat. III. Afferents from the lower brain stem. *Journal of Comparative Neurology, 202,* 335–356.

Ottersen, O. P. (1982). Connections of the amygdala of the rat. IV. Corticoamygdaloid and intra-amygdaloid connections as studied with axonal transport of horseradish peroxidase. *Journal of Comparative Neurology, 205,* 30–48.

Ottersen, O. P., & Ben-Ari, Y. (1979). Afferent connections to the amygdaloid complex of the rat and cat. I. Projections from the thalamus. *Journal of Comparative Neurology, 187,* 401-424.

Post, S., & Mai, J. K. (1980). Contribution to the amygdaloid projection field in the rat: A quantitative autoradiographic study. *Journal fur Hirnforsch, 21,* 199-225.

Price, J. L., & Amaral, D. G. (1981). An autoradiographic study of the projections of the central nucleus of the monkey amygdala. *Journal of Neuroscience, 1,* 1242-1259.

Roberts, G. W., Woodhams, P. L., Polak, J. M., & Crow, T. J. (1982). Distribution of neuropeptides in the limbic system of the rat: The amygdaloid complex. *Neuroscience, 7,* 99-131.

Roger, M., & Arnault, P. (1989). Anatomical study of the connections of the primary auditory area in the rat. *Journal of Comparative Neurology, 287,* 339-356.

Romanski, L. M., & LeDoux, J. E. (1991). Equipotentiality of thalamo-amygdala and thalamo-cortico-amygdala circuits in auditory fear conditioning. *Society for Neuroscience Abstracts, 17,* 658.

Romanski, L. M., Clugnet, M. C., Bordi, F., & LeDoux, J. E. (1990). Unconditioned stimulus transmission to the amygdala. *Society for Neuroscience Abstracts, 16,* 608.

Rosen, J. B., & Davis, M. (1988a). Enhancement of acoustic startle by electrical stimulation of the amygdala. *Behavioral Neuroscience, 102,* 195-202.

Rosen, J. B., & Davis, M. (1988b). Temporal characteristics of enhancement of startle by stimulation of the amygdala. *Physiology & Behavior, 44,* 117-123.

Rosen, J. B., & Davis, M. (1990). Enhancement of electrically elicited startle by amygdaloid stimulation. *Physiology & Behavior, 48,* 343-349.

Rosen, J. B., Hitchcock, J. M., Sananes, C. B., Miserendino, M. J. D., & Davis, M. (1991). A direct projection from the central nucleus of the amygdala to the acoustic startle pathway: Antero-grade and retrograde tracing studies. *Behavioral Neuroscience, 105,* 817-825.

Rosen, J. B., Hitchcock, J. M., Miserendino, M. J. D., Falls, W. A., Campeau, S., & Davis, M. (1992). Lesions of the perirhinal cortex, but not of the frontal, medial pre-frontal, visual or insular cortex block fear-potentiated startle using a visual conditioned stimulus. *Journal of Neuroscience, 12,* 4624-4633.

Russchen, F. T. (1982). Amygdalopetal projections in the cat. II. Subcortical afferent connections. A study with retrograde tracing techniques. *Journal of Comparative Neurology, 207,* 157-176.

Ryugo, D. K., & Killackey, H. P. (1974). Differential telencephalic projections of the medial and ventral divisions of the medial geniculate body of the rat. *Brain Research, 82,* 173-177.

Sananes, C. B., & Davis, M. (1992). N-Methyl-D-Aspartate lesions of the lateral and basolateral nuclei of the amygdala block fear-potentiated startle and shock sensitization of startle. *Behavioral Neuroscience, 106,* 72-80.

Sandrew, B. B., Edwards, D. L., Poletti, C. E., & Foote, W. E. (1986). Amygdalospinal projections in the cat. *Brain Research, 373,* 235-239.

Sarter, M., & Markowitsch, H. J. (1985). Involvement of the amygdala in learning and memory: A critical review, with emphasis on anatomical relations. *Behavioral Neuroscience, 99,* 342-380.

Schwaber, J. S., Kapp, B. S., Higgins, G. A., & Rapp, P. R. (1982). Amygdaloid and basal forebrain direct connections with the nucleus of the solitary tract and the dorsal motor nucleus. *Journal of Neuroscience, 2,* 1424-1438.

Smith, B. S., & Millhouse, O. E. (1985). The connections between basolateral and central nuclei. *Neuroscience Letters, 56,* 307-309.

Stanton, P. K., & Sejnowski, T. J. (1989). Associative long-term depression in the hippocampus induced by hebbian covariance. *Nature, 339,* 215-218.

Teich, A. H., McCabe, P. M., Gentile, C. G., Jarrell, T. W., Winters, R. W., Liskowsky, D. R., & Schneiderman, N. (1988). Role of auditory cortex in the acquisition of differential heart rate conditioning. *Physiology & Behavior, 44,* 405-412.

Teyler, T. J., & DiScenna, P. (1984). Long-term potentiation as a candidate mneomonic device. *Brain Research Reviews, 7,* 15-28.

Thatcher, R. W., & Kimble, D. P. (1966). Effects of amygdaloid lesions on retention of an avoidance response in overtrained and non-overtrained rats. *Psychonomic Science, 6,* 9–10.

Turner, B. J. (1981). The cortical sequence and terminal distribution of sensory related afferents to the amygdaloid complex of the rat and monkey. In Y. Ben-Ari (Ed.), *The amygdaloid complex* (pp. 51–62). Amsterdam: North-Holland.

Turner, B. H., & Herkenham, M. (1981). An autoradiographic study of thalamo-amygdaloid connections in the rat. *The Anatomical Record, 199,* 260A.

Turner, B. H., & Herkenham, M. (1991). Thalamoamygdaloid projections in the rat: A test of the amygdala's role in sensory processing. *Journal of Comparative Neurology, 313,* 295–325.

Turner, B. H., & Zimmer, J. (1984). The architecture and some of the interconnections of the rat's amygdala and lateral periallocortex. *Journal of Comparative Neurology, 227,* 540–557.

Van Hoesen, G. W. (1981). The differential distribution, diversity and sprouting of cortical projections to the amygdala in the Rhesus monkey. In Y. Ben-Ari (Ed.), *The amygdaloid complex* (pp. 77–90). Amsterdam: Elsevier/North-Holland.

Veening, J. (1978). Subcortical afferents of the amygdaloid complex in the rat: An HRP study. *Neuroscience Letters, 8,* 197–202.

2

Modulation of Emotional and Nonemotional Memories: Same Pharmacological Systems, Different Neuroanatomical Systems

PAUL E. GOLD

Experiences that elicit intense emotions are often remembered very well. On the basis of manipulations of hormonal and neurotransmitter systems, as well as correlations between functional measures in these systems with learning and memory, there is considerable support for the view that release of some hormones and neurotransmitters in response to experience regulate the formation of new memories. The main goal of this chapter is to integrate and to organize pharmacological studies of memory by searching for generalizations or "rules" about the roles of hormonal and neurotransmitter systems in the regulation of learning and memory processes. In doing so, it is important to examine carefully the extent to which these generalizations are similar and different for results obtained with systemic injections and those obtained with direct brain injections.

Consistently, systemic injections of epinephrine or of glucose, which may contribute to epinephrine effects on memory (see below), enhance memory when administered near the time of training. Similarly, systemically administered drugs that promote the functions of central cholinergic, glutaminergic, or noradrenergic systems enhance memory on later tests. Moreover, diminished release of the neurotransmitters or pharmacological blockade of their receptors can impair memory. There also appear to be some neurochemical systems, for example, opioid and GABA, for which activation impairs, and inactivation enhances, learning and memory.

In viewing these hormonal and neurotransmitter systems, it might be possible to identify one set of modulators that is a particularly important regulator of the processes that store memories for highly emotional experiences, and another set of regulators for less emotional experiences. The evidence available does not, however, support such a conclusion. Nor does current evidence suggest an identi-fication of sets of modulators responsible for memories sorted by task demands on other grounds. When injected systemically, drugs that enhance memory, and drugs that impair memory, do so for most tests of memory. The wide range of tasks on which a given treatment acts, retaining the direction of effect (enhance-ment or impairment), is characterized here as a lack of task specificity.

Particularly in recent years, many experiments examined memory after admin-istration of combined systemic injections of drugs that act not only within but also across neurotransmitter domains. One purpose of examining these interactions is to attempt to identify a sequence of neurotransmitter actions by which memories are regulated, that is, to determine whether modulators of memory act in linear fashion, with activation of some neurotransmitters relatively proximal to the events of memory formation. The evidence reviewed below suggests that interac-tions of drugs are readily observed both within and across neurotransmitters. For example, when injected systemically, an opiate antagonist can block not only the effects on memory of an opiate agonist but also the effects of a cholinergic antagonist. While the treatments considered here often have high specificity for particular neurotransmitters and, within a neurotransmitter system for particular receptor types, combinations of treatments within and across neurotransmitter and/or receptor domains are most often additive with respect to their effects on memory. The readily observed additivity of treatments with neurobiological actions across neurotransmitter and receptor domains is termed here a lack of pharmacological specificity for effects on memory.

Thus, the often high degree of neurotransmitter specificity of the treatments employed contrasts with the low degree of specificity for memory, defined either by task or by neurotransmitter. One view of such findings is that systemically administered drugs may have access to, and opportunity for acting in parallel on, a wide range of neural systems. For example, systemic injections of a treatment that modulates memory might enhance or impair several components of information that collectively contribute to memory for a particular experience. According to this view, pharmacological impairment of one component of information might be attenuated by another treatment that enhances memory of a different component. In an experiment using systemic injections, the consequence might be seen as an example of additivity across neurotransmitters. Much different patterns of results might be evident, however, if the drugs are administered directly into specific brain targets.

In comparison to experiments employing peripheral injections, tests of the ef-fects of direct brain injections are more incomplete. Still, there are some general-izations that seem to be emerging. The results obtained thus far with studies of the effects on learning and memory of direct brain injections resemble in part those obtained with systemically administered treatments and in part differ in some very important ways. One feature of the results obtained with systemic injections ap-pears to be retained with central injections. The direction of a drug's effects on memory, enhancement or impairment, appears to be retained with direct brain injections. When two drugs are injected in combination into a brain area, some additivity is retained but some is not. The absence of additivity is very important in defining a hierarchical organization of neurotransmitter actions on memory, as well as determining the extent to which neurotransmitters that modulate memory are organized in a serial or parallel manner.

A second important difference between results obtained with systemic and direct brain injections is that, in the latter case, task specificity often emerges. For example, injections of drugs into one brain region might influence memory for one set of tasks but not another. As described below, however, the task specificity maps well against task differences expected on the basis of lesion data for the brain structures tested. Thus, task differences seen with direct brain injections reflect differences based on anatomically defined systems more than on the particular drugs employed. These findings offer the promise of integrating studies of memory using a pharmacological level of analysis with those using a neuroanatomical systems level of analysis.

MODULATION OF MEMORY: SYSTEMIC INJECTIONS

One view of the reason that some neuroendocrine systems promote memory formation is that particular hormones add neural "significance" to the event eliciting the endogenous hormonal response, regulating memory storage so that the strength of the enduring memory is susceptible to the importance of the experience (e.g., Gold, 1992; Gold & McGaugh, 1975; Kety, 1972; McGaugh, 1989).

The idea that endogenous hormonal responses add neural significance to an experience can be illustrated easily with a description of studies designed to show hormonal enhancement of memory formation for inhibitory avoidance training. In an inhibitory avoidance task, a rat or mouse receives a single footshock upon crossing from a start compartment into a shock compartment. On a later test of retention, the animal will exhibit better avoidance performance (i.e., longer retention latency) if previously trained with a strong footshock than if trained with a weak footshock. It is important to distinguish the contributions to memory of neuroendocrine responses to training from the contributions of the stimulus properties per se. One strategy is to train the animal with a mild footshock followed by one of the hormonal consequences of a stronger footshock. This creates experimentally a situation in which all rats receive the same training procedures but postexperiential hormonal levels are modified, by injection, to match the endogenous consequences of a more intense training footshock. On memory tests administered later, if the rat avoids later as if it had received the stronger footshock, the findings suggest that the hormone enhanced the formation of memory.

This interpretation can be and has been stated in many ways. For example, the hormone promoted the storage of information; or the hormone tagged the information as salient and therefore worthy of storage. The general view is that a set of hormones, released by an experience, select from all events those that should be stored. Thus, an emotional experience would provide not only the information content that should be stored but would also provide a special neuroendocrine response, establishing an internal milieu that enhances memories for emotional events such as those initiated by shock avoidance procedures. Although the example thus far describes hormonal responses to an experience, the internal milieu would also include activation of central neurotransmitter systems that participate in regulation of memory storage processes.

In this manner, one might expect to find different neurotransmitter and hormonal effects on memory for emotional versus nonemotional experiences. It has long been evident, however, that this is not entirely accurate. Instead, hormonal responses, particularly those related to stress, select the *time* at which the mechanisms of memory formation should be engaged, not the *type* of memory that should be stored. As an initial illustration of this point, consider the possible roles of neuroendocrine and other emotional responses in the rather weakly understood phenomenon of flashbulb memories. Depending on the reader's age, memories shared by many people for some major societal events include the bombing of Pearl Harbor, the assassination of President Kennedy, and the Challenger space shuttle disaster. I, and others, have suggested that these memories are formed with particular intensity because of neuroendocrine responses elicited by these events (e.g., Gold, 1992). Yet, consider some common questions asked in order to identify flashbulb memories: What were you wearing when you heard . . . ? Who told you about . . . ? Where were you when you learned . . . ? These questions deal not with the significant event itself but with relatively minor circumstances surrounding the event. Thus, if stress-related hormones and neuromodulatory systems contribute to the formation of these intense memories, the modulators are demonstrably nonspecific when selecting the information to commit to permanent storage.

According to this view, the interplay of emotions and memory follows a scenario in which emotional experiences result in release of a set of hormones. The nature of the emotional experience may determine when and probably which hormones and neurotransmitters are released, as well as the magnitude of the responses. Once released, however, these neuroendocrine responses to the experience apparently enhance memory formation for many aspects of that moment's experience. In this sense, *neuroendocrine responses to experience select* when, *but not* which, *memories will be made.*

Epinephrine and Glucose

The hormone most studied as a modulator of memory processes is epinephrine, which appears to enhance memory, at least in part, by increasing blood glucose levels. This section describes the extent to which increases in circulating epinephrine and glucose levels select times when memory processes are augmented and the extent to which comparable effects are seen on a broad range of tasks. The subsequent two sections consider similarly the effects of other systemically administered drugs.

Epinephrine is released into the circulation from the adrenal medulla in response to a wide range of experiences, including graded responses to experiences such as handling, placement in a novel environment, and footshocks of varying intensities (Gold & McCarty, 1981; McCarty & Gold, 1981). When administered shortly after training, epinephrine injections, at doses that result in physiologically significant circulating epinephrine levels, enhance memory tested at a later time (see Gold, 1991, 1992). Because epinephrine does not enter the brain from blood in appreciable amounts (Axelrod, Weil-Malherbe, & Tomchick, 1959), it is likely that the effects of epinephrine on memory require a peripheral action as an intermediate step between release of the hormone and its actions on memory. A major physiological action of epinephrine is to liberate glucose stores from the liver, resulting in increased circulating glucose levels (Ellis, Kennedy, Eusebi, & Vincent, 1967). A substantial number of studies during the past several years suggest that increases in circulating glucose levels enhance memory and may mediate epinephrine effects on memory (see Gold, 1991, 1992; White, 1991). As described below, glucose enhances memory not only when injected systemically but also when injected directly into specific brain targets.

With regard to temporal specificity, both epinephrine and glucose are especially effective at modifying memory, assessed at a later time, when the treatments are administered near the time of training. Thus, the temporal relationship between an experience and the administration of epinephrine or glucose is a critical variable in determining whether the treatments will affect learning and memory. For example, injections of both epinephrine and glucose (Fig. 2.1) enhance memory for many avoidance tasks when the treatments are administered near the time of training in an inhibitory avoidance task comparable to the example given above (see: Gold, 1991, 1992; McGaugh, 1989; Wenk, 1989; White, 1991). The effec-

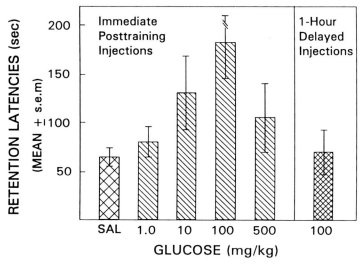

FIGURE 2.1.   Dose- and time-dependent enhancement of memory by glucose in rats trained in a one-trial inhibitory avoidance task. (From Gold, 1986)

tiveness of epinephrine and glucose in enhancing memory decreases as the time between training and treatment increases. Moreover, both epinephrine and glucose are released shortly after training with avoidance procedures, and injections of epinephrine and glucose, as well as other treatments, modify circulating epinephrine and glucose levels during the time shortly after training in a manner that predicts later performance of the learned response (Fig. 2.2) (Gold & McCarty, 1981; Hall & Gold, 1986, 1992; McCarty & Gold, 1981).

Thus, convergence between the time of training and administration or release of epinephrine and glucose is a requirement for their regulation of memory processes. This temporal constraint is consistent with the view that epinephrine and glucose are important determinants of when memories will be stored.

The temporal specificity demonstrated for epinephrine and glucose effects on memory is not paralleled by task specificity. There are no examples, to my knowledge, of experiments in which rats were tested for enhancement of memory for minor circumstances surrounding a highly salient event, that is, in the manner of testing flashbulb memories. The issue of selectivity by type of memory can be handled quite readily, however, by testing epinephrine and glucose effects on memory in a variety of tasks. The results indicate very clearly that both treatments enhance memories for a very broad range of tests. In addition to enhancing memory for highly emotional events, for example, avoidance tasks, epinephrine

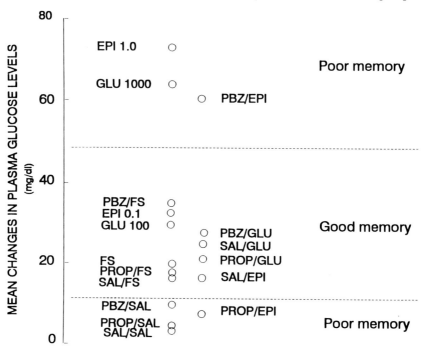

FIGURE 2.2.   Relationship between posttraining increases in blood glucose levels under a range of conditions in which memory for inhibitory avoidance training is poor or good. (From Hall & Gold, 1992)

and glucose also enhance memory for relatively less emotional events, such as appetitive operant tasks (Messier & Destrade, 1988; Packard & White, 1990), spatial tasks in rodents (Means & Fernandez, 1992; Sternberg, Isaacs, Gold, & McGaugh, 1985; Sternberg, Martinez, Gold, & McGaugh, 1985) and goldfish (Peretti & Nowak, 1974), spontaneous alternation performance (Ragozzino, Arankowsky-Sandoval, & Gold, 1992; Stone, Rudd, & Gold, 1992; Stone, Walser, Gold, & Gold, 1991; Walker & Gold, 1992), declarative memory in humans (e.g., Hall, Gonder-Frederick, Chewning, Silveira, & Gold, 1989; Manning, Hall, & Gold, 1990; Manning, Parsons, & Gold, 1992; Manning, Ragozzino, & Gold, 1993), and long-term potentiation (Gold, Delanoy, & Merrin, 1984). Some specific examples of glucose enhancement of memory under different conditions are shown in Figures 2.3, 2.4, and 2.5.

There are, to be sure, examples of failures of epinephrine or glucose to enhance memory with some tests. For example, glucose did not enhance memory for the Stone maze (Long, Davis, Garofalo, Spangler, & Ingram, 1990), and did not enhance memory for digit span or for implicit memory (priming) in humans (Hall et al., 1989; Manning, Hall, & Gold, 1990; Manning, Parsons, Cotter, & Gold, 1994). Still, the broad spectrum of memory tests susceptible to enhancement by epinephrine and glucose is striking compared to the short list of tests not affected by these treatments. These findings leave little reason to conclude that epinephrine and glucose are principally regulators of the formation of emotional memories, or more generally, that these circulating factors are specific to certain kinds of memory measures. Instead, the data support the conclusion that *modulators of memory formation are nonspecific with regard to the emotional content of an experience or to the particular memory test employed.*

Neurotransmitter-Related Drugs

The rules by which drugs targeted at specific neurotransmitter systems regulate memory appear to be the same as those found for epinephrine and glucose. The neurotransmitter-related drugs also exhibit time-dependent effects on memory (McGaugh, 1989; McGaugh & Gold, 1989) and, in addition, have effects on memory that are evident and consistent across a wide range of tasks. One difference is that activation of some neurotransmitter systems (e.g., acetylcholine, glutamate) promotes memory formation, while activation of others (e.g., opiate, GABA) impairs memory formation. Regardless of whether one chooses avoidance or appetitive tasks, spatial or nonspatial tasks, or classical or instrumental conditioning tasks, systemic injections of drugs that modulate memory generally have a positive or negative "valence" in terms of the direction of their effects on memories for all sorts of events.

In most instances, cholinergic agonists enhance memory and cholinergic antagonists impair memory, opioid and GABAergic agonists impair memory and their antagonists enhance memory, glutaminergic (in past studies of memory, principally N-methyl-D-aspartate (NMDA) receptor) antagonists impair and agonists enhance memory. In this scheme, epinephrine and glucose are both modulators of

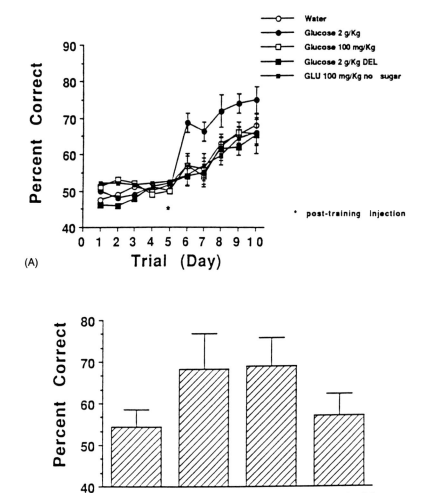

FIGURE 2.3.   Glucose enhancement of acquisition on two appetitive tasks. (A) Effects of posttraining glucose injections on acquisition with win-stay procedures in a radial arm maze. (B) Effects of glucose on acquisition with win-shift procedures in a radial arm maze. (From Packard & White, 1990)

memory with a positive valence. Thus, *hormones and neurotransmitters that modulate memory have a positive or negative "valence," enhancing or impairing learning and memory without regard to the particular test employed.*

Before proceeding, it is important to note that most drugs that enhance memory will also impair memory at higher doses; most enhancers of memory have an inverted-U dose-response curve. The basis for the inverted-U dose-response curve is unknown. One possibility is that, at high doses, drugs recruit actions on brain

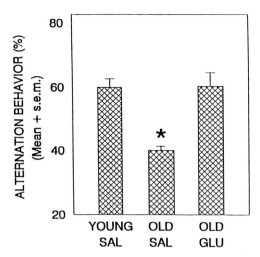

FIGURE 2.4.   Glucose facilitation of spontaneous alternation performance in 2-year-old rats. (From Stone, Rudd, & Gold, 1992)

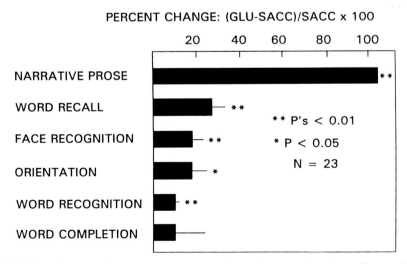

FIGURE 2.5.   Glucose enhancement on a range of cognitive tests in patients diagnosed as having Alzheimer's disease. (From Manning, Ragozzino, & Gold, 1992)

function beyond their "primary" actions and these additional effects impair memory. Another possibility is that enhancement of memory processes might, at very high drug levels, engage sufficient neural plasticity to store extraneous information (noise) as readily as the specific information contained (signal) in the experience. While the basis for inverted-U dose-response curves is an issue of considerable interest and importance, positive valence as used in this chapter refers to the effects on memory at low doses, with the embedded assumption that the effects on memory seen at low doses are the most selective effects for each treatment.

The assignment of modulators of memory to categories of positive or negative valence is a generalization with exceptions, but appears largely to represent the effects across a wide range of tasks and species. It is of course impossible to list here all of the relevant studies that have tested drug effects on memory, even if limiting the list only to cholinergic, GABAergic, opiate and NMDA drugs. However, some examples demonstrating measures on which all four classes of drugs (mostly using systemic injections) are effective include tests of classical conditioning (*ACh:* Moye & Rudy, 1987; *opiate:* Cicacla, Azorlosa, Estall, & Grant, 1990; Hernandez, Valentine, & Powell, 1987; McEchron & Gormezano, 1991; *GABA:* Alexandrov, Sabanov, & Samoylova, 1984; Haley, Thompson, & Madden, 1988; *NMDA:* Welzl, Alessandri, & Battig, 1990), fear and avoidance (*ACh and opiates:* for reviews see Gold & Zornetzer, 1983; McGaugh, 1989; McGaugh & Gold, 1989; Martinez et al., 1991; *GABA:* Castellano & McGaugh, 1989, 1991; Castellano, Introini-Collison, Pavone, & McGaugh, 1989; Swartzwelder, Tilson, McLamb, & Wilson, 1987; *NMDA:* Flood, Baker, & Davis, 1990; Kim, DeCola, Landeira-Fernandez, & Fanselow, 1991; Walker & Gold, 1991a), spatial (*ACh:* Levin, & Rose, 1991; Riekkinen, Sirvio, Aaltonen, & Riekkinen, 1990; *Opiate:* Canli, Cook, & Miczak, 1990; Decker, Introini-Collison, & McGaugh, 1989; Gallagher, King, & Young, 1983; *GABA:* Brioni & Arolfo, 1992; *NMDA:* Lyford & Jarrard, 1991; Ward, Mason, & Abraham, 1990; Pontecorvo, Clissold, White, & Ferkany, 1991; Robinson, Crooks, Shinkman, & Gallagher, 1989; Shapiro & Caramanos, 1990; Morris, Anderson, Lynch, & Baudry, 1986), spontaneous alternation (*ACh and opiate:* Stone et al., 1991; *GABA:* Grey, Lam, & Gold, 1992; *NMDA:* Walker & Gold, 1991a, 1992), and long-term potentiation (*ACh:* Lin & Phillis, 1991; *GABA:* Del Cerro, Jung, & Lynch, 1992; Mott & Lewis, 1991; *Opiate:* Shors, Levine, & Thompson, 1990; *NMDA:* see Collingridge & Bliss, 1987; Cotman, Monaghan, & Ganong, 1988; Morris, Halliwell, & Bowery, 1989). This list was restricted to measures for which there is evidence for all four drug classes reviewed here. There are, of course, many examples of other tests of memory—for example, nonspatial operant, habituation, olfactory—tested for each of these drug classes. In these instances as well, the general case is that the drugs retain their direction of effect, either enhancing or impairing learning and memory.

Where tested, comparable effects also appear to be seen with several tests of learning and memory in nonhuman primates (*ACh:* Aigner & Mishkin, 1986; *GABA:* Schulze, Slikker, & Paule, 1989; *Opiate:* Aigner & Mishkin, 1988) and in humans (*ACh:* Nissen, Knopman, & Schacter, 1987; Sevush, Guterman, & Villalon, 1991; *GABA:* Black & Barbee, 1987; *Opiate:* Kerr et al., 1991); tests of glutaminergic effects on memory in primates have not, to my knowledge, been performed. These findings provide not only increased breadth of tasks on which the drugs act, but also indicate that the drugs retain their generalized efficacy across species. In humans and monkeys as in rodents, the findings indicate that the drugs retain their valences with respect to effects on learning and memory; for example, cholinergic antagonists, and GABA and opiate agonists impair learning and memory.

Drug Interactions

The notion that each neurotransmitter system has a valence defining its participation in the formation of memory underlies the idea that interactions between drugs should also be evident. In the simplest cases, a neurotransmitter agonist and antagonist, each with opposite effects on memory, have no effect when administered concomitantly. For example, the opiate agonist, morphine, impairs several measures of learning and memory and the opiate antagonist, naloxone, reverses these impairments (Izquierdo, 1979; Mahalik & Fitzgerald, 1988; McNamara & Skelton, 1991; Schindler, Gormezano, & Harvey, 1987; Stone et al., 1991). [Note that the sentence could as easily be: Naloxone enhances memory and morphine reverses the enhancement.] Similarly, the cholinergic agonist, physostigmine, reverses deficits in memory produced by the cholinergic antagonist, scopolamine, on many tasks in rodents (e.g., Dawson et al., 1991; Itoh, Nabeshima, & Kameyama, 1990; Stone et al., 1991; Worms, Gueudet, Perio, & Soubrie, 1989), as well as in humans (Hrbek, Macakova, Komenda, & Siroka, 1989; Preston et al., 1989) and in nonhuman primates (Rupniak, Samson, Tye, Field, & Iverson, 1991). Thus, within a drug class, combined administration of an agonist and antagonist can be additive and cancel each other's effects.

In my view, the picture gets clearer, not muddier, when considering interactions *across* neurotransmitter domains because the results are predictable by simply summing the valences. Thus, a cholinergic agonist, for example, physostigmine or oxotremorine, can effectively reverse memory impairments not only after administration of a cholinergic antagonist, but also after administration of an opiate or GABAergic agonist (e.g., Castellano & McGaugh, 1991; Stone et al., 1991). Naloxone can attenuate the effects not only of morphine but also of cholinergic and NMDA antagonists (e.g., Rush, 1986; Walker & Gold, 1992). Glucose can reverse the effects on memory of cholinergic antagonists (scopolamine, atropine, mecamylamine), an opioid agonist (morphine), a GABA agonist (muscimol), and an NMDA antagonist (NPC 12626) (Messier, Durkin, Mrabet, & Destrade, 1990; Ragozzino, Arankowsky-Sandoval, & Gold, 1994; Ragozzino & Gold, 1992; Grey et al., 1992; Stone et al., 1991; Walker & Gold, 1992). Figure 2.6 illustrates the ability of several drugs to reverse the effects of scopolamine on spontaneous alternation performance.

Additivity is also evident with examinations of interactions between modulators of memory with the same valence. Subthreshold doses of two positive modulators

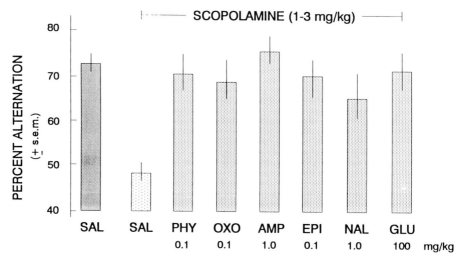

FIGURE 2.6.   Attenuation of scopolamine-induced impairments in mice for spontaneous alternation performance by cholinergic agonists (PHY = physostigmine; OXO = oxotremorine), adrenergic agonists (AMP = amphetamine; EPI = epinephrine), an opiate antagonist (NAL = naloxone), and glucose (GLU). (From data in Stone et al., 1991, & Walker et al., 1991)

or of two negative modulators are additive both within and across drug classes, resulting in memory enhancement or impairment, respectively (Decker, Gill, & McGaugh, 1990; Flood, Smith, & Cherkin, 1985; Ragozzino, Arankowsky-Sandoval, & Gold, 1992; Riekkinen et al., 1990; Riekkinen, Riekkinen, Sirvioe, & Riekkinen, 1992). In analogous manner, cholinergic and adrenergic agonists can act synergistically to facilitate the induction of long-term potentiation in visual cortex (Broecher, Artola, & Singer, 1992). This, then, leads to the next general conclusion: *When injected systemically, hormones and neurotransmitters which modulate memory have a valence (memory enhancement or impairment), but otherwise lack pharmacological specificity in terms of interactions with drugs directed at other neurotransmitter systems.*

It is important to note that this generalization appears to apply to several non-memory measures as well. For example, systemic injections of glucose reverse impairments in REM sleep produced by atropine (Stone & Gold, 1988). Glucose also reverses morphine-induced impairments in both slow wave and REM sleep (Arankowsky-Sandoval & Gold, 1994). Glucose and physostigmine reverse increased locomotor activity after scopolamine and morphine (Stone, Rudd, & Gold, 1990). In addition, glucose and naloxone augment tremors induced by physostigmine (Stone, Cottrill, Walker, & Gold, 1988; Walker, McGlynn, Grey, Ragozzino, & Gold, 1991).

When systemic treatments are employed, the extensive and predictable interactions between modulators of memory processes, and the preservation of the nature of these interactions across measures of memory and other aspects of brain function suggest two points. First, in order to affect a wide range of brain functions, each treatment is likely to have actions on multiple neural systems. Second, because additivity of treatments is retained across measures, the bases for the interactions between hormonal and neurotransmitter systems are likely to be repeated in multiple neural systems.

The main conclusion of studies of interactions of systemically administered drugs within and between hormonal and neurotransmitter systems is that the effects of combined treatments are predictable from the effects of individual treatments. It is important to note that this is not the only set of results that might have occurred. In particular, if the treatments did not interact so fully across hormonal and neurotransmitter domains, the results would support a serial pharmacological model, perhaps with a "final common modulator" proximally linked to the substrate mechanisms of memory formation. (An example of such a model can be seen in Gold, 1991.) A serial model predicts that the effects of drugs acting on some neurotransmitter systems, that is, those closer to the memory substrate mechanisms, will not be offset by drugs acting on others more distant to the substrate mechanisms. This pattern of results is not consistent, however, with the regularly observed interactions between systemically administered treatments across neurotransmitter domains. On the basis of less information, it appears likely that the full complement of interactions is not evident when the same drugs are injected into specific brain targets. These findings, described below, suggest that it will be possible to define the series of events responsible for modulation of memory processes using direct brain injections.

MODULATION OF MEMORY FORMATION: NEURAL SYSTEMS ANALYSES

The general rules derived from studies of systemic administration of treatments that enhance or impair memory—that the treatments have a valence with respect to their effects on memory, that the treatments are nonspecific in terms of the drugs with which they interact, that there is little specificity by memory task—offer issues that can be addressed by neural systems analyses of pharmacological modulation of memory. One type of experiment is designed to determine whether a lesioned brain area is a "target" or site of action for a systemic drug effect on memory. Importantly, however, these experiments also ask whether specific brain lesions block the efficacy of one, some, or all modulators of memory processing. A second type of experiment determines whether drugs injected directly into specific brain regions are able to modulate memory processes. As with lesion experiments, studies of injections into specific brain targets also address the question of pharmacological specificity by determining whether one, some, or all modulators tested are effective when administered directly to a specific brain area and, in addition, ask whether the valence identified with systemic administration of a class of drugs is retained. Thus, one issue is whether pharmacological specificity emerges after selective brain lesions or direct brain injections.

Another issue is that of task specificity. While the findings described previously, obtained with systemic treatments, suggest an absence of important distinctions between classes of memory, studies of memory dysfunctions after damage to specific brain areas suggest independent classes of memory (for examples and reviews, see Kesner, 1992; Kesner & Johnson, 1991; Mishkin & Appenzeller, 1990; Schacter, 1987; Squire, 1987). The absence of specificity by pharmacological treatment and by memory task for systemically administered drugs contrasts sharply with the often specific impairments evident after different brain lesions. Thus, another question considered in the sections below is the extent to which task specificity emerges when testing pharmacological modulation of memory after selective brain lesions or modulation by direct brain injections.

This chapter focuses on two brain regions, the amygdala and medial septum, to examine the effects of brain lesions on memory modulation by systemic drug injections, and subsequently to examine the effects of direct central injections.

Brain Lesions

Amygdala

As described by Davis (this volume), emotional memories are particularly sensitive to lesions of the amygdala. Lesions of the amygdala interfere with a wide range of emotional memories, including inhibitory avoidance, fear-potentiated startle, and conditioned fear (e.g., Davis, 1992; Helmstetter, 1992; Kesner, 1992; LeDoux, 1992), while amygdala lesions have little effect on acquisition of spatial memory assessed in the radial arm maze or the water maze (e.g., Becker, Walker, & Olton, 1980; Sutherland & McDonald, 1990; see also Kesner, 1992, for review).

Lesions of the amygdala or its output through the stria terminalis block modulation by systemically administered treatments across a broad range of pharmacological treatments. Lesions of the amygdala or stria terminalis block enhancement of memory for avoidance training produced by epinephrine, other adrenergic agonists, naloxone, bicuculline, muscimol, and oxotremorine, and also block impairment of memory for avoidance training produced by several amnestic treatments, including those of cholinergic antagonists, and opioid and GABA agonists (Ammassari-Teule, Pavone, Castellano, & McGaugh, 1991; Castellano, Libri, & Ammassari-Teule, 1988; Introini-Collison, Arai, & McGaugh, 1991; Liang & McGaugh, 1983; Liang, McGaugh, & Yao, 1990; McGaugh, Introini-Collison, Juler, & Izquierdo, 1986; Tomaz, Dickinson-Anson, & McGaugh, 1992). Thus, lesions of the amygdala or stria terminalis block the effects on memory of several classes of treatments that otherwise either enhance or impair memory. These findings offer compelling evidence for the view that pharmacological modulation of memory converges on the amygdala, with stria terminalis projections from the amygdala conveying the modulatory influences on memory storage at other brain sites (McGaugh, Introini-Collison, Cahill, Kim, & Liang, 1992).

While the evidence described earlier is remarkably consistent across drug classes, all of the findings are based on avoidance training procedures. The issue of task specificity for the lesion-drug interactions is still, to my knowledge, untested. For example, will lesions of the amygdala or stria terminalis, which are generally ineffective in influencing performance on appetitively motivated spatial tasks, nonetheless block the effects of these treatments on such tasks? The negative result—that is, demonstrating that amygdala lesions do not block the effects of memory-modulating treatments on nonavoidance tasks—would support the view that the amygdala integrates neuromodulatory influences on storage of memory for emotional, but not unemotional, events. The positive results would suggest that the amygdala more generally integrates the neuromodulatory influences on memory storage per se (Introini-Collison, Miyazaki, & McGaugh, 1991). My guess is that the negative will be true; amygdala lesions will *not* block pharmacological enhancement and impairment of memory for spatial tasks. If these anticipated results are correct, the findings would support the idea that the anatomical targets at which systemically administered drugs act may be diffuse, and that specific subsets of these targets are relevant for particular memory tasks. Such findings would support the generalization that there is little pharmacological specificity but substantial task specificity for those instances in which amygdala and stria terminalis lesions block pharmacological effects on memory. This is a readily tested issue needing resolution.

Medial Septum
While both the amygdala and medial septum have received considerable attention as targets for direct brain injections (described below), reversals of the effects of medial septum damage on learning and memory by acute pharmacological treatment have received far less attention. An advantage of examining manipulations of the medial septum is that the output to the hippocampus is relatively well defined anatomically and pharmacologically (Nicoll, 1985). The output is largely cholinergic and GABAergic (e.g., Amaral & Kurz, 1985; Frotscher & Leranth, 1985; Köhler, Chan-Palay, & Wu, 1984), offering the possibility of identifying transmitter and anatomical loci for the consequences of septal lesions, as well as providing a potential target for pharmacological attenuation of deficits in memory after septal damage. For studies of acute drug injections, most attempts to attenuate the extent of memory impairment after septal damage have employed cholinergic agonists. In addition, with the evidence (see earlier) that septal lesions impair performance on spatial tasks, attempts to reverse the consequences of medial septal lesions for learning and memory have largely been restricted to such tasks.

Systemic administration of cholinergic receptor agonists, both muscarinic and nicotinic, as well as the indirect agonists, cholinesterase inhibitors, reverse deficits in the eight-arm radial maze and water maze after medial septum or fornix damage (Decker, Majchrzak, & Anderson, 1992; Maho, Dutrieux, & Ammassari-Teule, 1988; Matsuoka, Maeda, Ohkubo, & Yamaguchi, 1991; Riekkinen, Aaltonen, Sirvio, & Riekkinen, 1991). We recently found that systemic injections of oxotremorine, but not physostigmine, also reversed deficits in spontaneous alternation performance (McGlynn, Lennartz, Gold, & Gold, 1994). These findings are shown in Figure 2.7. While the results obtained with a direct muscarinic

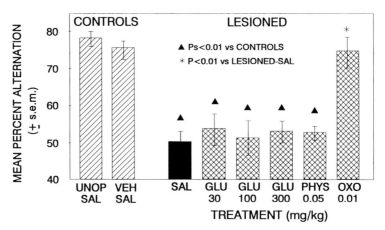

FIGURE 2.7. Deficits in spontaneous alternation performance in rats after ibotenic acid lesions of the medial septum. Oxotremorine (OXO), a direct muscarinic agonist, but not the cholinesterase inhibitor, physostigmine (PHYS) or glucose (GLU), attenuated these deficits. (McGlynn et al., 1994)

agonist are consistent across tasks, the conflicting results obtained with physostigmine may reflect differences between acquisition of maze learning and spontaneous alternation performance or may reflect differences in the extent to which the cholinergic input to hippocampus was removed. The issue of whether physostigmine is effective is an important one. Cholinesterase inhibitors require cholinergic terminals for their pharmacological action. If most of the cholinergic input to hippocampus is deafferented by the lesion, physostigmine reversal of the behavioral deficit would imply that cholinergic activation at nonhippocampal sites is sufficient (in lesioned animals) to compensate for the damage. Alternatively, residual cholinergic input to hippocampus may permit physostigmine to act within that brain area to reverse the consequences of medial septal damage. McGlynn et al. (1994) also examined the efficacy of glucose at enhancing spontaneous alternation performance. Glucose was ineffective in ameliorating the impaired alternation seen in rats with medial septal lesions. Together with results described below showing that direct intraseptal injections of glucose can reverse the effects of intraseptal morphine and muscimol on spontaneous alternation performance, the findings suggest that the medial septum is one brain area sensitive to glucose effects on memory.

Tests of modulation of memory in animals with lesions of medial septum are not as complete as those performed after amygdala lesions. Except for glucose, only drugs directed at cholinergic functions have, to my knowledge, been tested for efficacy in attenuating memory deficits after medial septal damage.

Conclusions
The issues of pharmacological and task specificity have been addressed only partially using these brain lesions. For amygdala and stria terminalis lesions, it is clear that the lesions interfere with the efficacy of a wide range of treatments,

suggesting that lesions do not interfere with modulation of memory in a neuro-transmitter-specific manner. Thus, for the amygdala, the rule appears to be that there is no pharmacological specificity for which drug classes lose efficacy in enhancing or impairing memory for aversive training conditions after amygdala lesions. For the medial septum, some pharmacological specificity—glucose versus cholinergic agonists—may appear, but the absence of examinations of other classes of drugs is striking, leaving the specificity of which treatment effects on memory are blocked by lesions of medial septum less clearly resolved.

Because comparable experiments have not been performed across tasks after lesions of either amygdala or medial septum, the findings do not address the question of whether drug effects on memory across tasks are blocked in animals with lesions or whether task specificity arises by area; the latter view is supported by results obtained when treatments are injected directly into specific brain regions.

Drug Injections into Specific Brain Targets

Many of the classes of drugs tested for effects on memory with systemic injections, as well as many of the interactions across neurotransmitter systems, have also been tested when administered directly into specific brain regions, in particular into the amygdala and medial septum. The overall findings lead to three general conclusions: (1) Drugs retain their valences as defined by systemic injections; a drug that enhances or impairs memory when injected systemically is likely to do the same when injected directly into a brain target (this first conclusion parallels the results obtained with systemic injections); (2) while some drug interactions seen with direct brain injections are similar to those seen with systemic injections, others are not evident when combined injections are administered to specific brain regions; (3) task specificity is evident when drug injections are aimed at specific brain regions. Importantly, this emergent task specificity appears to be defined by brain region rather than by treatment. Thus, treatments that enhance or impair memory do not do so for all tasks if the drugs are injected directly into specific brain targets. A corollary of this point is that if one drug (with either positive or negative valence) is effective in modulating memory on a particular task when injected into a brain area, other treatments injected into that brain area will also be effective in modulating memory for the same task. These points are addressed below for both amygdala and medial septum.

Amygdala Injections

Reversible lesions accomplished with bilateral injections of tetrodotoxin into the amygdala produce retrograde amnesia for inhibitory avoidance learning (Bucherelli, Tassoni, & Bures, 1992). In addition, there is a great deal known about the consequences, for learning and memory in avoidance tasks, of intra-amygdala injections of drugs directed at specific neurotransmitter systems (McGaugh et al., 1992). For example, posttraining injections of the beta-adrenergic antagonist, propranolol, produce retrograde amnesia for inhibitory avoidance training

(Gallagher, Kapp, Musty, & Driscoll, 1977). This effect can be reversed by additional administration into the amygdala of norepinephrine or phentolamine; phentolamine is an alpha-adrenergic antagonist that itself enhances memory when injected into the amygdala and that may act presynaptically to augment local release of norepinephrine (Gallagher & Kapp, 1981). Intra-amygdala injections of norepinephrine also enhance memory for inhibitory avoidance learning, an effect blocked by concomitant injections of propranolol (Liang, Juler, & McGaugh, 1986).

Analogous results have been observed with manipulations of both opiate, GABA, and glutamate receptor injections of drugs into the amygdala. Intra-amygdala injections of opiate and GABA agonists impair memory and the respective antagonists enhance memory for inhibitory avoidance training (Brioni, Nagahara, & McGaugh, 1989; Castellano, Brioni, Nagahara, & McGaugh, 1989; Ferreira, Da Silva, Medina, & Izquierdo, 1992; Gallagher & Kapp, 1978; Izquierdo et al., 1990; Izquierdo et al., 1992; Ragozzino, Parker, & Gold, 1992). Glutamate injections into the amygdala also enhance inhibitory avoidance memory, while injections of AP5 impair memory (Izquierdo et al., 1992). These latter findings are consistent with several other reports that NMDA antagonists injected into the amygdala shortly before training generally impair performance on later retention tests for inhibitory avoidance, fear-potentiated startle, and extinction of fear-potentiated startle (Falls, Miserendino, & Davis, 1992; Ferreira et al., 1992; Kim & McGaugh, 1992; Walker & Gold, 1991b).

Initial evidence from examinations of acute cholinergic manipulations of the amygdala near the time of training was unclear, with demonstrations, for example, that physostigmine enhances (Dumery, Derer, & Blozovski, 1988) or impairs (Todd & Kesner, 1978) memory, a discrepancy that may be based on dose. More recently, Izquierdo et al. (1992) demonstrated that posttraining intra-amygdala injections of scopolamine impaired retention on an inhibitory avoidance task, while the muscarinic agonist, oxotremorine, enhanced retention performance.

The effects on memory of drugs injected into the amygdala are well localized. For example, drugs that regulate memory when injected into the amygdala are not effective when injected into the caudate-putamen region dorsal to the amygdala (Brioni, Nagahara, & McGaugh, 1989; McGaugh, Introini-Collison, & Nagahara, 1988; Walker & Gold, 1991b).

Examinations of interactions across classes of treatments injected into the amygdala indicate, in some instances, summation of treatment valences. For example, enhancement of memory by either systemic or intra-amygdala injections of naloxone is blocked by concurrent injections of propranolol into the amygdala (Introini-Collison, Nagahara, & McGaugh, 1989; McGaugh, Introini-Collison, & Nagahara, 1988). Another B-adrenergic antagonist, timolol, blocked enhancement of inhibitory avoidance learning produced by the GABA antagonist, picrotoxin (Izquierdo et al., 1992). In analogous manner, injections of morphine into the amygdala impaired memory for inhibitory avoidance training; concomitant intra-amygdala injections of glucose reversed this impairment (Fig. 2.8) (Ragozzino

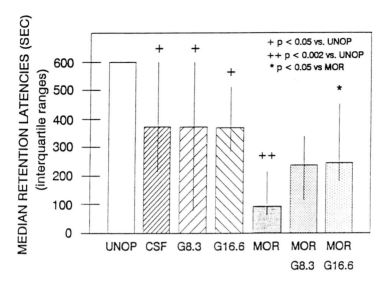

FIGURE 2.8.   Impairments in inhibitory avoidance acquisition in rats that received morphine injections into the amygdala. Concomitant intra-amygdala injections of glucose attenuated the impairments. (Ragozzino & Gold, 1994)

& Gold, 1994), findings consistent with additive properties of treatments with opposite valence.

In examining interactions of direct brain injections of glucose administered concurrently with other drugs, some failures to observe results predicted by studies of systemic injections appear. One example comes from examinations of potential interactions of amygdala injections of glucose and an NMDA antagonist. When injected into the amygdala, AP5- and propranolol-induced impairments in inhibitory avoidance learning do not appear to be reversed by glucose (unpublished). Thus, within the amygdala, glucose attenuates impairments in inhibitory avoidance learning after morphine (as noted earlier), but not impairments produced by other treatments. Other examples of limits on additivity with central injections are described below for the medial septum.

Several studies have addressed the issue of task specificity with direct central nervous system (CNS) drug injections. From these experiments, it appears that drug effects are specific to task according to the site of injection rather than the treatment injected. Levorphenol, an opiate agonist that impairs inhibitory avoidance learning when injected directly into the amygdala (Gallagher & Kapp, 1978), does not interfere with spatial learning when injected into the amygdala (Gallagher, Meagher, & Bostock, 1987). Similarly, while morphine injections into the amygdala impair inhibitory avoidance learning, the injections have no effect on spontaneous alternation performance (Ragozzino & Gold, 1994). Another example of task specificity is that a GABA agonist, chlordiazepoxide, does not impair spatial learning when injected into the amygdala, though it does so when injected into the medial septum (Stackman & Walsh, 1992). Although injections of many drugs into the amygdala, hippocampus, or medial septum have comparable effects on memory for inhibitory avoidance training, memory for habituation of exploration to a novel environment was modulated only if the drugs were injected into the hippocampus (Izquierdo et al., 1992). Importantly, when injected into the hippocampus, drugs that retained their valences with respect to the direction of effects on the habituation measure of memory were retained; AP5, scopolamine, and muscimol impaired memory on the habituation task, while glutamate, oxotremorine, picrotoxin, and norepinephrine enhanced memory.

While more studies of this type are needed, these findings suggest that task specificity emerges with direct brain injections of neurotransmitter-related drugs, in marked contrast to the results obtained with systemic administration of the same and similar drugs. Thus, the drug valence is retained, but task specificity is provided by neuroanatomical site of injection, not by the drug. The nature of the task specificity is what one would predict based on findings obtained with lesions of the same brain areas. While regional diversity of receptor localization suggests that, on a given task, some but not all modulators should be effective when injected into discrete brain areas, this pattern of results has not yet been reported. The collective findings obtained thus far suggest that similar neural mechanisms of modulation of memory are represented repeatedly in several brain regions.

Medial Septum Injections

Direct administration to the medial septum of the local anesthetics, lidocaine or procaine, interferes with spatial learning (Givens & Olton, 1990; Mizumori, Perez, Alvarado, Barnes, & McNaughton, 1990; Poucet, Herrmann, & Buhot, 1991). Drugs directed at opiate, cholinergic, and GABAergic receptors enhance or impair spatial learning in accord with the valence found with systemic injections of these and comparable drugs. Bostock, Gallagher, and King (1988) found that posttraining injections of naloxone into the medial septum enhance and injections of B-endorphin impair acquisition of radial maze learning in novel spatial environments. The opiate actions within the medial septum are not restricted to spatial learning. When administered to the medial septum, the opiate agonist levorphenol also impairs latent inhibition in rabbits (Gallagher, Meagher, & Bostock, 1987). Morphine injections into the medial septum interfere with spontaneous alternation performance and also impair acquisition of inhibitory avoidance learning (Ragozzino et al., 1992).

As with systemic injections, the cholinergic antagonist scopolamine impairs spatial learning when injected directly into the medial septum. Givens and Olton (1990) found that intraseptal scopolamine interferes with acquisition of a rewarded alternation task, as do intraseptal injections of galanin, a peptide colocalized with acetylcholine and that may inhibit acetylcholine release (Givens, Olton, & Crawley, 1992). Similarly, intraseptal injections of scopolamine impair spontaneous alternation performance (Grey et al., 1992).

GABAergic agonists administered to the medial septum also impair learning on spatial and other tasks. Pretraining injections of muscimol into the medial septum impair performance on spatial tasks (Brioni, Decker, Gamboa, Izquierdo, & McGaugh, 1990; Chrobak, Stackman, & Walsh, 1989), as well as on reinforced alternation (Givens & Olton, 1990), spontaneous alternation tasks (Grey et al., 1991), and inhibitory avoidance (Nagahara, Brioni, & McGaugh, 1992; Nagahara & McGaugh, 1992). When injected systemically or directly into the medial septum, the benzodiazepine, chlordiazepoxide, impairs working memory in a delayed non-match-to-sample version of the radial arm maze (Stackman & Walsh, 1992). As noted earlier, impairments on this task were not seen in rats that received the drug injected into the amygdala. In examining the effects on memory of several drugs injected into three brain targets, Izquierdo et al. (1992) found that a wide range of treatments affected inhibitory avoidance memory when injected into the medial septum, amygdala, or hippocampus; AP5, scopolamine, and muscimol impaired memory and glutamate, oxotremorine, picrotoxin, and norepinephrine enhanced memory for inhibitory avoidance training when injected into any of the three brain areas tested. As noted previously, only when injected into the hippocampus did these treatments modulate memory for habituation of exploration to a novel environment.

The tasks susceptible to septal manipulations are less restricted than those susceptible to amygdala injections. The results presented earlier indicate that injections into the medial septum of drugs that modulate memory influence not only spatial learning but also inhibitory avoidance and latent inhibition, but not habituation of exploration to a novel environment. There are several reasons these results might appear. The inhibitory avoidance tasks employed in these experiments all include a spatial component that might provide the basis for the effects on avoidance learning. Perhaps because specific task demands differ, perhaps because our categorizations of types of memory (e.g., spatial vs. avoidance) are not accurate, or perhaps because manipulations of the medial septum affect many types of memory, effects of drug injections into medial septum do not fit easily into a particular memory class. Still, it is important to note that the direction of effects of drugs injected into the medial septum, as well as amygdala or hippocampus, is consistent with the valence obtained with systemic injections.

Impairments on both spontaneous alternation and inhibitory avoidance measures produced by morphine injections into the medial septum are reversed by either systemic or intraseptal injections of glucose (Fig. 2.9) (Ragozzino et al., 1992). Together with analogous findings obtained in the amygdala for avoidance learning (Ragozzino & Gold, 1994), these findings suggest that glucose can act locally to reverse the effects of an opiate agonist on memory. However, not all potential interactions occur. In contrast to the findings obtained with morphine, glucose coadministered with scopolamine into the medial septum is ineffective in reversing the effects of scopolamine on spontaneous alternation performance. These findings, together with partial reversal of impaired spontaneous alternation performance after intraseptal muscimol are shown in Figure 2.10. The failure of glucose to reverse scopolamine actions contrasts again with glucose reversal of morphine impairments of spontaneous alternation performance when the two drugs are both injected into medial septum.

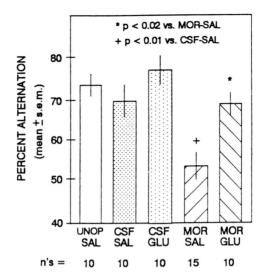

FIGURE 2.9. Impairments in spontaneous alternation performance in rats that received morphine injections into the medial septum. Concomitant intraseptal injections of glucose attenuated the impairments. (Ragozzino, Parker, & Gold, 1992)

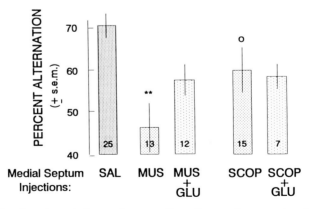

FIGURE 2.10. Impairments in spontaneous alternation performance in rats that received muscimol or scopolamine injections into the medial septum. Concomitant intraseptal injections of glucose partially attenuated the muscimol-induced impairments but not the scopolamine-induced impairments. (Grey, Lam, & Gold, 1991)

These results are not consistent with those obtained with systemic injections, which indicate that glucose does attenuate the effects of systemically administered scopolamine on spontaneous alternation performance, as well as on many other measures. The difference in the pharmacological specificity versus lack of specificity with central versus systemic injections presumably reflects glucose actions on multiple and redundant neural systems. More generally, the implication of this view is that systemic injections of two drugs acting on different classes of neurotransmitters might be additive because of actions on parallel neural systems, a possibility avoided with direct central injections. Thus, additivity across drug classes seen with systemic injections is only partially retained with central injections. One goal of experiments testing the effects of interactions across neurotransmitter systems on memory is to identify a sequential series of actions through which memory is modulated. There are now many examples of such interactions and, in my view, it is the failures to see interactions that become more revealing. Drug actions on those modulatory mechanisms proximal to the mechanisms of memory formation should not be susceptible to manipulations targeted at earlier steps.

While the motivation for studies of medial septum includes the extensive information defining, both neuroanatomically and pharmacologically, the septal input to hippocampus, studies that directly use this information are only beginning to appear. As one example, cholinergic activation, assessed by high-affinity choline uptake, is seen in mice trained in an eight-arm radial maze (Toumane, Durkin, Marighetto, & Jaffard, 1989). The activation is blocked and spatial learning is impaired in mice that receive intraseptal injections of the alpha-adrenergic antagonist, phenoxybenzamine (Marighetto, Durkin, Toumane, & Jaffard, 1989) or the GABA agonists, bicuculline or muscimol (Durkin, 1992).

These findings are consistent with evidence obtained with systemic injections as well. Messier, Durkin, Mrabet, and Destrade (1990) report that glucose injections interact with scopolamine in regulating hippocampal high-affinity choline uptake, though the pattern of results is complex. We have begun to use microdialysis measures of acetylcholine release in dorsal hippocampus after systemic morphine injections. Initial results, shown in Figure 2.11, indicate that morphine injections at doses that impair spontaneous alternation performance in rats reduce acetylcholine release in the dorsal hippocampus (Ragozzino, Wenk, & Gold, 1994). Analogous studies using direct septal injections have not yet been completed. Together, these findings offer the possibility that modulation of cholinergic activity may be an output process common to many treatments that modulate memory. Experiments of this type suggest that the septohippocampal system might prove useful as a model with which to dissect the nature of pharmacological interactions that regulate memory processing.

Conclusions

For both amygdala and medial septum injections, there appears to be a wide range of neurotransmitter-related drugs that can enhance or impair memory. Importantly, the valences with respect to effects of systemic injections on memory are

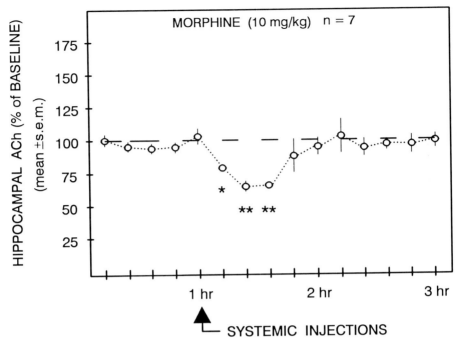

FIGURE 2.11.   Decrease in acetylcholine, assessed with microdialysis collection and HPLC analysis, released in dorsal hippocampus after systemic injection of morphine at a dose that impairs learning and memory. (Ragozzino et al., 1994)

retained when the drugs are injected directly into these brain regions. Thus, the general rule is: *When injected directly into specific brain sites, most drugs have a positive or negative valence consistent with that identified with systemic injections.*

In several examples of studies of interactions between drugs belonging to different neurotransmitter classes, the memory modulation valences are additive. The findings obtained with septal and amygdala injections of glucose, however, offer exceptions to straightforward additivity predicted by systemic injections, with demonstrations that glucose can reverse the impairments on memory with some (e.g., opiate, GABAergic) but not other (glutamatergic, cholinergic) neurotransmitter systems. In the case of glucose attenuation of morphine-induced impairments, comparable results are seen in two brain areas, the amygdala and medial septum, for different tasks, inhibitory avoidance and spontaneous alternation, respectively. The appearance of pharmacological specificity with direct brain injections offers hope for elucidating the nature of glucose effects on brain function as well as clarifying the sequential neurotransmitter actions responsible for modulating memory processes in different brain areas.

The findings reviewed here that compare effects on different tasks of treatments injected into different brain regions suggest that brain structure, rather than neurotransmitter class, conveys those task differences observed. While more demonstrations of this type are needed, it seems reasonable to conclude, albeit somewhat tentatively, that *task specificity for memory modulation is a property of the neural system targeted, not of the treatment itself.*

GENERAL CONCLUSIONS

This chapter has attempted to identify several concepts into which much of the evidence about the pharmacology of learning and memory can be placed. Studies using systemically administered treatments identify a direction, enhancement or impairment, of effects of several hormones and neurotransmitters on learning and memory, with little evidence of differences across tasks. Furthermore, these valences are additive for treatments acting both within and across neurotransmitter and receptor domains. For some endogenous modulators of memory formation, for example, epinephrine and glucose, the experimental procedures of systemic injections mirror systemic release of the modulators. Therefore, experiences that elicit release of modulators of learning and memory into the circulation are likely also to promote memory storage for any information reaching the nervous system at about the same time. This view suggests that systemically administered treatments might also enhance or impair memory across a wide range of tasks. These are the results obtained.

In applying these general concepts obtained with systemically administered treatments to findings obtained with direct brain injections, there are some similarities, but also some important differences. For a given drug, the valence identified with systemic administration appears to be retained in large part with direct injections into the medial septum or amygdala, as well as the hippocampus. When effects on memory are evident, they are well-localized to the brain target with comparable injections into neighboring or other control sites ineffective in modulating memory. Within the set of drugs that regulate memory, however, the brain target—more than the treatment—defines the task for which the drugs will be effective modulators. With the data available, this statement applies particularly well to the amygdala and perhaps hippocampus, and less well as of yet to the medial septum. Thus, differences in memory modulation by task reflect actions on different neural systems more than actions on different neurotransmitter systems.

A second important difference between results obtained with systemic and peripheral injections is that additivity is more readily evident with systemic injections than with central injections. Full examination of additivity of treatments, particularly those crossing neurotransmitter and receptor classes, is still quite incomplete. The initial demonstrations of restricted additivity suggest, however, that it will be possible to define the extent to which different neurotransmitters within a brain area act in series, or in parallel, or with hierarchical importance, to regulate learning and memory processes. Failures to see interactions are especially important for identifying the organization and integration of neurotransmitter regulation of memory formation.

One major question is whether the organization of neurotransmitters that regulate memory is similar in different brain regions. On the basis of very little data obtained thus far, the same neurotransmitter systems appear to act at each brain site tested thus far, though on memory for different behavioral tasks. Moreover, similar restrictions on additivity with injections into the medial septum or amygdala are seen in both brain targets, albeit with few examples. If comparable results are evident across brain areas for many drugs and many measures of memory, the implication is that there is a single organization of neurotransmitters that regulate memory in several brain regions.

The view that there is an integrated neurochemical system, recurring in different brain areas, that regulates memory formation may simplify the task of attaining several goals. One implication is that the substrates of memory are regulated in different neuroanatomical systems by the same modulatory mechanisms, and that the content-specific nature of memory is defined not by modulators but by those neuroanatomical systems engaged by specific experiences. A reasonable corollary of this view is that, like the modulatory systems, the mechanisms of memory formation might also be few in number and repeatedly represented in multiple neuroanatomical systems. This view offers great hope, I think, at unraveling the biological bases by which memories are made and regulated. In addition, with growing evidence that the same treatments that enhance memory in rodents also do so in humans and other primates, the prospects improve greatly for identifying cognitive enhancers (Wenk & Olton, 1989) that ameliorate memory loss during aging and in pathological conditions.

ACKNOWLEDGMENTS

Preparation of this manuscript and research from this laboratory was supported by research grants from the National Science Foundation (BNS-9012239), the Office of Naval Research (N0001489-J-1216), and the National Institute on Aging (AG 07648).

REFERENCES

Aigner, T. G., & Mishkin, M. (1986). The effects of physostigmine and scopolamine on recognition memory in monkeys. *Behavioral and Neural Biology, 45,* 81–87.

Aigner, T. G., & Mishkin, M. (1988). Improved recognition memory in monkeys following naloxone administration. *Psychopharmacology, 94,* 21–23.

Alexandrov, A. A., Sabanov, V.S., & Samoylova, L. A. (1984). The influence of microiontophoretic GABA application on the formation of the cellular analogue of the conditioned response. *Zhurnal Vysshei Nervnoi Deyatel'nosti, 34,* 1122–1127.

Amaral, D. G., & Kurz, J. (1985). An analysis of the origins of the cholinergic and noncholinergic septal projections to the hippocampal formation. *Journal of Comparative Neurology, 240,* 37–59.

Ammassari-Teule, M., Pavone, F., Castellano, C., & McGaugh, J. L. (1991). Amygdala and dorsal hippocampus lesions block the effects of GABAergic drugs on memory storage. *Brain Research, 551,* 104–109.

Arankowsky-Sandoval, G., & Gold, P. E. (1994). *Morphine-induced deficits in sleep patterns: Attenuation by glucose.* Manuscript submitted.

Axelrod, J., Weil-Malherbe, H., & Tomchick, R. (1959). The physiological disposition of 3H-epinephrine and its metabolite metanephrine. *Journal of Pharmacology and Experimental Therapeutics, 127,* 251–256.

Becker, J. T., Walker, J. A., and Olton, D. S. (1980). Neuroanatomical bases of spatial memory. *Brain Research, 200,* 307–320.

Black, I. L., & Barbee, J. G. (1987). Effect of diazepam upon verbal recall associated with simple picture recognition. *Psychological Reports, 60,* 1139–1149.

Bostock, E., Gallagher, M., & King, R. A. (1988). Effects of opioid microinjections into the medial septal area on spatial memory in rats. *Behavioral Neuroscience, 102,* 643–652.

Brioni, J. D., & Arolfo, M. P. (1992). Diazepam impairs retention of spatial information without affecting retrieval or cue learning. *Pharmacology Biochemistry and Behavior, 41,* 1–5.

Brioni, J. D., Decker, M. W., Gamboa, L. P., Izquierdo, I., & McGaugh, J. L. (1990). Muscimol injections into the medial septum impair spatial learning. *Brain Research, 522,* 227–234.

Brioni, J. D., Nagahara, A. H., & McGaugh, J. L. (1989). Involvement of the amygdala GABAergic system in the modulation of memory storage. *Brain Research, 487,* 105–112.

Broecher, S., Artola, A., & Singer, W. (1992). Agonists of cholinergic and noradrenergic receptors facilitate synergistically the induction of long-term potentiation in slices of rat visual cortex. *Brain Research, 573,* 27–36.

Bucherelli, C., Tassoni, G., & Bures, J. (1992). Time-dependent disruption of passive avoidance acquisition by post-training intra-amygdala injection of tetrodotoxin in rats. *Neuroscience Letters, 22,* 231–234.

Canli, T., Cook, R. G., and Miczek, K. A. (1990). Opiate antagonists enhance the working memory of rats in the radial maze. *Pharmacology Biochemistry and Behavior, 36,* 521–525.

Castellano, C., Brioni, J. D., Nagahara, A. H., & McGaugh, J. L. (1989). Post-training systemic and intra-amygdala administration of the GABA-B agonist baclofen impairs retention. *Behavioral and Neural Biology, 52,* 170–179.

Castellano, C., Introini-Collison, I. B., Pavone, F., & McGaugh, J. L. (1989). Effects of naloxone and naltrexone on memory consolidation in CD1 mice: Involvement of GABAergic mechanisms. *Pharmacology Biochemistry and Behavior, 32,* 563–567.

Castellano, C., Libri, V., & Ammassari-Teule, M. (1988). The amygdala mediates the impairing effect of the selective k-opioid receptor agonist U-50,488 on memory in CD1 mice. *Behavioural Brain Research, 30,* 259–263.

Castellano, C., & McGaugh, J. L. (1989). Retention enhancement with post-training picrotoxin: Lack of state dependency. *Behavioral and Neural Biology, 51,* 165–170.

Castellano, C., & McGaugh, J. L. (1991). Oxotremorine attenuates retrograde amnesia induced by post-training administration of the GABAergic agonists muscimol and baclofen. *Behavioral and Neural Biology, 56,* 25–31.

Chrobak, J. J., Stackman, R. W., & Walsh, T. J. (1989). Intraseptal administration of muscimol produces dose-dependent memory impairments in the rat. *Behavioral and Neural Biology, 52,* 357–369.

Cicacla, G. A., Azorlosa, J. L., Estall, L. B. & Grant, S. J. (1990). Endogenous opioids interfere with Pavlovian second-order fear conditioning. *Psychological Science, 1,* 312–315.

Collingridge, G. L., & Bliss, T. V. (1987). NMDA receptors: Their role in long-term potentiation. *Trends in Neuroscience, 10,* 288–293.

Cotman, C. W., Monaghan, D. T., & Ganong, A. H. (1988). Excitatory amino acid neurotransmission: NMDA and Hebb-type synaptic plasticity. *Annual Review of Neuroscience, 11,* 61–80.

Davis, M. (1992). The role of the amygdala in fear and anxiety. *Annual Review of Neuroscience, 15,* 353–375.

Dawson, G. R., Bentley, G., Draper, R., Rycroft, W., Iverson, S. D., & Pagella, P. G. (1991). The behavioral effects of heptyl physostigmine, a new cholinesterase inhibitor, in tests of long-term and working memory in rodents. *Pharmacology Biochemistry and Behavior, 39,* 865–871.

Decker, M. W., Gill, T. M., & McGaugh, J. L. (1990). Concurrent muscarinic and B-adrenergic blockade in rats impairs place-learning in a water maze and retention of inhibitory avoidance. *Brain Research, 513,* 81–85.

Decker, M. W., Introini-Collison, I. B., & McGaugh, J. L. (1989). Effects of naloxone on Morris water maze learning in the rat: Enhanced acquisition with pretraining but not posttraining administration. *Psychobiology, 17,* 270–275.

Decker, M. W., Majchrzak, M.J., & Anderson, D. J. (1992). Effects of nicotine on spatial memory deficits in rats with septal lesions. *Brain Research, 572,* 281–285.

Del Cerro, S., Jung, M., & Lynch, G. (1992). Benzodiazepines block long-term potentiation in slices of hippocampus and piriform cortex. *Neuroscience, 49,* 1–6.

Dumery, V., Derer, P., & Blozovski, D. (1988). Enhancement of passive avoidance learning through small doses of introamygdaloid physostigmine in the young rat: Its relation to the development of acetylcholinesterase. *Developmental Psychobiology, 21,* 553–565.

Durkin, T. P. (1992). GABAergic mediation of indirect transsynaptic control of septo-hippocampal cholinergic activity in mice. *Behavioural Brain Research, 50,* 155–165.

Ellis, S., Kennedy, B. L., Eusebi, A. J., & Vincent, N. H. (1967). Autonomic control of metabolism. *Annals of the New York Academy of Sciences, 139,* 826–832.

Falls, W. A., Miserendino, M. J. D., & Davis, M. (1992). Extinction of fear-potentiated startle: Blockade by infusion of an NMDA antagonist into the amygdala. *Journal of Neuroscience, 12,* 854–863.

Ferreira, M. B. C., Da Silva, R. C., Medina, J. H., & Izquierdo, I. (1992). Late posttraining memory processing by entorhinal cortex: Involvement of NMDA and GABAergic receptors. *Pharmacology Biochemistry and Behavior, 41,* 767–771.

Flood, J. F., Baker, M. L., & Davis, J. L. (1990). Modulation of memory processing by glutamic acid receptor agonists and antagonists. *Brain Research, 521,* 197–202.

Flood, J. F., Smith, G. E., & Cherkin, A. (1985). Memory enhancement: Supra-additive effect of subcutaneous cholinergic drug combinations in mice. *Psychopharmacology, 86,* 61–67.

Frotscher, M., & Leranth, C. (1985). Cholinergic innervation of the rat hippocampus as revealed by choline acetyltransferase immunocytochemistry: A combined light and electron microscopic study. *Journal of Comparative Neurology, 239,* 237–246.

Gallagher, M., & Kapp, B. S. (1978). Manipulation of opiate activity in the amygdala alters memory processes. *Life Sciences, 23,* 1973–1978.

Gallagher, M., & Kapp, B. S. (1981). Effect of phentolamine administration into the amygdala complex of rats on time-dependent memory processes. *Behavioral and Neural Biology, 31,* 90–95.

Gallagher, M., Kapp, B. S., Musty, R. E., & Driscoll, P. A. (1977). Memory formation: Evidence for a specific neurochemical system in the amygdala. *Science, 198,* 423–425.

Gallagher, M., King, R. A., & Young, N. B. (1983). Opiate antagonists improve spatial memory. *Science, 221,* 975–976.

Gallagher, M., Meagher, M. W., & Bostock, E. (1987). Effects of opiate manipulations on latent inhibition in rabbits: Sensitivity of the medial septal region to intracranial treatments. *Behavioral Neuroscience, 101,* 315–324.

Givens, B. S., & Olton, D. S. (1990). Cholinergic and GABAergic modulation of medial septal area: Effect on working memory. *Behavioral Neuroscience, 104,* 849–855.

Givens, B. S., Olton, D. S., & Crawley, J. N. (1992). Galanin in the medial septal area impairs working memory. *Brain Research, 582,* 71–77.

Gold, P. E. (1991). An integrated memory regulation system: From blood to brain. In R. C. A. Frederickson, J. L. McGaugh, & D. L. Felten (Eds.), *Peripheral signaling of the brain: Role in neural-immune interactions, learning and memory* (pp. 391–419). Toronto: Hogrefe & Huber.

Gold, P. E. (1992a). Modulation of memory processing: Enhancement of memory in rodents and humans. In N. Butters & L. R. Squire (Eds.), *Neuropsychology of memory* (pp. 402–414). New York: Guilford.

Gold, P. E. (1992b). A proposed neurobiological basis for regulating memory storage for significant events. In E. Winograd & U. Neisser (Eds.), *Affect and accuracy in recall: Studies of "flashbulb" memories* (pp. 141–161). New York: Cambridge University Press.

Gold, P. E., Delanoy, R. L., & Merrin, J. (1984). Modulation of long-term potentiation by peripherally administered amphetamine and epinephrine. *Brain Research, 305,* 103–107.

Gold, P. E., & McCarty, R. (1981). Plasma catecholamines: Changes after footshock and seizure-producing frontal cortex stimulation. *Behavioral and Neural Biology, 31,* 247–260.

Gold, P. E., & McGaugh, J. L. (1975). A single-trace, two-process view of memory storage processes. In D. Deutsch & J. A. Deutsch (Eds.), *Short-term memory* (pp. 355–390). New York: Academic Press.

Gold, P. E., & Zornetzer, S. F. (1983). The mnemon and its juices: Neuromodulation of memory processes. *Behavioral and Neural Biology, 38,* 151–189.

Grey, C.M., Lam, W. K. K., & Gold, P. E. (1991). Effects of peripheral and central injections of GABA agonists on spontaneous alternation performance. Presented at the Twenty-first Annual Meeting of the Society for Neuroscience, New Orleans, LA.

Haley, D. A., Thompson, R. F., & Madden, J. (1988). Pharmacological analysis of the magnocellular red nucleus during classical conditioning of the rabbit nictitating membrane response. *Brain Research, 454,* 131–139.

Hall, J. L., & Gold, P. E. (1986). The effects of training, epinephrine, and glucose injections on plasma glucose levels in rats. *Behavioral and Neural Biology, 46,* 156–176.

Hall, J. L., & Gold, P. E. (1992). Plasma glucose levels predict the susceptibility of memory enhancement to disruption by adrenergic antagonists. *European Journal of Pharmacology, 221,* 365–370.

Hall, J. L., Gonder-Frederick, L. A., Chewning, W. W., Silveira, J., & Gold, P. E. (1989). Glucose enhancement of performance on memory tests in young and aged humans. *Neuropsychologia, 27,* 1129–1138.

Helmstetter, F. J. (1992). Contribution of the amygdala to learning and performance of conditional fear. *Physiology and Behavior, 51,* 1271–1276.

Hernandez, L. L., Valentine, J. D., & Powell, D. A. (1987). Opioid modulation of Pavlovian learning in rabbits: Involvement of sublenticular pathways. *Behavioral Neuroscience, 105,* 431–442.

Hrbek, J., Macakova, J., Komenda, S., & Siroka, A. (1989). Effect of physostigmine and its combination with some drugs on the process of verbal learning. *Activitas Nervosa Superior, 31,* 74–75.

Introini-Collison, I. B., Arai, Y., & McGaugh, J. L. (1991). Stria terminalis lesions attenuate the effects of posttraining oxotremorine and atropine on retention. *Psychobiology, 17,* 397–401.

Introini-Collison, I. B., Miyazaki, B., & McGaugh, J. L. (1991). Involvement of the amygdala in the memory-enhancing effects of clenbuterol. *Psychopharmacology, 104,* 541–544.

Introini-Collison, I. B., Nagahara, A. H., & McGaugh, J. L. (1989). Memory enhancement with intra-amygdala post-training naloxone is blocked by concurrent administration of propranolol. *Brain Research, 476,* 94–101.

Itoh, J., Nabeshima, T., & Kameyama, T. (1990). Utility of an elevated plus-maze for the evaluation of memory in mice: Effects of nootropics, scopolamine and electroconvulsive shock. *Psychopharmacology, 101,* 27–33.

Izquierdo, I. (1979). Effect of morphine on various forms of memory in the rat: Possible role of endogenous opiate mechanisms in memory consolidation. *Psychopharmacology, 66,* 199–203.

Izquierdo, I., da Cunha, C., Huang, C. H., Walz, R., Wolfman, C., & Medina, J. H. (1990). Post-training down-regulation of memory consolidation by a GABA-A mechanism in the amygdala modulated by endogenous benzodiazepines. *Behavioral and Neural Biology, 54*, 105–109.

Izquierdo, I., da Cunha, C., Rosat, R., Jerusalinshky, D., Ferreira, M. B. C., & Medina, J. H. (1992). Neurotransmitter receptors involved in post-training memory processing by the amygdala, medial septum and hippocampus of the rat. *Behavioral and Neural Biology, 58*, 16–26.

Kerr, B., Hill, H., Coda, B., Calogero, M., Chapman, C.R., Hunt, E., Buffington, V., & Mackie, A. (1991). Concentration-related effects of morphine on cognition and motor control in human subjects. *Neuropsychopharmacology, 5*, 157–166.

Kesner, R. P. (1992). Learning and memory in rats with an emphasis on the role of the amygdala. In J. P. Aggleton (Ed.), *The amygdala: Neurobiological aspects of emotion, memory, and mental dysfunction* (pp. 379–399). New York: Wiley-Liss.

Kesner, R. P., & Johnson, D. L. (1991). An analysis of the basal forebrain contribution to learning and memory. In R. T. Richardson (Ed.), *Activation to acquisition: Functional aspects of the basal forebrain cholinergic system* (pp. 263–288). Boston: Birkäuser.

Kety, S. (1972). Brain catecholamines, affective states and memory. In J. L. McGaugh (Ed.), *The chemistry of mood, motivation and memory* (pp. 65–80). New York: Raven.

Kim, J. J., DeCola, J. P., Landeira-Fernandez, J., & Fanselow, M. S. (1991). N-methyl-D-aspartate (NMDA) receptor antagonist APV blocks acquisition but not expression of fear conditioning. *Behavioral Neuroscience, 105*, 126–133.

Kim, M., & McGaugh, J. L. (1992). Effects of intra-amygdala injections of NMDA receptor antagonists on acquisition and retention of inhibitory avoidance. *Brain Research, 585*, 35–48.

Köhler, C., Chan-Palay, V., & Wu, J.-Y. (1984). Septal neurons containing glutamic acid decarboxylase immunoreactivity project to the hippocampal region in the rat brain. *Anatomical Embryology, 169*, 41–44.

LeDoux, J. E. (1992). Emotion and the amygdala. In J. P. Aggleton (Ed.), *The amygdala: Neurobiological aspects of emotion, memory, and mental dysfunction* (pp. 339–351). New York: Wiley-Liss.

Levin, E. D., & Rose, J. E. (1991). Nicotinic and muscarinic interactions and choice accuracy in the radial-arm maze. *Brain Research Bulletin, 27*, 125–128.

Liang, K. C., Juler, R., & McGaugh, J. L. (1986). Modulating effects of posttraining epinephrine on memory: Involvement of the amygdala noradrenergic system. *Brain Research, 368*, 125–133.

Liang, K. C., & McGaugh, J. L. (1983). Lesions of the stria terminalis attenuate the enhancing effect of posttraining epinephrine on retention of an inhibitory avoidance response. *Behavioural Brain Research, 9*, 49–58.

Liang, K. C., McGaugh, J. L., & Yao, H. Y. (1990). Involvement of amygdala pathways in the influence of post-training intra-amygdala norepinephrine and peripheral epinephrine on memory storage. *Brain Research, 508*, 225–233.

Lin, Y., & Phillis, J. W. (1991). Muscarinic agonist-mediated induction of long-term potentiation in rat cerebral cortex. *Brain Research, 551*, 342–345.

Long, J., Davis, B., Garofalo, P., Spangler, E., & Ingram, D. (1990). Complex maze learning in aged rats is related to blood glucose levels and insulin response but is unresponsive to glucose treatment. *Society for Neuroscience Abstracts, 16*, 840.

Lyford, G. L., & Jarrard, L. E. (1991). Effects of the competitive NMDA antagonist CPP on performance of a place and cue radial maze task. *Psychobiology, 19*, 157–160.

Mahalik, T., & Fitzgerald, R. D. (1988). Morphine influences on classical aversive conditioned heart rate in rats. *Behavioral Neuroscience, 102*, 244–253.

Maho, C., Dutrieux, G., & Ammassari-Teule, M. (1988). Parallel modifications of spatial memory performances, exploration patterns, and hippocampal theta rhythms in fornix-damaged rats: Reversal of oxotremorine. *Behavioral Neuroscience, 102*, 601–604.

Manning, C. A., Hall, J. L., & Gold, P. E. (1990). Glucose effects on memory and other neuropsychological tests in elderly humans. *Psychological Science, 1*, 307–311.

Manning, C. A., Parsons, M. W., Cotter, E. M., & Gold, P. E. (1992). *Glucose effects on explicit and implicit memory in healthy elderly and young adults.* Manuscript in preparation.

Manning, C. A., Parsons, M. W., & Gold, P. E. (1992). Anterograde and retrograde enhancement of 24-hour memory by glucose in elderly humans. *Behavioral and Neural Biology, 58,* 125–130.

Manning, C. A., Ragozzino, M., & Gold, P. E. (1993). Glucose enhancement of memory in patients with Alzheimer's disease. *Neurobiology of Aging, 14,* 523–528.

Marighetto, A., Durkin, T., Toumane, A., Jaffard, R. (1989). Septal α-noradrenergic antagonism *in vivo* blocks the testing-induced activation of septo-hippocampal cholinergic neurones and produces a concomitant deficit in working memory performance in mice. *Pharmacology Biochemistry and Behavior, 34,* 553–558.

Martinez, J. L., Jr., Weinberger, S. B., Janak, P. H., Schulteis, G., Shibanoki, S., & Ishikawa, K. (1991). Peripheral signaling of the brain: How hormones influence learning and memory. In R. C. A. Frederickson, J. L. McGaugh, & D. L. Felten (Eds.), *Peripheral signaling of the brain: Role in neural-immune interactions, learning and memory* (pp. 365–378). Toronto: Hogrefe & Huber.

Matsuoka, N., Maeda, N., Ohkubo, Y., & Yamaguchi, I. (1991). Differential effects of physostigmine and pilocarpine on the spatial memory deficits produced by two septo-hippocampal deafferentations in rats. *Brain Research, 559,* 233–240.

McCarty, R., & Gold, P. E. (1981). Plasma catecholamines: Effects of footshock level and hormonal modulators of memory storage. *Hormones and Behavior, 15,* 168–182.

McEchron, M. D., & Gormezano, I. (1991). Morphine's effects on differential serial compound conditioning and reflex modification of the rabbit's (Oryctolagus cuniculus) nictitating membrane response. *Behavioral Neuroscience, 105,* 510–520.

McGaugh, J. L. (1989). Involvement of hormonal and neuromodulatory systems in the regulation of memory storage. Annual Review of Neuroscience, 12, 255–287.

McGaugh, J. L., & Gold, P. E. (1989). Hormonal modulation of memory. In R. Brush & S. Levine (Eds.), *Psychoendocrinology* (pp. 305–339). New York: Academic Press.

McGaugh, J. L., Introini-Collison, I. B., Cahill, L., Kim, M., & Liang, K. C. (1992). Involvement of the amygdala in neuromodulatory influences on memory storage. In J. P. Aggleton (Ed.), *The amygdala: Neurobiological aspects of emotion, memory, and mental dysfunction* (pp. 431–451). New York: Wiley-Liss.

McGaugh, J. L., Introini-Collison, I. B., Juler, R. G., & Izquierdo, I. (1986). Stria terminalis lesions attenuate the effects of posttraining naloxone and B-endorphin on retention. *Behavioral Neuroscience, 100,* 839–844.

McGaugh, J. L., Introini-Collison, I. B., & Nagahara, A. H. (1988). Memory-enhancing effects of posttraining naloxone: Involvement of *B*-adrenergic influences in the amygdaloid complex. *Brain Research, 446,* 37–49.

McGlynn, T. J., Lennartz, R., Gold, S. D., & Gold, P. E. (1994). *Ibotenic acid lesions of medial septum: Reversal of spontaneous alternation deficits with oxotremorine, but not glucose or physostigmine.* Manuscript submitted for publication.

McNamara, R. K., & Skelton, R. W. (1991). Pretraining morphine impairs acquisition and performance in the Morris water maze: Motivation reduction rather than amnesia. *Psychobiology, 19,* 313–322.

Means, L. W., & Fernandez, T. J. (1992). Daily glucose injections facilitate performance of a win-shift water-escape working memory task in mice. *Behavioral Neuroscience, 106,* 345–350.

Messier, C., & Destrade, C. (1988). Improvement of memory for an operant response by post-training glucose in mice. *Behavioural Brain Research, 31,* 185–191.

Messier, C., Durkin, T., Mrabet, O., & Destrade, C. (1990). Memory-improving action of glucose: Indirect evidence for a facilitation of hippocampal acetylcholine synthesis. *Behavioural Brain Research, 39,* 135–143.

Mishkin, M., & Appenzeller, T. (1990). The anatomy of memory. In R. R. Llinas (Ed.), *The workings of the brain: Development, memory and perception* (pp. 88–102). New York: Freeman.

Mizumori, S. J. Y., Perez, G. M., Alvarado, M. C., Barnes, C. A., & McNaughton, B. L. (1990). Reversible inactivation of the medial septum differentially affects two forms of learning in rats. *Brain Research, 512,* 12–20.

Morris, R. G. M., Anderson, E., Lynch, G. S., & Baudry, M. (1986). Selective impairment of learning and blockade of long-term potentiation by an N-methyl-D-aspartate receptor antagonist, AP5. *Nature, 319,* 774–776.

Morris, R. G., Halliwell, R. F., & Bowery, N. (1989). Synaptic plasticity and learning: II. Do different kinds of plasticity underlie different kinds of learning? *Neuropsychologia, 27,* 41–59.

Mott, D. D., & Lewis, D. V. (1991). Facilitation of the induction of long-term potentiation by GABA-sub(b) receptors. *Science, 252,* 1718–1720.

Moye, T. B., & Rudy, J. W. (1987). Visually mediated trace conditioning in young rats: Evidence for cholinergic involvement in the development of associative memory. *Psychobiology, 15,* 128–136.

Nagahara, A. H., Brioni, J. D., & McGaugh, J. L. (1992). Effects of intraseptal infusion of muscimol on inhibitory avoidance and spatial learning: Differential effects of pretraining and post-training administration. *Psychobiology, 20,* 198–204.

Nagahara, A. H., & McGaugh, J. L. (1992). Muscimol infused into the medial septum impairs long-term memory but not short-term memory in inhibitory avoidance, water maze place learning and reward alternation tasks. *Brain Research, 591,* 54–61.

Nicoll, R. A. (1985). The septo-hippocampal projection: A model cholinergic pathway. *Trends in Neuroscience, 8,* 533–536.

Nissen, M. J., Knopman, D. S., & Schacter, D. L. (1987). Neurochemical dissociation of memory systems. *Neurology, 37,* 789–794.

Packard, M. G., & White, N. M. (1990). Effect of posttraining injections of glucose on acquisition of two appetitive learning tasks. *Psychobiology, 18,* 282–286.

Peretti, P. O., & Nowak, C. (1974). Effects of epinephrine on the activity level and on the formation of learning of a maze in "carassius auratus." *Acta Neurologica, 29,* 715–719.

Pontecorvo, M. J., Clissold, D. B., White, D. B., & Ferkany, J. W. (1991). N-methyl-D-aspartate antagonists and working memory performance: Comparison with the effects of scopolamine, propranolol, diazepam, and phenylisopropyladenosine. *Behavioral Neuroscience, 105,* 521–535.

Poucet, B., Herrmann, T., & Buhot, M. C. (1991). Effects of short-lasting inactivations of the ventral hippocampus and medial septum on long-term and short-term acquisition of spatial information in rats. *Behavioural Brain Research, 44,* 53–65.

Preston, G. C., Ward, C., Lines, C. R., Poppleton, P., Haigh, J. R. M., & Traub, M. (1989). Scopolamine and benzodiazepine models of dementia: Cross-reversals by RO 15-1788 and physostigmine. *Psychopharmacology, 98,* 487–494.

Ragozzino, M. E., Arankowsky-Sandoval, G., & Gold, P. E. (1994). Glucose attenuation of the effect of combined muscarinic-nicotinic blockade on spontaneous alternation. *European Journal of Pharmacology, 256,* 31–36.

Ragozzino, M., & Gold, P. E. (1992). Glucose effects on mecamylamine-induced memory deficits and decreases in locomotor activity in mice. *Behavioral and Neural Biology, 56,* 271–282.

Ragozzino, M. E., & Gold, P. E. (1994). Task-dependent effects of intra-amygdala morphine injections: Attenuation by intra-amygdala glucose injections. *Journal of Neuroscience,* in press.

Ragozzino, M. E., Parker, M. E., & Gold, P. E. (1992). Spontaneous alternation and inhibitory avoidance impairments with morphine injections into the medial septum. Attenuation by glucose administration. *Brain Research, 597,* 241–249.

Ragozzino, M. E., Wenk, G. L., & Gold, P. E. (1994). Glucose attenuates morphine-induced decrease in hippocampal acetylcholine output: An *in vivo* microdialysis study in rats. *Brain Research,* in press.

Riekkinen, P., Jr., Aaltonen, M., Sirvio, J., & Riekkinen, P. (1991). Tetrahydroaminoacridine alleviates medial septal lesion-induced and age-related reference but not working memory deficits. *Physiology and Behavior, 49,* 1147–1152.

Riekkinen, P., Jr., Riekkinen, M., Sirvioe, J., & Riekkinen, P. (1992). Effects of concurrent nicotinic antagonist and PCPA treatments on spatial and passive avoidance learning. *Brain Research, 575*, 247–250.

Riekkinen, P., Sirvio, J., Aaltonen, M., & Riekkinen, P. (1990). Effects of concurrent manipulations of nicotinic and muscarinic receptors on spatial and passive avoidance learning. *Pharmacology Biochemistry and Behavior, 37*, 405–410.

Robinson, G. S., Jr., Crooks, G. B., Jr., Shinkman, P. G., & Gallagher, M. (1989). Behavioral effects of MK-801 mimic deficits associated with hippocampal damage. *Psychobiology, 17*, 156–164.

Rupniak, N. M., Samson, N. A., Tye, S. J., Field, M. J., & Iverson, S. D. (1991). Evidence against a specific effect of cholinergic drugs on spatial memory in primates. *Behavioural Brain Research, 43*, 1–6.

Rush, D. K. (1986). Reversal of scopolamine-induced amnesia of passive avoidance by pre- and post-training naloxone. *Psychopharmacology, 89*, 296–300.

Schacter, D. L. (1987). Memory, amnesia, frontal lobe dysfunction. *Psychobiology, 15*, 21–36.

Schindler, C. W., Gormezano, I., & Harvey, J. A. (1987). Effects of morphine, ethylketocyclazocine, U-50,488H and naloxone on the acquisition of a classically conditioned response in the rabbit. *Journal of Pharmacology and Experimental Therapeutics, 243*, 1010–1017.

Schulze, G. E., Slikker, W., & Paul, M. G. (1989). Multiple behavioral effects of diazepam in rhesus monkey. *Pharmacology Biochemistry and Behavior, 34*, 29–35.

Sevush, S., Guterman, A., & Villalon, A. V. (1991). Improved verbal learning after outpatient oral physostigmine therapy in patients with dementia of the Alzheimer type. *Journal of Clinical Psychiatry, 52*, 300–303.

Shapiro, M. L., & Caramanos, Z. (1990). NMDA antagonist MK-801 impairs acquisition but not performance of spatial working and reference memory. *Psychobiology, 18*, 231–243.

Shors, T. J., Levine, S., & Thompson, R. F. (1990). Opioid antagonist eliminates the stress-induced impairment of long-term potentiation (LTP). *Brain Research, 506*, 316–318.

Squire, L. R. (1987). *Memory and brain* (315 pp.). New York: Oxford University Press.

Stackman, R. W., & Walsh, T. J. (1992). Chlordiazepoxide-induced working memory impairments: Site specificity and reversal by flumazenil (R015-1788). *Behavioral and Neural Biology, 57*, 233–243.

Sternberg, D. B., Isaacs, K. R., Gold, P. E., & McGaugh, J. L. (1985). Epinephrine facilitation of appetitive learning: Attenuation with adrenergic receptor antagonists. *Behavioral and Neural Biology, 44*, 447–453.

Sternberg, D. B., Martinez, J. L., Gold, P. E., & McGaugh, J. L. (1985). Age-related memory deficits in rats and mice: Enhancement with peripheral injections of epinephrine. *Behavioral and Neural Biology, 44*, 213–220.

Stone, W. S., Cottrill, K., Walker, D., & Gold, P. E. (1988). Blood glucose and brain function: Interactions with CNS cholinergic systems. *Behavioral and Neural Biology, 50*, 325–334.

Stone, W. S., & Gold, P. E. (1988). Sleep and memory relationships in intact old and amnestic young rats. *Neurobiology of Aging, 9*, 719–727.

Stone, W. S., Rudd, R. R., & Gold, P. E. (1990). Glucose and physostigmine effects on morphine- and amphetamine-induced increases in locomotor activity in mice. *Behavioral and Neural Biology, 54*, 146–155.

Stone, W. S., Rudd, R. J., & Gold, P. E. (1992). Glucose attenuation of deficits in spontaneous alternation behavior and augmentation of relative brain 2-deoxyglucose uptake in old and scopolamine-treated mice. *Psychobiology, 20*, 276–279.

Stone, W. S., Walser, B., Gold, S. D., & Gold, P. E. (1991). Scopolamine- and morphine-induced impairments of spontaneous alternation performance in mice: Reversal with glucose and with cholinergic and adrenergic agonists. *Behavioral Neuroscience, 1991*, 264–271.

Sutherland, R. J., & McDonald, R. J. (1990). Hippocampus, amygdala, and memory deficits in rats. *Behavioural Brain Research, 37*, 57–79.

Swartzwelder, H. S., Tilson, H. A., McLamb, R. L., & Wilson, W. A. (1987). Baclofen disrupts passive avoidance retention in rats. *Psychopharmacology, 92*, 398–401.

Todd, J., & Kesner, R. P. (1978). Effects of posttraining injection of cholinergic agonists and antagonists into the amygdala on retention of passive avoidance training in rats. *Journal of Comparative and Physiological Psychology, 92,* 958–968.

Tomaz, C., Dickinson-Anson, H., & McGaugh, J. L. (1992). Basolateral amygdala lesions block diazepam-induced anterograde amnesia in an inhibitory avoidance task. *Proceedings of the National Academy of Sciences, 89,* 3615–3619.

Toumane, A., Durkin, T. P., Marighetto, A., & Jaffard, R. (1989). The durations of hippocampal and cortical cholinergic activation induced by spatial discrimination testing of mice in an eight-arm radial maze decrease as a function of acquisition. *Behavioral and Neural Biology, 52,* 279–284.

Walker, D. L., & Gold, P. E. (1991a). Effects of the novel NMDA antagonist, NPC 12626, on long-term potentiation, learning and memory. *Brain Research, 549,* 213–221.

Walker, D. L., & Gold, P. E. (1991b). Time-dependent impairment and enhancement of inhibitory avoidance learning by intra-amygdala 2-amino-5-phosphonopentanoic acid (AP5) infusion. Presented at the Twenty-first Annual Meeting of the Society for Neuroscience, New Orleans, LA.

Walker, D. L., & Gold, P. E. (1992). Impairment of spontaneous alternation performance by an NMDA antagonist: Attenuation with non-NMDA treatments. *Behavioral and Neural Biology, 58,* 69–71.

Walker, D. L., McGlynn, T., Grey, C., Ragozzino, M., & Gold, P. E. (1991). Naloxone modulates the behavioral effects of cholinergic agonists and antagonists. *Psychopharmacology, 105,* 57–62.

Ward, L., Mason, S. E., & Abraham, W. C. (1990). Effects of the NMDA antagonists CPP and MK-801 on radial arm maze performance in rats. *Pharmacology Biochemistry and Behavior, 35,* 785–790.

Welzl, H., Alessandri, B., & Battig, K. (1990). The formation of a new gustatory memory tract in rats is prevented by the noncompetitive NMDA antagonist ketamine. *Psychobiology, 18,* 43–47.

Wenk, G. L. (1989). An hypothesis on the role of glucose in the mechanism of action of cognitive enhancers. *Psychopharmacology, 99,* 431–438.

Wenk, G. L., & Olton, D. S. (1989). Cognitive enhancers: Potential strategies and experimental results. *Progress in Neuro-Psychopharmacology and Biological Psychiatry, 13,* S117–S139.

White, N. (1991). Peripheral and central memory-enhancing actions of glucose. In R. C. A. Frederickson, J. L. McGaugh, & D. L. Felten (Eds.), *Peripheral signaling of the brain: Role in neural-immune interactions and learning and memory* (pp. 421–441). Toronto: Hogrefe & Huber.

Worms, P., Gueudet, C., Perio, A., & Soubrie, P. (1989). Systemic injection of pirenzepine induces a deficit in passive avoidance learning in rats. *Psychopharmacology, 98,* 286–288.

3

Psychophysiology of Emotional Memory Networks in Posttraumatic Stress Disorder

ROGER K. PITMAN
SCOTT P. ORR

Psychiatrists and psychologists whose interests extent beyond the "what" (diagnosis) and "what's to be done?" (therapy) of mental disorders, to their "why" (etiology) and "how" (pathogenesis) have increasingly turned to evolutionary biology for explanations. In so doing, they have made use of the concepts of "proximate" and "ultimate" causation. According to this point of view, proximate causation involves events in the life of the individual that set into motion innate, ordinarily adaptive biobehavioral mechanisms, which eventuate in maladaptive disorders in unlucky individuals. Ultimate causation involves the events in the evolution of the species originally responsible for the selection of these mechanisms.

The capacity of evolutionary biology to inform various aspects of psychopathology is becoming increasingly recognized (Nesse, 1984). However, the reverse is less appreciated. Because psychopathologic phenomena often represent extreme forms of ordinary human behavior, evolutionary mechanisms may be cast in higher relief in the mentally disordered (Pitman, 1983). Their behaviors constitute potentially useful data often overlooked by basic behavioral scientists (Pitman, 1980). Darwin (1872/1965) was aware that the behavior of some insane patients reveals the "brute nature" within human beings, and he cited piloerection during maniacal paroxysms as one example. More than 40 years before Tinbergen (1949) described the phenomenon of displacement activities in animals, Janet (1903/1976) postulated that human compulsive behaviors result from the diversion of energy from other intended actions.

Information presented in this chapter suggests that findings from research into the mental disorder currently known as posttraumatic stress disorder (PTSD) may shed light on evolutionary biobehavioral mechanisms of memory and emotion.

POSTTRAUMATIC STRESS DISORDER

The current definition of posttraumatic stress disorder (PTSD), according to the *Diagnostic and Statistical Manual of Mental Disorders,* 3rd Ed.-Rev. (*DSM-III-R*) (American Psychiatric Association, 1987), appears in the box. It will be seen that for diagnostic criterion A, the *DSM-III-R* defines the proximate cause of PTSD as ". . . an event that is outside the range of usual human experience and that would be markedly distressing to almost anyone, e.g., serious threat to one's life or physical integrity. . . ." (p. 250)

Beyond its proximate causal event, PTSD is defined by its symptomatic manifestations, which comprise *DSM-III-R* criteria B–D (see box). Most important are the B (reexperiencing) criteria, which consist of recurrent distressing recollections, dreams, and flashbacks of the traumatic event. One striking feature of PTSD is its timelessness. A PTSD sufferer may repeatedly experience a traumatic event with emotion so fresh each time that it is as if the event were reoccurring. Although it is

---

DSM-III-R Diagnostic Criteria for PTSD (abridged)

A. An event outside the range of usual human experience that would be markedly distressing to almost anyone.

B. Reexperiencing criteria (one required)
1. Recurrent, intrusive, distressing recollections of the event
2. Recurrent, distressing dreams of the event
3. Flashbacks to the event
4. Intense psychological distress at exposure to events that symbolize or resemble the traumatic event

C. Avoidance criteria (three required)
1. Of thoughts and feelings associated with the trauma
2. Of activities or situations that arouse recollections of the trauma
3. Inability to recall an important aspect of the trauma
4. Markedly diminished interest in significant activities
5. Feelings of detachment or estrangement from others
6. Restricted range of affect (numbing)
7. Sense of a foreshortened future

D. Arousal criteria (two required)
1. Insomnia
2. Irritability or outbursts of anger
3. Difficulty concentrating
4. Hypervigilance
5. Exaggerated startle response
6. Physiological reactivity to events that symbolize or resemble the traumatic event

E. Duration at least one month

currently classified as an arousal criterion D.6 in *DSM-III-R,* "physiological reactivity upon exposure to events that symbolize or resemble an aspect of the traumatic event. . ." is likely to be reclassified among the reexperiencing criteria in *DSM-IV.*

LANG'S NETWORK THEORY OF EMOTION

Lang (1985) has proposed a theory of emotion that is relevant to PTSD. He suggests that emotion is defined by a specific information structure in memory, the content of which consists of three primary categories: (1) information about prompting external stimuli and the context in which they occur (stimulus propositions); (2) information about responding in this context, including expressive verbal behavior, overt acts, and the visceral and somatic events that mediate arousal and action (response propositions); and (3) information that defines the meaning of the stimulus and response data (meaning propositions). These propositions are organized into an associative network that is processed as a unit when a critical number of propositions is accessed.

PTSD may be conceptualized as consisting of one or more pathologic emotional memory networks that when activated produce its characteristic reexperiencing symptomatology (Pitman, 1988). These networks are considered pathologic because of their heightened accessibility or even capacity for spontaneous processing, interference with adaptive functioning, and associated emotional distress. The unitary nature of network processing in PTSD is best illustrated by the flashback phenomenon (B.3 in the boxed text), in which a full-blown experiential memory of the traumatic event may be activated with a concurrent loss of reality testing.

Lang and colleagues have operationalized emotional network theory through the technique of script-driven imagery (Cook, Melamed, Cuthbert, McNeil, & Lang, 1988; Lang, Levin, Miller, & Kozak, 1983). This method employs "scripts" portraying a variety of events, read one at a time to research subjects in the psychophysiology laboratory. Subjects are instructed to imagine as vividly as possible the event that each script portrays. Each script incorporates stimulus, response, and meaning propositions, making it capable of activating the presumed emotional memory network associated with the event. In research described below, Pitman and colleagues have utilized Lang's script-driven imagery technique for the investigation of emotional memory networks associated with traumatic events. The following is an example of a personal script constructed from the experience of a Vietnam combat veteran with PTSD.

> You have just received a signal for a hasty ambush. You sit in the elephant grass trying to figure out your field of fire. Then you hear them coming, talking and laughing and making jokes. You hold your breath, and your heart stops. You freeze, like you can't move. Their voices keep on getting louder and louder. When they get right in front of you, you can see them from the waist down, their AKs slung. You count them as they pass. When you get to four, all shit breaks loose. You pull your trigger and hold it

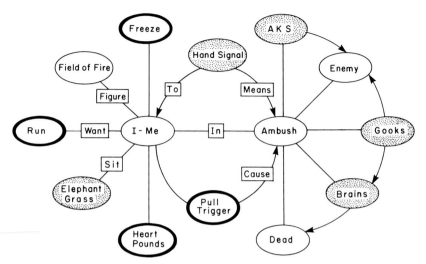

FIGURE 3.1.   Example of a theoretical PTSD emotional memory network. Shaded circles: Stimulus propositions; light circles: meaning propositions; heavy circles: response propositions.

down. The next thing you know, you're staring at a dead Gook's feet. Your teammates are yelling, "Get up. We gotta go!" Now your heart is pounding, and you feel jittery all over, like you want to run, but there's no place to go. You stand up and see the top of the Gook's head blown off, his brains glaring in the sun. You've never seen blood and guts before. You feel sick to your stomach and in a state of shock.

Figure 3.1 schematizes the preceding experience as an emotional memory network, utilizing the format suggested by Lang (1985). The stimulus propositions (elephant grass, hand signal, AKs, Gooks, brains) appear in shaded circles. The meaning propositions (field of fire, enemy, dead) appear in light circles. The response propositions (freeze, pull trigger, heart pounds, run) appear in heavy circles.

PSYCHOPHYSIOLOGIC STUDIES OF POSTTRAUMATIC STRESS DISORDER

Psychophysiologic studies of PTSD have mainly addressed criterion D.6 (see boxed text).

Posttraumatic Stress Disorder Studies Using Audiovisual, Trauma-Related Stimuli

Blanchard, Kolb, Pallmeyer, and Gerardi (1982) reported that Vietnam combat veterans with PTSD showed greater heart rate (HR) and blood pressure responses to combat-related sounds (machine gun fire, explosions) in the laboratory than did noncombat, non-PTSD, control subjects. These investigators subsequently replicated this finding in a study using combat, non-PTSD, control subjects (Blanchard, Kolb, Gerardi, Ryan, & Pallmeyer, 1986). Malloy, Fairbank, and Keane (1983) observed larger HR responses to combat pictures and sounds in Vietnam veterans with PTSD, in comparison to mentally healthy Vietnam combat veterans and non-PTSD psychiatric inpatients. Each of the preceding studies employed standard audiovisual stimuli, that is, the same stimuli were presented to all subjects within a study.

Posttraumatic Stress Disorder Studies Using Script-Driven Traumatic Imagery

A limitation of standard stimuli is that they may not effectively reproduce what was uniquely stressful about even a war veteran's particular traumatic combat experience. For example, pictures and sounds of ground combat may have little meaning for a pilot whose stressful event involved being shot down and held as a prisoner of war. Lang's script-driven imagery technique circumvents this difficulty. Pitman and colleagues have successfully employed this technique in four independent studies of medication-free PTSD and non-PTSD subjects, matched with regard to age, educational level, apparent severity of traumatic experience, and in the case of combat veterans, overall combat exposure. Heart rate, skin conductance (SC), and lateral frontalis electromyogram (EMG-frnt) were recorded during subjects' personal traumatic imagery.

A first study (Pitman, Orr, Forgue, de Jong, & Claiborn, 1987) found that 18 Vietnam combat veterans with PTSD produced markedly higher physiologic responses during imagery of their personal combat events than did 15 mentally healthy, non-PTSD, combat control subjects. A second study (Pitman et al., 1990) found higher physiologic responses during personal combat imagery in a new group of seven PTSD Vietnam combat veterans, compared with seven Vietnam combat veterans with non-PTSD anxiety disorders. An analysis (Orr et al., 1990) of the combined data from the first and second studies demonstrated significant correlations between subjects' physiologic responses and psychometric measures of PTSD. A third study (Orr, Pitman, Lasko, & Herz, 1993) found significantly higher physiologic responses during combat imagery in a group of 8 World War II and Korean veterans with PTSD in comparison to 12 mentally healthy combat veterans of the same wars. These studies all used male American combat veteran subjects. A fourth study (Shalev, Orr, & Pitman, in press), however, compared 9 male and 4 female PTSD, and 6 male and 7 female non-PTSD, civilian Israeli victims of road accidents, assaults, and other noncombat traumatic events. This study again found significantly higher physiologic responses during personal traumatic imagery in the PTSD subjects.

The combined data from the previous four studies, with the results of univariate analyses, appear in Figure 3.2. Multivariate analysis of variance between PTSD and non-PTSD groups, with HR, SC, and EMG responses during personal trau-

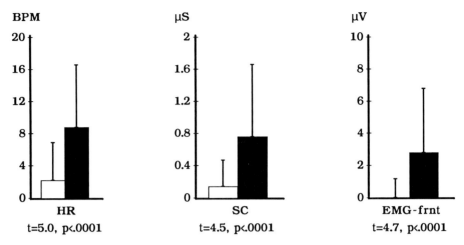

FIGURE 3.2. Mean physiologic responses during script-driven traumatic imagery. White bars indicate non-PTSD subjects; black bars indicate PTSD subjects; lines above bars indicate standard deviations. HR = heart rate; SC = skin conductance; EMG-frnt = lateral frontalis electromyogram.

matic imagery as simultaneous dependent variables, yielded $F(3, 90) = 13.8$, $p < .0001$.

In some PTSD subjects, for example, WW II veterans, highly elevated physiologic responses accompanied recall of traumatic experiences that had occurred more than half a lifetime earlier, dramatically demonstrating the "timelessness" of PTSD memories.

IMPLICATIONS FOR MEMORY AND EMOTION

The preceding findings in PTSD patients serve to illustrate in exaggerated, pathologic form the potentially lasting effects of stressful life events on emotional memory. Indeed, in extreme instances, the memory of the traumatic event may become a virtual "black hole" (Pitman & Orr, 1990) in the mental life of the PTSD patient, attracting all associations to it. As noted in the beginning of this chapter, psychopathologic phenomena often represent the result of innate adaptive biobehavioral mechanisms gone awry. This may be the case with regard to the psychologic and physiologic reexperiencing of PTSD.

Evolution appears to have endowed mammalian species with a memory storage mechanism that provides a means by which the importance of the experience, as reflected by its hormonal consequences, modulates the strength of its memory (McGaugh, Liang, Bennett, & Sternberg, 1984). The ultimate causation of this mechanism is assumed to have been natural selection of the ability to learn quickest and best that which is most essential for survival. A substantial body of animal research shows that several hormones, or what have been termed "stress-responsive neuromodulators" (Gold, 1988), enhance memory consolidation, whereas blockade of these hormones interferes with consolidation. These findings have involved adrenocorticotropic hormone (ACTH), ACTH fragments, vasopressin (reviewed by Zager & Black, 1985), and epinephrine and norepinephrine (McGaugh, 1985). The final common pathway for this effect may be noradrenergic influences on the amygdala (McGaugh et al., 1990), a neuroanatomic structure with theoretical relevance to PTSD (Shalev, Rogel-Fuchs, & Pitman, 1992).

The existence of a means by which the postevent activity of stress-responsive neurohormones enhances consolidation may confer upon traumatic events their power to produce pathologically intense and long-lasting memories. In the pathogenesis of PTSD, an extremely stressful event may release large amounts of endogenous, stress-responsive neurohormones, which modulate an overconsolidation of the memory trace of the event, producing a deeply engraved traumatic memory that subsequently manifests itself in the intrusive recollections and conditioned emotional responses of PTSD (Pitman, 1989). PTSD may represent an unhappy human confirmation of the proposition that ". . . emotional memory may be forever." (Ledoux, 1990, p. 41)

Such a model offers potential explanations for two puzzling clinical features of PTSD that are recognized in *DSM-III-R*. The first of these is the sometimes observed paradoxical amnesia for aspects of the trauma. Because the dose-response curve relating stress hormone activation to memory is typically an inverted U-shaped function (McGaugh et al., 1984), exceedingly high levels of stress hormonal activity at the time of the traumatic event may lead not to enhancement of, but rather interference with, consolidation of the memory trace, resulting in amnesia. An alternate possible explanation for paradoxical amnesia is suggested by findings that some stress-responsive neurohormones, for example, endorphins and oxytocin (reviewed by Zager & Black, 1985) appear not to facilitate but rather to inhibit consolidation.

The second puzzling clinical feature of PTSD is its capacity to occur with a delayed onset. A possible explanation for this clinical observation is offered by the hypothesis of Eysenck and Kelly (1987) that memory-enhancing neurohormones may be responsible for the phenomenon of incubation in anxiety disorders. Thus recall of the traumatic event may lead to re-releases of stress hormones that further enhance the strength of the memory trace, leading to a greater likelihood of its intruding again, with yet further releases of stress hormones. The result may be a positive feedback loop, in which subclinical PTSD may escalate into clinical PTSD.

Testing of the preceding theories in human subjects would involve prospective studies incorporating biologic data obtained at the time of traumatic events. For example, body fluid specimens, along with physiologic measures, might be collected immediately after combat, or at emergency room visits of accident, rape, or assault victims, who could then be followed for the development of PTSD. Immediate postevent biologic values could then be related to clinical outcome. Easier to perform would be analogue studies modeling PTSD through the presentation of ethically acceptable stressful events to nonclinical populations in the laboratory.

Because some hormones and pharmacologic hormonal blockers have the theoretical potential for inhibiting consolidation of traumatic memories, studies employing these agents in traumatized individuals shortly after the trauma, or in analogue designs, could conceivably lead to secondary pharmacologic preventions for PTSD.

REFERENCES

American Psychiatric Association (1987). *Diagnostic and statistical manual of mental disorders* (3rd ed., rev.) Washington, DC: American Psychiatric Association.

Blanchard, E. B., Kolb, L. C., Gerardi, R. J., Ryan, P., & Pallmeyer, T. P. (1986). Cardiac response to relevant stimuli as an adjunctive tool for diagnosing post-traumatic stress disorder in Vietnam veterans. *Behavior Therapy, 17,* 592–606.

Blanchard, E. B., Kolb, L. C., Pallmeyer, T. P., & Gerardi, R. J. (1982). A psychophysiological study of post traumatic stress disorder in Vietnam veterans. *Psychiatric Quarterly, 54,* 220–229.

Cook, E. W. III, Melamed, B. G., Cuthbert, B. N., McNeil, D. W., & Lang, P. J. (1988). Emotional imagery and the differential diagnosis of anxiety. *Journal of Consulting and Clinical Psychology, 56,* 734–740.

Darwin, C. (1965). *The expression of the emotions in man and animals.* Chicago: University of Chicago Press. (Reprinted from London: Murray, 1872.)

Eysenck, H. J., & Kelley, M. J. (1987). The interaction of neurohormones with Pavlovian A and Pavlovian B conditioning in the causation of neurosis, extinction, and incubation of anxiety. In D. Graham (Ed.), *Cognitive processes and Pavlovian conditioning in humans* (pp. 251–286). New York: Wiley.

Gold, P. W. (1988). Stress-responsive neuromodulators. *Biological Psychiatry, 24,* 371–374.

Janet, P. (1976). *Les obsessions et la psychasthenie* [Obsessions and psychasthenia] (Vol. 1). New York: Arno. (Reprinted from Paris: Alcan, 1903.)

Lang, P. J. (1985). The cognitive psychophysiology of emotion: Fear and anxiety. In A. Tuma & J. Maser (Eds.), *Anxiety and the anxiety disorders* (pp. 131–170). Hillsdale, NJ: Erlbaum.

Lang, P. J., Levin, D. N., Miller, G. A., & Kozak, M. J. (1983). Fear behavior, fear imagery, and the psychophysiology of emotion: The problem of affective-response integration. *Journal of Abnormal Psychology, 92,* 276–306.

LeDoux, J. E. (1990). Information flow from sensation to emotion: Plasticity in the neural computation of stimulus value. In M. Gabriel & J. Moore (Eds.), *Learning computational neuroscience: Foundations of adaptive networks* (pp. 3–51). Cambridge, MA: MIT Press.

Malloy, P. F., Fairbank, J. A., & Keane, T. M. (1983). Validation of a multimethod assessment of posttraumatic stress disorders in Vietnam veterans. *Journal of Consulting and Clinical Psychology, 51,* 488–494.

McGaugh, J. L. (1985). Peripheral and central adrenergic influences on brain systems involved in the modulation of memory storage. *Annals of the New York Academy of Sciences, 444,* 150–161.

McGaugh, J. L., Introini-Collison, I. B., Nagahara, A. H., Cahill, L., Brioni, J. D., & Castellano, C. (1990). Involvement of the amygdaloid complex in neuromodulatory influences on memory storage. *Neuroscience and Biobehavioral Reviews, 14,* 425–441.

McGaugh, J. L., Liang, K. C., Bennett, C., & Sternberg, D. B. (1984). Adrenergic influences on memory storage: Interaction of peripheral and central systems. In G. Lynch, J. L. McGaugh, & N. M. Weinberger (Eds.), *Neurobiology of learning and memory* (pp. 313–332). New York: Guilford.

Nesse, R. M. (1984). An evolutionary perspective in psychiatry. *Comprehensive Psychiatry, 25,* 575–580.

Orr, S. P., Claiborn, J. M., Altman, B., Forgue, D. F., de Jong, J. B., Pitman, R. K., & Herz, L. R. (1990). Psychometric profile of PTSD, anxious, and healthy Vietnam veterans: Correlations with psychophysiologic responses. *Journal of Consulting and Clinical Psychology, 58*, 329–335.

Orr, S. P., Pitman, R. K., Lasko, N. B., & Herz, L. R. (1993). Psychophysiologic assessment of post-traumatic stress disorder imagery in World War II and Korean combat veterans. *Journal of Abnormal Psychology, 102*, 152–159.

Pitman, R. K. (1980). Austro-German ethology and schizophrenia. *Behavioral and Brain Sciences, 3*, 627–628.

Pitman, R. K. (1983). Tourette's syndrome and ethology. *American Journal of Psychiatry, 140*, 652.

Pitman, R. K. (1988). Post-traumatic stress disorder, conditioning, and network theory. *Psychiatric Annals, 18*, 182–189.

Pitman, R. K. (1989). Post-traumatic stress disorder, hormones, and memory. *Biological Psychiatry, 26*, 221–223.

Pitman, R. K., & Orr, S. P. (1990). The black hole of trauma. *Biological Psychiatry, 27*, 469–471.

Pitman, R. K., Orr, S. P., Forgue, D. F., Altman, B., de Jong, J. B., & Herz, L. R. (1990). Psychophysiologic responses to combat imagery of Vietnam veterans with post-traumatic stress disorder versus other anxiety disorders. *Journal of Abnormal Psychology, 99*, 49–54.

Pitman, R. K., Orr, S. P., Forgue, D. F., de Jong, J. B., & Claiborn, J. M. (1987). Psychophysiologic assessment of posttraumatic stress disorder imagery in Vietnam combat veterans. *Archives of General Psychiatry, 44*, 970–975.

Shalev, A. Y., Orr, S. P., & Pitman, R. K. (1993). Psychophysiologic assessment of traumatic imagery in Israeli civilian post-traumatic stress disorder patients. *American Journal of Psychiatry, 150*, 620–624.

Shalev, A. Y., Rogel-Fuchs, Y., & Pitman, R. K. (1992). Conditioned fear and psychological trauma. *Biological Psychiatry, 31*, 863–865.

Tinbergen, N. (1949). *The social behavior of animals.* London: Methuen.

Zager, E. L., Black, P. M. (1985). Neuropeptides in human memory and learning processes. *Neurosurgery, 17*, 355–369.

4

Emotion's Multiple Effects on Memory

DANIEL REISBERG
FRIDERIKE HEUER

As the previous chapters have made clear, there has been extraordinary progress in the last few years in our understanding of the neurobiology of learning, particularly learning about emotional events. A measure of this progress can be found in the increasing "cross talk" in this domain between neurobiologists and psychologists. Indeed, the literature allows us to discuss a series of specific bridges between neurobiological events, on the one side, and a variety of complex molar phenomena concerning human emotional learning. This is evident, for example, in Gold's (Chapter 2) discussion of so-called flashbulb memories, Pitman and Orr's (Chapter 3) discussion of posttraumatic stress disorder, or Davis et al.'s (Chapter 1) discussion of the memory "triggers" for human anxiety and panic disorders.

There is no denying the parallels between the biological and psychological perspectives on emotional learning. We will argue in this chapter, however, that there are several levels of complexity in human emotional learning *not* captured by the known neurobiological mechanisms. Clearly, this takes nothing away from the value of the current work. This work, however, will need to be embedded in a much larger context if we hope to account for phenomena like flashbulb memories, posttraumatic stress disorder, and the like. In what follows, we seek to document this claim, but also to suggest ways in which these complex phenomena might be approached from a biological perspective.

EMOTION AND MEMORY: THE "SIMPLE" STORY

The emotional events of our lives are remembered with great clarity and detail. Although emotionality is by no means the only source of memory vividness, the correlation between emotionality and vividness is nonetheless quite strong. For example, in one of our early studies, we gave subjects a list of target events, such as getting one's first job; or graduating from college (Reisberg, Heuer, McLean, & O'Shaughnessy, 1988). For each event, we asked subjects to rate how vividly they remembered the event, and also how emotional the event was at the time that it occurred. This study yielded strong positive correlations between emotionality and memory vividness, and, interestingly, correlations that were independent of the type of emotion experienced. It did not matter if subjects were thinking back to a sad event or a happy one, or, for that matter, a public event or a private one. Across categories, the stronger the emotion attached to an event, the greater the memory vividness later on.

This study of "ordinary" remembering obviously dovetails nicely with two cases of extraordinary remembering, namely, the flashbulb memories mentioned by Gold (Chapter 2), and also the memories, mentioned by Pitman and Orr (Chapter 3), that accompany posttraumatic stress disorder. In both these cases, subjects are remembering events that were enormously emotional at the time they occurred, and, correspondingly, we observe recall that is complete, clear, and utterly compelling.

This pattern invites a straightforward account of the underlying neural mechanisms, and various versions of the account are already in the literature (see, for example, the chapters by Gold and by Pitman & Orr). In rough outline, the account is this: Emotional events are, of course, accompanied by strong arousal. The arousal is accompanied by (or perhaps consists of) a series of changes in body chemistry, and these changes promote brain processes responsible for the encoding of new information. With this enhanced encoding in place, it is no wonder that subsequent recollection is fuller and more detailed for emotional events. This kind of account is, of course, consistent with our correlational data, and also the obvious facts about flashbulb memories and posttraumatic stress disorder. And, of course, this claim is compatible with the many laboratory studies summarized in the previous three chapters.

The evidence favoring this theoretical picture is impressive. We know in some detail (from the animal evidence) how arousal promotes learning, both neurally (e.g., Davis et al., Chapter 1) and pharmacologically (e.g., Gold, Chapter 2). And it seems likely that these arousal-based mechanisms play an important role in human emotional memory. Nonetheless we argue in this chapter that this theoretical picture is, at best, incomplete, and that it simply cannot do justice to the full range of emotion's effects on memory. Our argument is empirically driven: A number of recent studies (including both laboratory studies and studies of eyewitness testimony) have examined subjects' memories for emotional events. These studies have revealed a web of effects, with emotion plainly having *diverse influences* on memory. We will, in what follows, document some of this diversity, but, from the outset, one thing seems clear: the evidence demands an account far more complicated than the picture we have in view so far.

THE SELECTIVITY OF EMOTIONAL MEMORY

Interestingly enough, the "simple" account offered so far may be more than incomplete; it may (in some ways) be misleading. Consider, for example, the application of this account to flashbulb recollection. Flashbulb memories typically concern highly emotional events; we would therefore expect, thanks to the mechanisms just sketched, enhanced encoding for these events. Consequently, our recall of these events should be accurate and complete. But is it?

To explore this point, Neisser & Harsch (1992) interviewed subjects one day after the space shuttle disaster, asking them where they were when they heard the news, who told them, and the like. Three years later, Neisser & Harsch located the same subjects, and asked them the same questions, allowing a comparison between the immediate and delayed reports. Quite remarkably these comparisons showed that the degree of agreement between the immediate and delayed reports was near zero for many subjects. At the same time, however, subjects were extremely confident in the accuracy of their delayed reports. So we once again observe the clarity and detail of flashbulb recollection, but in this case, we have reason to believe that the clear and detailed recollection is *false*.

Not surprisingly, this counterintuitive finding has sparked some controversy. For example, some early data suggested that subjects' 3-year recollection did agree with their reports one *week* after the original event, even if the 3-year recollection did not agree with reports collected one *day* after the event. This could be read as indicating that these emotional memories take some days to consolidate, but then, once consolidated, remain stable over time. A number of studies, however, have now replicated the original Neisser and Harsch pattern, using comparisons between one-week and then long-term reports. (For reviews, see Winograd & Neisser, 1992.) Thus the memory inaccuracies in flashbulb recollection seem easy to document and reliable across procedures.

One way to think about these flashbulb errors draws on a hypothesis that has been in the literature for many years, namely, the Easterbrook hypothesis (e.g., Bruner, Matter, & Papanek, 1955; Easterbrook, 1959; Eysenck, 1982; Mandler, 1975). Broadly speaking, Easterbrook's suggestion was that arousal, in all of its forms, leads to a narrowing of attention. Thus, with increasing levels of arousal, an organism decreases the range of cues it takes in. Exactly how this phenomenon transpires, given what we now believe about attention, is unspecified, but one could imagine realizing it in any of several different ways. To apply this finding to the space shuttle study, all we need to argue is that subjects hearing about this event were highly emotional, and therefore highly aroused, and therefore they encoded only a limited amount of information about the event. Consequently, if they recall a great deal later on, then much of the recall must be after-the-fact reconstruction, and so of course is open to error. No wonder then that we easily document errors in memories for emotional events.

The Easterbrook claim—that arousal narrows the range of encoding—has found support in a number of studies. To understand these data, we need to be clear about what the Easterbrook claim entails: If arousal narrows attention, then some aspects of an emotional event will obviously fall outside of this narrowed focus, and other aspects will be inside. Thus we should predict uneven effects of emotion on memory: aspects of the event outside the narrowed focus will presumably be excluded from memory, but, thanks to this focusing of attention, emotionality could *promote* memory for more "central" elements of the episode.

The difficulty in testing these claims obviously lies in locating the focus of attention, and, correspondingly, in defining the *center* of an episode, presumably favored by arousal, and the *periphery,* presumably excluded. In a recent study, we decided to treat this as an empirical matter, by treating to-be-remembered material as a parameter to be systematically varied, allowing us to ask how emotionality influences the different aspects of a remembered episode (Burke, Heuer, & Reisberg, 1992). Subjects in this study watched a brief story depicting a mother and son going to visit Dad at work. The son watches Dad performing a task, and then mother leaves, late for her own work. In the neutral version of the story, the father is a garage mechanic, and the son watches him working on a car. In the arousal version, the father is a surgeon, and the son watches a fairly gruesome surgery. The arousal and neutral stories were otherwise matched as closely as possible, in terms of plot complexity, photographic layout, structure of the narration, and so on. (Burke et al. provide a fuller description of this matching, designed to ensure that it was indeed emotionality that created the data pattern.)

Subjects' memories for these stories were tested either immediately after seeing the slides, or at a delay, allowing us to ask how these memories fare with the passage of time. More importantly, we probed subjects' memory for four types of material. First, we distinguished between *plot-relevant* and *plot-irrelevant* materials, in order to look at the effects of conceptual or semantic centrality to the story at hand. Within the plot-relevant material, we made a further distinction between gist—defined roughly as the answer to the question, What happened next in the story?—and what we called basic-level visual information— roughly the answer to the question, What does this slide show? Broadly speaking, the first of these defines the gist of the story independent of how the gist is packaged, and the second of these defines what we might call the visual gist of the story.

We also subdivided the plot-irrelevant materials, using a spatial, or perceptual distinction, rather than a conceptual one. We looked first at plot-irrelevant details that happened to be spatially attached to the story's central players. We looked separately at plot-irrelevant details that were truly in the background. Finally, the story materials themselves were divided into three phases, with the arousal manipulation in the middle phase, and the two stories identical in the first and third phases. (This was one element of the "matching" of the stories, mentioned earlier.)

Figure 4.1 provides a broad overview of the data. For the plot-relevant materials—the two top rows in the figure—subjects showed better memory for the arousal story. This advantage was primarily lodged in the middle phase of the

Phase

	1	2	3
Gist	*Weakly helps*	Emotion **helps** memory	*Weakly helps*
Basic-level visual information	*Weakly helps*	Emotion **helps** memory	*Weakly helps*
Central details (spatially contiguous with 'the action')	*No effect observed*	Emotion **helps** memory	*Weakly hurts*
Background details	*Weakly hurts*	Emotion **HURTS** memory	*Weakly hurts*

FIGURE 4.1.   Summary of results from Experiments 1 and 2 in Burke et al. (1992). *Note:* (1) Cells have been identified as "weakly" helped, or "weakly" hurt *if* (a) only one of the two procedures yielded a reliable effect or (b) both procedures yielded trends ($.10 > p > .05$). (2) The arousal manipulation was lodged in Phase 2; hence material in this phase was temporally contiguous with "the action."

story—the phase in which the arousal manipulation took place—but was also detectable in the other phases of the story.

The pattern is rather different for the plot-*ir*relevant materials. First consider the plot-irrelevant material that happens to be spatially associated with plot-relevant characters. Here we observe an advantage in remembering Phase 2 of the emotional story—again, the locus of the manipulation—but no advantage in the other phases. Indeed, we observe a slight *dis*advantage for the emotion story in remembering the story's final phase. The pattern is just the reverse of this when we consider plot-irrelevant material that happened to be truly in the background. Here we get a memory *dis*advantage associated with emotion, almost all of which is lodged in the story's second phase.

This is a complex pattern of data, but it lends itself to a reasonably simple account. Emotion seems to help memory for anything tied to the *action* in the event. But material can be "tied" to the action in several different senses: It can be *conceptually* tied, as it is in the top six cells of Figure 4.1. Material can also be *perceptually* tied to the action, via spatial and temporal contiguity. Notice, though, that we need *both* spatial and temporal contiguity. If the spatial link is severed (e.g., the bottom row in the figure), emotion undermines memory. Likewise, if the temporal link is severed (as it is in Phase 1 or Phase 3 in the figure's third row), again emotion undermines memory.

We should mention that this study also showed effects of retention interval. These effects were small but consistent in their direction: Memory advantages associated with emotion, when they occurred, tended to grow with the passage of time; disadvantages associated with emotion, when these occurred, tended to shrink with time. The obvious reading of this is that emotion serves to retard the process of forgetting. We have argued in other contexts that this is probably attributable to several different mechanisms, working in parallel (e.g., Heuer & Reisberg, 1992; Reisberg & Heuer, 1992), but we will leave the details of this aside for present purposes.

These data are broadly consistent with the Easterbrook claim, since plainly some sorts of material do seem to be excluded from these memories, while other sorts of memory are accentuated. The distinction between these categories is a complex one, depending both on conceptual and perceptual dimensions, but the distinction is certainly needed if we are to account for the data. Thus we simply cannot say that emotion works against memory, or that emotion helps memory, because both effects can be documented for the same event. (We note, in particular, that this seems incompatible with Gold's "when not which" principle, described in Chapter 2.) Moreover, we cannot account for this pattern by appeals to dose-response curves, or species of emotion, since of course those notions cannot handle the results we have just described.

OTHER EFFECTS OF EMOTION ON MEMORY

In an earlier study, we showed subjects either the mechanic or the surgeon sequence, and then asked them to recall the story (Heuer & Reisberg, 1990). As a memory measure, recall provides a relatively sparse assessment of subjects' recollection, but it allows us to assess what errors people make in recalling these emotional events. In particular, we can look at intrusion errors, that is, aspects of the remembered story that were, in fact, not present in the original story. Our data indicate that the sheer number of intrusion errors is not influenced by emotion, but the type of intrusion error is. Broadly put, subjects recalling the neutral story made many errors about plot (whether the mother brought the child to school or to the garage; whether the mother went grocery shopping after she left the garage, and so on). In general, these subjects seemed to be constructing sensible but false aspects of the tale, as if to fill gaps in the remembered sequence. In contrast, arousal subjects made very few plot errors, but tended instead to confabulate about the story's protagonists' motives or reactions. Subjects often exaggerated what the story had said about these, and frequently *falsified* what the story had said. In these cases, subjects seem to have projected their own emotions into their memories, and, crucially, to recall these emotions as being part of the original event.

All of this quite plainly moves us toward a complex picture, and indeed that is the point we are trying to make. Emotion has multiple effects on memory; we have so far mentioned four: the enhancement of memory for some sorts of material; the undercutting of memory for other materials; a generally slowed course of forgetting; and, it seems, a distinctive sort of intrusion errors. In fact, this list of effects can be extended further, as shown below. (Evidence for points 5 and 6 is discussed in Burke, Heuer, & Reisberg, 1992, Heuer & Reisberg, 1992; Reisberg & Heuer, 1992.)

1. Enhancement of memory for materials "tied to the action"
2. Undercutting of memory for materials not "tied to the action"
3. Slowed forgetting
4. Distinctive pattern of intrusion errors
5. State-dependency effects derived from emotional state
6. Effects of emotion on *test performance* (independent of emotional state during encoding)
7. Differences between "remembering *while emotional*" and "remembering *emotional materials*"

Item 7 on this list seems particularly worth noting: The simple account with which we began this comment presumes that it is *arousal* that leads to enhanced memory encoding; it should not matter, therefore, whether the arousal is induced by the to-be-remembered materials themselves, or whether the arousal is produced by some source extrinsic to the memory materials. A number of studies indicate that this is *not* the case, however; the source of the arousal does matter (e.g., Christianson & Mjörndal, 1985; Christianson, Nilsson, Mjörndal, Perris, & Tjellden, 1986; Dorman, 1989). This may reflect memory effects from the *meaning* of emotional materials. Alternatively, the arousal may interact once again with attention mechanisms, so that attention is drawn toward the source of the arousal. One way or the other, though, *remembering emotional materials* seems different from *remembering while emotional*. This plainly will demand complexity in our accounts, and will also rule out accounts of emotional memory that speak only of arousal mechanisms.

CONCLUSIONS

Where, then, does all this leave us? Our ultimate account of emotion's effects on memory seems certain to include the mechanisms described by Gold (Chapter 2), and by Pitman and Orr (Chapter 3), but without question, we will also need some further mechanisms. The known pharmacological systems may, for example, explain the slowed forgetting observed for emotional events, but will not account for many of the other effects listed in the previous section. Likewise, it seems plain that the amygdala serves crucial functions in the creation of fear-based learning (Davis et al., Chapter 1), and this seems certain to play a role in our accounts of emotional learning. However, this once again leaves unexplained many of the phenomena we have described.

Hand in hand with all this, we would suggest that the interpretation of flashbulb memories, or the flashbacks within posttraumatic stress disorder, is far from clear-cut. These examples of extraordinary recollection *may* reflect the enhanced encoding brought out by extraordinary levels of arousal. But this suggestion plainly takes these memories at face value—that is, *as memories.* The Neisser and Harsch data, however, at least open the possibility that what needs explaining here is not vivid, detailed recollection, but instead vivid, detailed *fictional* reconstruction. Therefore, we urge caution in interpreting some of the suggestions made, for example, by both Gold and by Pitman and Orr, about the connection between these phenomena and the known neural mechanisms.

We close this chapter, though, on a positive note. Nothing we have said diminishes the important work reported in the three previous chapters. In addition, the facts about emotional remembering suggest a number of lines for research at the neural or pharmacological level. For example, the contrast we have discussed between types of to-be-remembered materials should be translatable into animal studies, potentially providing a research inroad on that issue. Likewise, the *narrowing* of attention associated with arousal clearly implies a three-way interaction among arousal, learning, and mechanisms of attention. Specifically, we are suggesting that the distinction between the third and fourth rows of Figure 4.1 should be understood in terms of visual attention; the fourth row, on this conception, simply consists of those details outside the "spotlight beam" of visual attention. (Some data indicate that this purely spatial distinction is indeed appropriate [Burke, 1991]; this seems to implicate well-documented parietal mechanisms.) All of this suggests that the interaction among emotion, memory, and attention may be tractable at the neurobiological level, especially given the richness of current discussions of the brain mechanisms underlying attention.

We began this chapter by noting the increasing level of cross talk between psychological and neurobiological studies of emotional learning. That cross talk invites close comparison between the two enterprises, and, in this chapter, we have discussed levels of complexity that are apparent in one of these domains but not (yet) in the other. In no way, however, do we intend this as a criticism: it is a virtue of the cross talk that such comparisons are now possible between these two research enterprises. And it is a virtue indeed when we can locate discrepancies and use them to guide further research. Thus, from the psychologists' perspective, we are extraordinarily impressed by the neurobiological research, both because of what has been accomplished so far, and also because of what could well be accomplished soon. We hope these comments, focusing on the multifactorial nature of human emotional remembering, point a way for some of this future work.

REFERENCES

Bruner, J. S., Matter, J., & Papanek, M. L. (1955). Breadth of learning as a function of drive level and mechanization. *Psychological Review, 42,* 1–10.

Burke, A. (1991). *Emotion's effects on memory: A spatial narrowing of attention.* Unpublished bachelor's thesis, Reed College, Portland, OR.

Burke, A., Heuer, F., & Reisberg, D. (1992). Remembering emotional events. *Memory & Cognition, 20,* 277–290.

Christianson, S.-Å., & Mjörndal, T. (1985). Adrenalin, emotional arousal, and memory. *Scandinavian Journal of Psychology, 26,* 237–248.

Christianson, S.-Å., Nilsson, L.-G., Mjörndal, T., Perris, C., & Tjellden, G. (1986). Psychological versus physiological determinants of emotional arousal and its relation to laboratory induced amnesia. *Scandinavian Journal of Psychology, 27,* 300–310.

Dorman, C. (1989). *The effects of emotional arousal on memory.* Unpublished bachelor's thesis, Reed College, Portland, OR.

Easterbrook, J. A. (1959). The effect of emotion on cue utilization and the organization of behavior. *Psychological Review, 66,* 183–201.

Eysenck, M. W. (1982). *Attention and arousal: Cognition and performance.* Berlin: Springer-Verlag.

Heuer, F., & Reisberg, D. (1990). Vivid memories of emotional events: The accuracy of remembered minutiae. *Memory & Cognition, 18,* 496–506.

Heuer, F., & Reisberg, D. (1992). Emotion, arousal and memory for detail. In S.-Å. Christianson (Ed.), *Handbook of Emotion and Memory.* Hillsdale, NJ: Erlbaum Associates.

Mandler, G. (1975). *Mind and emotion.* New York: Wiley.

Neisser, U., & Harsch, N (1992). Phantom flashbulbs: False recollections of hearing the news about Challenger. In E. Winograd & U. Neisser (Eds.), *Affect and accuracy in recall.* New York: Cambridge University Press.

Reisberg, D., & Heuer, F. (1992). Remembering emotional events. In E. Winograd & U. Neisser (Eds.), *Affect and accuracy in recall.* New York: Cambridge University Press.

Reisberg, D., Heuer, F., McLean, J., & O'Shaughnessy, M. (1988). The quantity, not the quality, of affect predicts memory vividness. *Bulletin of the Psychonomic Society, 26,* 100–103.

Winograd, E., & Neisser, U., (Eds.) (1992). *Affect and flashbulb memories.* New York: Cambridge University Press.

5

Emotional Memory: Conceptual and Methodological Issues

NORMAN M. WHITE

Three of the previous four chapters deal in different ways with memory for emotions, or for emotional events. Michael Davis and his coworkers summarize the elegant work done in Davis's laboratory on the neural circuits and mechanism that mediate conditioned fear. Paul Gold presents us with an innovative and provocative synthesis of data on the pharmacology of memory, which has implications for several important issues in the field. Roger Pitman and Scott Orr show us how pyschiatrists can use basic information about the formation of memories to help in the understanding and treatment of a mental illness, posttraumatic stress disorder (PTSD). Five themes of importance for understanding memory run through these papers, and I comment on each of them in turn.

MULTIPLE MEMORY SYSTEMS

All of the chapters deal with aversive emotional memory, and all seem to accept the idea that the amygdala is involved in the acquisition and expression of this type of memory. There is considerable evidence in the literature for this idea (e.g., Davis, 1992; LeDoux, Cicchetti, Xagoraris, & Romanski, 1990), much of which is cited in Davis et al.'s paper. There is also evidence that parts of the amygdala mediate rewarding emotional memories (e.g., Cador, Robbins, & Everitt, 1989; Everitt, Cador, & Robbins, 1989; Gaffan & Murray, 1990; Hiroi & White, 1991).

Furthermore, all the authors discussed here recognize, either implicitly or explicitly, that these emotional memories are not the only kinds of memories that can be stored in the mammalian brain. All assume, Gold in an explicit manner, that each type of memory is mediated in an anatomically distinct system. Gold's hypothesis clearly suggests that the content of a memory, including its emotional content, may determine how and in what part of the brain it is stored. This concept is central to current thinking about multiple memory systems.

The idea that there may be more than one kind of memory may have been suggested first (in the modern literature) by Tolman (1949), and the first empirical evidence for the idea may have been provided by Milner, in her analysis of the memory deficits suffered by H.M. as a consequence of his hippocampectomy (Milner, Corkin, & Teuber, 1968; Penfield & Milner, 1958). Since the publication of these seminal papers, the idea of multiple memory systems has been the basis of several important theories of learning and memory by Hirsh (1974), by O'Keefe and Nadel (1978); and by Mishkin (Mishkin, Malamut, & Bachevalier, 1984; Mishkin & Petri, 1984). More recently, this idea has been the subject of a large number of papers containing data and theorizing (e.g., Butters, Martone, White, Granholm, & Wolfe, 1986; Horn, 1985; Nadel, 1992; Packard, Hirsh, & White, 1989; Sherry & Schacter, 1987; Squire, 1986; Squire et al., 1990). It is perhaps a tribute to the power of the idea that the mammalian brain contains more than a single memory system that none of the authors of the three papers under discussion here felt it necessary to state it explicitly, but simply used it as a framework within which to organize their thinking about emotional memory. At the same time, it is probably worth remembering that multiple independent memory systems is only one way of organizing the information available on the organization of the memory functions of the brain, and that the possibility of alternative interpretations (e.g., Kesner & Dimattia, 1987) should not be ignored.

REWARD VS. REINFORCEMENT

Representations of the properties of stimuli and events that make up any learning situation become the content of the memories that are stored in the brain. One of the properties of some stimuli and events, often called *reinforcers,* is the affective states these stimuli and events produce in the organisms that come into contact with them. The chapters under discussion here deal primarily with reinforcers that have negative, or aversive, affective properties. However, the main focus of the chapter by Gold and by Pitman and Orr is a different property of reinforcers: their tendency to *improve memory.* There are several lines of evidence suggesting that the affective and memory-improving properties of reinforcers act independently of each other in the mammalian nervous system (see White, 1989a; White, 1989b; White & Milner, 1992, for reviews).

Brief summaries of two experiments will illustrate the difference between the affective and memory-improving properties of reinforcers. Using a conditioned emotional response (CER) procedure Messier and White (1984) gave water-deprived rats a series of 10-sec tones that ended with 0.5-sec footshocks. The rats were then returned to their home cages and given either sucrose or saccharin solutions, or water, to drink. The next day the strength of the rats' memories for the tone–shock association was tested by measuring the suppression of drinking (water) produced by the tone. The rats that had drunk sucrose solutions after the tone–shock pairings were more suppressed by the tone than the rats that had drunk saccharin solutions. The rats that had drunk saccharin were suppressed by about the same amount as the rats that had drunk water. The sucrose and saccharin solutions were equally sweet and therefore equally rewarding, but only one of them improved the memory of the tone–shock association. This suggests that the effect of the sucrose solution on the neural substrate of reward was not the basis of its memory-improving action. Rather the memory-improving action of post-training consumption of the sucrose must have been the result of its action on some other substrate. In the present context it is worth noting that posttraining footshock has a memory-improving effect very similar to that of sucrose consumption (White & Legree, 1984).

Systemic injections of amphetamine also have a posttraining memory-improving effect similar to that of sucrose consumption (Doty & Doty, 1966; Krivanek & McGaugh, 1969; Martinez et al., 1980), as well as rewarding effects measured in self-administration (Hoebel et al., 1983; Pickens & Thompson, 1971) and conditioned place preference (CPP) (Phillips, Spyraki, & Fibiger, 1982; Reicher & Holman, 1977; Spyraki, Fibiger, & Phillips, 1982) paradigms. We used intracerebral microinjections of amphetamine to localize these memory-improving and rewarding effects. Posttraining injections of amphetamine into the caudate nucleus, but not into nucleus accumbens, improved retention of a CER (Carr, 1981; Carr &White, 1984) while intracerebral injections of amphetamine into nucleus accumbens, but not into caudate nucleus, produced a CPP (Carr & White, 1983). These findings suggest that the rewarding and memory-improving effects of amphetamine have different neural substrates.

It should be noted that the posttraining paradigm used in the laboratory to demonstrate the memory-improving action of reinforcers is only an experimental device for observing this effect independently of the reinforcer's affective consequences. In fact, simple temporal contiguity of a reinforcer with a learning situation is sufficient for the memory-improving property of the reinforcer to strengthen the memory of the situation (Gold & Stone, 1988; Gonder-Frederick et al., 1987; Parsons & Gold, 1992). As described by Pitman and Orr, PTSD is an example of a case in which the powerful memory-improving action of a highly stressful event serves to strengthen the memory of itself to the degree that it is recalled at inappropriate times and interferes with normal behavior.

The posttraining paradigm also provides a clue to the mechanism by which reinforcers improve memory, because it can be used to demonstrate that their effects are time dependent, like events that disrupt retention (Gold & McGaugh, 1975; McGaugh & Gold, 1989; McGaugh & Herz, 1972). Posttraining administration of reinforcers is effective immediately after a task has been learned, but ineffective minutes to hours later. This suggests that these treatments interact in some way with mechanisms of memory consolidation, the process whereby the storage of memories changes from a labile to a permanent form.

CONSERVATION OF STORAGE MECHANISMS

Starting with the idea that there are several independent memory systems in the brain, Gold analyzes the effects of certain drugs acting on catecholaminergic, acetylcholinergic, and glutamatergic neurotransmitter systems and makes the provocative suggestion that the pharmacology of the memory storage mechanism in each is identical. He further suggests that each drug has a "valence" with respect to memory such that it either improves or disrupts retention, and that these effects of various drugs summate algebraically. Davis et al. present some additional support for this hypothesis: the application of an *N*-methyl-D-aspartate (NMDA) blocker to the amygdala has the same effect on learning mediated in that structure as it has on spatial learning tasks that are mediated by the hippocampal system.

Even in the presence of the similarities in the effects of drugs on different systems described by Gold, I still have some reluctance to believe that the brain evolved in a way that is so convenient for the people who investigate its function. If Gold's hypothesis is correct, the most likely way that three such systems could have evolved is from some common origin within the developing brain. But if each of these forebrain structures attained its present structure at a different evolutionary time, Gold's hypothesis forces us to believe that the same mechanism evolved independently several times, a series of events that seems unlikely.

In addition to the forebrain structures that are the subjects of Gold's analysis, there is also evidence that the cerebellum mediates a form of memory (e.g., Thompson, 1990), but there is no reason to think that the common pharmacological mechanisms proposed are conserved in this memory system. Moreover, to the extent that they are understood, memory systems that have been studied in non-mammalian species (e.g., Alkon, 1990; Byrne, 1987) are also based on different mechanisms. So, if conservation of mechanisms in fact exists, it does so in a limited number of closely related forebrain systems in the mammalian brain. Although the data presented by Gold cannot be disputed, it is clear that more information will be required to interpret the coincidences he has brought to our attention.

CENTRAL VS. PERIPHERAL MEMORY-IMPROVING EFFECTS

Reinforcers, drugs, or manipulations of the CNS can produce changes in blood levels of certain endocrine substances and of glucose. These changes can influence central processes directly, or they can be detected in the periphery and initiate signals that are transmitted to the brain, probably via the autonomic nervous system. In either case, these peripheral changes can act on the consolidation process to improve or impair memory storage (Frederickson, McGaugh, & Felten, 1991). A mechanism of this type could explain the common effects of peripherally injected drugs on different types of memory. If we allow the possibility that a given drug could have similar effects on one or more circulating blood factors when injected into different brain areas, such a mechanism could also serve as a basis for the common effects of centrally injected drugs on memory. Accordingly, an alternative explanation for Gold's observation that some drugs have common effects on different kinds of memory when injected into different brain areas is that these effects are mediated by a common change in a memory-active substance in the periphery. Until more is known about the peripheral mechanisms that affect memory it will be difficult to evaluate either Gold's hypothesis or any alternatives to it.

A related issue is raised by Davis et al.'s demonstration that injection of an NMDA antagonist into the lateral-basolateral amygdaloid complex blocks acquisition (but not expression) of the memory that produces potentiation of startle. They suggest that the synaptic change representing this memory may occur at the injection site. This is a possible, even likely interpretation of these findings, but there are others as well. It could be that blocking NMDA receptors at this site in the amygdala either inhibits or activates processes at related (possibly nonamygdaloid) sites that are the actual location of the critical synaptic changes. Alternatively, injection of NMDA might produce peripheral changes that feed back to the brain to interfere with the consolidation process and weaken the storage of the memory. Once again, an improved understanding of the effects of peripheral changes on memory storage is required for an evaluation of this hypothesis.

INVERTED-U CURVE

Pitman and Orr's description of the posttraumatic stress syndrome and its possible etiology as an emotional memory that has been stamped in too hard by an accompanying emotional state seems to be a very useful way of understanding a psychiatric problem in psychological terms. Pitman mentions the fact that some individuals who experience very traumatic situations do not develop PTSD, but rather its converse—they develop amnesia for the event. Drawing on the animal literature, he points out that all known memory-improving events have inverted-U-shaped "dose"-effect curves (McGaugh, 1989; McGaugh & Herz, 1972). That is, all such events potentiate memory at some optimal dose or level, and fail to do so at doses or levels above or below the optimum. Thus, Pitman and Orr argue, it may be that those who exhibit amnesia have in fact experienced much higher levels of emotional arousal than those with PTSD, and therefore have not had the memory stamped in. Although this explanation can account for the fact that these patients do not exhibit PTSD, it does not necessarily explain why they exhibit amnesia for the events in question. The literature does not provide clear evidence on whether very high arousal events produce amnesia or simply fail to improve retention, and further investigation of the effects of such events in animals will be required to evaluate this hypothesis.

In terms of treatment, Pitman and Orr's analysis suggests some form of extinction of the learning that produces the debilitating memories. Davis et al. have begun to address the issue of extinction of this type of emotional memory by studying the conditions under which extinction of the potentiation of startle can occur. Their finding that injection of an NMDA receptor antagonist inhibits extinction of fear-potentiated startle suggests that extinction (in this case, at least) involves some kind of new learning. Based on this finding, Davis et al. have been studying a conditioned inhibition paradigm involving explicit training with a stimulus that signals safety. Elimination of conditioned fear (as measured by potentiation of startle) occurs only if the safety signal is presented together with the conditioned fear stimulus. These findings suggest that simple extinction will not be a successful treatment for PTSD. Rather, training involving a competing stimulus signaling "safety," based on the conditioned inhibition paradigm, may be required for successful behavioral treatment of this disorder.

REFERENCES

Alkon, D. L. (1990). Biophysics of memory. *Progress in Clinical and Biological Research, 334,* 273–278.

Butters, N., Martone, M., White, B., Granholm, E., & Wolfe, J. (1986). Clinical validators: Comparisons of demented and amnesic patients. In L. Poon (Ed.), *Handbook of clinical assessment of memory* (pp. 337–352). Washington, DC: American Psychological Association.

Byrne, J. H. (1987). Cellular analysis of associative learning. *Physiological Reviews, 67,* 329–439.

Cador, M., Robbins, T. W., & Everitt, B. J. (1989). Involvement of the amygdala in stimulus-reward associations: Interaction with the ventral striatum. *Neuroscience, 30,* 77–86.

Carr, G. D. (1981). *Relationships among amphetamine-induced locomotor activity, stereotypy, memory-facilitation and conditioned taste aversion.* Unpublished masters thesis, McGill University, Montreal, P.Q., Canada.

Carr, G. D., & White, N. M. (1983). Conditioned place preference from intra-accumbens but not intracaudate amphetamine injections. *Life Sciences, 33,* 2551–2557.

Carr, G. D., & White, N. M. (1984). The relationship between stereotypy and memory improvement produced by amphetamine. *Psychopharmacology, 82,* 203–209.

Davis, M. (1992). The role of the amygdala in fear and anxiety. *Annual Review of Neuroscience, 15,* 353–375.

Doty, B., & Doty, L. (1966). Facilitating effects of amphetamine on avoidance conditioning in relation to age and problem difficulty. *Psychopharmacology, 9,* 234–241.

Everitt, B. J., Cador, M., & Robbins, T. W. (1989). Interactions between the amygdala and ventral striatum in stimulus-reward associations: Studies using a second-order schedule of sexual reinforcement. *Neuroscience, 30,* 63–75.

Frederickson, R. C. A., McGaugh, J. L., & Felten, D. L. (1991). *Peripheral signalling of the brain: Neural, immune and cognitive function.* Toronto: Hogrefe & Huber.

Gaffan, D., & Murray, E. A. (1990). Amygdalar interaction with the mediodorsal nucleus of the thalamus and the ventromedial prefrontal cortex in stimulus-reward associative learning in the monkey. *Journal of Neuroscience, 10,* 3479–3493.

Gold, P. E., & McGaugh, J. L. (1975). A single trace, two process view of memory storage processes. In D. Deutsch & J. A. Deutsch (Eds.), *Short term memory.* New York: Academic Press.

Gold, P. E., & Stone, W. S. (1988). Neuroendocrine effects on memory in aged rodents and humans. *Neurobiology of Aging, 9,* 709–717.

Gonder-Frederick, L., Hall, J. L., Vogt, J., Cox, D. J., Green, J., & Gold, P. E. (1987). Memory enhancement in elderly humans: Effects of glucose ingestion. *Physiology and Behavior, 41,* 503–504.

Hiroi, N., & White, N. M. (1991). The lateral nucleus of the amygdala mediates expression of the amphetamine conditioned place preference. *Journal of Neuroscience, 11,* 2107–2116.

Hirsh, R. (1974). The hippocampus and contextual retrieval of information from memory: A theory. *Behavioral Biology, 12,* 421–444.

Hoebel, B. G., Monaco, A. P., Hernandez, L., Aulisi, E. F., Stanley, B. G., & Lenard, L.G. (1983). Self-injection of amphetamine directly into the brain. *Psychopharmacology, 81,* 158–163.

Horn, G. (1985). *Memory, imprinting and the brain: An inquiry into mechanisms,* Oxford: Clarendon.

Kesner, R. P., & Dimattia, B. V. (1987). Neurobiology of an attribute model of memory. *Progress in Psychobiology and Physiological Psychology, 12,* 207–278.

Krivanek, J., & McGaugh, J. L. (1969). Facilitating effects of pre- and post-training amphetamine administration on discrimination learning in mice. *Agents and Actions, 1,* 36–42.

LeDoux, J. E., Cicchetti, P., Xagoraris, A., & Romanski, L. M. (1990). The lateral amygdaloid nucleus: Sensory interface of the amygdala in fear conditioning. *Journal of Neuroscience, 10,* 1062–1069.

Martinez, J. L., Vasquez, B. J., Rigter, H., Messing, R. B., Jensen, R. A., Liang, K. C., & McGaugh, J. L. (1980). Attenuation of amphetamine-induced enhancement of learning by adrenal demedullation. *Brain Research, 195,* 433–443.

McGaugh, J. L. (1989). Involvement of hormonal and neuromodulatory systems in the regulation of memory storage. *Annual Review of Neuroscience, 12,* 255–287.

McGaugh, J. L., & Gold, P. E. (1989). Hormonal modulation of memory. In R. B. Brush & S. Levine (Eds.), *Psychoendocrinology* (pp. 305–339). New York: Academic Press.

McGaugh, J. L., & Herz, M. J. (1972). *Memory consolidation.* San Francisco: Albion.

Messier, C., & White, N. M. (1984). Contingent and non-contingent actions of sucrose and saccharin reinforcers: Effects of taste preference and memory. *Physiology and Behavior, 32,* 195–203.

Milner, B., Corkin, S., & Teuber, H.-L. (1968). Further analysis of the hippocampal amnesic syndrome: 14-year follow-up study of H.M. *Neuropsychologia, 6,* 215–234.

Mishkin, M., Malamut, B., & Bachevalier, J. (1984). Memories and habits: Two neural systems. In G. Lynch, J. L. McGaugh & N. M. Weinberger (Eds.), *Neurobiology of human memory and learning* (pp. 65–77). New York: Guilford.

Mishkin, M., & Petri, H. L. (1984). Memories and Habits: Some implications for the analysis of learning and retention. In L. R. Squire & N. Butters (Eds.), *Neuropsychology of memory* (pp. 287–296). New York: Guilford.

Nadel, L. (1992). Multiple memory systems: When and why. *Journal of Cognitive Neuroscience, 4,* 179–188.

O'Keefe, J., & Nadel, L. (1978). *The hippocampus as a cognitive map.* Oxford: Oxford University Press.

Packard, M. G., Hirsh, R., & White, N. M. (1989). Differential effects of fornix and caudate nucleus lesions on two radial maze tasks: Evidence for multiple memory systems. *Journal of Neuroscience, 9,* 1465–1472.

Parsons, M. W., & Gold, P. E. (1992). Glucose enhancement of memory in elderly humans: An inverted-U dose-response curve. *Neurobiology of Aging, 13,* 401–404.

Penfield, W., & Milner, B. (1958). Memory deficit produced by bilateral lesions in the hippocampal zone. *Archives of Neurology and Psychiatry, 79,* 475–497.

Phillips, A. G., Spyraki, C., & Fibiger, H. C. (1982). Conditioned place preference with amphetamine and opiates as reward stimuli: Attenuation by haloperidol. In B. G. Hoebel & D. Novin (Eds.), *The neural basis of feeding and reward* (pp. 455–464). Brunswik, ME: Haer Institute.

Pickens, R., & Thompson, T. (1971). Characteristics of stimulant drug reinforcement. In T. Thompson & R. Pickens (Eds.), *Stimulus properties of drugs* (pp. 177–192). New York: Appleton-Century-Crofts.

Reicher, M. A., & Holman, E. W. (1977). Location preference and flavor aversion reinforced by amphetamine in rats. *Animal Learning and Behavior, 5,* 343–346.

Sherry, D. F., & Schacter, D. L. (1987). The evolution of multiple memory systems. *Psychological Review, 94,* 439–454.

Spyraki, C., Fibiger, H. C., & Phillips, A. G. (1982). Dopaminergic substrates of amphetamine-induced place preference conditioning. *Brain Research, 253,* 185–193.

Squire, L. R. (1986). Mechanisms of memory. *Science, 232,* 1612–1619.

Squire, L. R., Zola-Morgan, S., Cave, C. B., Haist, F., Musen, G., & Suzuki, W. A. (1990). Memory: Organization of brain systems and cognition. *Cold Spring Harbor Symposia on Quantitative Biology, 55,* 1007–1023.

Thompson, R. F. (1990). Neural mechanisms of classical conditioning in mammals. *Philosophical Transactions of the Royal Society of London. B:Biological Sciences, 329,* 161–170.

Tolman, E. C. (1949). There is more than one kind of learning. *Psychological Review, 56,* 144–155.

White, N. M. (1989a). A functional hypothesis concerning the striatal matrix and patches: Mediation of S-R memory and reward. *Life Sciences, 45,* 1943–1957.

White, N. M. (1989b). Reward or reinforcement: What's the difference? *Neuroscience and Biobehavioral Reviews, 13,* 181–186.

White, N. M., & Legree, P. (1984). Effect of post-training exposure to an aversive stimulus on retention. *Physiological Psychology, 12,* 233–236.

White, N. M., & Milner, P. M. (1992). The psychobiology of reinforcers. *Annual Review of Psychology, 43,* 443–471.

II

Aging and Memory

6

Cognition and Hippocampal Systems in Aging: Animal Models

MICHELA GALLAGHER
ALAN H. NAGAHARA
REBECCA D. BURWELL

Life expectancy was just 47 years of age in America at the turn of the century. In recent decades an increasingly large proportion of the population survives beyond the age of 65, so that by the beginning of the next century it is estimated that 1 in 5 of our citizens will be elderly. These dramatic and well-publicized demographic changes are not yet matched by advances in the understanding of many essential features of aging. The term *normal aging* refers to this area of inquiry, contrasting with the term *senility* once used to denote an expected deterioration in mental faculties very late in life. Today it is recognized that the prevalence of diseases that cause cognitive impairment rises sharply with age. But in the absence of such diseases, what is the progression of the aging process and how does it affect the functioning of individuals in the later decades of life? The answers to these questions will be relevant for the majority of the elderly, since they will age free from dementing illness. The answers may also yield valuable information about the neurobiology of the aged brain, the setting that is most relevant to the occurrence of age-related dementia and one that may present special opportunities and/ or limitations for the development of therapeutic strategies, that is, insights that would not be gained from studies of the young adult nervous system.

The main aim of this chapter is to consider how research using laboratory animals contributes to our understanding of aging in mammals. It deals first with how such studies help to address some of the more vexing questions about the nature of aging that have arisen in research with humans. It also examines how an approach that combines the study of behavior and the brain in the same aged animals is more powerful that the application of these methods separately. It will become evident in this discussion that animal models of cognitive aging can provide a framework for research to address more fundamental questions about the mechanisms through which the aging process is regulated and expressed in neural systems.

INDIVIDUAL DIFFERENCES AND THE CONCEPT OF FUNCTIONAL AGING

One theme, reiterated in much research on aging with human subjects, is that greater interindividual variability emerges with increased age. The data in Figure 6.1 illustrate this observation. Despite substantial decline with advancing age as reflected by average performance across decades (shown in the top graph), individual scores (bottom panel) reveal that some aged subjects exhibit minimal loss, or none at all (Heron & Chrown, 1967). Thus, the range of performance in the later decades of life substantially exceeds the range observed in young adults. The phenomenon of larger individual differences among the aged has led some investigators to use the concept of functional or biological age, as distinct from chronological age, to index the gradual senescent decline characteristic of mammals (Reff & Schneider, 1982). According to this view, capacities near the end of the life span differ markedly among members of a population matched for chronological age due to individual differences in the rate and/or severity of underlying aging processes. Of course, these data are subject to other interpretations that have generated considerable further research using human subjects. The following discussion shows how the study of aging in laboratory animals helps to resolve some of the central issues in this debate.

There are a number of difficulties inherent in the interpretation of data from the types of studies most commonly conducted with human subjects. The vast majority of such studies, for example, use cross-sectional designs that are especially subject to confounding differences between generations. To illustrate this point, note that the oldest subjects in the research shown in Figure 6.1 were educated at the turn of the century, introducing the possibility that their educational background differed substantially from that of the 20- and 30-year-old participants. More specifically in the present context, greater variability in the aged might also reflect greater variability in educational background in those generations relative to more recent times. To extend this argument a bit further, perhaps increased variability late in life is a reflection of differences in many sorts of living conditions or experience within any generation that accrue over the course of a life span. All of these concerns lead to some uncertainty about whether differences in the elderly are actually due to aging processes that specifically emerge late in life, as well as uncertainty about the significance of greater disparities in performance with advancing age. Even longitudinal studies in humans are not likely to entirely resolve these issues. Research using laboratory animals, although not immune from either generational effects or the cumulative effects of subtle differences in living conditions, can be used to control for these factors to a much greater extent

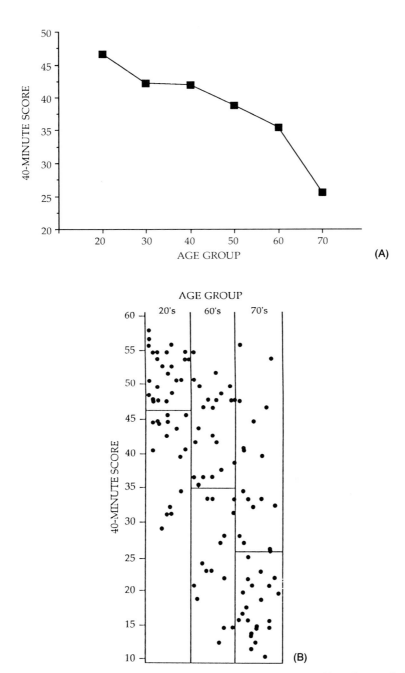

FIGURE 6.1.   Data in this figure are from Heron and Chrown (1967). The graph (A) shows an age-related decline in performance on Ravens Progressive matrices in a cross-sectional study of human subjects. The scores for individual subjects in several of the age groups are shown below the graph (B). Note the increased range of performance in the older age groups relative to young adults.

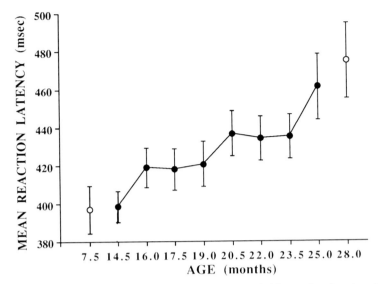

FIGURE 6.2.   Results from a longitudinal assessment (14–25 months of age) and a cross-sectional study (comparing 5-month- and 28-month-old groups) on a simple RT task. An age-related increase in RT latency was found in both experiments. (Adapted from Burwell & Gallagher, 1993; and Gallagher & Burwell, 1989).

than is possible in human studies. In turning to such research, we can ask whether greater interindividual variability becomes apparent during aging in animals maintained under relatively uniform and controlled conditions.

Figure 6.2 shows the results of two experiments from work in our laboratory that assessed reaction time (RT) performance in pathogen-free male Long-Evans rats. An age-related slowing of RT was observed in both a cross-sectional design (rats tested at 5 and 28 months of age) and a longitudinal study in which testing was repeated at 6-week intervals between the ages of 14 and 25 months (Burwell & Gallagher, 1993; Gallagher & Burwell, 1989). Note that early training and repeated exposure to the task appeared to have no protective effect against the age-related increase in response latency for subjects in the longitudinal study compared to those rats trained and tested at 28 months. The effect of age on RT performance in rats shown here agrees with numerous reports of age-related RT slowing in humans. Such studies have also indicated that this effect of aging in human subjects is quite variable. For example, in a study that screened over 5000 subjects, about one-third of the participants over 69 years of age had faster RT than the mean performance of the 20–29-year-old subjects (Wilkinson & Allison, 1989). Figure 6.3 shows the individual RT latencies for the rats included in our longitudinal experiment at the first and last assessments. Here too, the range of RT latencies increased substantially with age, and no discernible decrement in performance was found for some rats over the entire course of the experiment. These data indicate that some subjects remain stable over time while other aged cohorts decline quite markedly.

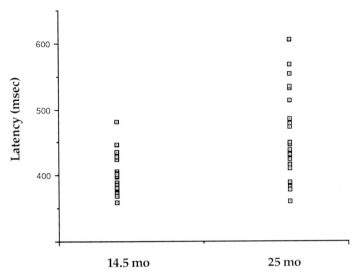

FIGURE 6.3.   Distribution of reaction-time performance for all rats in a longitudinal assessment at the first (14.5 months) and last (25 months) assessments. The data point for each rat represents the mean on 500 trials. Note the increased interindividual differences at 25 months relative to the younger age.

Data such as these from studies using laboratory animals support the notion that increased interindividual variability is observed with advancing age independent of the many confounds and possible artifacts that could account for this phenomenon in humans. Indeed, considerable evidence for pronounced individual differences in studies of aged laboratory animals has accumulated in recent years (see Collier & Coleman, 1991, for recent review). This work has given support to the notion that disparities in functional aging may reflect individual differences in the rate and/or severity of underlying aging processes. Within this framework, one important implication of the preserved function in some individuals late in life is that much of the decline associated with normal aging is not obligatory and might be subject to modification. The concept of successful aging has been introduced into the study of normal aging in recognition of this possibility and the need to consider factors that might mitigate or decelerate the course of aging (Rowe & Kahn, 1987).

FUNCTIONAL DECLINE AND BIOMARKERS OF AGING: RATIONALE FOR THE RESEARCH STRATEGY

A major thrust of research in recent years has been to examine whether functional differences in aged animals coincide with differences in biological markers of aging. Such studies have adopted the research strategy of conducting behavioral and neurobiological studies in the same animals. This work is designed to test the hypothesis that the severity of underlying aging processes accounts for variability in functional decline. Such studies are important because variability in functional decline might not be due to individual differences in decremental aging processes; many effects of aging might occur uniformly across animals with selective compensation accounting for differences in performance. Alternatively, an aging process that uniformly affects all animals might also yield different outcomes in functional impairment, depending on background levels of ability, that is, those individuals performing least well at younger ages showing more change than those with near optimal performance earlier in life. If this were the case, then individual differences in aging processes per se might be small, despite relatively large discrepancies in functional decline.

With respect to these possibilities, it is notable that a number of studies with human subjects have reported relatively high test–retest correlations in longitudinal assessments, providing some evidence for stable individual differences across time (for recent review, see Salthouse, 1991). For example, Schwartzman, Gold, Andres, Arbuckle, and Chaikelson (1987) reported a high correlation ($r = .76$) in performance for 260 Canadian veterans retested 40 years after their original assessment as World War II army recruits. Such findings suggest that increased variability in aging is largely due to an expanded range of performance with little change in rank ordering of subjects as the effects of aging become manifest. This pattern of results would seem to argue against the expectation that differences in functional ability will be systematically related to the severity of specific aging processes. It is important, however, to note that such data on human aging have come largely from studies using psychometric tests of intelligence, which are designed to yield high stability for individual differences. A different pattern of results can be found in data from aged laboratory animals. In our longitudinal assessment of RT latencies in rats, the correlation between performance as mature adults (14 months) and at the end of the study (25 months) was exceedingly low ($r = .09$). At least in this case, the age-related increase in variability is not merely an expansion of the range of individual differences evident at a younger age, but appears to reflect a process that occurs independent of such preexisting individual differences (Burwell & Gallagher, 1993).

A second aim of research that combines functional testing and neurobiological analysis in the same animals is to identify those biological changes that are most closely linked to impairment in aging. This goal takes on added significance from research demonstrating that individual differences in the effects of aging are highly task-specific. In studies in which the same animals were assessed across a range of tasks that are equally sensitive to aging, it has been found that those animals that exhibit marked decline in one sphere of behavioral function may exhibit preserved function in a different behavioral domain. A number of laboratories have shown this to be the case in comparing performance on sensorimotor tasks and tests of cognitive function. To illustrate this point, research conducted in our laboratory has indicated that substantial variability occurs in the effects of aging on spatial learning ability in rats. The data in Figure 6.4 are reminiscent of those shown previously for RT performance in that some aged rats learned as

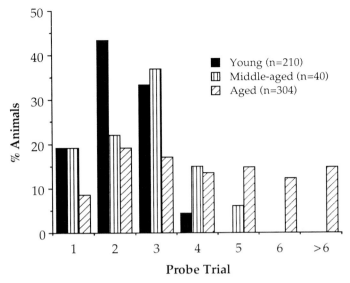

FIGURE 6.4. Acquisition of criterion performance for young (4–7 months), middle-aged (16–18 months), and aged (25–29 months) Long-Evans rats in the Morris water maze. Probe trials (30-sec duration) were interpolated after each block of five training trials. Bars represent the percentage of animals in each group that initially reached criterion at each probe trial. Criterion was reached on a probe trial when 30% of the path length was traversed in the maze quadrant that contained the escape platform during training and at least two annulus crossings occurred.

proficiently as young rats, while others fell outside the entire range of young performance. In studies in which both RT performance and spatial learning were assessed in the same-aged animals, no predictable relationship was found between age-related impairment in these two tasks (Burwell & Gallagher, 1993; Gallagher & Burwell, 1989). Others have reported similar results, suggesting that biological changes that lead to deficits in sensorimotor function may occur independent of those changes that underlie cognitive decline (Gage, Dunnett, & Björklund, 1984; Gage, Dunnett & Björklund, 1989; Markowska et al., 1989).

In light of such findings, the reasons for combining behavioral and neurobiological assessments in the study of aged animals become quite compelling. To the extent that variability in functional decline is due to individual differences in aging, biological comparisons that are made on the basis of chronological age alone are relatively insensitive: some proportion of the subjects in a chronologically defined group of aged animals is liable to show little evidence of either functional or biological aging. Because age-related decline can also be selective for a particular sphere of functioning, the characterization of specific types of impairment linked to those neural systems under study may provide the most useful background for assessing the effects of aging on the brain. Before discussing the research findings that demonstrate the utility of this approach, some methodological issues are addressed.

FUNCTIONAL DECLINE AND BIOMARKERS OF AGING: SOME METHODOLOGICAL ISSUES

There is a growing body of research in which both behavioral and neurobiological data are available for aged subjects (for recent reviews, see Collier & Coleman, 1991; Rapp & Amaral, 1992). This broad spectrum of work includes experiments conducted with a number of different mammalian species, including rodents, nonhuman primates, and humans. Our discussion targets a subset of these studies that have focused on cognitive decline and neurobiological changes in either of the two major inputs to the hippocampal formation, the septo-hippocampal projection and the perforant path. There is now a substantial amount of data from this work, permitting some assessment of the reliability and generality of findings. Of equal importance for the development of this research strategy, certain issues raised by these studies may point to ways in which the approach can be improved and strengthened for future investigations.

The results of studies examining the septo-hippocampal system and the status of the perforant path innervation of the hippocampal formation in behaviorally characterized aged subjects are summarized in Tables 6.1–6.3. Although some diversity in the behavioral tests used to define functional capacity is evident, there has been a heavy reliance on spatial learning tasks, particularly the Morris water maze. We will return to this feature of the behavioral data shortly. The selection of tasks, however, is reasonably well geared to assess the status of the neurobiological targets because experimental manipulations aimed at these systems, such as lesions or pharmacological treatments, are effective in altering the performance of young animals on these tests. Thus, it would be reasonable to expect that aged animals with preserved behavioral function would not exhibit marked decline in the integrity of these brain systems. By the same token, a substantial disruption of functional integrity in these pathways might well become evident in behavioral impairment. It is important to keep in mind, however, that such deficits in spatial learning in aged animals could be due to causes other than changes in the circuitry under study. This is important to acknowledge because each of the tasks used in these studies is sensitive to brain manipulations is other neural systems. Of equal concern is the possibility that deficits in some aged animals could reflect behavioral impairments that are unrelated to the specific memory/cognitive demands of the task under study. These factors would necessarily limit the ability to find a close correspondence between behavioral performance and measures in the target neural systems.

As noted earlier, it is evident that much of our information about behavioral/ brain correlates during aging in the studies shown in the summary tables has come from the use of a single behavioral paradigm, that is, the Morris water maze (Morris, Garrud, Rawlins, & O'Keefe, 1982). One advantage in the use of a single task is the ability to compare results across studies. It should be noted, however, that although the water maze apparatus was used in much of this research, different methods of behavioral analysis were employed in many of the experiments. Not all of these methods provide a comparable index of spatial learning ability

TABLE 6.1   Septo-Hippocampal Markers in the Septal Complex

Behavioral Task Strain and Species, (Ages), Reference	Neurobiological Change	Relationship to Functional Decline
Morris Water Maze		
Sprague-Dawley rats (3, 24 mo) *Fischer et al., 1989*	↓ Size of AChE cells in MS	Correlated with impaired performance (platform crossing, not escape latency)—within aged group
	↓ No.# of AChE cells in MS	Correlated with impaired performance (platform crossing and escape latency)—within aged group
	↓ Size and no.# of AChE cells in MS and VDB	In both impaired aged and severely impaired aged rats (subgrouped by escape performance)
Sprague-Dawley rats (3, 12, 18, 24, 30 mo) *Fischer et al., 1991*	↓ Size and no.# of ChAT/NGF-ir cells in MS and VDB	Correlated with impaired performance (platform crossing and escape latency)—across all age groups
Sprague-Dawley rats (3, 24 mo) *Fischer et al., 1991b*	↓ Size and no.# of NGF-ir cells in MS and VDB	In impaired aged, but not unimpaired aged rats (subgrouped by escape performance)
Long-Evans rats (10, 24, 32–35 mo) *Koh et al., 1989*	↓ No.# of NGF-ir-labeled cells in DB	In impaired aged, but not unimpaired aged rats (subgrouped by probe trial performance) Correlated with performance (% pathlength in training quadrant)—across all age groups
Long-Evans rats (7–8, 28–29 mo) *Gallagher et al., 1990*	↓ ChAT levels in basal forebrain	In impaired aged, but not unimpaired aged rats (subgrouped by probe trial performance)
Sprague-Dawley rats (3, 24 mo) *Hellweg et al., 1990*	÷ ChAT activity in septal region	No difference between severely impaired aged and impaired aged or young rats
	↑ NGF levels in septal region	In severely impaired aged, but not impaired aged rats (subgrouped by escape performance)
Sprague-Dawley rats (7, 25 mo) *Higgins et al., 1990*	↑ In amyloid protein precursor mRNA in basal forebrain	In impaired aged rats, but not unimpaired aged rats (subgrouped by escape performance)
Radial Arm Maze Fischer 344 rats (3, 24 mo) *Luine & Hearns, 1990*	↓ In ChAT level in VDB	Correlated with decline in memory performance (choice accuracy)— across both age groups
Delay-Nonmatch-to-Sample Rhesus monkeys (10–12, 23–25 yr) *Stoessner-Johnson et al., 1992*	↓ No.# ChAT cells in caudal MS	In impaired aged and unimpaired aged monkeys (subgrouped by DNMS performance)
	↑ Size of ChAT cells in rostral MS	In impaired aged, but not unimpaired aged monkeys

TABLE 6.2 Septo-Hippocampal Markers in the Hippocampal Formation

Behavioral Task Strain and Species, (Ages), References	Neurobiological Change	Relationship to Functional Decline
Morris Water Maze		
Sprague-Dawley rats (3, 24 mo) *Fischer et al., 1989*	÷ In ChAT activity in the hippocampus	No difference between severely impaired aged and impaired aged or young rats (subgrouped by escape performance)
Sprague-Dawley rats (3, 22–24 mo) *Hellweg et al., 1990*	÷ In ChAT activity in the hippocampus	No difference between severely impaired aged and impaired aged or young rats (subgrouped by escape performance)
	÷ In NGF level in the hippocampus	No difference between severely impaired aged and impaired aged or young rats (subgrouped by escape performance)
Long-Evans rats (7–8, 28–29 mo) *Gallagher et al., 1990*	÷ In ChAT activity in the hippocampus	No difference between impaired aged and unimpaired aged or young rats (subgrouped by probe trials)
	↓ In total muscarinic binding in hippocampus	In impaired aged, but not unimpaired aged rats (subgrouped by probe trials)
Sprague-Dawley rats (3, 24 mo) *Fischer et al., 1991b*	÷ In ACh release in the hippocampus (In vivo measure)	No difference between impaired aged rats and unimpaired aged rats or young rats (subgrouped by escape performance)
Long-Evans rats (4–5, 22–24 mo) *Gallagher & Pelleymounter, 1988*	Absence of ↓ in high-affinity choline uptake sites after place training	In impaired aged rats, but not unimpaired aged rats (subgrouped by probe trials)
Radial Arm Maze		
Wistar rat (8, 26 mo) *Ingram et al., 1981*	÷ In ChAT in hippocampus	Correlated with maze performance (choice accuracy)—within each age group
Fischer 344 rats (3, 24 mo) *Luine & Hearns, 1990*	↓ in ChAT in dentate gyrus of dorsal hippocampus, but not in ventral hippocampus and not in dorsal CA1	Not correlated with memory performance (choice accuracy)—across age groups
Wistar rats (3, 12, 17, 24) *Kadar et al., 1990*	↓ In M1 ([3H]-pirenzepine binding) in dentate gyrus	Correlated with maze performance (choice accuracy)—across age groups
T-maze		
ACE rats (8–9 mo vs. 22–24 mo) *Lowy et al., 1985*	÷ In ChAT activity in the hippocampus	Not correlated with memory performance in either working memory or reference memory phase of the task—within each age group

TABLE 6.3   Biomarkers in the Perforant/Dentate Gyrus Projection

Behavioral Task Strain and Species, (Ages), Reference	Neurobiological Aging Change	Relationship to Functional Decline
Morris Water Maze		
Long-Evans rat (4–5, 24 mo) *Jiang et al., 1989*	↑ In level of Dynorphin-A (1–8) and dynorphin mRNA in hippocampus	In impaired aged rats, but not unimpaired aged rats (subgrouped by probe trial performance)
Fischer 344 rats (3, 28 mo) *Clark et al., 1992*	↓ In NMDA and AMPA, but not KA and CPP, receptor binding in dentate gyrus molecular layer	In both nonachiever (severely impaired) aged and achiever (impaired) aged rats (subgrouped by escape performance)
Long-Evans rats (7–8, 27–29 mo) *Nagahara et al., (submitted)*	÷ In KA binding in dentate molecular layer	No difference between impaired aged rats and unimpaired aged rats or young rats (subgrouped by probe trial performance)
	↑ In width of high-density KA binding in dentate molecular layer	In both impaired aged rats and unimpaired aged rats (subgrouped by probe trial performance)
Circular Platform Maze		
Long-Evans rats (10–16, 28–34 mo) *Barnes, 1979*	↓ In LTE response to repeated high-frequency perforant path stimulation	Correlated with memory performance (distance and/or error measure)— within each age group
Radial Arm Maze		
Fischer 344 rats (3, 26 mo) *deToledo-Morrell et al., 1984*	↑ In number of perforant path stimulations required to induce hippocampal kindling	Correlated with memory performance (trials to criterion)—across age groups
Fischer 344 rats (4, 26 mo) *Geinisman et al., 1986a*	↓ In number of perforated axospinous synapses	In impaired aged rats, but not unimpaired aged rats (trials to criterion) Correlated with memory performance (trials to criterion and choice accuracy)—within aged group and (trials to criterion)—across age groups
Fischer 344 rats (5, 27 mo) *Geinisman et al., 1986b*	↓ In number of perforated axospinous synapses	In aged impaired, but not aged unimpaired rats (trials to criterion) Correlated with memory performance (trials to criterion and choice accuracy)—within aged group and (trials to criterion)—across age groups
	↓ In nonperforated axospinous synapses	In impaired aged, but not aged unimpaired rats (trials to criterion) Not correlated with memory performance (trials to criterion)— across age groups

113

with which to compare functional decline and neurobiological measures. As background to the neurobiological data, the following is a brief discussion of the strengths and weaknesses of the various approaches used for assessing functional decline in the water maze task.

The Morris maze apparatus consists of a large, circular pool filled with water that has been made opaque through the addition of powdered milk or some other substance. In the typical "hidden platform" version of the task, rats are trained to find a camouflaged escape platform that is positioned just below the water's surface, and that remains in the same location throughout training trials. Because there are no local cues that mark the position of the platform, the rat's ability to locate it efficiently depends on using a configuration of extramaze cues surrounding the pool. Indeed, young rats typically learn to swim directly to the escape platform within relatively few training trials from any of a number of start locations at the perimeter of the pool. Learning is reflected in shorter latencies to find the escape platform and by decreases in the length of the path that the rat traverses in reaching the platform.

One issue that applies equally to all of the studies under consideration concerns precautions that need to be taken to ensure the deficits reflect decline in cognitive ability rather than a more generalized impairment. One advantage of the water maze is that it permits a number of variations in training that can be used to distinguish cognitive impairment from more nonspecific performance deficits. For example, in addition to training animals in the typical place learning version of the task, rats can also be trained in an alternate version of the task in which a visible platform is used, that is, so-called cue learning. It has been well documented that rats with damage to the hippocampal formation and interconnected structures have deficits in "place learning," but perform normally in "cue learning" (e.g., Morris, Garrud, Rawlins, & O'Keefe, 1982), the latter result indicating that basic motivational and sensorimotor functions are intact. Some studies have reported a pattern of results with aged animals that closely resembles that found with hippocampal damage (e.g., Gallagher & Burwell, 1989). Not all studies on aging, however, have made this distinction either because cue training was not included in the behavioral analysis or because aged animals exhibited deficits in both versions of the task. It is possible that strain differences account for differences in cue-training performance: aged albino strains appear more likely to exhibit cue learning deficits. When deficits are evident in both place and cue learning, the impairment is not confined to conditions that depend on spatial information processing, and may reflect a more generalized behavioral deterioration.

When a selective deficit in place learning is observed in studies of aged animals, the next issue concerns the behavioral measures that should be used to characterize that impairment. Although optimal performance in the place training version of the task requires that the rat learn the location of the platform, it was recognized early on that this was not the only learning strategy that could yield improved performance during training. One alternate strategy that is often adopted by rats with hippocampal damage and by some aged animals is to search for the platform by swimming in concentric circles at a relatively fixed distance from the wall of the pool (DiMattia & Kesner, 1988; Gallagher & Holland, 1992; Morris, Schenk, Tweedie, & Jarrard, 1990). This is a less efficient strategy than learning the precise location of the platform, but supports considerably better performance than a random search, resulting in decreases on training trial measures of learning. Consequently, decreased latencies and path lengths to find the platform across a series of training trials need not reflect the accuracy of "place" learning. Thus, the use of those measures for aged rats may provide a relatively imprecise estimate of spatial learning ability with which to perform correlations with potential markers for aging in the hippocampus.

For the reasons just discussed, numerous studies have emphasized the importance of probe trials to analyze the learning strategy used by rats in the water maze: such trials are often incorporated into the design of studies on aging. Probe trial performance is assessed when trained animals are allowed to search during a fixed interval in the maze when the platform is unavailable for escape. Probe trial measures typically include the percentage of the total path length or time during the search that is traversed within the training quadrant and so-called platform crossings, which occur when the animal's path traverses the location where the escape platform was positioned during training. These measures are designed to reflect the spatial bias of an animal's search pattern. They do have, nonetheless, certain shortcomings when used for correlational analyses in neurobiological studies, as illustrated below.

Figure 6.5 shows three sample paths from probe trials. The accuracy of the animal's search relative to the escape platform location differs substantially in these three records. As shown by comparing the search patterns from probe trials (A) and (B) in Figure 6.5, the percentage of path length in the training quadrant provides a relatively imprecise measure of search accuracy; according to this measure, the search patterns shown in (A) and (B) are fairly comparable because roughly 50% of the total path length was located in the training quadrant on each trial. In contrast, the platform crossing measure distinguishes (A) from (B), but does not distinguish the performance shown in (B) from that in (C). In addition to

FIGURE 6.5.   Computer tracking of the paths taken on three 30-sec probe trials. The percentage of path length in the training quadrant for (A), (B), and (C) was 52%, 49%, and 15%. The average distance from the platform during the search was 36.9, 50.7, and 75.2 cm for (A), (B), and (C). Average proximity to the platform was calculated from 1-sec averages (sampled 10×/sec). See text for further description.

providing a rather limited measure of performance, platform crossings have the added disadvantage of yielding a rather narrow range of possible scores for correlational analyses.

Thus, the various measures of behavioral performance traditionally used in this task do not provide comparable information, and some are rather poorly suited for statistical analyses using correlational methods. In awareness of these problems, some investigators have elected not to use correlational approaches, but instead have adopted some criterion for classification of impairment in aged animals. The main aim using this approach is to identify those aged animals that are proficient in using the spatial learning strategy typical of young performance and to examine whether neurobiological markers differ for those aged rats relative to their "impaired" aged cohorts. While this method of analysis circumvents some of the shortcomings discussed for the available behavioral measures, it may constitute an inappropriate practice if the distribution of performance in aging is continuous rather than bimodally distributed (see Olton and Markowska, 1992, for further discussion of these issues).

In order to address the problems previously discussed for measures in the water maze, we have dedicated some effort to develop an improved graded measure of spatial learning in this task for use in correlational analyses. The method we recently adopted involves computing the distance of the animal from the escape platform location during probe trials. In essence, this method integrates the types of information provided with the traditional measures. As an illustration of the proximity measure, consider its application to the data in Figure 6.5. The average distance from the goal differs substantially for the three records; 36.9 cm in (A), 50.7 cm in (B), and 75.2 cm in (C). As shown in this example, the proximity measure of search accuracy can be used to reflect the entire distribution of the path, providing a more representative index of individual performance.

Finally, an important methodological issue concerns the statistical design used to examine the relationship between behavioral and neurobiological indices when correlational methods are used in studies of aging. It is apparent from the information provided in the summary tables that many studies have examined correlations between behavioral and neurobiological data when all animals (both young and aged groups) are included in the analysis. In other studies, correlations are reported for the aged animals alone, either in addition to, or independent from, correlations that include all subjects. If the goal is to determine whether functional variability in aging is associated with underlying differences on neurobiological measures, then a correlation that is limited to a consideration of the data for the aged subjects would seem appropriate. In addition, the inclusion of the data for young animals along with the aged subjects is also liable to spuriously inflate a correlation due to overall group differences on the variables in the analysis. Thus, it is of interest to know whether a correlation between the behavioral and brain data holds when aged subjects alone are considered in the analysis. In addition, it may be of interest to know whether a correlation that is found in aging likewise exists at a younger age (analysis of behavioral and brain data for young rats alone). Statistical models involving multivariate approaches permit comparisons of the relationships among variables for different groups, for example, testing whether the slope of the regression relating behavioral and neurobiological measures differs for young and aged groups. Analyses of this type, however, are not commonly used in this line of research.

Notwithstanding the cautionary comments offered in this section, a number of studies have indicated that cognitive deficits in aged animals are related to changes in hippocampal circuitry. Some salient features of the neurobiological findings involving the septo-hippocampal projection and the perforant path input to the hippocampal formation are discussed in the following section.

FUNCTIONAL DECLINE AND BIOMARKERS OF AGING: THE DATA

The septal complex gives rise to one of the major projections to the hippocampal formation, providing input of subcortical origin. These neurons, located in the medial septal nucleus (MS) and the vertical limb of the diagonal band (VDB) innervate all subregions of the hippocampal formation. A substantial component of the input is cholinergic, with estimates ranging from 30% to 55% of the septal cells labeled as projection neurons to the hippocampus (Amaral & Kurz, 1985; Rye, Wainer, Mesulan, Mufson, & Saper, 1984). This component of the septo-hippocampal pathway, along with the cholinergic neurons in the nucleus basalis (NBM), have figured prominently in the neuropathology of Alzheimer's disease (McGeer, McGeer, Suzuki, Dolman, & Nagai, 1984; Rossor et al., 1982; Whitehouse, Price, Clark, Coyle, & Delong, 1981), and also have been implicated in the memory decline associated with normal aging (Bartus, Dean, Beer, & Lippa, 1982; Drachman & Leavitt, 1974). As indicated in Table 6.1, cognitive decline in aged animals appears to coincide with age-related neurobiological changes in this system, a relationship that is particularly evident with markers for the cholinergic cell bodies.

One line of research has focused on the relationship between the status of cholinergic neurons in the septal complex and performance in the water maze using aged female Sprague-Dawley rats (Fisher, Chen, Gage, & Björklund, 1991; Fischer, Gage, & Björklund, 1989; Fischer, Nilsson, & Björklund, 1991). These morphological studies used several different methods to label cholinergic neurons, including choline acetyltransferase (ChAT) and nerve growth factor-immunoreactivity (NGF-ir), and acetylcholinesterase (AChE) histochemistry. Two different approaches were generally employed to assess the relationship between the behavioral and neurobiological data. In one method, correlations were performed using either average escape latency at the end of training or a measure of spatial bias during a final probe trial, that is, platform crossings in a 60-sec test. Alternatively, aged subjects were subdivided into different subpopulations (e.g., unimpaired, impaired, severely impaired) based on escape performance relative to the young group. Subgrouping aged rats by severity of impairment yielded differences in cell size/number within some regions of the septal complex, for example, the size of AChE-positive cells in MS was more reduced in severely impaired aged subjects relative to aged rats with more modest impairment. In addition, platform crossings and the average final escape performance were generally found to correlate with age-related decline in both size and number of cells in MS and VDB. Koh, Chang, Collier, and Loy (1989) also reported a significant correlation between decreased number of neurons in the VDB labeled with NGF-ir and an age-related decline in performance in the water maze using male Long-Evans rats. The behavioral index used in their study was the percentage of path length in the training quadrant during a 2-min probe at the end of training.

These findings are in basic agreement with other studies that have reported decreased ChAT activity in the septal complex in aged rats with spatial learning impairment (Gallagher et al., 1990; Luine & Hearn, 1990). In one of these studies, aged male Long-Evans rats were subgrouped as either impaired or unimpaired with reference to young rat performance on probe trials (Gallagher et al., 1990). ChAT activity in a tissue sample that included both the MS and VDB was significantly decreased in impaired aged but not in unimpaired aged rats relative to the young group. Hellweg et al. (1990), using the behavioral methods described earlier for studies by Fisher and colleagues, shows a similar decrease in ChAT activity in the medial septum of severely impaired aged rats, but this was not statistically reliable given the small sample size ($n = 5$ per group). Luine and Hearns (1990) also report a modest, but reliable, correlation between ChAT activity in the VDB and choice accuracy in the radial arm maze using young and aged female Fisher 344 rats. Finally, Higgins, Oyler, Neve, Chen, and Gage (1990), using in situ hybridization techniques, described an elevated expression of amyloid protein precursor mRNA (inserted Kunitz-type serine protease inhibitor form) in the basal forebrain of rats with spatial learning impairment relative to unimpaired aged and young rats. The increase in this marker was found throughout the MS, VDB, and NBM, suggesting that it may be associated with the septo-hippocampal projection system, as well as other components of the basal forebrain cholinergic system.

In summary, these studies provide a remarkably consistent pattern of findings indicating that age-related spatial learning impairment is associated with a decline in the integrity of the cholinergic component of the septo-hippocampal pathway. It should be noted, however, that these kinds of neurobiological changes and their relationship to behavior are not necessarily confined to the septal complex. Comparable results held for the NBM in some of these investigations (Fisher et al., 1989; Koh et al., 1989).

A recent study provides the first report that age-related changes in this system in the nonhuman primate brain may also be associated with functional decline in memory performance (Stroessner-Johnson, Rapp, & Amaral, 1992). A subset of the aged rhesus monkeys in this study had recognition memory deficits on a delayed nonmatching to sample task that resemble the effects of medial temporal lobe damage. Although a decline in the number of cholinergic neurons identified by ChAT immunoreactivity was observed in both unimpaired aged and impaired aged subjects, only behaviorally impaired aged monkeys showed a marked hypertrophy of ChAT-positive neurons at rostral levels of the MS, a region where minimal cell loss was found. The nature of the change reported here differs from that described in rodent studies: the finding, nonetheless, indicates a functional/ biological correspondence in the effects of aging on this system.

In contrast to the evidence discussed previously, markers for the cholinergic innervation of the hippocampal formation do not appear to correlate with age-related behavioral decline. Thus, a number of studies—some reporting results for the same animals used to examine the septal complex—have failed to find any relationship between hippocampal ChAT activity and age-related declines in spatial learning (Fisher et al., 1989; Gallagher et al., 1990; Hellweg et al., 1990; Lowy et al., 1985; Luine & Hearns, 1990, but see Ingram, London, & Goodrick, 1981). Moreover, with the exception of Luine and Hearns (1990), these studies did not find an age-related decrease in hippocampal ChAT activity, suggesting that the complement of cholinergic innervation may be maintained in the hippocampus. In addition, Fisher et al., (1991) reported that the release of acetylcholine in the hippocampus was unaltered in aged rats with spatial learning deficits, even though these same animals showed degenerative changes in the basal forebrain.

Notwithstanding the negative findings already discussed, an effect on the presynaptic element of the septo-hippocampal cholinergic pathway has been described by assessment of dynamic change in high-affinity choline uptake (HACU) in the hippocampus. Alterations in HACU can be induced by training on spatial learning tasks in both C57BL/6 mice and Long-Evans rats, an effect that was found to be absent in aged subjects (Decker, Pelleymounter, & Gallagher, 1988; Lebrun, Durkin, Marighetto, & Jarrard, 1990). The specific pattern of change in hippocampal HACU in young rats was shown to occur under conditions in which animals use spatial information processing: no comparable effect on HACU was found in yoked control rats given a nonspatial version of the water maze task (Decker et al., 1988). The effect of aging on HACU in rats, moreover, was found to depend on learning ability. No effect of training on HACU was found in impaired aged rats, but unimpaired aged rats showed a change comparable to that seen in young rats (Gallagher & Pelleymounter, 1988).

Additional research indicates that cholinoceptive mechanisms may be altered in hippocampus of learning-impaired aged rodents. Gallagher et al. (1990) found a small but reliable decrease in B_{max} for total muscarinic binding in hippocampus of impaired aged rats, but no difference between unimpaired aged subjects and young rats. Kadar, Silbermann, Weissman, and Levy (1990) reported that M1 sites, defined in an autoradiography study by [3H]pirenzepine binding, were significantly correlated with errors in the radial arm maze task, but only within the dentate gyrus: greater reduction in binding was associated with poorer performance.

In addition to the studies that have indicated some changes in cholinergic markers within the hippocampal formation that are related to cognitive decline, neurobiological changes associated with another input pathway have also yielded evidence of a relationship between hippocampal aging and spatial learning impairment. Cortical input reaches the hippocampus through the perforant path.

This projection originates in layer II neurons of the entorhinal cortex that innervate the dendrites of granule cells in the molecular layer of the dentate gyrus. In Alzheimer's disease there is a profound loss of perforant path input due to degeneration of neurons in entorhinal cortex (Hyman, Kromer, & Van Hoesen, 1987a; Hyman, Van Hoesen, & Damasio, 1987b; Hyman, Van Hoesen, Damasio, & Barnes, 1984). Several lines of evidence also indicate a more modest loss of this innervation in normal aging (e.g., Barnes, 1979; Geinisman & Bondareff, 1976). In addition to the direct consequences for information processing caused by a loss of input, much research has shown that removal of perforant path innervation normally induces sprouting of the commissural/associational (C/A) fibers and the cholinergic septal input to the dentate (Cotman, Nieto-Sampedro, & Harris, 1981; Hoff, Scheff, Benardo, & Cotman, 1982). Similar evidence for sprouting has also been reported in the dentate gyrus of brains from patients with Alzheimer's disease (Geddes et al., 1985). It is therefore possible that normal aging may include not only decremental effects on this system but may also induce reactive processes.

A number of age-related changes in the morphology and function of the perforant path/dentate system have been found to correlate with cognitive decline. The results from these studies are summarized in Table 6.2. In a pioneering study using the approach highlighted in this chapter, Barnes (1979) reported changes in long-term enhancement (LTE) produced by electrophysiological stimulation of the perforant path that were correlated with the performance of aged Long-Evans rats on a circular maze. In a different type of analysis, acquisition and decay rates in the LTE paradigm and in learning/retention of the spatial task were compared for groups of young and aged rats (Barnes & McNaughton, 1985). Relative to young rats, aged rats exhibited slower acquisition and more rapid decay characteristics. Age differences in the behavioral and neurobiological data were closely matched, particularly in comparing the rate of LTE decay with forgetting assessed in the spatial task. Using the radial arm maze to characterize functional decline in aged Fisher 344 rats, de Toledo-Morrell, Morrell, and Fleming (1984) also reported a correspondence between behavioral decline and another form of long-term physiological change in the perforant path/dentate system, that is, kindling induced by perforant path stimulation. Although the physiological mechanisms underlying these age-related neurobiological changes are not yet understood, the findings point to alterations in neural plasticity that might be particularly relevant to the loss of memory/cognitive function.

The loss of perforant input to the dentate in aging, noted earlier in this section, has also been found to exhibit variability that coincides with individual differences in the effects of aging on behavior. An electronmicroscopic investigation originally revealed an age-related decline in synaptic contacts within the region of the dentate molecular layer that is innervated by the perforant path (Geinisman & Bondareff, 1976). Subsequent studies showed a significant correlation for aged animals between the number of a specific type of contact/neuron (perforated axospinous synapses) and two measures of performance on the radial arm maze, that is, trials to criterion and choice accuracy (Geinisman, de Toledo-Morell, & Morell, 1986a; 1986b).

Morphological evidence for loss of input to the dentate could be connected to other effects of aging in this system that may reflect reactive processes. One example comes from studies examining the regulation of the opioid peptide dynorphin. This peptide is largely confined within the hippocampal formation to the dentate granule cells. Jiang, Owyang, Hong, and Gallagher (1989) reported that hippocampal dynorphinA(1-8)-immunoreactivity (dynA(1-8)ir) was elevated in impaired aged rats relative to their unimpaired aged cohorts and to young rats. A corresponding increase in the expression of hippocampal prodynorphin mRNA was also observed in aged rats that were impaired in the water maze. This effect of aging is interesting in light of other research showing that this peptide is negatively regulated by perforant path input. Stimulation of the perforant path normally decreases both dynorphin content and the expression of prodynorphin mRNA in the hippocampal formation (Mitchell, Grimes, Hudson, & Hong, 1987; Morris, Feasey, Bruggencate, Herz, & Hollt, 1988; Xie, Mitchell, & Hong, 1990). Additional experiments have indicated that lesions of the perforant path produce an increase in hippocampal dynA(1-8)ir in young rats that resembles the change found in learning-impaired aged rats (Thai, Hong, & Gallagher, 1991). Dysregulation of hippocampal dynorphin in aging may thus reflect a reactive process associated with diminished input and/or activity in the perforant path. Other evidence for reactive reorganization comes from a study showing that a change in the topography of [^{3}H]kainate ([^{3}H]Ka) binding, which normally reflects C/A sprouting after perforant path lesions, is evident in aged rats, but this change was not correlated with functional decline in spatial learning (Nagahara, Nicolle, & Gallagher, 1993).

Given the morphological and functional evidence for age-related neurobiological changes in perforant path transmission through the dentate, recent studies that have examined the status of glutamate receptors in this system are noteworthy. Two studies using in vitro autoradiography techniques reported comparable results indicating that the density of [^{3}H]Ka binding in the dentate gyrus was not altered during aging, irrespective of cognitive decline (Clark, Magnusson, & Cotman, 1992; Nagahara et al., 1993). The study by Clark et al. (1992) also included an analysis of AMPA and *N*-methyl-D-aspartate binding. An age-related decrease in these subpopulations of binding sites was observed in the dentate gyrus, but the magnitude of change was unrelated to the behavioral classification of aged rats. According to their classification, aged rats that failed to show any evidence of place learning were designated *nonachievers* and aged rats that exhibited some learning, albeit deficient relative to the young rats, were designated *achievers*. The apparent lack of difference in binding according to this classification should be viewed with some caution because the two aged subgroups had parallel deficits in nonspatial cue learning. However, one important feature of these data, as noted by the investigators, is the differential effect of aging on different glutamate receptor subtypes. This suggests that loss of binding sites is not secondary to changes in morphology (cell loss or changes in neuron density). This conclusion is supported by other morphometric data for dentate granule cells indicating no differences in aged rats even when cognitive decline was considered in the analysis (Geinisman et al., 1986a).

CONCLUSION

This brief review of the neurobiological results of studies on the perforant path/ dentate system highlight the fact that both decremental and reactive/reorganizational changes in the brain may be a feature of aging. Together with the results of studies on the septo-hippocampal projection, it also becomes apparent that aging has an impact on different neural elements within this circuitry. Indeed, aside from the research discussed in this review, studies have also shown significant neurobiological changes within the hippocampus proper that are correlated with cognitive decline during aging (e.g., Gage, Kelly & Björklund, 1984; Issa, Rowe, Gauthier, & Meaney, 1990; Kadar, Silbermann, Brandeis, & Levy, 1990; Meaney, Aitken, van Berkel, Bhatnagar, & Sapolsky, 1988; Pelleymounter, Beatty, & Gallagher, 1990). One issue that needs to be resolved is how changes in different parts of this circuitry might be related to one another. Indeed, it is not yet clear whether there is a functional relationship among these changes—for example, a cascading effect—or whether independent mechanisms underlie the effects of aging in different parts of the system. It is also noteworthy that both of the major input pathways to the hippocampal formation considered in this review, as well as the integrity of neurons within the hippocampus, are afflicted during the course of Alzheimer's disease. In this context, the findings on normal aging from studies of laboratory animals could signal a vulnerability in particular neural elements/circuits that provides an important background for understanding the pathophysiology of age-related dementia.

To return to the original question posed at the outset of this chapter, it is apparent that much can be learned from studies that combine behavioral assessment and neurobiological analysis in the same aged subjects. As noted previously this approach provides an alternative in the study of aging to one in which comparisons are based on chronological age alone. The assessment of functional decline and concomitant biological changes is more sensitive: a number of the neurobiological observations in this review would have been obscured in a simple comparison of young and aged brains. In yielding evidence about those changes that are most tightly coupled to cognitive decline, this approach points to loci where mechanisms involved in the regulation and expression of aging can be studied. In addition, there is growing evidence that large interindividual differences do indeed occur in aged animals, and that these can be related to underlying individual differences in age-related changes in the brain. This phenomenon has important implications for interventions that are aimed at loss of cognitive function in aging. Screening for cognitive impairment, as done by some investigators, may yield a clearer picture of the therapeutic potential of innovative treatments (e.g., Gage &

Björklund, 1986). In addition, the basis for the apparent variability in aging processes poses one of the most interesting topics for future research.

REFERENCES

Amaral, D. G., & Kurz, J. (1985). An analysis of the origins of the cholinergic and noncholinergic septal projections to the hippocampal formation of the rat. *Comparative Journal of Neurology, 240,* 37–59.

Barnes, C. A. (1979). Memory deficits associated with senescence: A neurophysiological and behavioral study in the rat. *Journal of Comparative Physiology and Psychology, 93,* 74–104.

Barnes, C. A., & McNaughton, B. L. (1985). An age comparison of the rates of acquisition and forgetting of spatial information in relation to long-term enhancement of hippocampal synapses. *Behavioral Neuroscience, 99,* 1040–1048.

Bartus, R. T., Dean, R. L. III, Beer, B., & Lippa, A. S. (1982). The cholinergic hypothesis of geriatric memory dysfunction. *Science, 217,* 408–417.

Burwell, R., & Gallagher, M. (1993). A longitudinal study of reaction time performance in Long-Evans rats. *Neurobiology of Aging, 14,* 57–64.

Clark, A. S., Magnusson, K. R., & Cotman, C. W. (1992). In vitro autoradiography of hippocampal excitatory amino acid binding in aged Fischer 344 rats: Relationship to performance on the Morris water maze. *Behavioral Neuroscience 2,* 324–335.

Collier, T. J., & Coleman, P. D. (1991). Divergence of biological and chronological aging: Evidence from rodent studies. *Neurobiology of Aging, 12,* 685–693.

Cotman, C. W. Nieto-Sampedro, M., & Harris, E. W. (1981). Synapses replacement in the nervous system of adult vertebrates. *Physiological Review, 61,* 684–784.

Decker, M., Pelleymounter, M. A., & Gallagher, M. (1988). The effects of training on a spatial memory task on high affinity choline uptake in hippocampus and cortex in young adult and aged rats. *Journal of Neuroscience, 8,* 90–99.

de Toledo-Morrell, L., Morrell, F., & Fleming, S. (1984). Age-dependent deficits in spatial memory are related to impaired hippocampal kindling. *Behavioral Neuroscience, 98,* 902–907.

DiMattia, B. D., & Kesner, R. P. (1988). Spatial cognitive maps: Differential role of parietal cortex and hippocampal formation. *Behavioral Neuroscience, 102,* 471–480.

Drachman, D. A., & Leavitt, J. L. (1974). Human memory and the cholinergic system. A relationship to aging? *Archives of Neurology, 30,* 113–121.

Fischer, W., Chen, K. S., Gage, F. H., & Björklund, A. (1991). Progressive decline in spatial learning and integrity of forebrain cholinergic neurons in rats during aging. *Neurobiology of Aging, 13,* 9–23.

Fischer, W., Gage, F. H., & Björklund, A. (1989). Degenerative changes in forebrain cholinergic nuclei correlate with cognitive impairments in aged rats. *European Journal of Neuroscience, 1,* 34–45.

Fischer, W., Nilsson, O. G., & Björklund, A. (1991). In vivo acetylcholine release as measured by microdialysis is unaltered in the hippocampus of cognitively impaired aged rats with degenerative changes in the basal forebrain. *Brain Research, 556,* 44–52.

Gage, F. H., & Björklund, A. (1986) Cholinergic septal grafts into the hicampal formation improve sy in aged rats by an atropine sensitive mechanism. *Journal of Neuroscience, 6,* 2837–2847.

Gage, F. H., Dunnett, S. B., & Björklund, A. (1984). Spatial learning and motor deficits in aged rats. *Neurobiology of Aging, 5,* 43–48.

Gage, F. H., Dunnett, S. B., & Björklund, A. (1989). Age-related impairments in spatial memory are independent of those in sensorimotor skills. *Neurobiology of Aging, 10,* 347–352.

Gage, F. H., Kelly, P. A. T., & Björklund, A. (1984). Regional changes in brain glucose metabolism reflect cognitive impairments in aged rats. *Journal of Neuroscience, 4,* 2856–2865.

Gallagher, M. & Burwell, R. D. (1989). Relationship of age-related decline across several behavioral domains. *Neurobiology of Aging, 10,* 691–708.

Gallagher, M., Burwell, R. D., Kodski, M. H., McKinney, M., Southerland, S., Vella-Roundtree, L., & Lewis, M. H. (1990). Markers for biogenic amines in the aged rat brain: Relationship to decline in spatial learning ability. *Neurobiology of Aging, 11*, 507–514.

Gallagher, M., & Holland, P. C. (1992). Preserved configural learning and spatial learning impairment in rats with hippocampal damage. *Hippocampus, 2*, 81–88.

Gallagher, M., & Pelleymounter, M. A. (1988). An age-related spatial learning deficit: Choline uptake distinguishes "impaired" and "unimpaired" rats. *Neurobiology of Aging, 9*, 363–369.

Geddes, J. W., Monaghan, D. R., Cotman, C. W., Lott, I. T., Kim, R. C., & Chui, H. C. (1985). Plasticity of hippocampal circuitry in Alzheimer's disease. *Science, 230*, 1179–1181.

Geinisman, Y., & Bondareff, W. (1976) Decrease in the number of synapses in the senescent brain: A quantitative electron microscopic analysis of the dentate gyrus molecular layer in the rat. *Mechanisms of Ageing and Development, 5*, 11–23.

Geinisman, Y., deToledo-Morrell, L., & Morrell, F. (1986a). Loss of perforated synapses in the dentate gyrus: Morphological substrate of memory deficit in aged rats. *Proceedings of the National Academy of Sciences of the United States of America, 83*, 3027–3031.

Geinisman, Y., deToledo-Morrell, L., & Morrell, F. (1986b). Aged rats need a preserved complement of perforated axospinous synapses per hippocampal neuron to maintain good spatial memory. *Brain Research, 398*, 266–275.

Hellweg, R., Fischer, W., Hock, C., Gage, F. H., Björklund, A., & Thoenen, H. (1990). Nerve growth factor levels and choline acetyltransferase activity in the brain of aged rats with spatial memory impairments. *Brain Research, 537*, 123–130.

Heron, A., & Chown, S. (1967). *Age and function.* Boston: Little, Brown.

Higgins, G. A., Oyler, G. A., Neve, R. L., Chen, K. S., & Gage, F. H. (1990). Altered levels of amyloid protein precursor transcripts in the basal forebrain of behaviorally impaired aged rats. *Proceedings of the National Academy of Sciences of the United States of America, 87*, 3032–3036.

Hoff, S. F., Scheff, S. W., Benardo, L. S., & Cotman, C. W. (1982). Lesioned-induced synaptogenesis in the dentate gyrus of aged rats. I. Loss and reacquisition of normal synaptic density. *Journal of Comparative Neurology, 205*, 246–252.

Hyman, B. T., Kromer, L. J., & Van Hoesen, G. W. (1987a). Reinnervation of the hippocampal perforant pathway zone in Alzheimer's disease. *Annals of Neurology, 21*, 259–267.

Hyman, B. T., Van Hoesen, G. W., & Damasio, A. R. (1987b). Alzheimer's disease: Glutamate depletion in the hippocampal perforant pathway zone. *Annals of Neurology, 22*, 37–40.

Hyman, B. T., Van Hoesen, G. W., Damasio, A. R., & Barnes, C. L. (1984). Alzheimer's disease: Cell-specific pathology isolates the hippocampal formation. *Science, 225*, 1168–1179.

Ingram, D. K., London, E. D., & Goodrick, C. L. (1981). Age and neurochemical correlates of radial maze performance in rats. *Neurobiology of Aging, 2*, 41–47.

Issa, A. M., Rowe, W., Gauthier, S., & Meaney, M. J. (1990). Hypothalamic-pituitary-adrenal activity in aged, cognitively impaired and cognitively unimpaired rats. *Journal of Neuroscience, 10*, 3247–3254.

Jiang, H. K., Owyang, V., Hong, J. S., & Gallagher, M. (1989). Elevated dynorphin in the hippocampal formation of aged rats: Relation to cognitive impairment on a spatial learning task. *Proceedings of the National Academy of Sciences of the United States of America, 86*, 2948–2951.

Kadar, T., Silbermann, M., Brandeis, R., & Levy, A. (1990). Age-related structural changes in the rat hippocampus: Correlation with working memory deficiency. *Brain Research, 512*, 113–120.

Kadar, T., Silbermann, M., Weissman, B. A., & Levy, A. (1990). Age-related changes in the cholinergic components within the central nervous system. II. Working memory impairment and its relation to hippocampal muscarinic receptors. *Mechanisms of Ageing and Development, 55*, 139–149.

Koh, S., Chang, P., Collier, T. J., & Loy, R. (1989). Loss of NGF receptor immunoreactivity in basal forebrain neurons of aged rats: Correlation with spatial memory impairment. *Brain Research, 498*, 397–404.

Lebrun, C., Durkin, T., Marighetto, A., & Jaffard, R. (1990). A comparison of the working memory performances of young and aged mice combined with parallel measures of testing and drug-induced activations of septo-hippocampal and nbm-cortical cholinergic neurones. *Neurobiology of Aging, 11*, 515–521.

Lowy, A., Ingram, D. K., Olton, D. S., Waller, S. B., Reynolds, M. A., & London, E. D. (1985). Discrimination learning requiring different memory components in rats: Age and neurochemical comparisons. *Behavioral Neuroscience, 99*, 638–651.

Luine, V., & Hearns, M. (1990). Spatial memory deficits in aged rats: Contributions of the cholinergic system assessed by ChAT. *Brain Research, 523*, 321–324.

Markowska, A. L., Stone, W. S., Ingram, D. K., Reynolds, J., Gold, P. E., Conti, L. H., Pontecorvo, M. J., Wenk, G. L., & Olton, D. S. (1989). Individual differences in aging: Behavioral and neurobiological correlates. *Neurobiology of Aging, 10*, 31–43.

McGeer, P. L., McGeer, E. G., Suzuki, J., Dolman, C. E., & Nagai, T. (1984). Aging, Alzheimer's disease, and the cholinergic system of the basal forebrain. *Neurology, 34*, 741–745.

Meaney, M. J., Aitken, D. H., van Berkel, C., Bhatnager, S., & Sapolsky, R. M. (1988). Effect of neonatal handling on age-related impairments associated with the hippocampus. *Science, 239*, 766–768.

Mitchell, C. L., Grimes, L., Hudson, P. M., & Hong, J.-S. (1987). Stimulation of the perforant path alters hippocampal levels of opioid peptides, glutamine and GABA. *Brain Research, 435*, 343–347.

Morris, B. J., Feasey, K. J., Bruggencate, G., Herz, A., & Hollt, V. (1988). Electrical stimulation in vivo increases the expression of proenkephalin mRNA and decreases the expression of prodynorphin nRNA in rat hippocampal granule cells. *Proceedings of the National Academy of Sciences of the United States of America, 85*, 3226–3230.

Morris, R. G. M., Garrud, P., Rawlins, J. N. P., & O'Keefe, J. (1982). Place navigation impaired in rats with hippocampal lesions. *Nature, 297*, 681–683.

Morris, R. G. M., Schenk, F., Tweedie, F., & Jarrard, L. E. (1990). Ibotenate lesions of hippocampus and/or subiculum: Dissociating components of allocentric spatial learning. *European Journal of Neuroscience, 2*, 1016–1028.

Nagahara, A. H., Nicolle, M. M., & Gallagher, M. (1993). Alterations in [3H]-kainate receptor binding in the hippocampal formation of aged Long-Evans rats. *Hippocampus, 3*, 269–277.

Olton, D. S., & Markowska, A. L. (1992). The aging septo-hippocampal system: Its role in age-related memory impairments. In L. Squire & N. Butters (Eds.), *Neuropsychology of memory* (pp. 378–385). New York: Oxford University Press.

Pelleymounter, M. A., Beatty, G., & Gallagher, M. (1990). Hippocampal 3H-CPP binding and spatial learning deficits in aged rats. *Psychobiology, 18*, 198–304.

Rapp, P. R., & Amaral, D. G. (1992). Individual differences in the behavioral and neurobiological consequences of normal aging. *Trends in Neuroscience, 15*, 340–345.

Reff, M. E., & Schneider, E. L. (1982). Biological markers of aging. *Proceedings of the Conference on Nonlethal Biological Markers of Physiological Aging.* NIH Publication No. 82-2221. Washington, DC: U.S. Department of Health and Human Services.

Rossor, M. N., Garrett, N. J., Johnson, A. L., Mountjoy, C. Q., Roth, M., & Iversen, L. L. (1982). A post-mortem study of the cholinergic and GABA systems in senile dementia. *Brain, 105*, 313–330.

Rowe, J. W., & Kahn, R. L. (1987). Human aging: Usual and successful. *Science, 237*, 143–149.

Rye, D. B., Wainer, B. H., Mesulan, M.-M., Mufson, E. J., & Saper, C. B. (1984). Cortical projections arising from the basal forebrain: A study of cholinergic and noncholinergic components employing combined retrograde tracing and immunohistochemical localization of choline acetyltransferase. *Neuroscience, 13*, 627–643.

Salthouse, T. A. (1991). *Theoretical perspectives on cognitive aging.* Hillsdale, NJ: Erlbaum.

Schwartzman, A. E., Gold, D., Andres, D., Arbuckle, T. Y., & Chaikelson, J. (1987). Stability of intelligence: A 40-year follow-up. *Canadian Journal of Psychology, 41,* 244–256.

Stroessner-Johnson, H. M., Rapp, P. R., & Amaral, D. G. (1992). Cholinergic cell loss and hypertrophy in the medial septal nucleus of the behaviorally characterized aged rhesus monkey. *Journal of Neuroscience, 12,* 1936–1944.

Thai, L., Hong, J. S., & Gallagher, M. (1991). Perforant path deafferentation alters hippocampal dynorphin and enkephalin content in rats. *Society of Neuroscience Abstracts, 17,* 395.

Whitehouse, P. J., Price, D. L., Clark, A. W., Coyle, J. T., & DeLong, M. R. (1981). Alzheimer's disease: Evidence for selective loss of cholinergic neurons in the nucleus basalis. *Annals of Neurology, 10,* 122–126.

Wilkinson, R. T. & Allison, S. (1989). Age and simple reaction time: Decade differences for 5,325 subjects. *Journal of Gerontology, 44,* 29–35.

Xie, C., Mitchell, C. L., & Hong, J. (1990). Perforant path stimulation differentially alters prodynorphin mRNA and proenkephalin mRNA levels in the entorhinal cortex-hippocampal region. *Molecular Brain Research, 7,* 199–205.

7

Animal Models of Multiple Neurotransmitter Interactions in Alzheimer's Disease

V. HAROUTUNIAN
W. WALLACE
A. C. SANTUCCI
K. L. DAVIS

Animal model systems for diseases with unknown etiology must, by definition, be restricted to modeling some or all of the known features of the disease entity. Modeling strategies are constrained further by the availability of techniques to duplicate the features and symptoms of interest. Alzheimer's disease (AD) represents one neurodegenerative disorder the etiology of which is as yet unknown. The animal model systems that have emerged for this disease have therefore been limited to model systems aiming to duplicate some of the observed behavioral and neurobiological changes that occur in the disease (Dekker, Connor, & Thal, 1991; Olton & Wenk, 1987). Animal model systems for AD are further hampered by the absence of the tools necessary to duplicate some of the known neurodegenerative changes. For example, slow progressive neurodegeneration has been difficult to reproduce. Similarly, with the exception of some recent and as yet under-scrutinized systems (Kowall, Beal, Busciglio, Duffy, & Yankner, 1991; Marx, 1991; Wirak et al., 1991), the reproduction of some of the classical neuropathological hallmarks of the disease, such as neuritic plaques and neurofibrillary tangles, has been difficult (Thal, Mandel, Terry, Buzsaki, & Gage, 1990). These limitations have forced the development of incomplete model systems. One example of such an incomplete model system(s) is the experimental reproduction of some of the neurochemical deficits noted in the AD brain (Decker & McGaugh, 1991; Dekker et al., 1991; Olton et al., 1987). Although it is generally recognized and accepted that such model systems are gross approximations at best, it must also be recognized that these model systems may lead to some insights into the role of the affected systems in AD and its symptoms and may provide avenues for symptom reduction.

The studies presented in this chapter were conducted to determine whether (1) the neurochemical deficits noted in AD could produce some of the cognitive symptoms of AD in animals, and (2) whether the cognitive deficits so produced would be amenable to pharmacological alleviation. As a result of these series of investigations, we have also determined that some of the neurochemical deficits noted in AD may be intimately linked to another hallmark of the AD brain, namely the synthesis of β-amyloid precursor protein (β-APP).

FOREBRAIN CHOLINERGIC LESIONS IN ANIMAL MODEL SYSTEMS

During the past decade and a half it has become definitively established that forebrain cholinergic system deficits are among the most severely affected systems in AD (Bird, Stranahan, Sumi, & Raskind, 1983; Davies & Maloney, 1976; Gottfries, 1985; Lehericy et al., 1989; McGeer, McGeer, Suzuki, Dolman, & Nagai, 1984; Perry, 1980, 1987; Perry et al., 1978; Price et al., 1985). The neuropathological studies reported by Coyle, Price, & DeLong (1983) and Whitehouse, Price, Struble, Clark, & Coyle (1982) demonstrated the degeneration of magnacellular cholinergic neurons in the basal forebrain to be responsible for this massive cortical cholinergic deficit.

Hundreds of studies have now been reported demonstrating that similar cortical cholinergic deficits can be reproduced by lesioning homologous forebrain regions in non-human primates and other mammalian species such as the rat (see Decker & McGaugh, 1991; Dekker et al., 1991; Olton & Wenk, 1987 for review). These studies have employed a variety of lesioning techniques, including electrolytic, excitotoxic, and neurotoxic methods. One example of the dependence of cortical cholinergic activity on basal forebrain nucleus basalis of Meynert integrity is a study that we recently conducted in collaboration with Dr. S. Ahlers (Haroutunian et al., 1992). Rather than permanently lesioning the nbM, we infused a 20% lidocaine solution unilaterally into the region of the rat nbM and recorded basal acetylcholine release in the cerebral cortex by in vivo microdialysis. Figure 7.1 demonstrates that the infusion of 20% lidocaine into the nbM of rats results in a significant ($ns = 6$, $ps < 0.01$) decrease in the extracellular release of ACh in the frontal cortex. ACh levels return to near baseline levels within approximately 60 minutes of lidocaine infusion.

A very large body of literature can also be cited in support of the hypothesis that lesions of the nbM lead to significant deficits in learning and memory. These studies have been amply summarized by a number of authors (Decker & McGaugh, 1991; Dekker et al., 1991; Olton & Wenk, 1987). The results of one such study are presented in Figure 7.2. In this study, different groups of rats ($ns = 8$–10) received neurotoxin-induced lesions of the nbM or sham operations. Ten to fourteen days later each rat was trained on a one trial step through passive

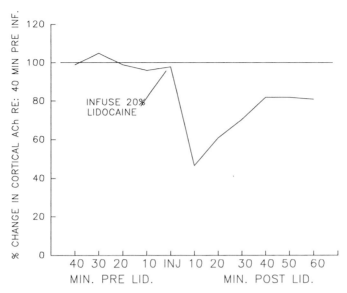

FIGURE 7.1.   Effects of 20% lidocaine infusion into the nbM of rats on spontaneous cortical release of acetylcholine.

avoidance task using a 0.65 mA footshock as the UCS. Seventy-two hours later each rat was tested for the retention of passive avoidance using procedures that were identical to those used during training. Latency to step into the previously shock-associated compartment of the passive avoidance apparatus served as the dependent measure. As Figure 7.2 indicates, the nbM lesioned rats, irrespective of the neurotoxin used, stepped into the shock associated compartment of the passive avoidance apparatus with significantly shorter latencies than the sham operated controls. Assessment of cortical ChAT activity shortly after the completion of the passive avoidance task showed that the infusion of NMDA into the nbM had led to an approximately 27–32% depletion of cortical ChAT activity. Results similar to these have been reported in dozens of experiments.

It can be and has been argued (Fibiger, 1991; Wenk, Markowska, & Olton, 1989) that the lesion studies cited above suffer from a lack of neurochemical specificity, and that other systems that might also have been damaged by the lesioning process could be involved in the learning and memory deficits (Dunnett, Whishaw, Jones, & Bunch, 1987; Wenk et al., 1989). Although no one study can be cited to refute such an argument, the plethora of studies reporting similar findings with a variety of different lesioning techniques, agents, and outcome measures argue that the cholinergic cells of the nbM are at the very least among those neural systems that influence cortically mediated mnemonic functions. In addition, we and others have found that nbM-lesioned rats are particularly susceptible to the disruptive effects of low doses of antimuscarinic agents such as scopolamine. In one such study, rats were trained on a spatial working memory task. Each rat was permitted to find food reinforcement (Kellogg's Frootloop cereal) in

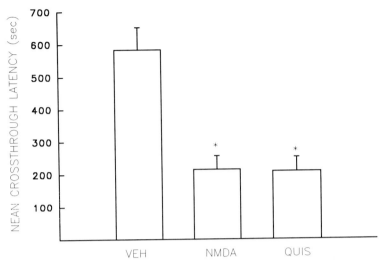

FIGURE 7.2.   Effects of NMDA and quisqualic acid lesions of the nbM on the 72-hour retention of a one trial passive avoidance task (* vs. VEH, *ps* < 0.01).

the only exposed well of a rectangular apparatus. The rat was removed from the apparatus, the remaining three wells were exposed, the original well was rebaited, and the rat was allowed to search for reinforcement. Head pokes into the previously unbaited wells were used as the dependent measure. nbM-lesioned and sham operated rats were trained to the same criterion (3 of 4 correct trials). After reaching criterion each rat received one subcutaneous (sc) injection of a low dose of scopolamine HBr (0.1 mg/kg). This dose of scopolamine produced no adverse effects on performance in the spatial maze for the sham operated rats (mean errors = 1.3), whereas the nbM-lesioned rats made an average of 14 incorrect head pokes before obtaining the Frootloop pellet ($p < .001$). This increase in sensitivity to the disruptive effects of scopolamine argues in favor of a central role of the lesioned cholinergic system in controlling the observed performance deficits.

CHOLINOMIMETIC POTENTIATION OF MNEMONIC ACTIVITY IN nBM LESIONED RATS AND IN AD

One implication of the dramatic cortical cholinergic deficits in AD and the cholinergic deficits produced by lesions of the nbM is that the resulting cognitive deficits should be amenable to amelioration by cholinomimetic therapy. This hypothesis is supported by animal model system experiments where cholinomimetics have been administered to nbM-lesioned rats. The administration of physostigmine, arecoline, pilocarpine, 4-aminopyridine, all alleviate, at least partially, the nbM-induced learning and memory deficits (Dekker et al., 1991; Haroutunian, Kanof, Tsuboyama, Campbell, & Davis, 1986; Haroutunian, Mantin, & Kanof, 1990; Mandel, Chen, Connor, & Thal, 1989; Murray & Fibiger, 1985; Ridley, Murray,

Johnson, & Baker, 1986). The results of one series of studies using physostigmine, 4-aminopyridine, and oxotremorine are presented as examples of cholinomimetic effects on the 72-hour retention of a passive avoidance task (Haroutunian et al., 1986) (Fig. 7.3). In these studies, rats received bilateral lesions of the nbM using ibotenic acid. Approximately two weeks later each rat was trained on a single trial step-through passive avoidance task using a single 0.65-mA scrambled footshock as the UCS. Immediately following the shock experience different groups of rats received different sc doses of each of the three cholinomimetics mentioned earlier. Retention of passive avoidance was assessed 72 hours later. As Figure 7.3 demonstrates, each of the cholinomimetics was able to enhance retention test performance at a specific dose range. In general, retention test performance was enhanced to at least the level of sham operated rats receiving saline.

Unlike the almost complete normalization of passive avoidance retention test performance observed in nbM-lesioned rats receiving cholinomimetics, the results of cholinomimetic therapy studies in AD patients have been less pronounced. In general, the administration of cholinomimetics to AD patients has led to significant, but modest improvements in some measures of cognitive function (Davis & Mohs, 1982; Mohs et al., 1985; Stern, Sano, & Mayeux, 1983; Thal, Fuld, Masur, & Sharpless, 1983). The reasons for the modest effects of cholinomimetics in AD have been discussed in several sources (Mohs & Davis, 1987), but the presence of other, noncholinergic lesions and deficits in AD may be among the most likely (Haroutunian et al., 1986; Haroutunian, Santucci, & Davis, 1990; Santucci, Haroutunian, Tsuboyama, Kanof, & Davis, 1989). Noradrenergic, serotonergic, and somatostatinergic deficits observed in AD may be among the factors that contribute to not only the cognitive deficits observed, but to the efficacy of cholinomimetics in alleviating the mnemonic deficits.

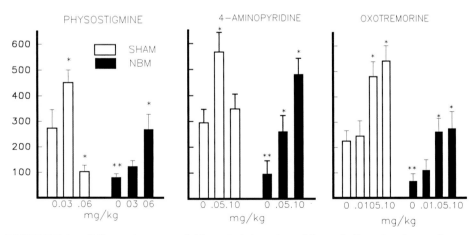

FIGURE 7.3.   Effects of post-acquisition administration of three cholinomimetics on the 72-hour retention test performance of a one trial passive avoidance task by nbM-lesioned and sham operated rats (* vs. 0 dose, *ps* < 0.01; ** vs. sham operated rats receiving the same dose of drug, *ps* < 0.01).

SOMATOSTATINERGIC DEFICITS
AND MNEMONIC FUNCTION

There is a significant body of evidence suggesting that (1) cortical somato-statinlike immunoreactivity (SLI) is decreased in AD (Beal et al., 1985; Beal, Uhl, Mazurek, Kowall, & Martin, 1986; Davies, Katzman, & Terry, 1980; Davies & Terry, 1981; Rossor, Emson, Montjoy, Roth, & Iversen, 1980) and (2) the depletion of central SLI may lead to substantial learning and memory deficits in animal model systems (Bakhit, Benoit, & Bloom, 1983; Haroutunian, Mantin, Campbell, Tsuboyama, & Davis, 1987; Vecsei et al., 1984). The results of these studies have been reviewed in detail (Haroutunian, Kanof, and Davis, 1989; Haroutunian et al., 1987). The significant reduction in cortical SLI levels in AD have been confirmed in our own laboratories by Dr. S. Gabriel in postmortem cortical tissues obtained from well-characterized and neuropathologically confirmed AD cases. It is difficult to draw firm conclusions regarding the role of somatostatin in learning and memory because of the paucity of tools for manipulating central somatostatinergic function. The most frequently used agent for influencing central SLI has been cysteamine. A number of laboratories have reported that the parenteral or central administration of cysteamine to rats leads to (1) pronounced decrements in central SLI (Bakhit et al., 1983; Haroutunian et al., 1987; Sagar et al., 1982) and (2) significant learning and memory deficits (Haroutunian et al., 1989; Haroutunian et al., 1987; Vecsei et al., 1984; Walsh et al., 1985). In a series of studies investigating the neurochemical and behavioral effects of cysteamine in the rat, we found that cysteamine effects on mnemonic function may depend more on the mechanism by which cysteamine depletes central SLI stores than on the depletion of SLI per se (Haroutunian et al., 1987). Simultaneous analysis of CSF and cortical SLI at different times following cysteamine administration revealed that cysteamine depleted cortical SLI stores by causing a massive release of somatostatin that was detectable in CSF. Subsequent behavioral studies revealed that cysteamine (50 mg/kg) interfered with learning and memory function only when the acquisition phase of the learning task was coincident with this period of rapid somatostatin release. When rats were trained on our standard passive avoidance task after CSF somatostatin levels had returned to baseline, but cortical levels of SLI were still depressed, learning and memory functions were intact (Haroutunian et al., 1987).

Somatostatinergic deficits, at least those deficits induced by the administration of cysteamine, do not adversely affect responsivity to cholinomimetics in nbM-lesioned or sham operated rats. In a large 2 × 2 balanced design, we administered several doses of physostigmine (0.0–0.24 mg/kg) immediately after passive avoidance training to rats with or without nbM lesions and with or without extensive (3 consecutive days) pretreatment with cysteamine. Upon testing 72 hours later, it was revealed that cysteamine (50 mg/kg) pretreatment failed to affect the retention test enhancing properties of posttrial physostigmine in either nbM-lesioned or sham operated rats (Haroutunian et al., 1989). These results suggest that although somatostatinergic activity may play a significant role in the processes that subserve learning and memory, the partial depletion of central SLI stores with cysteamine does not influence passive avoidance retention test performance and responsivity to cholinomimetics in sham or nbM-lesioned rats. These conclusions must be approached with caution, however, because of inadequacies in the tools available for controlled and anatomically specific somatostatinergic lesions. Somatostatinergic cells are widely distributed in the forebrain and lack a distinct nucleus of origin, making anatomically specific lesions difficult to produce. Furthermore, cysteamine-induced lesions are indirect (release mediated), generally incomplete (depleting cortical SLI by 50–60%), and temporary (only days in duration) (Haroutunian et al., 1989). Thus, the validity of the conclusions reached earlier must await the availability of pharmacological and experimental tools that permit the manipulation of this system in a more defined and controlled manner.

SEROTONERGIC DEFICITS AND MNEMONIC FUNCTION

Indices of serotonergic function have been reported to be reduced in AD by dozens of different studies (Cross, 1990; Gottfries, 1990a; Reinikainen et al., 1988; Reinikainen, Soininen, & Riekkinen, 1990). There is little question that serotonergic neurotransmission plays a significant role in the processes that subserve learning and memory. The precise nature of serotonergic influences on learning and memory is less clear. Mnemonic function can be enhanced or diminished by serotonergic agonists, antagonists, and lesions (Altman & Normile, 1988; Ogren, 1985, 1986a). Precisely which action these agents have appears to depend on and vary from task to task. There is some reason to believe that the serotonergic deficits contribute to the alterations in attentional and emotional functions (Fornal & Jacobs, 1988; Palmer, Stratmann, Procter, & Bowen 1988; Reinikainen et al., 1990).

In the rat model systems that we have used most frequently, serotonergic influences on mnemonic function have been most readily demonstrable when the depletion of central 5-HT stores has been achieved through or accompanied by the release of serotonin (Santucci, Kanof, & Haroutunian, 1990). We have produced serotonergic depletions by (1) the systemic administration of *p*-chloroamphetamine (PCA); (2) the infusion of the serotonergic toxin 5-7-DHT into the nbM; and (3) the infusion of 5-7-DHT into the dorsal raphe nucleus.

Our initial studies of the effects of PCA administration on passive avoidance behavior (Santucci et al., 1990) generally confirmed previous results showing that the pretreatment of rats with the PCA (2.5 mg/kg) 60–30 minutes prior to the acquisition phase of a passive avoidance response led to significant retention tests deficits 72 hours later. These results were obtained, however, only when PCA administration preceded passive avoidance training by approximately 60 minutes, and not when PCA was administered immediately following acquisition. These findings suggested that the passive avoidance deficits observed with PCA could be a result of the well-known serotonin-releasing property of PCA (Adell, Sarna,

Hutson, & Curzon, 1989; Ogren, 1986a, 1986b), rather than to the depletion of serotonin per se. By administering PCA (2.5 mg/kg) to rats at different times prior to training (i.e., 15, 30, 45, 120 minutes, and 1 and 7 days), we confirmed that retention test performance was disrupted at short intervals following PCA administration (<120 minutes) and not at longer intervals. The failure of PCA to affect passive avoidance behavior at long time periods was not due to the recovery of serotonergic function, since neurochemical analyses documented severe 5-HT depletion even two weeks after the PCA treatment. This pattern of results is not specific to the passive avoidance paradigm, but also extends to a Morris water maze task. In this experiment different groups of rats ($n = 8$) were treated with either saline or 2.5 mg/kg PCA one week prior to training on the water maze task. Each animal received 4 days of training with 4 trials run per day. All animals, irrespective of PCA treatment, learned to escape the water maze with equal facility. Neither escape latencies nor distances swum were affected by the PCA pretreatment. These experiments provided support for the hypothesis that PCA-induced amnesia is mediated through the rapid release of serotonin within a time frame to interfere with the acquisition of the passive avoidance response.

To test this hypothesis directly we lesioned the serotonergic system centrally by infusing 2 μl of 5-7-DHT (15 μg/μl) into the dorsal raphe nucleus. Two weeks later different groups of lesioned and sham operated rats (Ns = 10–12) received sc injections of either saline or 2.5 mg/kg PCA and were trained on the passive avoidance response 30 minutes later. Upon retention testing 72 hours later, only those rats that had received sham lesions showed significant PCA-induced retention test deficits. Raphe lesioned rats were not impaired on this passive avoidance task. These results confirm our earlier hypothesis that PCA-induced passive avoidance deficits are caused by the release of serotonin rather than the resultant depletion of serotonin. At the same time this study confirmed our prediction that PCA-induced passive avoidance deficits could be blocked by more global lesions of central 5-HT systems.

Perturbations of the forebrain serotonergic system do affect responsivity to acetylcholinesterase inhibitors, but as with serotonergic influences on passive avoidance behavior, these effects appear to be related to excessive 5-HT release rather than to 5-HT depletion. When nbM-lesioned and sham operated rats were pretreated with PCA (2.5 mg/kg) and were administered physostigmine immediately after passive avoidance training, physostigmine enhancement of retention test performance was disrupted in the PCA pretreated rats (Santucci et al., 1990). But when physostigmine (0.0–0.12 mg/kg) was administered to rats with combined NMDA-induced lesions of the nbM and 5-7-DHT-induced lesions of the dorsal raphe, its retention test performance-enhancing properties were undiminished (Haroutunian et al., 1990).

This pattern of results suggests that PCA-induced a 5-7-DHT-induced serotonergic perturbations, like somatostatinergic perturbations, affect learning and memory, but the effects (1) are not necessarily attributable to the 5-HT depletion, and (2) do not alter cholinomimetic influences on mnemonic function in intact or mnemonically impaired rats.

NORADRENERGIC INFLUENCES ON LEARNING AND MEMORY AND THEIR INTERACTION WITH FOREBRAIN CHOLINERGIC SYSTEMS

Our interest and studies of the influence of forebrain noradrenergic lesions on learning and memory have been guided by postmortem studies in AD and by the desire to find potential therapeutic avenues to enhance the efficacy of cholinomimetics in AD patients. Forebrain noradrenergic systems, like the cholinergic, somatostatinergic, and serotonergic systems discussed earlier, have been repeatedly shown to be compromised in AD (Adolfsson, Gottfries, Roos, & Winblad, 1979; Chan-Palay & Asan, 1989a, 1989b; Gottfries, 1990b; Palmer et al., 1987; Perry, 1987; Zweig et al., 1988). There is also evidence that sizable deficits occur in this system in aged rodents and nonhuman primates (Arnsten & Goldman-Rakic, 1985a, 1985b; Decker & McGaugh, 1991; Gold & Zornetzer, 1983). Like the forebrain somatostatinergic system and the forebrain serotonergic system, the degree to which forebrain noradrenergic deficits influence mnemonic function directly is not clear (Arnsten & Goldman-Rakic, 1985a; Decker, Gill, & McGaugh, 1990; Decker & McGaugh, 1990; Haroutunian et al., 1986). Although many experiments have shown that direct lesions of the forebrain noradrenergic system impair learning and memory on some tasks (Gold & Zornetzer, 1983; McNaughton & Mason, 1980), these impairments are often revealed under conditions of strong provocation, or conditions that place substantial demands on mnemonic functions (Arnsten & Goldman-Rakic, 1985a; Decker et al., 1990; Decker & McGaugh, 1990). In our studies we have focused more on the interactive effects of forebrain NE depletion with cholinergic lesions than on the direct influences of the NE system on mnemonic function.

In an initial series of experiments we studied the effects of 6-OHDA-induced lesions of the ascending dorsal noradrenergic bundle (DB) alone or in combination with concurrent ibotenic acid-induced lesions of the nbM (Haroutunian et al., 1986). Groups of 8 to 10 rats each were prepared with either sham lesions, lesions of the nbM alone, lesions of the DB alone, or concurrent lesions of the nbM and DB. Two weeks later the rats were trained on a standardized step-through one trial passive avoidance task using a 0.6-mA scrambled footshock UCS. Retention of passive avoidance was assessed 72 hours later, the rats were sacrificed within 3 weeks of lesioning and cortical cholinergic and noradrenergic marker activity, and levels were measured.

The results of the passive avoidance retention test performed 72 hours after training are shown in Figure 7.4. Passive avoidance retention test deficits were apparent only in animals that had sustained lesions of the nbM, either alone or in combination with lesions of the DB. Lesions of the NE system alone did not influence retention test performance on this measure. Since nbM lesions alone severely disrupted retention test performance, it is difficult to ascertain whether the combination of nbM + DB lesions produced even greater deficits; however, no evidence for an additive effect was obtained in two ancillary studies. Table 7.1 indicates that nbM and DB lesions both produced significant cortical deficits in

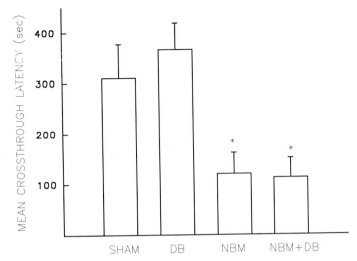

FIGURE 7.4.   Effects of nbM, DB and nbM + DB lesions on the 72-hour retention test performance of a one trial passive avoidance task (* vs. sham operated rats, *ps* < 0.01).

cholinergic and noradrenergic markers that were lesion-specific. The concurrent lesions of the nbM and DB led to significant deficits in cholinergic and noradrenergic markers. Although the degree of NE depletion produced by combined nbM + BD lesions was not significantly different from the NE deficits produced by DB lesions alone, the NE deficits produced by DB alone lesions were nominally more profound than the NE deficits induced by lesions of the nbM + DB. The significance of these nominal effects are discussed below.

TABLE 7.1   Effects of NMDA Lesions of the nbM, 6-OHDA Lesions of the Ascending Noradrenergic Bundle (ANB), 5-7-DHT Lesions of the Dorsal Raphe Nucleus, and Combined Lesions of the nbM with ANB and DR Lesions, on Various Neurochemical Markers in the Cortex

Marker	nbM	DB	nbM + DB	DR	nbM + DR
ChAT	**26.3***	2.4	**27.7***	6.14	**28.9***
AChE	**29.1***	1.9	**26.4***	7.06	**27.5***
NE	3.2	**93.7***	**88.4***	16.4	15.7
DA	5.2	3.8	11.2	+7.7	15.9
5-HT	9.9	4.3	3.2	**84.8***	**83.7***
SLI	2.6				
CRF	3.1				

Note that the nbM lesion effects in these studies are less profound than those reported in subsequent tables because for these studies rats received single bilateral lesions as opposed to the double unilateral lesions described in subsequent sections. In addition to the markers listed, neurotransmitter metabolites (HVA, DOPAC, MHPG, 5-HIAA) were also measured, but because they correlated highly with their respective transmitters, they are not presented here. Since these results were obtained in different discrete studies, values are reported as % depletion relative to sham operated controls. Data are based on Ns of 8–12 rats per lesion condition. Choline acetyltransferase (ChAT); acetylcholinesterase (AChE); norepinephrine (NE); dopamine (DA); serotonin (5-HT); somatostatinlike immunoreactivity (SLI); corticotrophin releasing factorlike immunoreactivity (CRF).

*vs. Sham operated controls, *ps* < 0.05.

As was the case with our studies of cholinergic/somatostatinergic and choliner-gic/serotonergic interactions, we investigated the consequences of combined cho-linergic/noradrenergic lesions on responsivity to cholinomimetics. The results of these studies have been extensively discussed (Haroutunian et al., 1986; Haroutu-nian et al., 1990; Haroutunian, Tsuboyama, Kanof, & Davies, 1988; Sautucci et al., 1989) and will only be summarized here. Different groups of rats were prepared with either sham lesions or concurrent lesions of the nbM and DB. After a 2-week recovery interval all rats were trained on the previously discussed one trial passive avoidance task. Immediately following training different groups of sham operated and lesioned rats (*ns* = 8–10) received different doses of the acetylcholinesterase inhibitor physostigmine (0.0–0.24 mg/kg). These doses were selected because they covered the entire dose range at which we and others have observed significant retention-test-enhancing properties for physostigmine (Dekker et al., 1991; Haroutunian et al., 1990; Mandel et al., 1989; Murray & Fibiger, 1985). The results of the 72-hour retention test performance scores are presented in Figure 7.5. Physostigmine failed to affect the performance of nbM + DB-lesioned rats at any of the doses tested. The retention test perform-ance on the nbM + DB-lesioned rats was significantly worse than that of sham-lesioned rats irrespective of physostigmine dose. Subsequent studies demonstrated that DB lesion-induced blockade of responsivity to physostigmine was not limited to physostigmine but generalized to the blockade of oxotremorine-induced en-hancement as well. An additional study confirmed the generality of NE depletion-

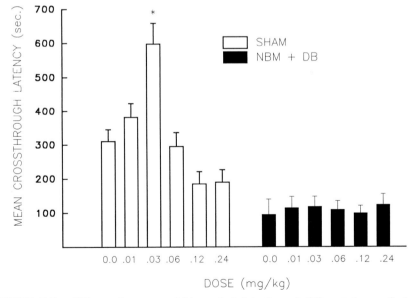

FIGURE 7.5. Effects of post-acquisition administration of different doses of physos-tigmine on the 72-hour retention test performance of a one trial passive avoidance task in sham operated rats and rats with combined lesions of the nbM and the DB (* vs. 0.0 dose, *p* < 0.01).

induced blockade of cholinomimetic influences on behavior by showing that the cataleptic response to 0.5-mg/kg oxotremorine was blocked by doses of the parenterally administered toxin, DSP-4 (0.0–75 mg/kg), which depleted cortical NE levels by 50% or more (50 and 75 mg/kg versus saline-injected rats, $ps < 0.01$). These results, taken together with complementary results reported by several other laboratories (Decker & Gallager, 1987; Decker et al., 1990; Decker & McGaugh, 1989; Mason & Fibiger, 1979; Riekkinen et al., 1990) strongly suggest that the cholinergic and noradrenergic systems interact dynamically and that the efficacy of cholinomimetics to affect mnemonic function is at least in part dependent upon the integrity of the noradrenergic system. These results viewed in light of the significant deficits in cortical cholinergic and noradrenergic function in AD and old age suggest that deficits in these two neurochemical systems are intimately involved in the cognitive deficits evident in these populations.

Recent neurochemical evidence suggests that the interaction of the cholinergic and noradrenergic systems might be even stronger and more complex than that which is apparent from the studies described earlier. It was previously mentioned that the cortical NE deficits resulting from nbM + DB lesions were nominally less profound than the NE deficits observed in animals with DB lesions alone. To study this possibility further we prepared different groups of rats ($ns = 7$–8) with bilateral or unilateral lesions of the nbM and DB either alone or in combination. Four weeks later the rats were sacrificed, and frontal, temporal, and parietal cortices were dissected and assayed for ChAT, NE, DA, and 5-HT. Cortical DA and 5-HT levels were not significantly affected by any of the lesion procedures. Cortical ChAT activity was significantly reduced by nbM lesions and was not differentially affected by DB lesions. Strong evidence for an interaction between nbM and DB lesions was obtained when cortical NE levels were examined.

The results of combined lesions of the nbM and DB on cortical NE levels are shown in Figure 7.6. The most important feature of this complex figure is the consistent elevation of cortical NE levels evident in nbM + DB-lesioned rats versus the DB-alone-lesioned rats. This attenuation of 6-OHDA lesion effects on cortical NE levels by nbM lesions is evident irrespective of whether unilateral or bilateral lesions are considered. We are currently conducting detailed neuroanatomical and neurochemical studies to determine the underlying compensatory mechanisms involved in this apparent "protective" effect of nbM lesions on cortical NE levels; however, one possibility is that these protective effects are gained through an alteration in the turnover of NE. Irrespective of the mechanism through which nbM lesions partially counter the effects of 6-OHDA lesions, it is clear that the functions of the cortical NE and ACh systems are intertwined and that the two systems interact dynamically at a behavioral, pharmacological, and neurochemical level.

One implication of the results of the behavioral and pharmacological studies described so far is that noradrenergic lesions may significantly impair or retard the ability of cholinomimetics to affect mnemonic function. It is possible that the cortical noradrenergic deficits that are apparent in a significant proportion of AD victims contribute to the efficacy with which cholinomimetic agents enhance their

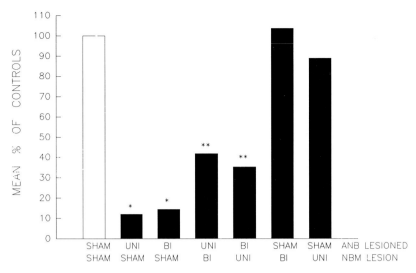

FIGURE 7.6.   Effects of lesions of the nbM and DB alone or in combination with each other on the levels of norepinephrine in the cerebral cortex (* vs. sham operated rats, *ps* < 0.01, ** vs. DB lesions alone, *ps* < 0.01).

cognitive deficits. Two pharmacological studies conducted in nbM + DB-lesioned rats address this issue (Haroutunian, Kanof, Tsuboyama, & Davis, 1990). Based on previous studies in rats, humans and in nonhuman primates (Arnsten, Cai, & Goldman-Rakic, 1988; Mair & McEntee, 1986; McEntee & Mair, 1980; Quartermain, Freedmen, Botwinick, & Gutwein, 1977; Quartermain, Judge, & Leo, 1988; Quartermain & Botwinick, 1975), we assessed the ability of the α_2-adrenergic receptor agonist clonidine to enhance retention test performance in nbM + DB-lesioned rats when administered alone or in combination with one of two cholinomimetics, physostigmine, or oxotremorine. Rats were prepared with either sham lesions or combined nbM + DB lesions. All rats were trained on the previously described passive avoidance task. In two separate studies, the rats received sc injections of different doses of clonidine and physostigmine alone or in combination, or different doses of clonidine and oxotremorine, alone or in combination. Retention of passive avoidance was assessed 72 hours after training and post-acquisition drug administration. The results of these studies are summarized in Figures 7.7 and 7.8. As predicted by the previously discussed studies, retention test performance was not enhanced by physostigmine or oxotremorine when either drug was administered alone. A very high dose of clonidine (0.5 mg/kg) alone was able to enhance retention test performance; however, clonidine at such high doses is neither pharmacologically specific nor clinically useful (this dose was selected for inclusion because some previous studies (Quartermain et al., 1977, 1988; Quartermain & Botwinick, 1975) had shown this dose to be effective in reversing experimentally induced retrograde amnesia). The most significant findings in these experiments were obtained in those lesioned rats that received low doses of clonidine (0.1 mg/kg) combined with low doses of physos-

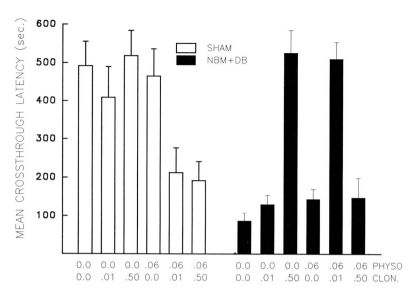

FIGURE 7.7. Effects of post-acquisition injection of physostigmine and clonidine administered alone or in combination with each other on the 72-hour retention test performance of a one trial passive avoidance task in sham operated rats and rats with combined lesions of the nbM and the DB.

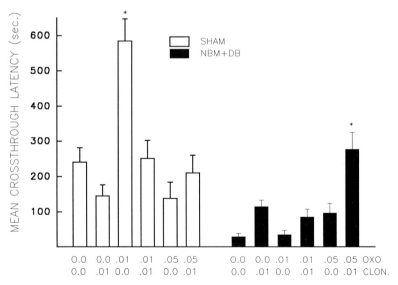

FIGURE 7.8. Effects of post-acquisition injection of oxotremorine and clonidine administered alone or in combination with each other on the 72-hour retention test performance of a one trial passive avoidance task in sham operated rats and rats with combined lesions of the nbM and the DB.

140

tigmine (0.06 mg/kg) or oxotremorine (0.1 mg/kg). In both of these studies, doses of physostigmine, oxotremorine, and clonidine when administered alone were ineffective in enhancing retention test performance. But when either physostigmine or oxotremorine were administered in combination with 0.1-mg/kg physostigmine, retention test performance was significantly enhanced.

The question of the efficacy of combined treatment with cholinomimetics and noradrenergic agents as a treatment strategy for AD is currently being investigated at our center and other laboratories. These difficult studies are not yet completed. Irrespective of their outcome, however, the experiments detailed previously demonstrate that cholinergic and noradrenergic systems participate and interact dynamically to modulate learning, memory, and cortical neurochemical function.

INVOLVEMENT OF FOREBRAIN CHOLINERGIC AND NORADRENERGIC SYSTEMS IN THE INDUCTION AND SYNTHESIS OF CORTICAL β-AMYLOID PRECURSOR PROTEIN

The deposition of neuritic plaques with β-amyloid protein cores and the accumulation of β-amyloid protein in the brain vasculature are among the hallmarks of the aged brain and, in a much exaggerated fashion, of AD. Brain β-amyloid protein is derived from a much larger molecule, β-amyloid precursor protein (β-APP) (Kang et al., 1987). The importance of β-amyloid and neuritic plaques to learning and memory is underscored by the prominence their densities in the aged and AD brain (Armstrong, Myers, Smith, Cairns, & Luthert, 1991; Cohen, Golde, Usial, Younkin, & Younkin, 1988; Cole et al., 1991; Delaere, Duyckaerts, He, Piette, & Hauw, 1991; Joachim et al., 1991; Lewis et al., 1988; Selkoe, 1991; Wisniewski, Barcikowska, & Kida, 1991), their inclusion as among the most prominent diagnostic features of AD, and the apparent correlation of plaque densities with cognitive function (Perry et al., 1978). Experimental evidence suggestive of a change in the expression of β-APP isoforms in the nbM of mnemonically impaired aged rats (Higgins, Oyler, Neve, Chen, & Gage, 1990) lends additional support to the pivotal role that this family of proteins may play in aging and AD. Although the deposition of amyloid peptide and profound deficits in cortical neurotransmitter systems have been recognized as characteristic of AD and aging, in general, the relationship between these neurotransmitter deficits and β-APP expression has not been elucidated and a unitary paradigm for studying these apparently diverse neuropathological features has not emerged. The induction of β-APP in the cortex by a variety of different subcortical lesions has been the focus of a number of our recent studies.

In an initial series of studies (Wallace et al., 1991) we investigated the relationship between cortical cholinergic deficits produced by subcortical NMDA lesions of the nbM and the synthesis of β-APP in the cortex. Rats received unilateral lesions of the nbM using NMDA (50 nM). An infusion cannula was lowered into the region of the nbM on the nonlesioned side, but NMDA was not infused. The side of the lesion was counterbalanced between different rats. After a one-week survival period they were sacrificed and their cortices were rapidly dissected and frozen on dry ice. Different aliquots of cortical tissues were used either for ChAT assays or for the study of β-APP and the glial marker glial fibrillary acidic protein (GFAP) synthesis by a previously described polysome translation assay. The results of this study have been reported in detail (Wallace et al., 1991) and are summarized in Table 7.2.

The most prominent feature of the data presented in this table is the increase in the amount of β-APP protein being actively synthesized by the cortex ipsilateral to the nbM lesion at the time of sacrifice. The elevated synthesis exhibited specificity to β-APP in that numerous other proteins, including glial fibrillary acidic protein, were not affected. Despite the approximately 2.5-fold increase in the rate of synthesis of β-APP, Western blot studies of mature protein showed that at 7 days postlesion β-APP did not accumulate in the cortex, indicating that the turnover rate of β-APP was also increased after the lesion. These results represented the first documentation of an association between neurotransmitter deficits in the cortex and increased synthesis of β-APP by cortical neurons. It is important to emphasize that the increase in β-APP synthesis occurred in the cortex, at the level of the projection site of the lesioned nbM cells. Whether or not there is an analogous increase in β-APP synthesis in the region of the lesioned nbM is not known.

In more recent studies we have found that the increase in the synthesis of β-APP following nbM lesions is due to a significant ($ps < 0.01$) increase in the cortical content of mRNA coding for β-APP (Wallace et al., 1993). These results were obtained using Northern blot analysis of β-APP mRNA expression in the cortex ipsilateral to the unilaterally lesioned nbM of rats sacrificed one week after lesioning. The cDNA probe used recognizes all β-APP mRNA isotypes (Anderson et al., 1989) suggesting that the single message detected in the samples reflects the β-APP$_{695}$ mRNA, which is the predominant β-APP mRNA in the rat (Anderson et al., 1989). No significant changes were apparent when identical RNA samples

TABLE 7.2   Effects of NMDA-induced Lesions of the nbM on Cortical Cholinergic Markers and Cortical Polysome Content and Translational Activity

	ChAT nmolsACh/hr /mg protein	AChE nmolsACh/hr /mg protein	Polysome Translation		
			Content A260 /gm	Activity X10 ^{35}S Meth /A260	β-APP** Arbitrary Units
Control	47.1 ± 12.1	1967 ± 160	15.4 ± 5.6	4.43 ± 1.9	100
	n = 14	n = 14	n = 7	n = 12	n = 11
Lesioned	25.7 ± 5.9*	871 ± 176*	15.2 ± 6.0	4.57 ± 1.2	258 ± 47*
	n = 14	n = 14	n = 7	n = 12	n = 11
Depletion	53.4 ± 8.6%	55.5 ± 9.2%	—	—	—

*vs. control $p < 0.002$.

**After densitometry of immunoprecipitated ^{35}S β-APP autoradiograms.

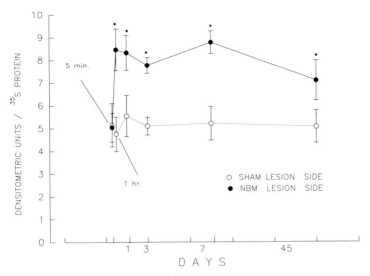

FIGURE 7.9.   Time course of β-APP induction in the cortex of nbM-lesioned rats.

were probed with actin cDNA. These results combined with the results of the previously described experiment (Wallace et al., 1991) indicate that nbM lesions lead to an overall elevation of β-APP mRNA concomitant with an increase in the synthesis of the protein.

Subsequent studies using identical procedures to those previously described have shown that the induction of cortical β-APP by nbM lesions is rapid (within 1 hour of NMDA infusion) and persists for at least 6 weeks (Fig. 7.9). In this study all rats received unilateral lesions of the nbM using NMDA. Different groups of rats ($n = 6$) were then sacrificed at different times (5 minutes–45 days) following lesioning and the levels of β-APP synthesized by polysomes were quantitated. Aliquotes of issues from the same cortices as those used earlier were also assayed for ChAT activity. The results of this analysis showed that cortical ChAT was significantly depleted one day after lesioning, continued to decrease until day 3 postlesion, and thereafter remained stably depleted by approximately 45% for the duration of the 6-week-long experiment (all *ps* < 0.01). It is noteworthy that the ChAT depletion following NMDA infusion did not become apparent until postlesion day 1, whereas β-APP was maximally induced within one hour of lesioning. The rapid induction of β-APP in the absence of ChAT deficits suggests that factors other than the reductions in cortical ChAT activity are responsible for β-APP induction.

Recent evidence obtained from a preliminary study conducted in collaboration with Dr. S. Ahlers (Haroutunian et al., 1992) suggests that the triggering and perhaps maintaining signal for the induction of β-APP may be the absence or reduction of acetylcholine at the cortical synapse. In this study, two groups of rats received unilateral infusion cannulae directed at the nbM. Approximately 1.5 hours after anesthesia a 20% solution of lidocaine was infused into the nbM. One-half of the rats were also implanted with microdialysis probes in the frontal cortex ipsilateral to the lidocaine-infused nbM. Dialysate was collected throughout the study and was assayed for ACh by HPLC. These animals were sacrificed 1.5 hours after the first infusion of lidocaine and their brains dissected and frozen. The remaining animals did not receive microdialysis probes at this time and were allowed to recover from anesthesia after lidocaine infusion. These animals were anesthetized 7 days later, were implanted with microdialysis probes, and ACh collected in the dialysate was quantified in a manner identical to their previously sacrificed counterparts for approximately 3 hours before they too were sacrificed. RNA was isolated from the cortex ipsilateral and contralateral to the nbM receiving lidocaine infusions and was probed with cDNA probes specific to β-APP and actin. Analysis of the dialysate obtained from the cortex showed that the spontaneous release of ACh was acutely attenuated shortly after the first infusion of lidocaine into the nbM, and returned to near normal levels within 45 minutes of infusion (Fig. 7.1). Northern blot analysis of RNA isolated from the cortices of the rats in this study showed that cortical β-APP was induced only in those animals that were sacrificed within 1.5 hours of lidocaine infusion. Cortical β-APP was not induced in those rats that were sacrificed one week following lidocaine infusion at a time when cortical ACh had returned to prelidocaine infusion levels. These results, though preliminary, strongly suggest that the signal for the initial induction and subsequent maintenance of elevated rates of synthesis of cortical β-APP following nbM lesions is the absence of neurotransmitter at the cortical synapse.

Other studies have extended the generality of these findings to the induction of cortical β-APP following lesions of other cortically projecting neurotransmitter systems. In studies identical to the NMDA lesion studies of the nbM described earlier, we have examined the effects of 6-OHDA lesions of the DB and 5-7-DHT lesions of the dorsal raphe. Both lesions induce cortical β-APP in a manner apparently similar to lesions of the nbM. Although the induction of cortical β-APP appears to be a general characteristic of lesions affecting cortical neurotransmitter levels, other perturbations of the CNS such as agonist-induced stimulation of central type I glucocorticoid receptor with RU 28362 (Coirini, Magarinos, DeNicola, Rainbow, & McEwen, 1985) in adrenalectomized rats, the sustained inhibition of acetylcholinesterase with 0.5- and 0.25-mg/kg daily doses of physostigmine for 2 weeks, or the depression of central metabolic activity with intracerebro-ventricular administration of either aCSF or aCSF plus 1.25 μg/gm body weight of the diabetogenic compound streptozotocin (Hoyer, 1990) for 42 days failed to affect cortical synthesis of β-APP (data not shown).

These studies (Haroutunian, Bragin, Gotlieb, Davis, & Wallace, 1991) have demonstrated that a potentially strong link exists between cortical neurotransmitter activity and the synthesis of β-APP. As the integrity of cortically projecting neurotransmitter systems (ACh, NE, and 5-HT) becomes compromised, cortical β-APP becomes induced. We have not as yet determined whether cortical β-APP remains induced for as long as neurotransmitter levels are depressed, but it is clear that this induction persists for at least 6 weeks following nbM lesioning. These results raise the possibility that age-related or AD-related decreases in cortical neurotransmission could be related to the accumulation of β-amyloid in the cortex. The studies conducted to date indicate, however, that at least one other, as yet unidentified, variable must be involved in the deposition of cortical β-APP as amyloid plaques. This conclusion is based on our results, which show that even 6 weeks after nbM lesions, cortical levels of mature amyloid protein are not increased (data not shown). Furthermore our studies, as well as those of others (Haroutunian, Wallace, & Davis, 1991; Thal et al., 1990), have clearly shown that neuritic plaques do not form in the brains of rats, even 14–18 months after lesions of the nbM. Thus these studies have indicated that neurotransmitter deficits can lead to the sustained increase in the synthesis of β-APP in the rat cortex, but that other factors must be responsible for the accumulation and deposition of the secreted mature protein.

These results taken as a whole reemphasize the centrality of neurotransmitter deficits as not only contributory factors to mnemonic dysfunction, but that these same neurotransmitter deficits might also contribute to neuropathologic features of the aged or AD brain. These results also demonstrate that neurotransmitter deficits not only interact to directly affect mnemonic function and responsivity to pharmacological agents, but that they interact with factors and proteins thought to possess neurotrophic and neurotoxic properties (Yankner, Caceres, & Duffy, 1990; Yankner et al., 1989; Yankner, Duffy, & Kirschner, 1990).

SUMMARY AND GENERAL CONCLUSIONS

In this chapter we have outlined our findings regarding the effects of deficits in a number of neurotransmitter systems on a limited series of learning and memory function tasks. We have restricted our analysis to some of the neurotransmitter and neuropeptide systems known to be adversely affected in old age and in AD. We have also demonstrated that the mnemonic functions that have been experimentally disrupted in animal model systems can be reversed or at least moderated by pharmacological agents related to the systems affected. In addition, we have found that although perturbations of somatostatinergic and serotonergic systems can profoundly affect learning and memory, they do not necessarily affect the learning and memory deficits induced by forebrain cholinergic lesions. Furthermore, somatostatinergic and serotonergic lesions do not adversely affect the ability of cholinomimetic agents to reverse the learning and memory deficits induced by forebrain cholinergic lesions. Forebrain noradrenergic and cholinergic systems, on the other hand, interact more dynamically, such that noradrenergic deficits diminish the ability of cholinomimetic agents to enhance retention test performance in animals with concurrent lesions of the two systems. The efficacy of cholinomimetic agents to enhance retention test performance in rats with combined forebrain cholinergic and noradrenergic lesions can, however, be restored by the concurrent administration of the α_2 noradrenergic receptor agonist clonidine. Recent experiments suggest that the interaction between these systems extends to the neurochemical deficits produced after lesioning, such that cholinergic lesions diminish the noradrenergic deficits produced by 6-OHDA lesions.

The results summarizing the effects of some of these same neurotransmitter deficits on the cortical synthesis of β-amyloid precursor protein reemphasize the link between neurotransmitter system deficits and other neuropathologic features of the aged and AD brain that have been found to be correlated with mnemonic dysfunction. These studies have shown that an "immediate" response of the rat cortex to a disruption in neurotransmitter function is an increase in the synthesis of a precursor protein, one product of which accumulates in the aged and AD brain to form pathologic deposits of β-amyloid protein, though to be associated with cognitive deficits. This increased synthesis of β-APP is maintained along with neurotransmitter deficits for at least 6 weeks. It remains to be determined by ongoing and future studies whether pharmacological and constitutive treatments such as the administration of cholinomimetic agents or neurotrophic factors can affect β-APP synthesis in a manner similar to their effects on learning and memory function and lesion-induced neurotransmitter deficits.

REFERENCES

Adell, A., Sarna, G. S., Hutson, P. H., & Curzon, G. (1989). An in vivo dialysis and behavioural study of the release of 5-HT by p-chloroamphetamine in resperine-treated rats. *British Journal of Pharmacology, 97,* 206–212.

Adolfsson, R., Gottfries, C. G., Roos, B. E., & Winblad, B. (1979). Changes in the brain catecholamines in patients with dementia of Alzheimer type. *British Journal of Psychiatry, 135,* 216–223.

Altman, H. J., & Normile, H. (1988). What is the nature of the role of the serotonergic nervous system in learning and memory: Prospects for development of an effective treatment strategy for senile dementia. *Neurobiology of Aging, 9,* 627–638.

Anderson, J. P., et al. (1989). Differential brain expression of the Alzheimer's amyloid precursor protein. *European Molecular Biology Organization Journal, 8,* 3627–3632.

Armstrong, R. A., Myers, D., Smith, C. U., Cairns, N., & Luthert, P. J. (1991). Alzheimer's disease: The relationship between the density of senile plaques, neurofibrillary tangles and A4 protein in human patients. *Neuroscience Letters, 123,* 141–143.

Arnsten, A. F., & Goldman-Rakic, P. S. (1985a). Catecholamines and cognitive decline in aged nonhuman primates. *Annals of the New York Academy of Sciences, 444,* 218–234.

Arnsten, A. F. T., & Goldman-Rakic, P. S. (1985b). α2-adrenergic mechanisms in prefrontal cortex associated with cognitive decline in aged nonhuman primates. *Science, 230,* 1273–1279.

Arnsten, A. F. T., Cai, J. X., & Goldman-Rakic, P. S. (1988). The alpha-2 adrenergic agonist guanfacine improves memory in aged monkeys without sedative or hypotensive side effects: Evidence for alpha-2 receptor subtypes. *Journal of Neuroscience, 8,* 4287–4298.

Bakhit, C., Benoit, R., & Bloom, F. E. (1983). Effects of cysteamine on pro-somatostatin related peptides. *Regulatory Peptides, 6,* 169–177.

Beal, M. F., Mazurek, M. F., Tran, V. T., Chattha, G., Bird, E. D., & Martin, J. B. (1985). Reduced numbers of somatostatin receptors in the cerebral cortex in Alzheimer's disease. *Science, 229,* 289–291.

Beal, M. F., Uhl, G., Mazurek, M. F., Kowall, N., & Martin, J. B. (1986). Somatostatin: Alterations in the central nervous system in neurological diseases. *Research Publication of the Association of Nervous and Mental Disorders, 64,* 215–257.

Bird, T. D., Stranahan, S., Sumi, S. M., & Raskind, M. (1983). Alzheimer's disease: Choline acetyltransferase activity in brain tissue from clinical and pathological subgroups. *Annals of Neurology, 14,* 284–293.

Chan-Palay, V., & Asan, E. (1989a). Alterations in catecholamine neurons of the locus coeruleus in senile dementia of the Alzheimer type and in Parkinson's disease with and without dementia and depression. *Journal of Comparative Neurology, 287,* 373–392.

Chan-Palay, V., & Asan, E. (1989b). Quantitation of catecholamine neurons in the locus coeruleus in human brains of normal young and older adults and in depression. *Journal of Comparative Neurology, 287,* 357–372.

Cohen, M. L., Golde, T. E., Usial, M. F., Younkin, L. H., & Younkin, S. G. (1988). In situ hybridization of nucleus basalis neurons shows increased B-amyloid mRNA in Alzheimer disease. *Proceedings of the National Academy of Sciences of the United States of America, 85,* 1227–1231.

Coirini, H., Magarinos, A. M., DeNicola, A. F., Rainbow, T. C., & McEwen, B. S. (1985). *Brain Research, 361,* 212–216.

Cole, G. M., Masliah, E., Shelton, E. R., Chan, H. W., Terry, R. D., & Saitoh, T. (1991). Accumulation of amyloid precursor fragment in Alzheimer plaques. *Neurobiology of Aging, 12,* 85–91.

Coyle, J. T., Price, D. L., & DeLong, M. R. (1983). Alzheimer's disease: A disorder of cortical cholinergic innervation. *Science, 219,* 1184–1190.

Cross, A. J. (1990). Serotonin in Alzheimer-type dementia and other dementing illnesses. *Annals of the New York Academy of Sciences, 600,* 405–415 (discussion).

Davies, P., Katzman, R., & Terry, R. D. (1980). Reduced somatostatin-like-immunoreactivity in cerebral cortex from cases of Alzheimer's disease Alzheimer's senile dementia. *Nature (London), 288,* 279–280.

Davies, P., & Maloney, A. J. F. (1976). Selective loss of central cholinergic neurons in Alzheimer's disease. *Lancet, 2,* 1403.

Davies, P., & Terry, R. D. (1981). Cortical somatostatin-like immunoreactivity in cases of Alzheimer's disease and senile dementia of Alzheimer's type. *Neurobiology of Aging, 2,* 9–14.

Davis, K. L., & Mohs, R. C. (1982). Enhancement of memory processes in Alzheimer's disease with multiple-dose intravenous physostigmine. *American Journal of Psychiatry, 139,* 1421–1424.

Decker, M. W., & Gallager, M. (1987). Scopolamine-disruption of radial arm maze performance: Modification by noradrenergic depletion. *Brain Research, 417,* 59–69.

Decker, M. W., Gill, T. M., & McGaugh, J. L. (1990). Concurrent muscarinic and beta-adrenergic blockade in rats impairs place-learning in a water maze and retention of inhibitory avoidance. *Brain Research, 513,* 81–85.

Decker, M. W., & McGaugh, J. L. (1989). Effects of concurrent manipulations of cholinergic and noradrenergic function on learning and retention in mice. *Brain Research, 477,* 29–37.

Decker, M. W., & McGaugh, J. L. (1991). The role of interactions between the cholinergic system and other neuromodulatory systems in learning and memory. *Synapse, 7,* 151–168.

Dekker, A. J. A. M., Connor, D. J., & Thal, L. J. (1991). The role of cholinergic projections from the nucleus basalis in memory. *Neuroscience Behavior Review, 15,* 299–317.

Delaere, P., Duyckaerts, C., He, Y., Piette, F., & Hauw, J. J. (1991). Subtypes and differential laminar distributions of beta A4 deposits in Alzheimer's disease: Relationship with the intellectual status of 26 cases. *Acta Neuropathology (Berlin), 81,* 328–335.

Dunnet, S. B., Whishaw, I. Q., Jones, G. H., & Bunch, S. T. (1987). Behavioral, biochemical and histochemical effects of different neurotoxic amino acids injected into nucleus basalis magnocellularis of rats. *Neuroscience, 20,* 653–669.

Fibiger, H. C. (1991). Cholinergic mechanisms in learning, memory and dementia: A review of recent evidence. *Trends in Neuroscience, 14,* 220–223.

Fornal, C. A., & Jacobs, B. L. (1988). Physiological and behavioral correlates of serotonergic single-unit activity. In N. N. Osborn & M. Hamon (Eds.), *Neuronal serotonin* (pp. 305-345). New York: Wiley.

Gold P. E., & Zornetzer, S. F. (1983). The mnemon and its juices: Neuromodulation of memory processes. *Behavioral and Neural Biology, 38,* 151-189.

Gottfries, C. G. (1985). Alzheimer's disease and senile dementia: Biochemical characteristics and aspects of treatment. *Psychopharmacology (Berlin), 86,* 245-252.

Gottfries, C. G. (1990a). Disturbance of the 5-hydroxytryptamine metabolism in brains from patients with Alzheimer's dementia. *Journal of Neural Transmissions, 30* (Suppl.), 33-43.

Gottfries, C. G. (1990b). Brain monoamines and their metabolites in dementia. *Acta Neurologica Scandinavia, 129* (Suppl.), 8-11.

Haroutunian, V., Ahlers, S., Bragin, V., Girenkova, Ns, Davis, K. L., & Wallace, W. C. (1992). Transmitter dependent induction of β-APP mRNA. *Society for Neuroscience Abstracts, 18,* 1464.

Haroutunian, V., Bragin, V., Gotlieb, J., Davis, K. L., & Wallace, W. C. (1991). Induction of the beta amyloid precursor protein in the subcortically lesioned rat cortex. *Society for Neuroscience Abstracts, 17,* 1066.

Haroutunian, V., Kanof, P. D., & Davis, K. L. (1989). Interactions of forebrain cholinergic and somatostatinergic systems in the rat. *Brain Research, 496,* 98-104.

Haroutunian, V., Kanof, P. D., Tsuboyama, G., & Davis, K. L. (1990). Restoration of cholinomimetic activity by clonidine in cholinergic plus noradrenergic lesioned rats. *Brain Research, 507,* 261-266.

Haroutunian, V., Kanof, P. D., Tsuboyama, G. K., Campbell, G. A., & Davis, K. L. (1986). Animal models of Alzheimer's disease: Behavior, pharmacology, transplants. *Canadian Journal of Neurological Science, 13,* 385-393.

Haroutunian, V., Mantin, R., Campbell, G. A., Tsuboyama, G. K., & Davis, K. L. (1987). Cysteamine-induced depletion of central somatostatin-like immunoactivity: Effects on behavior, learning, memory and brain neurochemistry. *Brain Research, 403,* 234-242.

Haroutunian, V., Mantin, R., & Kanof, P. D. (1990). Frontal cortex as the site of action of physostigmine in nbM-lesioned rats. *Physiology and Behavior, 47,* 203-206.

Haroutunian, V., Santucci, A. C., & Davis, K. L. (1990). Implications of multiple transmitter system lesions for cholinomimetic therapy in Alzheimer's disease. *Progress in Brain Research, 84,* 333-346.

Haroutunian, V., Tsuboyama, G. K., Kanof, P. D., & Davis, K. L. (1988). Pharmacological consequences of cholinergic plus noradrenergic lesions. In E. Giacobini & R. Becker (Eds.), *Current research in Alzheimer therapy* (pp. 63-72). New York: Taylor Francis.

Haroutunian, V., Wallace, W. C., & Davis, K. L. (1991). Nucleus basalis lesions and recovery. In E. Giacobini & R. Becker (Eds.), *Cholinergic basis for Alzheimer therapy* (pp. 120-125). Boston: Birkhauser.

Higgins, G. A., Oyler, G. A., Neve, R. L., Chen, K. S., & Gage, F. H. (1990). Altered levels of amyloid protein precursor transcripts in the basal forebrain of behaviorally impaired aged rats. *Proceedings of the National Academy of Sciences of the United States of America, 87,* 3032-3036.

Hoyer, S. (1990). Brain glucose and energy metabolism during normal aging. *Aging (Milano), 2,* 245-258.

Joachim, C., Games, D., Morris, J., Ward, P., Frenkel, D., & Selkoe, D. (1991). Antibodies to non-beta regions of the beta-amyloid precursor protein detect a subset of senile plaques. *American Journal of Pathology, 138,* 373-384.

Kang, J., et al. (1987). The precursor of Alzheimer's disease amyloid A4 protein resembles a cell-surface receptor. *Nature, 325,* 733-736.

Kowall, N. W., Beal, M. F., Busciglio, J., Duffy, L. K., & Yankner, B. A. (1991). An in vivo model for the neurodegenerative effects of beta amyloid and protection by substance P. *Proceedings of the National Academy of Sciences of the United States of America, 88,* 7247-7251.

Lehericy, S., et al. (1989). Selective loss of cholinergic neurons in the ventral striatum of patients with Alzheimer disease. *Proceedings of the National Academy of Sciences of the United States of America, 86,* 8580–8584.

Lewis, D. A., et al. (1988). Distribution of precursor amyloid-beta-protein messenger RNA in human cerebral cortex: Relationship to neurofibrillary tangles and neuritic plaques. *Proceedings of the National Academy of Sciences of the United States of America, 85,* 1691–1695.

Mair, R. G., & McEntee, W. J. (1986). Cognitive enhancement in Korsakoff's psychosis by clonidine: A comparison with l-dopa and ephedrine. *Psychopharmacology, 88,* 374–380.

Mandel, R. J., Chen, A. D., Connor, D. J., & Thal, L. J. (1989). Continuous physostigmine infusion in rats with excitotoxic lesions of the nucleus basalis magnocellularis: Effects on performance in the water maze task and cortical cholinergic markers. *Journal of Pharmacology and Experimental Therapy, 251,* 612–619.

Marx, J. (1991). Alzheimer's research moves to mice [news]. *Science, 253,* 266–267.

Mason, S. T., & Fibiger, H. C. (1979). Possible behavioral function for noradrenaline-acetylcholine interaction in brain. *Nature (London), 277,* 396–397.

McEntee, W. J., & Mair, R. G. (1980). Memory enhancement in Korsakoff's psychosis by clonidine: Further evidence for a noradrenergic deficit. *Annals of Neurology, 7,* 466–470.

McGeer, P. L., McGeer, E. G., Suzuki, J., Dolman, C. E., & Nagai, T. (1984). Aging, Alzheimer's disease, and the cholinergic system of the basal forebrain. *Neurology, 34,* 741–745.

McNaughton, N., & Mason, S. T. (1980). The neuropsychology and neuropharmacology of the dorsal ascending noradrenergic bundle—A review. *Progress in Neurobiology, 14,* 157–219.

Mohs, R. C., et al. (1985). Oral physostigmine treatment of patients with AD. *American Journal of Psychiatry, 142,* 28–33.

Mohs, R. C., & Davis, K. L. (1987). The experimental pharmacology of Alzheimer's disease and related dementias. In H. Y. Meltzer (Ed.), *Psychopharmacology: The third generation of progress* (pp. 921–928). New York: Raven Press.

Murray, C. L., & Fibiger, H. C. (1985). Learning and memory deficits after lesions of the nucleus basalis magnocellularis: Reversal by physostigmine. *Neuroscience, 19,* 1025–1032.

Ogren, S. O. (1985). Evidence for a role of brain serotonergic neurotransmission in avoidance learning. *Acta Physiologica Scandinavia, 544* (Suppl.), 1–71.

Ogren, S. O. (1986a). Serotonin receptor involvement in the avoidance learning deficits caused by p-chloroamphetamine-induced serotonin release. *Acta Physiologica Scandinavia, 126* (Suppl.), 449–462.

Ogren, S. O. (1986b). Analysis of the avoidance learning deficit induced by serotonin releasing compound p-chloroamphetamine. *Brain Research Bulletin, 16,* 645–660.

Olton, D. S., & Wenk, G. L. (1987). Dementia: Animal models of the cognitive impairments produced by degeneration of the basal forebrain cholinergic system. In H. Y. Meltzer (Ed.), *Psychopharmacology: The third generation of progress* (pp. 941–954). New York: Raven Press.

Palmer, A. M., Francis, P. T., Bowen, D. M., Neary, J. S., Mann, D. M. A., & Snowden, J. S. (1987). Catecholaminergic neurons assessed ante-mortem in Alzheimer's disease. *Brain Research, 414,* 365–375.

Palmer, A. M., Stratmann, G. C., Procter, A. W., & Bowen, D. M. (1988). Possible neurotransmitter basis of behavioral changes in Alzheimer's disease. *Annals of Neurology, 23,* 616–620.

Perry, E. K. (1980). The cholinergic system in old age and Alzheimer's disease. *Age and Ageing, 9,* 1–8.

Perry, E. K. (1987). Cortical neurotransmitter chemistry in Alzheimer's disease. In H. Y. Meltzer (Ed.), *Psychopharmacology: The third generation of progress* (pp. 887–896). New York: Raven Press.

Perry, E. K., Tomlinson, B. E., Blessed, G., Bergmann, K., Gibson, P. H., & Perry, R. H. (1978). Correlation of cholinergic abnormalities with senile plaques and mental test scores in senile dementia. *British Medical Journal, 2,* 1457–1459.

Price, D. L., Cork, L. C., Struble, R. G., Whitehouse, P. J., Kitt, C. A., & Walker, L. C. (1985). The functional organization of the basal forebrain cholinergic system in primates and the role of this system in Alzheimer's disease. *Annals of the New York Academy of Sciences, 444,* 287–295.

Quartermain, D., Freedmen, L. S., Botwinick, C. Y., & Gutwein, B. M. (1977). Reversal of cycloheximide-induced amnesia by adrenergic receptor stimulation. *Physiology, Biochemistry and Behavior, 7,* 259–267.

Quartermain, D., Judge, M. E., & Leo, P. (1988). Attenuation of forgetting by pharmacological stimulation of aminergic neurotransmitter systems. *Pharmacy, Biochemistry and Behavior, 30,* 77–81.

Quartermain, D., & Botwinick, C. Y. (1975). Role of biogenic amines in the reversal of cycloheximide-induced amnesia. *Journal of Comparative Physiology and Psychology, 88,* 386–401.

Reinikainen, K. J., Paljarvi, L., Huuskonen, M., Soininen, H., Laakso, M., & Reikkinen, P. J. (1988). A post-mortem study of noradrenergic, serotonergic and GABAergic neurons in Alzheimer's disease. *Journal of Neurological Sciences, 84,* 101–116.

Reikkinen, P., Jr., Sirvio, J., Valjakka, A., Pitkänen, A., Partanen, J., & Riekkinen, P. (1990). The effects of concurrent manipulations of cholinergic and noradrenergic systems on neocortical EEG and spatial learning. *Behavior and Neural Biology, 54,* 204–210.

Reinikainen, K. J., Soininen, H., & Reikkinen, P. J. (1990). Neurotransmitter changes in Alzheimer's disease: implications to diagnostics and therapy. *Journal of Neuroscience Research, 27,* 576–586.

Ridley, R. M., Murray, T. K., Johnson, J. A., & Baker, H. F. (1986). Learning impairment following lesions of the basal nucleus of Meynert in the marmoset: Modification by cholinergic drugs. Brain Research, 376, 108–116.

Rossor, M. N., Emson, P. C., Montjoy, C. Q., Roth, M., & Iversen, L. L. (1980). Reduced amounts of immunoreactive somatostatin in the temporal cortex in senile dementia of Alzheimer's type. *Neuroscience Letters, 20,* 373–377.

Sagar, S. M., Landry, D., Millard, W. J., Badger, T. M., Arnold, M. A., & Martin, J. B. (1982). Depletion of somatostatin-like immunoreactivity in the rat central nervous system by cysteamine. *Journal of Neuroscience, 2,* 225–231.

Santucci, A. C., Haroutunian, V., Tsuboyama, G. K., Kanof, P. D., & Davis, K. L. (1989). Therapeutics of Alzheimer's disease for clinical and pre-clinical issues. In K. Iqbal, N. M. Wishiewski, & B. Winblad (Eds.), *Progress in clinical and biological research* (pp. 1111–1120). New York: Alan R. Liss.

Santucci, A. C., Kanof, P. D., & Haroutunian, V. (1990). Serotonergic modulation of cholinergic systems involved in learning and memory in rats. *Dementia, 1,* 151–155.

Selkoe, D. J. (1991). The molecular pathology of Alzheimer's disease. *Neuron, 6,* 487–498.

Stern, Y., Sano, M., & Mayeux, R. (1983). Effects of oral physostigmine and lecithin improve memory in Alzheimer's disease. *Annals of Neurology, 13,* 419–496.

Thal, L. J., Fuld, P. A., Masur, D. M., & Sharpless, N. S. (1983). Oral physostigmine and lecithin improve memory in Alzheimer's disease. *Annals of Neurology, 13,* 491–496.

Thal, L. J., Mandel, R. J., Terry, R. D., Buzsaki, G., & Gage, F. H. (1990). Nucleus basalis lesions fail to induce senile plaques in the rat. *Experiments in Neurology, 108,* 88–90.

Vecsei, L., et al. (1984). Comparative studies with somatostatin and cysteamine in different behavioral tests with rats. *Pharmacology, Biochemistry and Behavior, 21,* 833–837.

Wallace, W. C., et al. (1991). Increased biosynthesis of Alzheimer amyloid precursor protein in the cerebral cortex of rats with lesions of the nucleus basalis of Meynert. *Molecular Brain Research, 10,* 173–178.

Wallace, W., Ahlers, S. T., Gotlib, J., Bragin, V., Sugar, J., Gluck, R., Shea, P. A., Davis, K. L., & Haroutunian, V. (1993). Amyloid precursor protein in the cerebral cortex is rapidly and persistently induced by loss of subcortical innervation. *Proceedings of the National Academy of Sciences of the United States of America, 90,* 8712–8716.

Walsh, T. L., Emerich, D. F., Winocur, A., Banki, C., Bissette, G., & Nemeroff, C. B. (1985). Intrahippocampal injection of cysteamine depletes somatostatin and produced cognitive impairments in the rat. *Society for Neuroscience Abstracts, 11,* 621.

Wenk, G. L., Markowska, A. L., & Olton, D. S. (1989). Basal forebrain lesions and memory: Alterations in neurotensin, not acetylcholine, may cause amnesia. *Behavioral Neuroscience, 103,* 765–769.

Whitehouse, P. J., Price, D. L., Struble, R. G., Clark, A. W., & Coyle, J. T. (1982). Alzheimer's disease and senile dementia: Loss of neurons in the basal forebrain. *Science, 215,* 1237–1239.

Wirak, D. O., et al. (1991). Deposits of amyloid beta protein in the central nervous system of transgenic mice. *Science, 253,* 323–325.

Wisniewski, H. M., Barcikowska, M., & Kida, E. (1991). Phagocytosis of beta/A4 amyloid fibrils of the neuritic neocortical plaques. *Acta Neuropathology (Berlin), 81,* 588–590.

Yankner, B. A., Caceres, A., & Duffy, L. K. (1990). Nerve growth factor potentiates the neurotoxicity of B amyloid. *Proceedings of the National Academy of Sciences of the United States of America, 87,* 9020–9023.

Yankner, B. A., Dawes, L. R., Fisher, S., Villa-Komaroff, L., Oster-Granite, M. L., & Neve, R. L. (1989). Neurotoxicity of a fragment of the amyloid precursor associated with Alzheimer's disease. *Science, 245,* 417–420.

Yankner, B. A., Duffy, L. K., & Kirschner, D. A. (1990). Neurotrophic and neurotoxic effects of amyloid B protein: Reversal by tachykinin neuropeptides. *Science, 250,* 279–282.

Zweig, R. M., et al. (1988). The neuropathology of aminergic nuclei in Alzheimer's disease. *Annals of Neurology, 24,* 233–242.

8

Retention of Function in the Aged Brain: The Pivotal Role of β-Amyloid

CARL W. COTMAN
AILEEN J. ANDERSON

In 1907 Dr. Alois Alzheimer reported the case history of a 51-year-old woman suffering from declarative and spatial memory impairments, temporal disorientation, and changes in affect. Upon autopsy, Alzheimer described what are now recognized as the pathological hallmarks of Alzheimer's disease (AD): neurofibrillary tangles (NFTs) and senile plaques (SPs) (Alzheimer, 1907). In the ensuing 85 years we have made considerable progress in identifying the nature of the pathology in AD, including the identification of the major protein component of SPs, β-amyloid (Aβ) (Glenner & Wong, 1984; Masters et al., 1985b). More recently, current epidemiological data suggest that Alzheimer's disease is much more prevalent than was previously thought, affecting 11% of the population over 65 years of age and 47% of the population over 85 years of age. In fact, these figures likely represent a slight underestimate of the true disease rate (Evans et al., 1989). These data highlight the social and medical consequences of AD, both at present and in the future, as we confront the needs of an aging population in the United States.

One goal of basic research in learning and memory is to elucidate the mechanisms that underlie normal, as well as abnormal, function in the brain. Although at the most basic level it is the disconnection of functional circuitry that results in the severity and diversity of the cognitive deficits in AD, the pathology underlying this disconnection may be inseparable from the mechanisms that protect the brain from other forms of injury and serve it in normal functioning.

In the normal brain, plasticity provides for the storage of new information and the reorganization of synapses to compensate for loss or disruption of functional circuitry (Fig. 8.1A). Plasticity in this context is an adaptive response designed to meet challenges to the functional capacity of the system. The ability of adaptive plasticity to compensate for such losses is influenced by the threshold for dysfunction; this threshold is in turn set by a variety of genetic and environmental risk

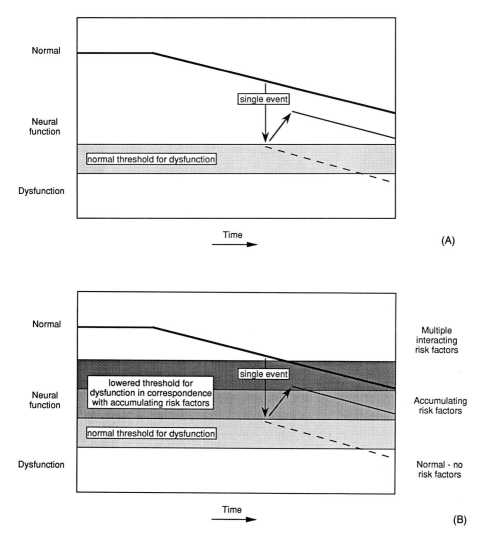

FIGURE 8.1. (A) Adaptive plasticity mechanisms may be initiated to minimize the consequences of functional losses from single events such as strokes, thus maintaining function within the normal range. (B) Over time, the aged brain successfully maintains some mechanisms essential for neuronal function, while others are impaired by a combination of cumulative risk factors, for example, risk factors associated with genetic or environmental influences. Risk factors can lower the threshold at which neuronal function is impaired, thus also lowering the capacity of the brain to recover from single events. The consequence of a single event will vary depending on the threshold for neuronal dysfunction in the brain.

factors. For example, an individual prone to strokes might be more likely to experience ischemic events and subtle amounts of focal damage to vulnerable brain areas, potentially impairing the capacity of adaptive plasticity to maintain function following other independent deleterious events (Fig. 8.1B). In the AD brain, it may be that adaptive plasticity is misdirected, and contributes to an acceleration of the cognitive decline associated with this disease. As we have outlined previously (Cotman, Cummings, & Pike, 1992; Cotman, Cummings, & Whitson, 1991; Cotman, Pike, & Cummings, 1993), our suggestion is that mechanisms of plasticity that are initially adaptive, ironically become a part of a set of molecular risk factors and cascades that contribute to AD pathology. We further suggest that Aβ plays a central role in this cascade.

We begin this chapter by briefly describing the basic deficits in learning and memory observed in AD, and the functional disconnection of cortical–hippocampal circuitry associated with its pathology. We then proceed to discuss the mechanisms driving pathology, and the pivotal role that Aβ may play in the disconnection of neuronal circuitry. β-amyloid exists in multiple assembly states: a soluble form and several aggregated forms with β sheet structures. In its soluble form Aβ appears to have trophic properties, participating in plasticity events. As it assembles into aggregates, Aβ gathers other molecules and can lower the threshold for neuronal degeneration via secondary mechanisms, for example, excitotoxicity. Furthermore, the accumulation of Aβ over time may initiate apoptosis (programmed cell death) in neurons exposed to such an increased Aβ load. In this context, Aβ may play a pivotal role in the events leading to neuron dysfunction and loss in AD.

THE NATURE OF MEMORY LOSS IN ALZHEIMER'S DISEASE

Neuropsychological Measures of Alzheimer's Disease

Alzheimer's disease results in a progressive decline in the capacity to store and recall new information; the cognitive dysfunction typical of this decline can be clinically assessed by neuropsychological testing. A diagnosis of probable AD remains a combined process of exclusion by previous medical history and classification based on neuropsychological testing. In general, AD appears to affect primarily declarative memory, largely sparing procedural memory (Eslinger & Damasio, 1986). The performance of AD patients is most affected on tasks requiring delayed recall, select visual–spatial skills, and those that are sequencing dependent (e.g., trails A and B) (McKhann et al., 1984). Some patients with moderate dementia, however, suffer deficits in perception, including a loss of visual–spatial orientation (Rosen, 1983), and it is necessary to take this factor into account when evaluating individuals.

While there is agreement on the basic types of neurological impairments found in patients with AD, there is frequently a large degree of variation between the types of impairments detected in individual patients. In practice, a clinical diagnosis of probable AD is dependent on a battery of tests that are used to construct a profile of neurological impairment for a given patient. This profile is then analyzed in combination with the patient's medical history, physiological symptoms, and brain state derived from imaging data to aid in the discrimination of AD from other causes of dementia, such as vascular and Pick's disease (McKhann et al., 1984; Morris, Mohs, Rogers, Fillenbaum, & Heyman, 1988). This test battery can also be used to follow the progress of an individual patient in the clinical setting.

Figure 8.2 shows a partial neuropsychological profile of the clinical progression of J. F., a patient who presented with relatively minor cognitive deficits in 1988. An initial look at J. F.'s performance using the Mini-Mental State Exam (MMSE) as a global index of cognitive impairment reveals some mild cognitive dysfunction at this time; a score of 22/30 where a score below 24 represents cognitive deficits. Although J. F. maintains function as assessed by some measures, it is clear from other tests of specific capacities that he shows an overall deterioration between 1988 and 1993. For example, deficits in visual–spatial abilities are a classical indicator of AD-type cognitive involvement. J. F.'s performance deteriorates markedly from 1988 to 1993 on all of the tasks that measure this ability in Figure 8.2. Significant deficits in performance on tests of memory such as delayed recall are perhaps most commonly associated with AD-like pathological processes. Indeed, J. F. is impaired on all of the tests of memory shown here.

J. F.'s 1988 neuropsychological profile illustrates the cognitive deterioration, and pattern of intermingled deficits and maintained function often observed in early AD cases. Many of the tasks in this profile can be interpreted in light of dysfunction related to particular brain areas, such as the frontal and parietal lobe associational cortices. Given the diversity of pathology observed in AD, it is critical to define the anatomical common ground underlying the basic deficits associated with the disease.

The Functional Disconnection of Cortical–Hippocampal Circuitry

It is well established that neuronal populations exhibit varying degrees of susceptibility to pathologic involvement in AD (McGeer et al., 1990; Terry et al., 1981); correspondingly, the pattern of brain-area vulnerability correlates to some degree with clinical assessments of dementia. For example, limbic and paralimbic pathology may correlate with the affective changes characteristic of late-stage AD, and diminished capacity for the performance of olfactory discriminations may be associated with NFTs and SPs in the piriform/prepiriform cortex, and atrophy of the olfactory epithelium. Furthermore, in agreement with the relative sparing of motor capacities in AD, there is a general lack of pathology in primary sensory and motor cortex. For review, see Chui (1989).

The core of the cognitive and memory deficits in AD appears to be tied to a functional disconnection of the ventromedial temporal lobe and associational cortices. The extensive cell loss and presence of large numbers of NFTs in layers II–III and V of the entorhinal cortex (Cajal's nomenclature) has been suggested to

SUMMARY PSYCHOMETRIC PROFILE

Name_____ CID _____ Date _____

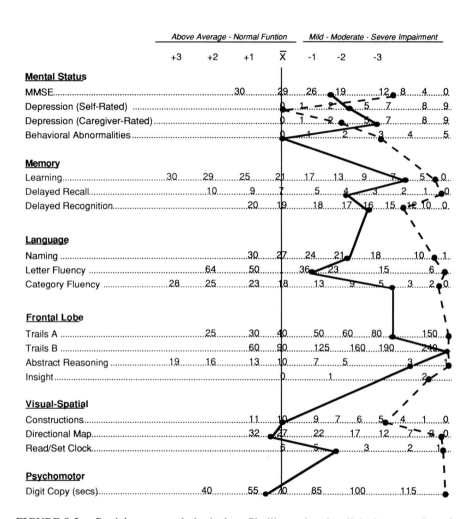

FIGURE 8.2. Partial neuropsychological profile illustrating the clinical progression of a patient, J. F., first evaluated in the U. C. Irvine AD clinic in 1988 with relatively minor cognitive defects. The vertical line illustrates the average score of age-controlled normal patients. The solid line represents the pattern of J. F.'s performance in 1988. The dashed line represents the pattern of J. F.'s performance in 1993. Note the overall decline in most areas of cognitive function.

disrupt the entorhinal–hippocampal connection mediated by layers II–III. This is compounded by CA1/subicular pathology, and the limbic and associational cortical connections mediated by layer V and CA1/subiculum projections, thereby disconnecting both input and output elements of this key circuit (Hyman, Van Hoesen, & Damasio, 1990; Hyman, Van Hoesen, Damasio, & Barnes, 1984).

The Relationship of Pathology and Dementia

The first study to demonstrate a specific correlation between morphological changes in AD and a psychological measure of cognitive impairment was conducted by Blessed in 1968; this study found a significant correlation between dementia and cortical SP number (Blessed, Tomlinson, & Roth, 1968; Roth, Tomlinson, & Blessed, 1966). These findings have since been extended, confirming a correlation between AD pathology and clinical dementia ratings; for review, see Coleman and Flood (1987). In particular, good correlations between NFT number (Arrigada, Growdon, Hedley-White, & Hyman, 1992) and synapse loss (Terry et al., 1991) have been reported; however, it is important to consider that the conclusions drawn from all of these studies are dependent on the methods used to identify SPs and NFTs. For example, recent data have shown that formic acid pretreatment can significantly enhance the detection of NFTs and SPs by antibodies to Aβ (Perry, Cras, Siedlak, Tabaton, & Kawai, 1992). Techniques that are capable of examining critical initiating mechanisms in the generation of AD pathology are necessary to clarify the precise relationship and evolution of these structure–function changes. One of the most challenging issues in this area of research remains the identification of the types of changes in brain state that best correlate to functional losses in cognition.

Recently, McKee, Kosik, and Kowall (1991) reported that neuritic pathology revealed by immunoreactivity for Tau, a protein localized within axonal membranes and abnormally phosphorylated in AD, is strongly correlated with clinically assessed dementia. This finding was consistent even in brains with few NFTs. In this study, both dystrophic neurite and NFT number were highly correlated with Blessed Dementia Scale scores in CA1, entorhinal cortex, superior temporal cortex, superior frontal cortex, and inferior parietal cortex; SP numbers and dementia were significantly correlated only in superior temporal cortex. These authors suggest that dystrophic neurites may in fact be a more sensitive correlate of clinical dementia than either NFTs or SPs.

A key index of the functional status of a neuronal circuit should be the number of intact synapses within it. In fact, the general connection of neuritic dystrophy with a loss of functional circuitry is supported by examinations of synaptic content in AD cortex (Davies, Mann, Sumpter, & Yates, 1987). See Coleman and Flood (1987) for review. Studies of the synaptic terminal proteins synapsin I and synaptophysin also support this connection; these findings suggest a decrease in the number of synapses in cortical areas and in the outer portion of the molecular layer of the dentate gyrus in the AD brain (Hamos, DeGennare, & Drachman, 1989; Masliah, Terry, DeTheresa, & Hansen, 1989; Weiler, Lassmann, Fischer,

Jellinger, & Winkler, 1990). The decrease in immunoreactivity for these proteins could reflect one locus of neuronal dysfunction/damage in the form of decreased synthesis of synaptically associated proteins. Additionally, it could reflect the disruption of functional circuitry in the form of neuronal, and therefore synaptic, loss. In either case, it is likely that there is a causal relationship between neuritic dystrophy and synapse loss. It is thus important to identify the nature of the cellular and molecular mechanisms responsible for the induction of neuritic dystrophy and synaptic loss.

ADAPTIVE PLASTICITY:
RECOVERY VS. DISRUPTION OF FUNCTION

In Alzheimer's disease, neurites not only become dystrophic, but also appear to sprout. The juxtaposition of these two processes raises questions as to whether they may in fact be related. Perception of the ongoing processes involved in the pathology of the AD brain has evolved over time from that of a phenomenon predominantly or exclusively involving degeneration, to a more active process involving both regeneration and degeneration (Geddes, Anderson, & Cotman, 1986). Interestingly, in his original description of the senile plaque, Cajal stated: "It appears as though the sprouts had been attracted toward the region of the plaque under the influence of some special neurotropic substance" (Cajal, 1928). In fact, there is now considerable evidence in support of a role for plasticity in AD. One of the most studied systems for these processes is the entorhinal–hippocampal system.

The middle to outer molecular layer of the dentate gyrus represents the terminal zone of the perforant pathway projection from entorhinal cortex to the hippocampus; entorhinal cortex layer II projections form 86% of the synapses in this zone (Matthews, Cotman, & Lynch, 1976a; Matthews, Cotman, & Lynch, 1976b). The outer two-thirds of the dentate gyrus molecular layer has been shown to undergo significant neuronal sprouting in response to deafferentiation in animal models (Cotman, Matthews, Taylor, & Lynch, 1973). Sprouting in these models is correlated with functional recovery of memory impairments and synapse formation, as assessed by quantitative electron microscopy (Matthews et al., 1976a; Matthews et al., 1976b; Scheff & Cotman, 1977). Sprouting may also help to maintain synaptic number and preserve trophic interactions between healthy neurons in this system. As predicted from animal models, the dentate gyrus shows increased cholinergic innervation as demonstrated by acetylcholinesterase (AChE) histochemical staining in the AD brain compared to controls (Geddes, et al., 1985). These data suggest the involvement of a plastic response to deafferentation in AD as well as in animal models (Geddes et al., 1985; Hyman, Kromer, & Van Hoesen, 1987).

In contrast to what is observed in animal models of deafferentation, however, much of the sprouting in the AD brain appears to be aberrant. In addition to an increase in dentate gyrus AChE staining, there are numerous cholinergic fibers that appear to sprout into AChE-positive plaques in the AD brain (Geddes et al., 1985). The activation of a sprouting response into a locus of neuritic degeneration does not seem to be an effective example of adaptive plasticity. Rather, we have suggested that this response is an aberrant one that contributes to the progression of pathology. The synaptic loss associated with AD supports the view that this is an aberrant process that does not play a successful compensatory role in entorhinal–hippocampal circuitry. Interestingly, the majority (94% by one estimate) of plaques in the dentate gyrus molecular layer are located in the middle and outer portions of this area (Crain & Burger, 1988; Hyman, Van Hoesen, Kromer, & Damasio, 1986). This implies that the increase in AChE staining in AD brain may be closely related to SPs. If sprouting fibers are attracted by the plaque environment, this process may play a central role in the progression of AD pathology (Fig. 8.3). The presence of SPs in the terminal fields of cell populations prominently affected by NFTs has been discussed by several authors; it has been suggested that the colocalization of neuritic pathology and Aβ in this regard implies that Aβ deposition may be a causative event in the progression of neuronal loss in AD (Hyman et al., 1990; Mann, Yates, & Marcynuik, 1985).

These points are consistent with the misdirected plasticity we suggest is associated with AD pathology. Thus, Aβ located in plaques may attract and stimulate

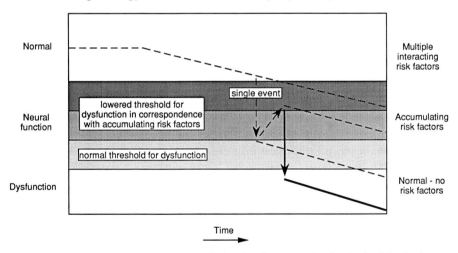

FIGURE 8.3. As illustrated in Figure 8.1, adaptive sprouting in the healthy brain may help to adjust connections and to maintain synaptic connectivity within normal ranges (dashed arrows). This may preserve function for a longer period of time than would be the case if neurons were simply lost and no additional connections formed. Pathological plasticity mechanisms may arise from a combination of initially adaptive responses to exacerbate the losses associated with single or multiple events (plain arrow). In AD it appears as if sprouting contributes to plaque formation, driving disease pathology and compromising neuronal function by leading to inappropriate connections, possibly abnormal trophic interactions, and neurite degeneration. Thus Alzheimer's disease is not the result of a single event, but rather a set of interacting events, some of which may have the ability to reset the threshold between normal function and dysfunction.

fiber sprouting, while at the same time the aberrant nature of this plasticity interrupts the functional circuitry repairs normally mediated by this response. In this way, pathological plasticity could drive disease pathology, leading to a further compromise of neuronal function (Fig. 8.3). According to this hypothesis, cognitive deficits in AD are a result of the initiation of a set of pathways or cascades leading to Aβ deposition, and the concurrent disconnection of neuronal circuitry by a combination of dystrophic neurite formation, NFT formation, and cell death. In this context we are examining the precise role of Aβ in the progression of these events.

RETENTION OF FUNCTION IN THE AGED BRAIN:
THE PIVOTAL ROLE OF β-AMYLOID

β-Amyloid

In contrast to the normal aged brain, there are massive accumulations of Aβ in abnormal structures in the AD brain. Prior to examining the possible biological activity of Aβ it is appropriate to provide the reader with background on Aβ and its metabolism.

Beta-amyloid is a 40–43 amino acid protein derived from the cleavage of (presumably) any one of a set of alternatively spliced β-amyloid precursor proteins (βAPPs). Currently, four primary alternatively spliced mRNA species containing the sequence for Aβ have been identified; for review see Ishiura (1991). βAPP is normally present with moderate abundance in a variety of tissues and species, which it appears to be predominantly associated with axonal membranes (Selkoe et al., 1988). The synthesis of βAPP is increased in response to injury in rat brain (Nakamura, Takeda, Niigawa, Hariguchi, & Nishimura, 1992; Otsuka, Tomonaga, & Ikeda, 1991; Wallace et al., 1991), and βAPP is secreted in response to neurotransmitter stimulation (Nitsch, Slack, Wurtman, & Growdon, 1992). Two processing mechanisms have been identified for βAPP, a secretory pathway (Palmert et al., 1989; Schubert, LaCorbiere, Saitoh, & Cole, 1989) and a lysosome/endosome shuttle pathway (Benowitz et al., 1989; Cole, Huynh, & Saitoh, 1989). It has been thought that the overproduction and/or abnormal processing of βAPP is responsible for the accumulation of Aβ. Recently, however, the normal secretion of Aβ by cell lines transfected with full or partial length βAPP has been reported by several groups (Haass et al., 1992; Seubert et al., 1992; Shoji et al., 1992); these data suggest an alternative pathway for the deposition and regulation of Aβ.

The overexpression of βAPP in Down's syndrome (trisomy 21), the similarity of AD pathology to that of Down's, and the identification of the βAPP gene on chromosome 21 fueled speculation that a gene dosage effect caused AD-type pathology (Goldgaber, Lerman, McBride, Saffioti, & Gajdusek, 1987; Kang et al., 1987; Tanzi et al., 1987). In fact, mutations of the APP gene have been tied to familial Alzheimer's disease (FAD) in some instances. However, the identification of several alternate gene loci involved in FAD, including one on chromosome 14 (Schellenberg et al., 1992), make it unlikely that there is a direct connection between all forms of FAD and mutation of the βAPP gene per se. Thus, there does not appear to be a simple solution to the etiology of AD within these findings, that is, it is clear that amyloid cannot be considered as the single cause of the disease. Perhaps more likely, these data may indicate multiple pathways that contribute to a common pivotal point in the pathogenesis of AD; such a pivotal role may be played by Aβ.

β-Amyloid Assembly States

Central to the role that we are suggesting for amyloid in AD pathogenesis, Aβ has multiple assembly states that affect its biological activity. The tendency of Aβ to adopt solution conformations that promote its self-association into dimer, tetramer, and ultimately, multimer assemblies is the critical process in the formation of aggregated Aβ. Aβ isolated from AD brains shows patterns characteristic of aggregation into an insoluble β-pleated sheet conformation on reducing gels (Masters et al., 1985a; Selkoe, Abraham, Podlisny, & Duffy, 1986); these findings have been extended to synthesized peptides in vitro (Barrow & Zagorski, 1991; Burdick et al., 1992; Hilbich, Kisters-Woike, Reed, Masters, & Beyreuther, 1991). Peptide components of Aβ that do not contain the hydrophobic-rich end of Aβ, such as amino acids 1–28, do not form stable aggregates (Burdick et al., 1992; Pike, Burdick, Walencewicz, Glabe, & Cotman, 1992). Additionally, aggregated Aβ peptides in vitro demonstrate positive Congo red and thioflavine S staining (Burdick et al., 1992; Hilbich et al., 1991) similar to that observed in plaques in vivo. After the incubation of full-length Aβ peptides in vitro, sheetlike structures are visible at the light microscopic level and an altered electrophoresis profile is evident on reducing gels, these observations are indicative of the formation of insoluble aggregates (Burdick et al., 1992; Pike, Walencewicz, Glabe, & Cotman, 1991b).

β-Amyloid Has Neurotrophic Properties

Soluble Aβ is neurotrophic to low-density hippocampal cultures optimized for the observation of trophic responses. These cultures display short-term survival enhancement in response to soluble synthetic Aβ 1–28 and 1–42 (Whitson, Selkoe, & Cotman, 1989), and a significant increase in axonal elongation and dendritic arborization in response to Aβ 1–42 (Whitson, Glabe, Shintani, Abcar, & Cotman, 1990). Similar results have been reported by other groups (Yankner, Duffy, & Kirschner, 1990). When Aβ is present in an aggregated assembly state, it retains its neurite outgrowth promoting properties; however, the neurites in contact with Aβ aggregates exhibit dystrophic morphology.

Aggregated β-Amyloid Induces Neuritic Dystrophy

The accumulation of Aβ in the AD brain over time likely involves the formation of insoluble aggregates similar to those isolated from AD brain at autopsy, and observed in vitro. Processes that extend into SPs are frequently dystrophic, exhibiting beaded, thickened, fragmenting fibers. These dystrophic neurites contain abnormally phosphorylated tau, a protein normally involved in the stabilization of structural elements such as microtubules. In correspondence with these observations the processes of hippocampal cultures exposed to aggregated Aβ 1–42 peptide exhibit the thickening, swelling, and fragmentation characteristic of dystrophic neurites in SP (Fig. 8.4). These processes appear to be axons by morphological criteria, and show growth cone retraction in addition to their other morphological alterations. Neurites from cultures treated with Aβ, but not in direct contact with aggregated Aβ 1–42, appear to be morphologically normal (Pike, Cummings, & Cotman, 1992).

β-Amyloid as a Risk Factor for Neuronal Injury

As the brain ages Aβ inevitably accumulates; the consequences of an increased Aβ load for neuronal vulnerability are therefore of interest. Numerous potential risk factors for the nonfamilial form of AD have been examined to date, including age, parental age, educational level, sex, race, antecedent disease conditions (e.g., stroke, hypertension, etc.), head injury, and exposure to various toxins. For review see Henderson (1988). The lack of consensus in the results of these studies suggests that no clear connection exists between AD and any one potential contributing factor. This in itself implies a complex etiology in which multiple risk factors at the physiological and molecular/cellular level may ultimately contribute to an initiation and progression of the disease state. Here we present in vitro evidence in support of an interaction between Aβ and two sources of neurological insult, excitotoxicity, and hypoglycemia.

Excitotoxicity

L-Glutamate mediates the majority of the excitatory signaling pathways in the brain. The systems associated with these pathways are particularly vulnerable in AD (Maragos, Greenamyre, Penney, & Young, 1987). Additionally, glutamate has been identified as a potent neurotoxin. Exposure of cultured neurons to as little as 100-μM glutamate can result in significant degeneration; furthermore, excitotoxicity has been identified as a contributing factor in the neuronal loss resulting from stroke/ischemia, anoxia, hypoglycemia, epilepsy, and head trauma. For review see Choi (1988). Other investigators have suggested that some or all of these neurologic insults may be risk factors for AD. In light of the implications of this suggestion, and the effect of Aβ in vitro, the interaction of Aβ and excitotoxicity was examined. Mature high-density mouse cortical cultures exposed to soluble Aβ 1–42 for one to four days, and then treated with a sublethal dose of glutamate, exhibit massive cell death. Control cultures exposed to soluble Aβ 1–42 alone do

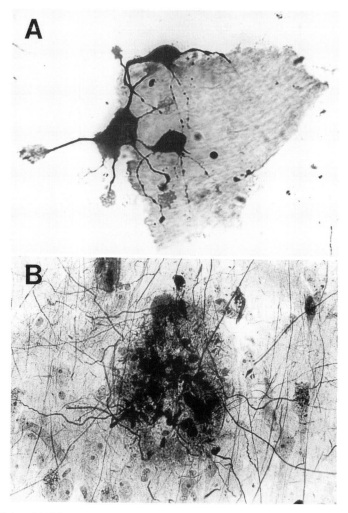

FIGURE 8.4.   (A) Neurons grown on low-density culture in the presence of small aggregates of Aβ appear to sprout toward these aggregates, and the processes show a swelling and fragmentation similar to the appearance of dystrophic neurites in the AD brain. (B) Dystrophic neurites in a plaque of an AD brain. The processes are beaded and thickened, with bulbous endings, and appear to be degenerating.

not exhibit neuronal degeneration (Fig. 8.5A) (Koh, Yang, & Cotman, 1990). The increase in susceptibility of these neurons to excitotoxic damage is dependent on the length of exposure to soluble Aβ 1–42; no enhancement of excitotoxic-induced degeneration is observed prior to 2 days of exposure to soluble Aβ 1–42. Similarly, soluble Aβ potentiates the toxicity of sublethal doses of the non-NMDA agonist kainate (Koh et al., 1990). Subtoxic doses of aggregated Aβ also enhance excitotoxic vulnerability (unpublished observations). These findings have been

(A)

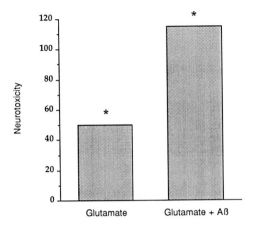

(B)

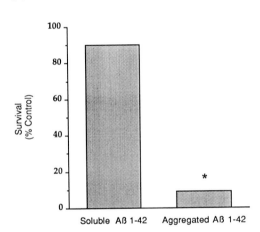

(C)

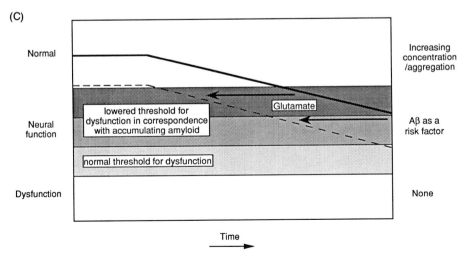

confirmed in long-term cultures of human neurons, and extended by the definition of a potential role of calcium homeostasis in altering the threshold for excitotoxic damage (Mattson et al., 1992). These data suggest that both NMDA and non-NMDA receptors may participate in the molecular pathway mediating the potentiation of excitotoxic damage by Aβ 1–42.

Hypoglycemia

A second potential risk factor in AD is hypoglycemia. Low cerebral glucose metabolism has been identified in early AD in several studies, and proposed as a contributing factor in AD pathology and dementia (Hoyer, Oesterreich, & Wagner, 1988). This suggested a strong possibility that hypoglycemia could represent an additional risk factor for cell death when combined with Aβ. In fact, the exposure of mature mouse cortical cultures to a brief period of glucose deprivation in combination with soluble Aβ 1–42 results in severe cell loss, while control cultures exposed to glucose deprivation alone exhibit only mild damage (Copani, Koh, & Cotman, 1991). Interestingly, cell death induced by hypoglycemia is mediated by excitotoxic mechanisms in vivo (Wieloch, 1985) and in vitro (Monyer & Choi, 1988). In accordance with these data, the administration of a noncompetitive NMDA receptor antagonist (MK801) in conjunction with glucose deprivation and soluble Aβ as described previously is almost 100% neuroprotective (Copani et al., 1991). These results support a role for unaggregated Aβ in the initiation of neuronal damage by increasing the vulnerability of neurons to other risk factors.

Aggregated β-Amyloid Has Toxic Properties

These results imply that the assembly state of Aβ may determine its biological activity: soluble Aβ 1–28 and 1–42 eliciting trophic responses from cultured neurons but potentiating their vulnerability to damage by excitotoxic mechanisms,

---

FIGURE 8.5. Aβ may alter the threshold of neurons to various potentially detrimental stimuli such as excessive glutamate. (A) Exposure of neurons in culture to a subtoxic dose (100 μg/ml) of β-amyloid increases the extent of cell loss following sublethal doses (100 μM) of glutamate, or other excitatory amino acid agonists. Neurotoxicity was assessed by measuring the activity of lactate dehydrogenase released into the culture media. ($P < 0.01$.) (B) When Aβ assembles into aggregates it becomes a further risk factor, and can trigger cells to degenerate in the absence of other insults. Newly synthesized, soluble Aβ 1–42 aggregates over time; new Aβ 1–42 thus produces no neuronal damage, whereas aged (aggregated) Aβ 1–42 is highly toxic. Cell survival was assessed by morphological criteria, and is shown as percent of control. ($P < 0.01$.) (C) Aβ may change the neuronal threshold to insult as a function of its concentration and assembly state. Since Aβ appears to be relatively metabolically inert, it represents a cumulative risk factor, resetting the threshold for neuronal vulnerability over time. Events such as glutamate excitotoxicity may shift normal function into the range of dysfunction when the threshold for neuronal vulnerability has been reset by Aβ accumulation.

aggregated Aβ-inducing neuritic dystrophy in the processes of cultured neurons exposed to it. The induction of neuritic dystrophy in the processes of neurons exposed to Aβ suggests more directly toxic effects on the cells themselves. In fact, a toxic response to Aβ peptides follows the initial period of trophic interactions observed with soluble Aβ; after several days in vitro Aβ 1–42 exposure results in decreased cell survival in the same low-density culture system used for the assessment of trophic interactions (Pike, Walencewicz, Glabe, & Cotman, 1991a). Aβ 1–40 exposure over several days also results in neurite retraction and cell death in hippocampal cultures (Yankner et al., 1990). This effect is likely due to the formation of insoluble aggregates over time in vitro; for discussion see Cotman, Pike, & Copani (1992).

Exposure of high-density immature hippocampal cultures to aggregated Aβ 1–42 causes severe cell death and degeneration (Fig. 8.5B). Neither soluble Aβ 1–42 nor 1–28 exhibit toxic cellular effects in this culture paradigm, although the increased neuritic outgrowth noted in low-density immature hippocampal cultures in response to soluble Aβ 1–42 is apparent (Pike et al., 1991a). In a more recent study, the variety of Aβ peptide fragments examined was expanded. Of ten different Aβ peptide lengths, only peptides that formed an aggregated assembly state were toxic in the high-density developing hippocampal culture system; prevention or reversal of the aggregated assembly state was effective in attenuating this toxicity (Pike et al., 1992). It is interesting to consider that different portions of the Aβ peptide may in fact have different biological activities.

These data show that there are damaging consequences of Aβ for neuronal function, and imply that these consequences may be dependent on contact with or uptake of Aβ. In fact, Aβ appears to be a molecule that may organize and catalyze subsequent pathology, perhaps by altering the threshold of neurons to dysfunction and degeneration (Fig. 8.5C). The toxic effects on neurites in contact with Aβ imply that this peptide plays a critical role in the progression of AD and the functional disconnection of areas of the brain critical for learning and memory, resulting in the profound cognitive decline typical of AD.

The Mechanism of β-Amyloid Catalyzed Neuronal Death

Although it is clear that Aβ can initiate neuronal death and degeneration, the mechanism by which the cells die is not. It is essential to clarify this mechanism in order to identify the precise role of the risks contributing to AD pathology and the molecular events being activated.

Apoptosis vs Necrosis

In general, cells die by following one of two pathways, necrosis or apoptosis; see Wyllie, Kerr, & Currie (1980) for review. Necrosis is typically responsible for cell loss following acute external insults, for example, head trauma. Apoptosis occurs in response to internal metabolic cues that trigger a molecular program of cellular self-destruction. In necrosis there is a gross swelling of the mitochondria, rupture of nuclear, organelle, and plasma membranes, and a corresponding dissolution of lysosomes and ribosomes. In contrast, apoptosis is characterized by condensation of the nucleus, cytoplasm, and chromatin, and the formation of cell-surface protrusions termed blebs; consequently, cells undergoing apoptosis maintain the integrity of their membranes until quite late in the degenerative process. An additional component of the apoptotic pathway is the activation of endogenous endonucleases resulting in DNA fragmentation. As a result of the confinement of the degenerative process to a single cell and the orderly maintenance of membrane integrity, there is little effect on surrounding cells following the initiation of apoptosis. This is again in contrast to necrosis, which generally involves a local inflammatory response and increases the stress on neighboring cells.

Apoptosis in Alzheimer's Disease

Recently, we have found that a series of morphologic and biochemical changes characteristic of apoptosis are induced in cultured neurons exposed to Aβ. These cells exhibit a variety of ultrastructural phenomena characteristic of apoptosis including shrinking, membrane blebbing, chromatin condensation, the maintenance of intact organelles, and the presence of isolated pyknotic nuclei. Furthermore, these cells exhibited a classic apoptotic pattern of DNA fragmentation that could be inhibited by blocking endonuclease activity with aurintricarboxylic acid. Aurintricarboxylic acid was also effective in delaying neuronal death (Loo et al., 1993). These findings suggest that apoptosis may be a significant mechanism of neuronal loss in AD.

As a gene-directed pathway of cell suicide, apoptosis provides a mechanism for the controlled regulation of neuronal number and survival. Although the role of programmed cell death in neurons has typically been associated with the developing central nervous system, it may be that apoptosis has broader implications for the response of mature neurons to less acute injuries and disease states. Indeed, apoptosis has now been described in a variety of neuronal paradigms, including trophic factor deprivation and glutamate toxicity (Kure, Tominaga, Yoshimoto, Tada, & Narisawa, 1991; Martin et al., 1988; Oppenheim, Prevette, Tytell, & Homma, 1990; Scott & Davies, 1990). The hypothesis that apoptosis could contribute to AD is attractive for a variety of reasons. In contrast to the simultaneous loss of groups of neurons typical of lesion-induced necrosis, the prolonged and progressive loss of isolated neurons in AD pathology is consistent with an apoptotic mechanism of cell death. Similarly, the identification of a relationship between some toxins and apoptosis suggests that environmental risk factors may contribute to the induction of cell death in some instances. For example, dioxin activates an apoptotic pathway in thymocytes (Orrenius, McConkey, Bellomo, & Nicotera, 1989). More closely related to the case of neurodegenerative disease, 1-methyl-4-phenylpyridinium (MPP+), a toxin that causes Parkinson's-type pathology in rats, monkeys, and humans, also produces changes characteristic of apoptosis in cerebellar granule cell cultures (Dipasquale, Marini, & Youle, 1991). It is of interest to speculate that the controlled removal of neurons that have become dystrophic and dysfunctional could be an adaptive mechanism in AD, and that an apoptotic pathway could be initiated in an attempt to retain function in a disintegrating neuronal circuitry without damaging the connections of nearby, but unaffected, neurons.

MOLECULAR CASCADES AND RISK FACTORS

Misdirected Plasticity and Senile Plaque Components

From the previous sections it is clear that Aβ can play a critical role in determining the fate of neurons. In these sections, we have illustrated several of the risks that can result from Aβ deposition. In this context, it is possible to envision several situations that could accelerate the development of pathology in AD, and further stimulate misdirected neuronal growth. One of these might be the presence of factors in the Aβ plaque environment that could interact to increase neuronal involvement. Another might be the enhancement of Aβ formation.

It is now well established that neurotrophic factors enhance the survival of neurons and stimulate the growth of their processes. One of the neurotrophic factors that appears to affect the majority of brain neurons is basic fibroblastic growth factor (bFGF). Recent experiments have shown that bFGF is increased following injury, including deafferentation of the hippocampus (Gomez-Pinilla, Lee, & Cotman, 1992). Additionally, there is an increase in bFGF in AD brains (Gomez-Pinilla, Cummings, & Cotman, 1990; Stopa et al., 1990). Although increased levels of bFGF may be providing additional trophic support to neurons under stress in the AD brain, the highest concentrations of bFGF in the AD brain appear to be in SPs. The localization of bFGF within pathological structures is likely involved in the stimulation of neuronal growth into the plaque, thereby enhancing the contact between Aβ and neurons and placing these cells at risk. Thus, bFGF likely represents one aspect of a cycle of degenerative responses within the SP.

The concentration of bFGF in the plaque environment could be the result of other events, occurring either earlier or concurrently, that could modulate the activity and accumulation of bFGF in the plaque environment. For example, the accumulation of a molecule with high affinity for bFGF in the plaque environment could result in the increases in bFGF observed. One such molecule is heparan sulfate proteoglycan (HSPG), which has a high affinity for bFGF and other growth factors (Gospodarowicz, Cheng, Lui, Baird, & Böhlent, 1984) and has been localized to plaques (Snow, Lara, Nochlin, & Wight, 1989; Snow et al., 1988; Snow et al., 1990). In fact, bFGF binding to NFTs and SPs is HSPG dependent (Kato et al., 1991; Perry et al., 1991), indicating the functional importance of HSPG in AD pathology. Interestingly, HSPG interacts with bFGF to promote its trophic effects (Damon, D'Amore, & Wagner, 1988; Flaumenhaft, Moscatelli, & Rifkin, 1990; Saksela, Moscatelli, Sommer, & Rifkin, 1988; Walicke, 1988), and an affinity of both Aβ (Schubert et al., 1989) and extracellular matrix APP (Klier, Cole, Stallcup, & Schubert, 1990) for HSPG has been reported. These interactions seem to be typical of the molecular cascades activated within the AD brain. It is becoming increasingly apparent that these cascades not only have the potential to be adaptive in response to normal brain injury, but also that they have equal potential to accelerate AD pathology.

In this context of cascades, the participation of a positive feedback cycle would further accelerate the progression of pathological change by initiating a set of recurrent molecular loops. Since current epidemiological data suggests that increasing age may correspond to an increased probability of the events leading to AD pathology, it seems intuitive that the initiation of such a recurrent set of events could drive these pathological processes with an ever increasing degree of probability over time. Indeed, there is evidence to support a potential role for positive feedback loops in AD pathology. bFGF induces a 5–10-fold increase in βAPP mRNA (Quon, Catalano, & Cordell, 1990), and a 2-fold increase in NGF secretion (Yoshida & Gage, 1991). In return, both bFGF and NGF have been reported to increase βAPP secretion (Schubert, Jin, Saitoh, & Cole, 1989), and NGF may potentiate the toxicity of Aβ 1–40 in vitro (Yankner, Caceres, & Duffy, 1990).

Given these pathways, we investigated the possibility that Aβ itself might stimulate cells in the plaque environment to produce more bFGF. Indeed, exposure of primary astrocytes and microglia to Aβ 1–42 increased the amount of bFGF (Araujo & Cotman, 1992). Thus one potential molecular feedback loop might be as follows: bFGF stimulates an increase in APP levels, APP in turn increases the probability of Aβ production, Aβ then increases bFGF production in the plaque environment—further stimulating APP production (Fig. 8.6). The initiation of this type of cascade illustrates how isolated events, which might have a normal regulatory role, could participate in a destructive sequence.

This may appear to be an isolated example; however, there are other factors in the plaque environment that may modulate the interactions of growth factors and plaque formation. For example, interleukin-1 is a cytokine that is elevated in glial cells in AD (Griffin et al., 1989), and that potentiates the induction of NGF by bFGF (Yoshida & Gage, 1991). Interleukin-1 also induces increases in βAPP mRNA (Goldgaber et al., 1989) in vitro. Additionally, α1-Antichymotrypsin has been identified in plaques in AD (Abraham, Selkoe, & Potter, 1988), and shown to promote neuronal survival (Mizuguchi & Kim, 1991; Shoji et al., 1991). Similarly, another injury-induced growth factor, transforming growth factor-β, has recently been localized to plaques (van der Wal, Gomez-Pinilla, & Cotman, 1993). These data suggest a complex series of interregulated molecular cascades contributing to the induction and progression of pathology in the AD brain.

CONCLUSIONS

The physiological basis for the loss of learning and memory function associated with AD appears to lie in the neuritic dysfunction described by Alzheimer. Indeed, it has long been accepted that neuritic dysfunction, typified by neuritic dystrophy, is a central pathological event in this disease. In our model of pathological plasticity in AD, the adaptive plasticity of neurons attracted to senile plaques

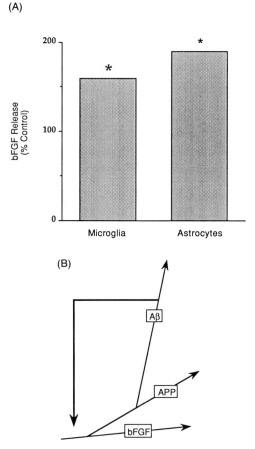

FIGURE 8.6.   (A) Cultured glial cells produce bFGF, exposure of these cells to Aβ increases the amount of bFGF detectable in the media. Induction of bFGF shown as percent control. (P < 0.001.) (B) This effect may illustrate a molecular cascade that contributes to the accumulation of Aβ and the development of pathology in AD. In this sense it is an example of a mechanism of adaptive plasticity that has become pathological.

is undermined by the toxic consequences of their proximity to aggregated Aβ. The end result of this interaction is the formation of dystrophic neurites, and the degeneration and loss of these neurons. Risk factors may shift the threshold at which neurons become vulnerable to a particular combination of insults, culminating in irreparable injury. The progressive dysfunction and eventual loss of neurons involved in these events could be the key to the functional disconnection of neuronal circuitry underlying the cognitive decline associated with AD.

As noted at the beginning of this chapter, the progressive nature of AD and its increasing incidence with age is unlikely to be due to a single factor. Rather, it may be that a series of altered regulatory mechanisms can ironically turn adaptive responses into pathological processes. As illustrated in Figure 8.1, multiple insults may combine with genetic risk factors unique to the individual to lower the threshold for dysfunction. Alternatively, an individual's genetic makeup could shift the threshold for dysfunction in the opposite direction, exerting a neuroprotective influence. This threshold model of vulnerability to neuronal insult suggests that over time, a series of less critical events could combine to initiate more severe pathological processes. In this chapter we have illustrated several specific examples of these processes, focusing on Aβ as a pivotal element. Some of these mechanisms appear to convert to molecular cascades, perhaps when events coincide in time or location to drive the formation of pathological loci such as plaques. The identification of these molecular cascades and key regulatory steps at the earliest stages of the disease will lead to a better understanding of AD. In the long run, this knowledge will allow the development of therapeutic interventions, and help preserve learning and memory in the aging population.

REFERENCES

Abraham, C. R., Selkoe, D. J., & Potter, H. (1988). Immunochemical identification of the serine protease inhibitor α1-antichymotrypsin in the brain amyloid deposits of Alzheimer's disease. *Cell, 52,* 487–501.

Alzheimer, A. (1907). A characteristic disease of the cerebral cortex. *Allgemeine Zeitschrift für Psychiatria und Psychisch-Gerichtliche Medizin, 44,* 146–148.

Araujo, D. M., & Cotman, C. W. (1992). β-Amyloid stimulates glial cells *in vitro* to produce growth factors that accumulate in senile plaques in Alzheimer's disease. *Brain Research, 569,* 141–145.

Arrigada, P. V., Growdon, J. H., Hedley-White, E. T., & Hyman, B. T. (1992). Neurofibrillary tangles but not senile plaques parallel duration and severity of Alzheimer's disease. *Neurology, 42,* 631–639.

Barrow, C. J., & Zagorski, M. G. (1991). Solution structures of β peptide and its constituent fragments: Relation to amyloid deposition. *Science, 253,* 179–181.

Benowitz, L. I., Rodriguez, W., Paskevich, P., Mufson, E. J., Shenk, D., & Neve, R. L. (1989). The amyloid precursor protein is concentrated in neuronal lysosomes in normal and Alzheimer disease subjects. *Experimental Neurology, 106,* 237–250.

Blessed, G., Tomlinson, B. E., & Roth, M. (1968). The association between quantitative measures of dementia and of senile change in the cerebral grey matter of elderly subjects. *British Journal of Psychiatry, 114,* 797–811.

Burdick, D., Soreghan, B., Kwon, M., Kosmoski, J., Knauer, M., Henschen, A., Yates, J., Cotman, C., & Glabe, C. (1992). Assembly and aggregation properties of synthetic Alzheimer's A4/β amyloid peptide analogs. *Journal of Biological Chemistry, 267,* 546–554.

Cajal, R. S. (1928). *Degeneration and regeneration of the nervous system* (R. M. May, Trans.). London: Oxford University Press.

Choi, D. W. (1988). Glutamate neurotoxicity and diseases of the nervous system. *Neuron, 1,* 623–634.

Chui, H. C. (1989). Dementia. A review emphasizing clinicopathologic correlation and brain-behavior relationships. *Archives of Neurology, 46,* 806–814.

Cole, G. M., Huynh, T. V., & Saitoh, T. (1989). Evidence of lysosomal processing of amyloid beta-protein precursor in cultured cells. *Neurochemical Research, 14*(10), 933–939.

Coleman, P. D., & Flood, D. G. (1987). Neuron numbers and dendritic extent in normal aging and Alzheimer's disease. *Neurobiology of Aging, 8,* 521–545.

Copani, A., Koh, J., & Cotman, C. W. (1991). β-amyloid increases neuronal susceptibility to injury by glucose deprivation. *NeuroReport, 2,* 763–765.

Cotman, C. W., Cummings, B. J., & Pike, C. J. (1993). Molecular cascades in adaptive versus pathological plasticity. In A. Goria (Ed.), *Neuro regeneration* New York: Raven Press.

Cotman, C. W., Cummings, B. J., & Whitson, J. S. (1991). The role of misdirected plasticity in plaque biogenesis and Alzheimer's disease pathology. In F. Hefti, P. Brachet, B. Will, & Y. Christen (Eds.), *Growth factors and Alzheimer's disease* (pp. 222–233). Berlin: Springer-Verlag.

Cotman, C. W., Matthews, D. A., Taylor, D., & Lynch, G. (1973). Synaptic rearrangement in the dentate gyrus: Histochemical evidence of adjustments after lesions in immature and adult rats. *Proceedings of the National Academy of Sciences, USA, 70,* 3473–3477.

Cotman, C. W., Pike, C. J., & Copani, A. G. (1992). β-amyloid neurotoxicity: A discussion of *in vitro* findings. *Neurobiology of Aging, 13*(5), 587–590.

Cotman, C. W., Pike, C. J., & Cummings, B. J. (1993). Adaptive versus pathological plasticity: Possible contributions to age-related dementia. In F. J. Seil (Ed.), *Advances in neurology* (pp. 35–45). New York: Raven Press.

Crain, B. J., & Burger, P. C. (1988). The laminar distribution of neuritic plaques in the fascia dentata of patients with Alzheimer's disease. *Acta Neuropathologica, 76,* 87–93.

Damon, D. H., D'Amore, P. A., & Wagner, J. A. (1988). Sulfated glycosaminoglycans modify growth factor-induced neurite outgrowth in PC12 cells. *Journal of Cell Physiology, 135,* 293–300.

Davies, C. A., Mann, D. M. A., Sumpter, P. Q., & Yates, P. O. (1987). A quantitative morphometric analysis of the neuronal and synaptic content of the frontal and temporal cortex in patients with Alzheimer's disease. *Journal of Neurological Science, 78,* 151–164.

Dipasquale, B., Marini, A. M., & Youle, R. J. (1991). Apoptosis and DNA degradation induced by 1-methyl-4-phenylpyridinium in neurons. *Biochemical Biophysical Research Communications, 181,* 1442–1448.

Eslinger, P. J., & Damasio, A. R. (1986). Preserved motor learning in Alzheimer's disease: Implications for anatomy and behavior. *Journal of Neuroscience, 6,* 3006–3009.

Evans, D. A., Funkenstein, H. H., Albert, M. S., Scher, P. A., Cook, N. R., Chown, M. J., Hebert, L. E., Hennekens, C. H., & Taylor, J. O. (1989). Prevalence of Alzheimer's disease in a community population of older persons. *Journal of the American Medical Association, 262*(18), 2551–2556.

Flaumenhaft, R., Moscatelli, D., & Rifkin, D. B. (1990). Heparin and heparan sulfate increase the radius of diffusion and action of basic fibroblast growth factor. *Journal of Cell Biology, 111,* 1651–1659.

Geddes, J. W., Anderson, K. J., & Cotman, C. W. (1986). Senile plaques as aberrant sprout-stimulating structures. *Experimental Neurology, 94,* 767–776.

Geddes, J. W., Monaghan, D. T., Cotman, C. W., Lott, I. T., Kim, R. C., & Chui, H. C. (1985). Plasticity of hippocampal circuitry in Alzheimer's disease. *Science, 230,* 1179–1181.

Glenner, G. G., & Wong, C. W. (1984). Alzheimer's disease: Initial report of the purification of a novel cerebrovascular amyloid protein. *Biochemical and Biophysical Research Communications, 120,* 885–890.

Goldgaber, D., Harris, H. W., Hla, T., Maciag, T., Donnelly, R. J., Jacobsen, J. S., Vitek, M. P., & Gajdusek, D. C. (1989). Interleukin 1 regulates synthesis of amyloid beta-protein precursor mRNA in human endothelial cells. *Proceedings of the National Academy of Sciences, USA, 86,* 7606–7610.

Goldgaber, D., Lerman, M. I., McBride, O. W., Saffioti, U., & Gajdusek, D. C. (1987). Characterization and chromosomal localization of a cDNA encoding brain amyloid of Alzheimer's disease. *Science, 235,* 877–880.

Gomez-Pinilla, F., Cummings, B. J., & Cotman, C. W. (1990). Induction of basic fibroblast growth factor in Alzheimer's disease pathology. *NeuroReport, 1*(3 & 4), 211–214.

Gomez-Pinilla, F., Lee, J. W., & Cotman, C. W. (1992). Basic FGF in adult rat brain: Cellular distribution and response to entorhinal lesion and fimbria-fornix transection. *Journal of Neuroscience 12*(1), 345–355.

Gospodarowicz, D., Cheng, J., Lui, G. M., Baird, A., & Böhlent, P. (1984). Isolation of brain fibroblast growth factor by heparan-sepharose affinity chromatography: Identity with pituitary fibroblast growth factor. *Proceedings of the National Academy of Sciences, USA, 81,* 6963–6967.

Griffin, W. S., Stanley, L. C., Ling, C., White, L., MacLeod, V., Perrot, L. J., White, C. L., & Araoz, C. (1989). Brain interleukin 1 and S-100 immunoreactivity are elevated in Down syndrome and Alzheimer disease. *Proceedings of the National Academy of Sciences, USA, 86,* 7611–7615.

Haass, C., Schlossmacher, M., Hung, A. Y., Vigo-Pelfrey, C., Mellon, A., Ostaszewski, B. L., Lieberberg, I., Koo, E. H., Schenk, D., Teplow, D. B., & Selkoe, D. (1992). Amyloid β-peptide is produced by cultured cells during normal metabolism. *Nature, 359,* 322–325.

Hamos, J. E., DeGennare, L. J., & Drachman, D. A. (1989). Synaptic loss in Alzheimer's disease and other dementias. *Neurology, 39,* 355–360.

Henderson, A. S. (1988). The risk factors for Alzheimer's disease: A review and a hypothesis. *Acta Psychiatry Scandinavia, 78,* 257–275.

Hilbich, C., Kisters-Woike, B., Reed, J., Masters, C. L., & Beyreuther, K. (1991). Aggregation and secondary structure of synthetic amyloid βA4 peptides of Alzheimer's disease. *Journal of Molecular Biology, 218,* 149–163.

Hoyer, S., Oesterreich, K., & Wagner, O. (1988). Glucose metabolism as the site of the primary abnormality in early-onset dementia of Alzheimer type? *Journal of Neurology, 235,* 143–148.

Hyman, B. T., Kromer, L. J., & Van Hoesen, G. W. (1987). Reinnervation of the hippocampal perforant pathway zone in Alzheimer's disease. *Annals of Neurology, 21,* 259–267.

Hyman, B. T., Van Hoesen, G. W., & Damasio, A. R. (1990). Memory-related neural systems in Alzheimer's disease. *Neurology, 40,* 1721–1730.

Hyman, B. T., Van Hoesen, G. W., Damasio, A. R., & Barnes, C. L. (1984). Alzheimer's disease: Cell-specific pathology isolates the hippocampal formation. *Science, 225,* 1168–1170.

Hyman, B. T., Van Hoesen, G. W., Kromer, L. J., & Damasio, A. R. (1986). Perforant pathway changes and the memory impairment of Alzheimer's disease. *Annals of Neurology, 20,* 472–481.

Ishiura, S. (1991). Proteolytic cleavage of the Alzheimer's disease amyloid A4 precursor protein. *Journal of Neurochemistry, 56,* 363–369.

Kang, J., Lemaire, H. G., Unterbeck, A., Salbaum, J. M., Master, C. L., Grezeschik, K. H., Multhaup, G., Beyruther, K., & Müller-Hill, B. (1987). The precursor of Alzheimer's disease amyloid A4 protein resembles a cell-surface receptor. *Nature, 325,* 733–736.

Kato, T., Sasaki, H., Katagiri, T., Sasaki, H., Koiwai, K., Youki, H., Totsuka, S., & Ishii, T. (1991). The binding of basic fibroblast growth factor to Alzheimer's neurofibrillary tangles and senile plaques. *Neuroscience Letters, 122,* 33–36.

Klier, F. G., Cole, G., Stallcup, W., & Schubert, D. (1990). Amyloid β-protein precursor is associated with extracellular matrix. *Brain Research, 515,* 336–342.

Koh, J. Y., Yang, L. L., & Cotman, C. W. (1990). β-amyloid protein increases the vulnerability of cultured cortical neurons to excitotoxic damage. *Brain Research, 533,* 315–320.

Kure, S., Tominaga, T., Yoshimoto, T., Tada, K., & Narisawa, K. (1991). Glutamate triggers internucleosomal DNA cleavage in neuronal cells. *Biochemistry and Biophysics Research Communications, 179*(1), 39–45.

Loo, D., Copari, A. G., Pike, C. J., Whiltemore, E. R., Walencewicz, A. J., & Cotman, C. W. (1993). Apoptosis is induced by beta-amyloid in cultured central nervous system neurons. *Proceedings of the National Academy of Sciences, USA, 90*(17), 7951–7955.

Mann, D. M. A., Yates, P. O., & Marcynuik, B. (1985). Correlation between senile plaque and neurofibrillary tangle counts in cerebral cortex and neuronal counts in cortex and subcortical structures in Alzheimer's disease. *Neuroscience Letters, 56,* 51–55.

Maragos, W. F., Greenamyre, J. T., Penney, J. B., & Young, A. B. (1987). Glutamate dysfunction in Alzheimer's disease: An hypothesis. *Trends in Neurosciences, 10,* 65–68.

Martin, D. P., Schmidt, R. E., DiStefano, P. S., Lowry, O. H., Carter, J. G., & Johnson, E. M. (1988). Inhibitors of protein synthesis and RNA synthesis prevent neuronal death caused by nerve growth factor deprivation. *Journal of Cell Biology, 106,* 829–844.

Masliah, E., Terry, R. E., DeTheresa, R. M., & Hansen, L. A. (1989). Immunohistochemical quantification of the synapse related protein synaptophysin in Alzheimer's disease. *Neuroscience Letters, 103,* 234–239.

Masters, C. L., Multhaup, G., Simms, G., Rottgiesser, J., Martins, R. N., & Beyreuther, K. (1985a). Neuronal origin of a cerebral amyloid: Neurofibrillary tangles of Alzheimer's disease contain the same protein as the amyloid of plaque cores and blood vessels. *European Molecular Biology Organization Journal, 4,* 2757–2763.

Masters, C. L., Simms, G., Weinman, N. A., Multhaup, G., McDonald, B. L., & Beyreuther, K. (1985b). Amyloid plaque core protein in Alzheimer disease and Down syndrome. *Proceedings of the National Academy of Sciences, USA, 82,* 4245–4249.

Matthews, D., Cotman, C., & Lynch, G. (1976a). An electron microscopic study of lesion-induced synaptogenesis in the dentate gyrus of the adult rat. I. Magnitude and time course of degeneration. *Brain Research, 115,* 1–21.

Matthews, D., Cotman, C., & Lynch, G. (1976b). An electron microscopic study of lesion-induced synaptogenesis in the dentate gyrus of the adult rat. II. Reappearance of morphologically normal synaptic contacts. *Brain Research, 115,* 23–41.

Mattson, M. P., Cheng, B., Davis, D., Bryant, K., Lieberberg, I., & Rydel, R. E. (1992). β-amyloid peptides destabilize calcium homeostasis and render human cortical neurons vulnerable to excitotoxicity. *Journal of Neuroscience, 12*(2), 376–389.

McGeer, P. L., McGeer, E. G., Akiyama, H., Itagaki, S., Harrop, R., & Peppard, R. (1990). Neuronal degeneration and memory loss in Alzheimer's disease and aging. In E. J. C. Creutzfeldt & O. Creutzfeldt (Eds.), *The principles of design and operation of the brain* (pp. 413–431). Berlin: Springer-Verlag.

McKee, A. C., Kosik, K. S., & Kowall, N. W. (1991). Neuritic pathology and dementia in Alzheimer's disease. *Annals of Neurology, 30*(2), 156–165.

McKhann, G., Drachman, D., Folstein, M. F., Katzman, R., Price, D., & Stadlan, E. M. (1984). Report of the NINCDS-ADRDA work group under the auspices of Department of Health and Human Services Task Force on Alzheimer's Disease. *Neurology, 34,* 939–944.

Mizuguchi, M., & Kim, S. U. (1991). α-antichymotrypsin supports short-term survival of neurons in culture. *Neuroscience Letters, 124,* 166–168.

Monyer, H., & Choi, D. W. (1988). Morphinians attenuate cortical neuronal injury induced by glucose deprivation *in vitro. Brain Research, 446,* 144–148.

Morris, J. C., Mohs, R. C., Rogers, H., Fillenbaum, G., & Heyman, A. (1988). Consortium to establish a registry for Alzheimer's disease (CERAD) clinical and neuropsychological assessment of Alzheimer's disease. *Psychopharmacology Bulletin, 24,* 641–644.

Nakamura, Y., Takeda, M., Niigawa, H., Hariguchi, S., & Nishimura, T. (1992). Amyloid β-protein precursor deposition in rat hippocampus lesioned by ibotenic acid injection. *Neuroscience Letters, 136,* 95–98.

Nitsch, R. M., Slack, B. E., Wurtman, R. J., & Growdon, J. H. (1992). Release of Alzheimer amyloid precursor derivatives stimulated by activation of muscarinic acetylcholine receptors. *Science, 258,* 304–306.

Oppenheim, R. W., Prevette, D., Tytell, M., & Homma, S. (1990). Naturally occurring and induced neuronal death in the chick embryo *in vivo* requires protein and RNA synthesis: Evidence for the role of cell death genes. *Developmental Biology, 138,* 104–113.

Orrenius, S., McConkey, D. J., Bellomo, G., & Nicotera, P. (1989). Role of Ca + + in toxic cell killing. *Trends in Pharmacological Sciences, 10,* 281–285.

Otsuka, N., Tomonaga, M., & Ikeda, K. (1991). Rapid appearance of β-amyloid precursor protein immunoreactivity in damaged axons and reactive glial cells in rat brain following needle stab injury. *Brain Research, 568,* 335–338.

Palmert, M. R., Siedlak, S. L., Podlisny, M. B., Witker, D. S., Oltersdorf, T., Younkin, L. H., Selkoe, D. J., & Younkin, S. G. (1989). The beta-amyloid protein precursor of Alzheimer's disease has soluble derivatives found in human brain and cerebrospinal fluid. *Proceedings of the National Academy of Sciences, USA, 86*(16), 6338–6342.

Perry, G., Cras, P., Siedlak, S. L., Tabaton, M., & Kawai, M. (1992). β protein immunoreactivity is found in the majority of neurofibrillary tangles of Alzheimer's disease. *American Journal of Pathology, 140*(2), 283–289.

Perry, G., Siedlak, S. L., Richey, P., Kawai, M., Cras, P., Kalaria, R., Galloway, P., Scardina, J. M., Cordell, B., Greenberg, B. D., Ledbetter, S., & Gambetti, P. (1991). Association of heparan sulfate proteoglycan with the neurofibrillary tangles of Alzheimer disease. *Journal of Neuroscience 11*(11), 3679–3683.

Pike, C. J., Burdick, D., Walencewicz, A., Glabe, C. G., & Cotman, C. W. (1993). Neurodegeneration induced by β-amyloid peptides in vitro: The role of peptide assembly state. *Journal of Neuroscience, 13*(4), 1676–1687.

Pike, C. J., Cummings, B. J., & Cotman, C. W. (1992). β-amyloid induces neuritic dystrophy in vitro: Similarities with Alzheimer pathology. *NeuroReport, 3*, 769–772.

Pike, C. J., Walencewicz, A. J., Glabe, C. G., & Cotman, C. W. (1991a). Aggregation-related toxicity of synthetic β-amyloid protein in hippocampal cultures. *European Journal of Pharmacy, 207*, 367–368.

Pike, C. J., Walencewicz, A. J., Glabe, C. G., & Cotman, C. W. (1991b). In vitro aging of β-amyloid protein causes peptide aggregation and neurotoxicity. *Brain Research, 563*, 311–314.

Quon, D., Catalano, R., & Cordell, B. (1990). Fibroblast growth factor induces beta-amyloid precursor mRNA in glial but not neuronal cultured cells. *Biochemical and Biophysical Research Communications, 167*, 96–102.

Rosen, W. G. (1983). Neuropsychological investigations of memory, visuoconstructural, visuo-perceptual, and language abilities in senile dementia of the Alzheimer types. In R. Mayeux (Ed.), *The dementias* (pp. 65–73). New York: Raven Press.

Roth, M., Tomlinson, B. E., & Blessed, G. (1966). Correlation between scores for dementia and counts of senile plaques in cerebral grey matter of elderly subjects. *Nature, 206*, 109–110.

Saksela, O., Moscatelli, D., Sommer, A., & Rifkin, D. (1988). Endothelial cell-derived heparan sulfate binds basic fibroblast growth factor and protects it from proteolytic degradation. *Journal of Cell Biology, 107*, 743–751.

Scheff, S. W., & Cotman, C. W. (1977). Recovery of spontaneous alternation following lesions of the entorhinal cortex in adult rats: Possible correlation to axon sprouting. *Behavioral Biology, 21*, 286–293.

Schellenberg, G. D., Bird, T. D., Wijsman, E. M., Orr, H. T., Anderson, L., Nemens, E., White, J. A., Bonnycastle, L., Weber, J. L., Alonso, E., Potter, H., Heston, L. L., & Martin, G. M. (1992). Genetic linkage evidence for a familial Alzheimer's disease locus on chromosome 14. *Science, 258*, 668–671.

Schubert, D., Jin, L. W., Saitoh, T., & Cole, G. (1989). The regulation of amyloid beta protein precursor secretion and its modulatory role in cell adhesion. *Neuron, 3*, 689–694.

Schubert, D., LaCorbiere, M., Saitoh, T., & Cole, G. (1989). Characterization of an amyloid beta-precursor protein that binds heparin and contains tyrosine sulfate. *Proceedings of the National Academy of Sciences, USA, 86*, 2066–2069.

Scott, S. A., & Davies, A. M. (1990). Inhibition of protein synthesis prevents cell death in sensory and parasympathetic neurons deprived of neurotrophic factor *in vitro*. *Journal of Neurobiology, 21*(4), 630–638.

Selkoe, D. J., Abraham, C. R., Podlisny, M. B., & Duffy, L. D. (1986). Isolation of low molecular weight proteins from amyloid plaque fibers in Alzheimer's disease. *Journal of Neurochemistry, 46*, 1820–1834.

Selkoe, D. J., Podlisny, M. B., Joachim, C. L., Vickers, E. A., Lee, G., Fritz, L. C., & Oltersdorf, T. (1988). β-amyloid precursor protein of Alzheimer's disease occurs as 110- to 135-kilodalton membrane-associated proteins in neural and non-neural tissues. *Proceedings of the National Academy of Sciences, USA, 85*, 7341–7345.

Seubert, P., Vigo-Palfrey, C., Esch, F., Lee, M., Dovey, H., Davis, D., Sinha, S., M., S., Whaley, J., Swindlehurst, C., McCormack, R. M., Wolfert, R., Selkoe, D., Lieberberg, I., & Schenk, D. (1992). Isolation and quantification of soluble Alzheimer's β-peptide from biological fluids. *Nature, 359,* 325–327.

Shoji, M., Golde, T. E., Ghiso, J., Cheung, T. T., Estus, S., Shafer, L. M., Cai, X., McKay, D. M., Tintner, R., Frangione, B., & Younkin, S. G. (1992). Production of the Alzheimer amyloid β protein by normal proteolytic processing. *Science, 258,* 126–129.

Shoji, M., Hirai, S., Yamaguchi, H., Harigaya, Y., Ishiguro, K., & Matsubara (1991). Alpha 1-antichymotrypsin is present in diffuse senile plaques. *American Journal of Pathology, 138,* 247–257.

Snow, A. D., Lara, S., Nochlin, D., & Wight, T. N. (1989). Cationinc dyes reveal proteoglycans structurally integrated within the characteristic lesions of Alzheimer's disease. *Acta Neuropathologica, 78,* 113–123.

Snow, A. D., Mar, H., Nochlin, D., Kimata, K., Kato, M., Suzuki, S., Hassell, J., & Wight, T. N. (1988). The presence of heparan sulfate proteoglycans in the neuritic plaques and congophillic angiopathy in Alzheimer's disease. *American Journal of Pathology, 133*(3), 456–463.

Snow, A. D., Mar, H., Nochlin, D., Sekiguchi, R. T., Kimata, K., Koike, Y., & Wight, T. N. (1990). Early accumulation of heparan sulfate in neurons and in the beta-amyloid protein-containing lesions of Alzheimer's disease and Down's Syndrome. *American Journal of Pathology, 137,* 1253–1270.

Stopa, E. G., Gonzalez, A., Chorsky, R., Corona, R. J., Alvarez, J., Bird, E. D., & Baird, A. (1990). Basic fibroblast growth factor in Alzheimer's disease. *Biochemical and Biophysical Research Communications, 171*(2), 690–696.

Tanzi, R. E., Gusella, J. F., Watkins, P. C., Bruns, G. A. P., St George-Hyslop, P., Van-Keuren, M. L., Patterson, D., Pagan, S., Kurnit, D. M., & Neve, R. L. (1987). Amyloid β protein gene: cDNA, mRNA distribution, and genetic linkage near the Alzheimer locus. *Science, 235,* 880–884.

Terry, R. D., Maslieh, E., Salmon, D. P., Butters, N., DeTheresa, R., Hill, R., Hansen, L. A., & Katzman, R. (1991). Physical basis of cognitive alterations in Alzheimer's disease: Synapse loss is the major correlate of cognitive impairment. *Annals of Neurology, 4,* 572–580.

Terry, R. D., et al. (1981). Some morphometric aspects of the brain in senile dementia of the Alzheimer type. *Annals of Neurology, 10,* 184–192.

Van der Wal, E. A., Gomez-Pinilla, F., & Cotman, C. W. (1993). Transforming growth factor-β1 is in plaques in Alzheimer and Down pathologies. *NeuroReport, 4,* 69–72.

Walicke, P. A. (1988). Interactions between basic fibroblast growth factor (FGF) and glycosaminoglycans in promoting neurite outgrowth. *Experimental Neurology, 102,* 144–148.

Wallace, W. C., Bragin, V., Robakis, N. K., Sambamurti, K., VanderPutten, D., Merril, C. R., Davis, K. L., Santucci, A. C., & Haroutunian, V. (1991). Increased biosynthesis of Alzheimer amyloid precursor protein in the cerebral cortex of rats with lesions of the nucleus basalis of Meynert. *Molecular Brain Research, 10,* 173–178.

Weiler, R., Lassmann, H., Fischer, P., Jellinger, K., & Winkler, H. (1990). A high ratio of chromogranin A to synapsin/synaptophysin is a common feature of brains in Alzheimer's and Pick disease. *Federation of European Biochemical Societies Letters, 263*(2), 337–339.

Whitson, J. S., Glabe, C. G., Shintani, E., Abcar, A., & Cotman, C. W. (1990). β-amyloid protein promotes neuritic branching in hippocampal cultures. *Neuroscience Letters, 110*(3), 319–324.

Whitson, J. S., Selkoe, D. J., & Cotman, C. W. (1989). Amyloid beta protein enhances the survival of hippocampal neurons in vitro. *Science, 243*(4897), 1488–1490.

Wieloch, T. (1985). Hypoglycemia-induced neuronal damage prevented by an N-methyl-D-aspartate antagonist. *Science, 230,* 681–683.

Wyllie, A. H., Kerr, J. F. R., & Currie, A. R. (1980). Cell death: The significance of apoptosis. *International Review at Cytology, 68,* 251–306.

Yankner, B. A., Caceres, A., & Duffy, L. K. (1990). Nerve growth factor potentiates the neurotoxic-ity of β-amyloid. *Proceedings of the National Academy of Sciences, USA, 87,* 9020–9023.

Yankner, B. A., Duffy, L. K., & Kirschner, D. A. (1990). Neurotrophic and neurotoxic effects of amyloid β-protein: Reversal by tachykinin neuropeptides. *Science, 250,* 279–282.

Yoshida, K., & Gage, F. H. (1991). Fibroblast growth factors stimulate nerve growth factor synthesis and secretion by astrocytes. *Brain Research, 538,* 118–126.

9

Models of Age-Related
Memory Decline

FRED H. GAGE

"Brain and Memory: Modulation and Mediation of Neuroplasticity" was the overall topic of the Fifth Conference on the Neurobiology of Learning and Memory. The second session of the conference focused on aging and memory. The three speakers (Michela Gallagher, Vahram Haroutunian, and Carl Cotman) dealt with different aspects of the topic, focusing primarily on the underlying biological bases of the decline in memory that occurs with age and disease. Michela Gallagher (Gallagher, Nagahara, & Burwell, 1992) discussed the natural decline with age, whereas Vaharm Haroutunian (Haroutunian, Wallace, Santucci, & Davis, 1992) and Carl Cotman (Cotman & Anderson, 1992) focused attention on the memory decline associated with the neurodegenerative changes associated with Alzheimer's disease.

When considering aging as a variable of memory, several decisions need to be made regarding the conclusions that can be drawn from the data that are presented in chapters 6, 7, and 8. First, one needs to decide if the aim of the study is to understand *comparative* aging, that is, to study the underlying common biological principles of aging as they affect memory, as opposed to a desire to understand *human memory* as affected by aging. In the latter case animal studies are often designed and conducted with an assumption that a clear relationship exists between underlying mechanisms of memory between animals and humans. By contrast, a comparative approach would focus on the diversity of the animal kingdom, drawing on different species to reflect unique and particularly interesting or relevant aspects of the aging process and its influence on memory. All three of the presenters in this session were either implicitly or admittedly interested in extrapolating their findings to human aging and memory.

The second consideration in designing and discussing aging and memory is the evaluation of *naturally occurring* age-related decline as distinguished from *pathological aging*, as in the case of Alzheimer's disease (AD). The distinction is not trivial since, in the case of pathological aging, the control group represents age-matched healthy aging, and the type of analysis is usually parametric ANOVA based. By contrast, investigations of naturally occurring aging focus on individual differences and the type of analysis is usually correlational. In naturally occurring aging, pathology is often used as a reason to exclude individuals from analysis if the pathology does not conform to the preexisting thesis of the underlying cause of aging impairment. Of the three presenters in this session, Michela Gallagher focused on naturally occurring aging in rodents with the expectation that the changes observed were relevant to the human condition. Vaharm Haroutunian and Carl Cotman clearly stated and overtly explored the pathologies that are commonly correlated with AD, focusing less on the chronological aspects of aging, and emphasizing that AD is an age-related pathological condition.

The third decision to be made when investigating age-related changes in learning and memory is choice of a model system to explore the underlying neurobiological mechanisms that affect memory with age. Since all three investigators are interested in cellular and chemical mechanisms, and are furthermore interested in human aging and memory, then *animal* models are required. However, as with most neurobiological studies, there are different types of models available, depending on the level of question being asked. There are at least three categories of animal models, each of which is useful in its own way, but clearly hierarchical in their relationship to the human condition, as can be seen in the following list.

1. Homologous model—etiological equivalence
   (a) Aging
   (b) Development
2. Isomorphic or analogous model—behavioral and physiological variables are similar
   (a) Anatomical or chemical lesion
   (b) Genetic manipulation (transgenic)
3. Equivalence model—outcome of treatment is predictive
   (a) Isolated cells
   (b) Tissue slice

The *homologous* model is the most rigorous and probably the most desirable. This is an animal model that not only represents the biological and behavioral manifestation of the human condition, but also assumes that the etiology of the conditions in the human and animal model is the same. There are a few examples of this type of model in neurobiology. One example is MPTP-induced Parkinsonism in monkeys and humans, caused by the ingestion of MPTP. Even in this case, however, the humans took the drug knowingly, while the monkeys are administered MPTP. The second type of model is an *isomorphic* model, which requires close resemblance of biological and behavioral manifestations to the human condition, but the cause of these manifestations can be quite different in the animal and the human. An example of this model is the unilateral 6-0HDA lesion, which results in rotational asymmetry in response to apomorphine or amphetamine. While some of the morphological and behavioral changes are related to the human condition of Parkinsonism, one could not examine the cause of PD with this approach. The third level of model is an *equivalency* model, which could have no resemblance to the human condition and certainly no common etiology, but may have significant predictive value of the human condition or predictive value of a therapy that might influence the human condition. An example of this model would be evaluating the effect of various trophic factors on culture cells from the ventral mesencephalon. Some of these neurons are dopaminergic and study of the neurons may lead to some discovery of a factor that supports the survival of dopamine neurons, but results from dopamine cells in vitro require additional model application before extrapolations to disease are warranted. Interestingly, the three chapters in this book on aging and memory make use of each of these three levels of models. In my comments about each of the chapters, I make reference to the type of model used and the utility and limitations of the data imposed by various models.

The stated purpose of Chapter 6 by Gallagher and her coworkers is to investigate how research in animals contributes to our understanding of aging. It seems clear that these authors are interested in a comparative approach to aging, but they have chosen to study the rat and extrapolate to humans in several instances. Their focus appears to be naturally occurring aging as opposed to pathological aging, as in AD. In some sense, these authors are using the aged rat as a homologous model of aging, since in fact the cause of naturally occurring age-related decline is time, which is a common cause for all species. Whether ultimately the changes that cause (or result in) cognitive decline in other species are the same as those in the rat remains to be discovered, but this question of aging along with the study of development are two of the few clearly homologous model systems that allow for the investigation of causal factors. A major theme in Chapter 6 is the attempt to find "biomarkers" of age-related cognitive decline. To this extent the authors have emphasized the individual differences that exist between animals as they age. Thus much of their analysis is correlational in nature and an argument is made that young animals should not be included in these analyses. A drawback in the use of correlational analysis is that one is left with correlations. In order to test or determine whether the correlations are indeed causal, some experimental test is needed. An assumption can be made that once enough of the appropriate correlations are established, then some test of the importance of these correlates in the memory decline will be made. However, the experimental test may require picking extremes of impaired versus nonimpaired aged animals and enhancing or accelerating various measures to determine whether the memory process is accelerated or ameliorated in the aged animals. Clearly Gallagher et al. have provided some of the most complete behavioral and chemical analyses of aging in the rat that currently exist in the literature.

Chapter 7 by Haroutunian and his coworkers makes it clear from the beginning that the objective is to understand pathological aging and in particular AD. Furthermore the authors are not interested in compartive aging but in human aging, specifically pathological human conditions. Given the admitted absence of homologous models of AD in animals at present, and the clear need for experimental studies to develop strategies for therapeutic intervention, these authors make the argument, as have many others, that by damaging the structures in rats that are damaged in AD patients one can explore the role that these structures play in the disease process. Furthermore, if the damage to these structures leads to behavioral or functional deficits that are analogous to those in the human condition, then an isologous model can be established that will be useful for the development of therapeutic drugs and other strategies. A strong case has already been made for an involvement of the cholinergic system in learning and memory as being at least partially responsible for some of the deficits in AD. In this presentation the interaction of the other neurochemical systems is explored, and a role for nor-adrenaline as a system interacting with cholinergic degeneration is made. Further-more, primary data linking damage to the cholinergic system and induction of beta amyloid are presented that would tie together two pathologies that have indepen-dently been considered to cause the impairments of AD. The use of isologous models has limitations to the extent that the cause of the disease or target behavior cannot be investigated. With reliable and robust biochemical, behavioral, and morphological changes as a baseline, however, experimental strategies that result in clear improvement in function reveal much about the role that these structures play in AD and provide clear opportunities for developing therapeutics.

Chapter 8 by Cotman and Anderson overtly states that in naturally occurring aging the plasticity that occurs is appropriate and participates in repair processes as well as learning and memory. The emphasis in these studies is on the aberrant plasticity that occurs in AD and is postulated to be at the core of the problem of the disease. In other words, it is not the absence of plasticity that is detrimental, but rather the inappropriate plasticity that leads to aberrant pathology and behavior. In this regard the expressed interest is in human aging and also in pathological, not comparative, aging. Once again, however, the absence of adequate homologous models of AD requires that other levels of models be developed or utilized. Using the loss of cells in layers 2 and 4 of the entorhinal cortex and the accumulation of amyloid and aberrant sprouting in the hippocampus as a starting point, Cotman and Anderson use the entorhinal lesion in the rat and the subsequent sprouting of fibers in the outer molecular layer of the dentate gyrus as an isologous model of AD. We can think of this model as isologous because there is damage to this area in AD and there is a sprouting response that does occur. A missing element in this model is a behavioral deficit with any analogy to the deficits in AD. Compelling data are presented, however, that argue that an aberrant increase in basic fibroblast growth factor is casual to the increase in amyloid accumulation in the hippocam-pus following entorhinal damage. Whether this occurs in humans with AD, and whether it is responsible for the observed behavioral deficits, is not known at present, but the use of these models is heuristic in developing the relevant hypoth-eses. In several instances Cotman and Anderson also make use of cultured fetal rat hippocampal neurons to test the role of trophic and toxic molecules, and then use these results to extrapolate to the potential toxicity or trophism of these models in the AD during the course of the disease. This is a common use of an equivalency model which, in conjunction with isologous models, provides valuable and more efficiently and reliably produced data. In isolation, correlational models are less useful in modeling human disease.

SUMMARY

Chapters 6, 7, and 8 represent a range of approaches to the understanding of aging and memory. While some focus is placed on naturally occurring aging, most of the emphasis is on pathological aging and how specific pathologies result in memory decline. Furthermore, there is an expressed emphasis on human aging and learning with little attention focused on the comparative nature of underlying common principles of aging. This latter focus evolves from the interest in pathological aging. Finally, the authors use a variety of model systems to address their questions. When investigating naturally occurring aging, a homologous model of aging in the rat is at least appropriate if not optimal. Several isologous models using the experimental destruction of specific areas of the brain that are damaged in AD provide clear insights into potential therapeutic opportunities. Even the in vitro culture of equivalency models of cells that are vulnerable in AD provide important if not essential data to form reliable and coherent theories of pathological changes in disease. The study of aging and memory has been greatly stimulated by the interest in AD, and while at present much of the focus may be on models of the disease, the need for understanding the underlying principles of naturally occurring aging and the changes that aging causes on memory processes remain dynamic and unresolved questions, whose answer will no doubt lead to insights into pathological aging in humans.

10

Nongenetic Factors in the Individuality of Brain Aging: Cell Numbers, Developmental Environment, and Disease

CALEB E. FINCH

Individual rodents and humans differ widely in brain functions during aging, as demonstrated by the preceding chapters by Gallagher, Haroutunian, and Cotman. Genetic variations within a population have major influences on brain functions later in life, as exemplified by Alzheimer's disease and other familial organic brain syndromes, as well as by the familial lipid and vascular disorders that predispose to stroke. Twin studies also indicate genetic factors that contribute to variance in cognitive functions (Pederson, Plomin, Nesselroade, & McClearn, 1992).

Nonetheless, highly inbred rodent strains show remarkable differences between individuals in brain aging, whether assessed in terms of behavior, neuroendocrine function, or anatomy. As an example, Figure 10.1 shows wide differences between female mice in their age changes in estrous cycles. Figure 10.2 shows individual difference in ovarian oocyte numbers, which range twofold in young mice and even greater spreads at later ages when oocyte exhaustion is approaching at midlife. As is often noted, the variance tends to increase with aging (Finch, Felicio, Mobbs, & Nelson, 1984; Gosden, Laing, Felicio, Nelson, & Finch, 1983).

How can this phenotypic variance occur in genetically nearly indistinguishable individuals after 100 generations of inbreeding? Standard calculations show that 30 generations are within an asymptotic limit of $<1\%$ residual genetic variance (Klein, 1986). I suggest several factors that partly explain the biological potential for individual outcomes of aging. For the user of lab rodents, an important and practical issue is the individual profile of major organ pathology. More intellectu-

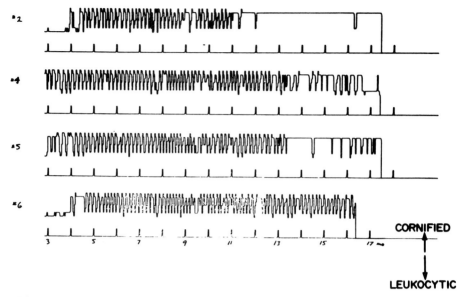

FIGURE 10.1.   Individual differences in female reproductive aging in C57BL/6J mice, a highly inbred and long-lived mouse strain. Vaginal cytology from longitudinal daily vaginal smears. The position of the horizontal lines indicates the type of vaginal smear, based on a composite scale that represents the density of leukocytes (bottom) and cornified epithelial cells (top). (From Finch et al., 1980.)

ally enticing perhaps are developmental and environmental influences on all mammals that are superimposed upon the genetic substrates. The following discussion is by no means comprehensive.

CELL NUMBER VARIATIONS THROUGH EPIGENETIC CAUSES

Variations in cell number between individuals of the same chromosomal genotype may contribute importantly to aging, as shown in the preceding example of ovarian oocytes. Some precedent for extensive individual variations of cell numbers through epigenetic causes comes from analyses of the lateral line system in *Xenopus*, which shows 10-fold or more variations in the numbers of neurons among the clusters of lateral line organ neurons in an individual (Winklbauer & Hausen, 1983).

This remarkable heterogeneity in number occurs through stochastic mechanisms during development, in which in these and other neuron lineages, there is a fixed probability at each replication that a daughter cell will remain in the lineage (Winklbauer & Hausen, 1983; Jacobson, 1985). In the lateral line of *Xenopus*, the distribution of neuron numbers is accurately modeled by the binomial distribution. More generally, conditional specification of cell fate is characteristic of

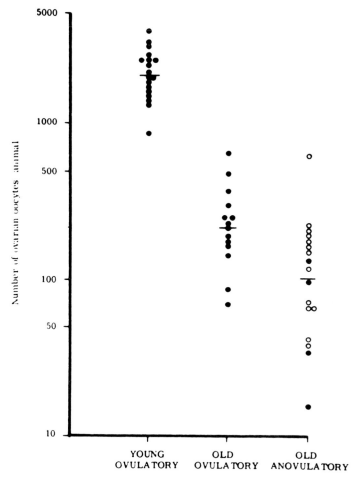

FIGURE 10.2.   Ovarian oocyte numbers in mice at two ages: young, at 4–5 months (the age of maximum fertility), and "old," 13–14 months (more accurately middle age, when fertility is vanishing in the population). The old were divided into ovulatory and anovulatory subgroups. (From Gosden et al., 1983; Finch et al., 1984.) Oocyte exhaustion ultimately limits the duration of fertility in rodents as in humans. Mice and rats, however, differ importantly from humans in the influence of the aging ovary on hypothalamic-pituitary functions during oocyte exhaustion.

vertebrates and is in complete contrast to the invariant determination of cell fate found in *Caenorhabditis* (Davidson, 1991).

An important and quite open question is the extent of variation between individuals in the numbers of brain neurons. While no ad hoc study has been made of interindividual variations in spinal or other neuron numbers in young inbred rodents, conversations with colleagues give the impression that a 20% or more range of neuron numbers would not be surprising. Even a 20% range of neuron numbers could alter the neuron reserve for the impact of changes during aging, in which some neural systems are more susceptible. On the one hand, the nigrostriatal pathway has a well-known capacity to sustain damage up to 80% with few functional consequences (e.g., Bernheimer, Birkmayer, Hornykiewicz, Jellinger, & Seitelberger, 1973). Contrarily, lesions of the A2 brain-stem nucleus have a low threshold for effects on blood pressure lability, with proportionate effects when >25% of the A2 nucleus is lesioned (Talman, Snyder, & Reis, 1980).

FETAL AND POSTNATAL ENVIRONMENT

Events during pre- and postnatal development have important effects on the outcomes of behavior and endocrine function during aging. In the first example, asymmetries in the intrauterine environment introduce another source of epigenetic influence from the interactions of adjacent fetuses. In particular, the sex of the neighboring fetus in polytocous rodents has many influences on the shadings of adult gender and on the outcomes of reproductive aging. Gender influences operate between both chromosomal sexes to influence the characteristics of young adults (vom Saal, Finch, & Nelson, 1994; Kinsley et al., 1986). For example, female mice that are flanked by males in utero (2M females, MFM) are more aggressive than 0M females (FFF or 0FF, etc.). Moreover, 0M females become infertile at an earlier age and have smaller litters (vom Saal & Moyer, 1985). There is no information on whether fetal neighbor effects extend to age changes in cognitive functions. Another unknown epigenetic outcome of fetal neighbor effects is how they interact with adult ovarian steroid memory effects, through which ovarian steroids, presumably estrogens, have an irreversible impact on hypothalamic pituitary functions that might vary between individuals according to their developmental exposure to steroids (Finch et al., 1980; Finch, Felicio, Mobbs, & Nelson, 1984; Kohama, Anderson, Osterburg, May, & Finch, 1989; Mobbs & Finch, 1992; Nelson, Felicio, Osterburg, & Finch, 1992).

The handling of neonatal rats has important influences on hippocampal aging (Meany, Aitken, Bhatnager, & Sanolsky, 1990; Meany, Aitken, Bhatnager, Van Berkel, & Sapolsky, 1988). Handled rats show smaller responses to stress throughout their life spans, with faster return to basal ACTH and corticosterone. Moreover, at 2 years, handled rats learned better and had a smaller loss of hippocampal neurons. Both examples show important epigenetic influences on brain-related aging phenomena that contribute to the nongenetic variance in age-related changes.

DISEASE

The last source of individual variation to be considered is through diseases outside of the brain. Rodents show many age-related pathological conditions that are characteristic of each genotype. Major age-related lesions in laboratory rodents include various types of tumors, particularly prolactin and growth hormone secreting pituitary tumors in females; kidney degeneration to various degrees that causes elevations of plasm parathyroid hormone and calcitonin; and autoimmune disorders (Bronson, 1990; Finch, 1990, pp. 317–339; Kalu, Hardin, Cockerham, & Yu, 1988). Yet, the age-related manifestation of these gross pathological lesions is not synchronous, even in a birth cohort of highly inbred rodents of the same gender.

This scattered distribution of age-related pathological lesions can have important influences on the outcome of studies on brain functions. As a neuroendocrine example, subsets of inbred mice at all adult ages that had tumors, wasting conditions, or other gross lesions, also had very low plasma testosterone (Nelson, Latham, & Finch, 1975) and diverse impairments in mating behavior (Huber, Bronson, & Desjardins, 1984). Another example is the different electrical activities in septo–hippocampal neurons of old rats with pituitary tumors with reference to 2-year-old rats without enlarged pituitaries (Lamour, Dutar, & Jobert, 1987). However, Gage, Kelly, and Björklund (1984) characterized the heterogeneity in aging rats by behavioral measures and cerebral glucose utilization, but could not account for different degrees of impairments with "physical signs of aging." These 22–24-month-old female Sprague-Dawley rats were observed to have two pathological lesions: pituitary tumors and respiratory difficulties.

These diverse effects of pathological lesions outside of the brain suggest the value of doing a careful postmortem examination for the *particular* gross organ pathology typical of that genotype. Few studies on aging rodents describe autopsy results. As a working rule, old rodents that loose or gain >10% body weight within a week before experimentation or sacrifice have a health condition that may be pertinent to the interpretation of aging changes (Finch, Foster, & Mirsky, 1969). The *Neurobiology of Aging* has editorial guidelines to further consideration of these issues.

With the continued emphasis on a small number of rodent genotypes as models for studying aging, we can anticipate the identification of lesions with particular impact on brain functions. In the study of human brain aging, the most attention has been given to the identification of specimens showing multiinfarct dementia or Alzheimer disease. However, little attention has yet been given to organ lesions outside of the brain. Although the age-related increase of diverse lesions is a general feature of aging in humans, as in all mammals, we may in the future recognize certain lesions with particular impact on brain functions. For further discussion of these subtle issues, see Kohn (1982), Fries and Crapo (1981, pp. 99–100), and Finch (1990, pp. 159–162 and 360–362).

CONCLUSIONS

There are many nongenetic sources of variation in brain functional changes during aging that may become important to experimental design. The long-range interest in these sources of variance is to identify individual factors that might optimize the trajectories of aging in any genotype.

REFERENCES

Bernheimer, H., Birkmayer, W., Hornykiewicz, O., Jellinger, K., & Seitelberger, F. (1973). Brain dopamine and the syndromes of Parkinson and Huntington: Clinical, morphological, and neurochemical correlations. *Journal of Neurological Science, 20,* 415-455.

Bronson, R. T. (1990). In D. E. Harrison (Ed.), *Genetics effects on aging II, (pp. 279-358).* Caldwell N.J.: Telford Press.

Davidson, E. H. (1991). Spatial mechanisms of gene regulation in metazoan embryos. *Development, 113,* 1-26.

Finch, C. E. (1990). *Longevity, senescence, and the genome.* Chicago: University of Chicago Press.

Finch, C. E., Felicio, L. S., Flurkey, K., Gee, D. M., Mobbs, C., Nelson, J. F., & Osterburg, H. H. (1980). Studies on ovarian-hypothalamic-pituitary interactions during reproductive aging in C57BL/6J mice. In D. Scott & J. L. Sladek, Jr. (Eds.), *Brain-endocrine interaction, IV: Neuropeptides in development & aging: Vol. 1, Suppl. 1 Peptides* (pp. 163-175). Fayetteville, N.Y.: ANKHO International.

Finch, C. E., Felicio, L. S., Mobbs, C. V., & Nelson, J. F. (1984). Ovarian and steroidal influences on neuroendocrine aging processes in female rodents. *Endocrine Review, 5,* 467-497.

Finch, C. E., Foster, J. R., & Mirsky, A. E. (1969). Aging and the regulation of cell activities during exposure to cold. *Journal of Genetics and Physiology, 54,* 690-712.

Fries, J. F., & Crapo, L. M. (1981). *Vitality and aging.* San Francisco: Freeman.

Gage, F. H., Kelly, P. A. T., & Björklund, A. (1984). Regional changes in brain glucose metabolism reflect cognitive impairments in age rats. *Journal of Neuroscience, 4,* 2856-2865.

Gosden, R. G., Laing, S. C., Felicio, L. S., Nelson, J. F., & Finch, C. E. (1983). Imminent oocyte exhaustion and reduced follicular recruitment mark the transition to acyclicity in aging C57BL/6J mice. *Biology of Reproduction, 28,* 255-260.

Huber, M. H. R., Bronson, F. H., & Desjardins, C. (1980). Sexual activity of aged male mice: Correlation with the level of arousal, physical endurance, pathological status, and ejaculatory capacity. *Biology of Reproduction, 23,* 305-316.

Jacobsen, M. (1985). Clonal analysis of the vertebrate CNS. *Trends in Neurosciences, 8,* 151-155.

Kalu, D. N., Hardin, R. R., Cockerham, R., & Yu, B. P. (1984). Aging and dietary modulation of rat skeleton parathyroid hormone. *Endocrinology, 115,* 1239-1247.

Kinsley, C., Miele, J., Konen, C., Ghiraldi, L., Broida, J., & Svare, B. (1986). Intrauterine hormone contiguity influences regulatory activity in adult female and male mice. *Hormones and Behavior, 20,* 7-19.

Klein, J. (1986). *Natural history of the major histocompatibility complex.* New York: Wiley.

Kohama, S. G., Anderson, C. P., Osterburg, H. H., May, P. C., & Finch, C. E. (1989). Oral administration of estradiol to young C57BL/6J mice induces age-like neuroendocrine dysfunctions in the regulation of estrous cycles. *Biology of Reproduction, 41,* 227-232.

Kohn, R. R. (1982). Causes of death in very old people. *Journal of the American Medical Association, 247,* 2793-2797.

Lamour, Y., Dutar, P., & Jobert, A. (1987). Septo-hippocampal neurons: Altered properties in the aged rat. *Brain Research, 416,* 277-282.

Meaney, M. J., Aitken, D. H., Bhatnagar, S., and Sapolsky, R. M. (1990). Postnatal handling attenuates certain neuroendocrine, anatomical and cognitive dysfunctions associated with aging in female rats. *Neurobiology of Aging, 12,* 31-38.

Meaney, M. J., Aitken, D. H., Bhatnagar, S., Van Berkel, C., and Sapolsky, R. M. (1988). Postnatal handling attenuates neuroendocrine, anatomical and cognitive impairments related to the aged hippocampus. *Science, 238,* 766-768.

Mobbs, C. V., & Finch, C. E. (1992). Estrogen-induced neuroendocrine impairment as a mechanism of senescence in female C57BL/6J mice. *Journal of Gerontology, 47,* B48-B51.

Nelson, J. F., Felicio, L. S., Osterburg, H. H., & Finch, C. E. (1992). Differential contributions from ovarian and extraovarian factors to age-related reductions in plasma estradiol and progesterone during the estrous cycle of C57BL/6J mice. *Endocrinology, 130,* 805-810.

Nelson, F. J., Latham, K. R., & Finch, C. E. (1975). Plasma testosterone levels in C57BL/6J male mice: Effects of age and disease. *Acta Endocrinology, 80,* 744–752.

Pederson, N. L., Plomin, R., Nesselroade, J. R., & McClearn, G. E. (1992). A quantitative genetic analysis of cognitive abilities during the second half of the life span. *Developmental Psychology, 29,* 110–118.

Talman, W. T., Snyder, D., and Reis, D. J. (1980). Chronic lability of arterial pressure produced by destruction of A2 catecholamine neurons in rat brain stem. *Circulation Research, 46,* 842–853.

Vom Saal, F. S., Finch, C. E., & Nelson, J. F. (1994). The natural history of reproductive aging in humans, laboratory rodents, and selected other vertebrates. In E. Knobil (Ed.), *Physiology of reproduction,* 2nd ed. (Vol. 2, pp. 1213–1314). New York: Raven Press.

Vom Saal, F. S., & Moyer, C. L. (1985). Prenatal effects on reproductive capacity during aging in female mice. *Biology of Reproduction, 32,* 1111–1126.

Winklbauer, R., & Hausen, P. (1983). Development of the lateral line system in *Xenopus laevis.* II. Cell multiplication and organ formation in the supraorbital system. *Journal of Embryology and Experimental Morphology, 76,* 283–296.

III

Cortical Plasticity

11

The Dynamic Nature
of Adult Visual Cortex

CHARLES D. GILBERT
CORINNA DARIAN-SMITH

The ability to change cortical connections and receptive field properties is a well-established characteristic of the cortex early in development. As shown by Hubel and Wiesel (1974), after a short period of plasticity extending from birth to about 6 months of age, which they named the critical period, the connections from thalamus to cortex become fixed. It has been tempting to extend the idea of a critical period for thalamocortical projections to all connections and functional properties of primary sensory cortex, leaving the dynamic changes necessary for information storage to higher cortical areas. Current evidence, however, shows that receptive field characteristics and cortical topography, even in primary sensory cortex and even in the adult, are surprisingly dynamic. These properties are subject to several influences—the context within which a feature is presented, long-term changes in sensory input, and attention toward stimulus attributes. The dynamic nature of cortical function has profound implications for understanding the mechanisms underlying many aspects of visual perception: the unification of an object's component contours into a single percept, separation of a figure from its background, perceptual constancies, the storage of visual information by neuronal ensembles, the mechanism of recovery of function following lesions of the central nervous system, and the role of top-down processes (expectation or attention) in perception. What is perhaps most striking is that the dynamic properties of cortex can be observed over a time scale of minutes.

LONG-TERM CHANGES IN CORTICAL TOPOGRAPHY

The visual cortex is topographically organized, with retinal coordinates mapped systematically on the cortical surface. When sensory input to the cortex is removed by making retinal lesions, the corresponding area of cortex is left devoid of functioning visual input. A similar situation applies to the somatosensory cortex, which is mapped according to position on the body surface. There, peripheral nerve transection or digit amputation silences the cortical region representing that body part. Depending on the size of the silenced cortical area, over time the cortex becomes reorganized, and develops a representation of a different body part, or different part of the retina, than it represented before the lesion (Calford & Tweedale, 1988; Gilbert & Wiesel, 1990; Heinen & Skavenski, 1991; Kaas et al., 1990; Merzenich et al., 1984; Merzenich, Recanzone, Jenkins, Allard, & Nudo, 1988; Sanes, Suher, Lando, & Donoghue, 1988; Rasmusson, 1982; Rasmusson, Turnbill, & Leech, 1985). In the experiments involving visual cortex, a cortical "scotoma" (the silenced region) up to 6 to 7 mm in diameter can completely fill-in within 2 to 3 months. Larger scotomata are generally left with a residual silent area in the center for periods up to 1 year.

In these experiments, the cortical area is effectively remapped, with an enlarged representation of the somatotopic or visuotopic areas immediately surrounding the lesioned sites. Figure 11.1 schematically illustrates the nature of the reorganization. The cells with receptive fields originally located within the lesioned area are initially silenced, and then over a period of 2 months regain visual input. The renewed receptive fields have shifted to positions outside of the lesioned area, effectively producing an expanded representation of the part of the retina just marginal to the lesion. In cortical terms, the representation of a shift of this size is on the order of 2.5 to 3.5 mm, comparable to the shift in the boundary of the edge of the cortical scotoma. This degree of mutability of the cortical map is quite a surprising finding for adult animals, where one would have expected that cortical organization would be fully developed and fixed early in life.

At what stage along the sensory pathway does this reorganization first occur? The possibilities are illustrated in Figure 11.2. Some of the reorganization seen in the cortex may be due to changes at earlier levels in the visual pathway, such as the lateral geniculate nucleus of the thalamus. In the somatosensory system, sensory information travels from sensory receptor to afferent fiber, dorsal horn and spinal cord, brainstem, thalamus, and finally to primary somatosensory cortex. Even in the dorsal horn of the spinal cord, there are widespread connections formed by sensory fibers, and spinal cord sensory maps have been shown to change following peripheral nerve injury (Devor & Wall, 1978; Wall & Werman, 1976). In one experiment where the sensory nerve was transected, substantial reorganization was observed in the ventrobasal complex of the thalamus (Garraghty & Kaas, 1991). A larger number of stages between periphery and cortex may in part account for apparent differences observed between visual and somatosensory systems.

As shown in Figure 11.2, there are several potential sets of connections capable of sending visual input into the cortical scotoma. The retina first sends signals along the optic nerve to the lateral geniculate nucleus (LGN). The terminal fibers of retinal ganglion cells are quite limited in their lateral extent, and the intrinsic connections of the LGN are also quite local (Friedlander, Lin, Stanford, & Sherman, 1981; Hamos, Horn, Raczkowski, Uhlrich, & Sherman, 1985), but any fill-

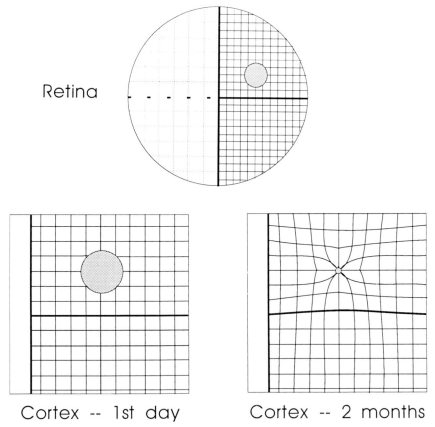

FIGURE 11.1.   Schematic diagram of reorganization of cortical map following retinal lesion. The visuotopic axes are represented as the Cartesian grid superimposed on the retina, and the corresponding maps on the cortex in surface view. A lesion, made with a diode laser, destroys the photoreceptor layer in a restricted part of the retina (shaded area, top), effectively removing visual input from the cortical region representing that retinal area (lower left). To get an idea of the dimensions involved, in the primate, a lesion subtending 5° of visual field, centered about 4° in the periphery, silences an area of cortex 10 mm in diameter. Over a period of 2 months the topography of the cortex is reorganized (lower right), with a decreased representation of the silenced input, and an increased representation of the perilesion retina. (Gilbert & Wiesel, 1990, 1992; Heinen & Skavenski, 1991; Kaas et al., 1990) (Reprinted from Gilbert, 1992.)

in of the scotoma at the level of the LGN would be propagated to the cortex. Most of the topographical changes reported in the visual cortex, however, must be mediated by intrinsic cortical connections: at a time when the cortical scotoma completely fills in, there is still a visually inactive region in the lateral geniculate nucleus (Darian-Smith, Gilbert, & Wiesel, 1992; Gilbert & Wiesel, 1992). Though earlier studies have shown a degree of reorganization in the LGN following retinal lesions (Eysel, Gonzalez-Aguilar, & Mayer, 1981), both the size of the

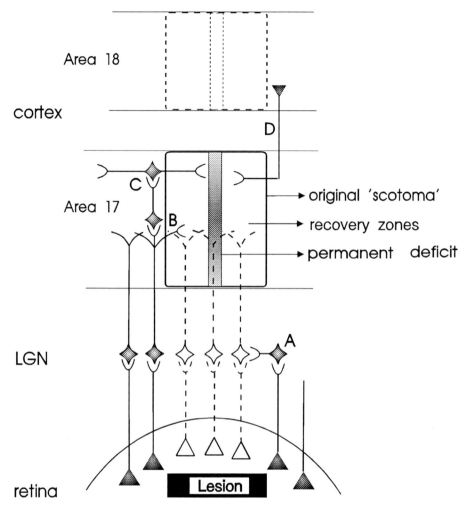

FIGURE 11.2. Visual pathway representing possible connections invòlved in cortical reorganization. The retinal lesion removes visual input from retinal ganglion cells (open triangles), which are left intact by the lesioning procedure. The ganglion cells project to the lateral geniculate nucleus, where lateral connections by interneurons (A) allow a small amount of lateral spread of visual information. The principal cells of the LGN project to cortical layer 4; a subset of these have terminal fields spreading horizontally in the cortex for distances of roughly 2 mm (B). Current evidence suggests that connections operating through this stage are not responsible for the fill-in of the cortical scotoma. Horizontal connections of cortical pyramidal cells (C) extend up to 6 to 7 mm, approximating the extent of the maximum cortical fill-in. Another possible source of the reorganization are feedback projections from higher cortical areas, such as area 18 (D). The area of the original cortical scotoma in area 17 is represented by the bold outline, and the area of the residual deficit after recovery is represented by the shaded area.

lesion and the scale of the reorganization were an order of magnitude smaller than that required to account for the cortical reorganization following larger retinal lesions.

Reorganization in the cortex could be mediated by the spread of geniculocortical afferents within the cortex. In a normal cortex these afferents maximally span a distance of 2 mm end to end, which is too small a distance to account for the cortical reorganization (Blasdel & Lund, 1983; Ferster & LeVay, 1978; Gilbert & Wiesel, 1979; Humphrey, Sur, Uhlrich, & Sherman, 1985). Visual input propagating from the edge of the scotoma toward its center would be expected to travel roughly half of the side-to-side spread of the axonal field mediating this process, assuming that the axon collaterals are distributed symmetrically about the main trunk. For geniculocortical afferents this would be a distance of 1 mm. The reorganization seen after 2 months, however, is 3 to 3.5 mm from the edge of the scotoma, allowing a complete fill-in of scotomata 6 to 7 mm in diameter, and consequently too great a distance to be achieved by normal afferents. If, on the other hand, these afferents were to sprout into the region of the cortical scotoma, they could then mediate the reorganization. But experiments involving injection of retrograde tracers at different positions within the cortical scotoma indicate that there is insufficient spread of the collateral arbors of geniculocortical afferents, even after topographic reorganization of the cortex, to account for the reorganization (Darian-Smith et al., 1992, and unpublished data; Gilbert & Wiesel, 1992). One therefore has to look for intrinsic cortical connections, arising from within cortex, as the source of the change.

In fact, there exists within the cortex a plexus of widespread connections that extend much more widely than the geniculocortical afferents—the axon collaterals of cortical pyramidal cells (Gilbert & Wiesel, 1979, 1983, 1989; Martin & Whitteridge, 1984; Rockland & Lund, 1982, 1983). An example of one of these cells, with its characteristic horizontally projecting clustered collateral arbor, is shown in Figure 11.3. These connections allow the target cells to integrate information from a wide area of cortex, and as a consequence of the topographical architecture of cortex, from a large part of the visual field, including loci outside the receptive field. In any one column of the primary visual cortex, cells have overlapping receptive fields. Taking together the receptive field area and the scatter in receptive field position, the receptive fields of all the cells in the column will cover a tiny fraction of the visual field. A rough rule of thumb governing topographic order in this area is that there is no overlap in the receptive fields of cells separated by a distance of 1.5 mm, taking into account the receptive field size and scatter for cells within a cortical column [a distance corresponding to two complete cycles of orientation columns, or two "hypercolumns," (Hubel & Wiesel, 1974)]. Thus horizontal connections spanning 6 to 7 mm allow communication between cells with widely separated receptive fields. This raises the puzzling finding that cells integrate information over a larger part of visual space than that covered by their receptive fields, and calls into question the very definition of receptive field. The explanation for this seeming contradiction between cortical topography and receptive field structure is that the definition of the receptive field is stimulus depen-

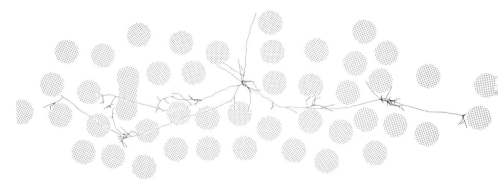

FIGURE 11.3.   Example of the axon from a pyramidal cell in a primate visual cortex forming long-range clustered horizontal connections. The cell is located in layer 3 and its axon extends for 6 mm parallel to the cortical surface. The axon gives off several clusters of collaterals within the superficial layers. As a reference, the cytochrome oxidase blobs are shown (shading). The blobs are aligned in rows along ocular dominance columns (vertically oriented in this view). Cells receiving input from axons such as these would be capable of integrating information over a substantial area of cortex representing an area of visual field that would be much larger than the cells' receptive fields. (Reprinted from Gilbert, 1992.)

dent, and that a cell's response can be modulated by stimuli lying outside the classic receptive field. Put another way, a cell's response to a complex visual stimulus cannot be fully predicted from its response to a simple stimulus, such as a single short line segment.

Since the extent of fill-in in the cortex is large relative to the spread of geniculo-cortical afferents within the cortex, it is tempting to think of the long-range horizontal connections as the source of visual input to the region of the original cortical scotoma. Another potential source is the feedback input from higher order visual cortical areas, such as area 18 or V2. No experiments have yet been done to discriminate the relative roles of horizontal and feedback connections in the phenomenon of cortical reorganization. At this point, however, it seems clear that the reorganization observed in visual cortex is largely due to changes intrinsic to cortex, and are most likely mediated by connections of cortical cells.

SHORT-TERM EFFECTS OF PERIPHERAL LESIONS

In the somatosensory system, changes in cortical topography following peripheral lesions have been observed within a short period. One observation was made in rats following section of the facial motor nerve that innervates the vibrissae (whiskers). Within a period of hours following transection, stimulating the original vibrissal representation of cortex evokes forelimb muscle activation (Donoghue, Suner, & Sanes, 1990). Digit amputation in the flying fox leads to an expansion in the sensory receptive fields of cortical cells originally representing the digit alone to the arm and wing, and this change occurs within 15 minutes (Calford & Tweedale, 1991).

In the visual cortex, following retinal lesions, there are striking changes in cortical receptive fields within minutes of the lesioning procedure: Those located near the boundary of the lesion expand in size by an order of magnitude. There is even a measure of remapping of cortical topography within this short time span, with a fill-in spanning a couple of millimeters (Gilbert & Wiesel, 1992). Another demonstration of the immediate effects of visual deprivation involved placing a laser lesion in one retina, waiting a period of time ranging from minutes to months, and then enucleating the other eye. Immediately following the enucleation, the area of cortex initially silenced to stimulation of the lesioned area recovers input from the surrounding retinal area (Chino, Kaas, Smith, Langston, & Cheng, 1992). Both studies showed shifts in topographic representation over a cortical distance of approximately 2 mm, as compared to reorganization of 6 to 10 mm seen in the longer term recoveries (Darian-Smith et al., 1992, unpublished data; Gilbert & Wiesel, 1992; Kaas et al., 1990; Pons et al., 1991).

These findings might reflect the fact that under ordinary circumstances cells are capable of integrating information over a large part of visual space. Usually the inputs from outside the classical receptive field serve to modulate the response of the cell, but under the appropriate pattern of stimulation they can be boosted to a suprathreshold level. Removing input to the receptive field center, for example, may "unmask" and enable the expression of portions of the receptive field that are peripheral to the original receptive field center.

CORTICAL CHANGES UNDER NORMAL SENSORY AND BEHAVIORAL EXPERIENCE

Though much of the earlier work on cortical reorganization has employed various lesioning procedures, it is now evident that altered patterns of sensory stimulation can have profound effects on the functional properties of cortical cells, without requiring actual damage of the periphery.

Use-dependent changes caused by altering tactile experience have been reported in somatosensory cortex. The documented changes were observed after several weeks of training. Though they do not fall under the rubric of the short-term changes that we have described earlier, they do represent an important departure from the experiments involving lesions (digit amputation, sensory nerve transection), in that they raise the possibility of shifting maps with normal sensory experience. For example, animals trained to detect differences in the frequency of a vibrating tactile stimulus develop larger cortical representations of the stimulated digits, and larger receptive fields in the expanded areas (Recanzone, Merzenich, Jenkins, Kamil, & Dinse, 1992). This develops further the earlier finding of changes in the representation of passively stimulated areas (Jenkins, Merzenich, Ochs, Allard, & Guic-Rocbles, 1990). Tactile stimulation alone can pro-

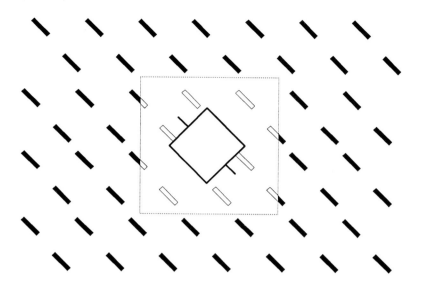

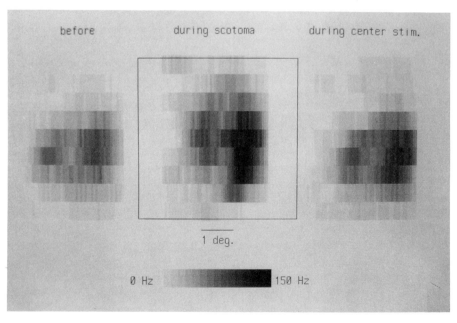

FIGURE 11.4. Effect of an artificial scotoma on receptive field size. Just as the retinal lesions are capable of producing a considerable expansion in receptive field size within minutes after making the lesion (Gilbert & Wiesel, 1992), mimicking the lesion by occluding a small part of the visual field also causes receptive fields located within the occluded area to expand (Pettet & Gilbert, 1992). The upper part of the figure shows the condition

duce changes in cortical responsivity over tens of presentations, spanning a time period of seconds (both increases and decreases have been observed), with no corresponding effect on the mechanoreceptor afferents (Lee & Whitsel, 1992). A degree of plasticity has likewise been reported in the auditory system, where one can shift the best frequency of a unit toward a conditioned stimulus frequency (Weinberger, Ashe, & Edeline, in press).

In the motor cortex, changes in the cortical representation of motor activity can be induced by postural changes. These maps are assessed by measuring EMG activity while electrically stimulating different cortical sites. Cortical regions that ordinarily are not associated with forearm movement when the elbow is kept flexed can, within 20 to 30 minutes after holding the elbow in extension, cause forelimb movement. In effect, the forelimb area expanded into an area originally representing the vibrissae (Sanes, Wang, & Donoghue, 1992).

In visual cortex, given the short time course of some of the changes following retinal lesions, and the ability to elicit changes with a restricted amount of damage (changes could be observed simply by destroying the photoreceptor layer, therefore not requiring a physical deafferentation of the target nuclei of the retina), it was reasonable to assume that the changes resulted from a particular pattern of retinal stimulation. This was mimicked by an "artificial scotoma," in which the area surrounding the receptive field was stimulated visually, but the receptive field itself was masked with a visual occluder. After a 10-minute period of conditioning the cell with this stimulus, its receptive field expanded severalfold in length (Pettet & Gilbert, 1992). Consequently, the size of the receptive field could be altered by the pattern of visual stimulation, and the relatively short time course of the effect suggested an ongoing process of modulation of field size, adapting in different ways to different scenes. The conditioning procedure and its effect on receptive field dimensions is shown in Figure 11.4. Though the changes in receptive field structure that have been documented have been shown after minutes of conditioning, this does not preclude the possibility of changes within seconds, but the appropriate experiments remain to be done. In human psychophysical experi-

---

ing stimulus: a pattern of lines moving outside the receptive field (the square with a solid outline, with the orientation specificity indicated by the two lines protruding from the square). The lines disappear when they move within the masked area (the mask is indicated by the dotted line, but is not explicitly drawn in the stimulating pattern; the stimulating lines are shown as the blackened rectangles, and their disappearance indicated by the open rectangles). After 10 minutes of conditioning, the receptive field expands. This is illustrated in the bottom part of the figure, which gives a two-dimensional response profile of the cell, with the darker portions showing the greater response. The size and position of the occluder is indicated by the outline in the center, and the enlarged receptive field is indicated within the outline. Stimulating the center of the receptive field causes it to collapse in size, as indicated in the lower right. The receptive field can be caused to alternately expand and contract by a sequence of surround followed by center stimulation. (Adapted from Pettet & Gilbert, 1992, Figs. 1 and 4, and reprinted from Gilbert, 1992.)

ments, however, possible perceptual correlates of the receptive field expansion have been shown to occur within one second (Kapadia, Gilbert, & Westheimer, 1994).

These changes are likely to be cortically based, since they show interocular transfer. When recording from a binocular cortical cell, presenting the conditioning stimulus with the artificial scotoma to one eye (while the other eye is occluded) leads to an expansion of the receptive fields of both eyes (Volchan & Gilbert, 1992). Since the merging of binocular information occurs at the single-cell level in the cortex, with the cells in the LGN being monocular, the interocular transfer of the conditioning effect suggests that the expansion is due to cortical mechanisms, which likely involves intrinsic long-range cortical connections.

The perceptual consequences of the context-dependent changes in receptive field properties could be related to a host of context-dependent effects that have been demonstrated psychophysically. The perception of the position of a point within the focal plane, or of its position in depth, or of the orientation of a line, is influenced by the presence of nearby points or lines. Perceptual fill-in may be related to the artificial scotoma experiment described earlier: information about color, texture, or movement in one part of the visual field is propagated to parts of the visual field that are occluded (Paradiso & Nakayama, 1991; Ramachandran & Gregory, 1991). Illusory contours might be a subset of this tendency to fill in or link contours in the visual scene. In addition, our sense of the position of a feature can be altered by conditioning routines similar to those used to elicit receptive field expansion (Kapadia et al., 1994).

The cortical plasticity that has been observed physiologically may also have a correlate in learning effects, that is, changes in perceptual performance over time resulting from repeated discrimination trials. Hyperacuity is subject to training, so that after a few hundred trials of attempting to make a judgment of whether two lines are aligned or offset, one's ability to see tiny offsets (as little as 15 seconds of arc) improves markedly, and the improvement seems specific to the orientation of the stimulus pattern (McKee & Westheimer, 1978; Poggio, Fahle, & Edelman, 1992). Stereoacuity also improves with training, and the training is specific for stimulus size and visual field position (Fendick & Westheimer, 1983; Westheimer & Truong, 1988). A third example is training effects for texture segmentation [picking out a pattern of oriented lines from a background of differently oriented lines (Karni & Sagi, 1991)]. The specificities of these training routines for stimulus pattern and visual position are suggestive of a process occurring early in the visual pathway.

Though the underlying mechanisms of short-term cortical plasticity are as yet unknown, it must involve in some way a change in the synaptic weight of existing connections, altering the patterns of activation of intrinsic circuits. It now seems quite likely that mutability of receptive fields and cortical architectures is associated with normal sensory experience, not just peripheral lesions, and that the changes can take place on a brief time scale of minutes. The mechanisms involved in the effects occurring at different time scales might be distinct. The shortest term changes could reflect a potentiation of excitatory connections (analogous to the long-term potentiation observed in hippocampus and cortex) and/or an adaptation of inhibition, either of which can occur within seconds, leading to an unmasking of existing circuits. The longer term changes could involve processes requiring transcription and protein synthesis, such as sprouting of axon collaterals.

Though the forms and sites of cortical plasticity discussed in this chapter are based in the primary sensory cortex, it is tempting to think that they may involve the same mechanisms, in terms of connections and synaptic changes, as those one normally associated with learning and memory. Both occur over a short time scale, and both occur after increased exposure to a given pattern of sensory stimulation. The functional significance of the "learning" occurring in the primary visual cortex could be a normalization or calibration of the response properties of cells to particular visual attributes, depending on the amount and kind of experience one receives. In the instance of a retinal scotoma, for example, there is a change in the amount of input one receives from different parts of visual space. Cortex contracts its representation of locations providing less input, and expands its representation of the remaining areas. An analogous model might apply to inferotemporal cortex, which is thought to be involved with recognition of objects such as faces. There, the extent of cortical representation of a given set of objects depends on the number of objects within the set that can be discriminated. The intriguing possibility raised by the experiments discussed here is that all cortex operates by stereotyped mechanisms and common algorithms, including those involved with different types of information storage.

ACKNOWLEDGMENTS

Parts of this review are adapted from earlier publications (Gilbert, 1992, 1993).

REFERENCES

Blasdel, G. G., & Lund, J. (1983). Termination of afferent axons in macaque striate cortex. *Journal of Neuroscience, 3*, 1389–1413.

Calford, M. B., & Tweedale, R. (1988). Immediate and chronic changes in responses of somatosensory cortex in adult flying-fox after digit amputation. *Nature, 332*, 446–448.

Calford, M. D., & Tweedale, R. (1991). Acute changes in cutaneous receptive fields in primary somatosensory cortex after digit denervation in adult flying fox. *Journal of Neurophysiology, 65*, 178–187.

Chino, Y. M., Kaas, J. H., Smith, E. L., III, Langston, A. L., & Cheng, H. (1992). Rapid reorganization of cortical maps in adult cats following restricted deafferentation in retina. *Vision Research, 32*, 789–796.

Darian-Smith, C., Gilbert, C. D., & Wiesel, T. N. (1992). Cortical reorganization following binocular focal retinal lesions in the adult cat and monkey. *Society for Neuroscience Abstracts, 18*, 11.

Devor, M., & Wall, P. D. (1978). Reorganization of spinal cord sensory map after peripheral nerve injury. *Nature, 276*, 75–76.

Donoghue J. P., Suner, S., & Sanes, J. N. (1990). Dynamic organization of primary motor cortex output to target muscles in adult rats II. Rapid reorganization following motor nerve lesions. *Experimental Brain Research, 79*, 492–503.

Eysel, U. T., Gonzalez-Aguilar, F., & Mayer, U. (1981). Time-dependent decrease in the extent of visual deafferentation in the lateral geniculate nucleus of adult cats with small retinal lesions. *Experimental Brain Research, 41,* 256–263.

Fendick, M., & Westheimer, G. (1983). Effects of practice and the separation of test targets on foveal and peripheral stereoacuity. *Vision Research, 23,* 145–150.

Ferster, D., & LeVay, S. (1978). The axonal arborizations of lateral geniculate neurons in the striate cortex of the cat. *Journal of Comparative Neurology, 182,* 923–944.

Friedlander, M. J., Lin, C.-S., Stanford, L. R., & Sherman, S. M. (1981). Morphology of functionally identified neurons in the lateral geniculate nucleus of the cat. *Journal of Neurophysiology, 46,* 80–129.

Garraghty, P. E., & Kaas, J. H. (1991). Functional reorganization in adult monkey thalamus after peripheral nerve injury. *NeuroReport, 2,* 747–450.

Gilbert, C. D. (1992). Horizontal integration and cortical dynamics. *Neuron, 9,* 1–20.

Gilbert, C. D., & Wiesel, T. N. (1979). Morphology and intracortical projections of functionally identified neurons in cat visual cortex. *Nature, 280,* 120–125.

Gilbert, C. D., & Wiesel, T. N. (1983). Clustered intrinsic connections in cat visual cortex. *Journal of Neuroscience, 3,* 1116–1133.

Gilbert, C. D., & Wiesel, T. N. (1989). Columnar specificity of intrinsic horizontal and corticocortical connections in cay visual cortex. *Journal of Neuroscience, 9,* 2432–2442.

Gilbert, C. D., & Wiesel, T. N. (1990). The influence of contextual stimuli on the orientation selectivity of cells in primary visual cortex of the cat. *Vision Research, 30,* 1689–1701.

Gilbert, C. D., & Wiesel, T. N. (1992). Receptive field dynamics in adult primary visual cortex. *Nature, 356,* 150–152.

Hamos, J. E., Horn, S. C., Raczkowski, D., Uhlrich, D. J., & Sherman, S. M. (1985). Synaptic connectivity of a local circuit neuron in the cat's lateral geniculate nucleus. *Nature, 317,* 618–621.

Heinen, S. J., & Skavenski, A. A. (1991). Recovery of visual responses in foveal V1 neurons following bilateral foveal lesions in adult monkey. *Experimental Brain Research, 83,* 670–674.

Hubel, D. H., & Wiesel, T. N. (1974). Uniformity of monkey striate cortex: A parallel relationship between field size, scatter and magnification factor. *Journal of Comparative Neurology, 158,* 295–306.

Humphrey, A. L., Sur, M., Uhlrich, D. J., & Sherman, S. M. (1985). Projection patterns of individual X- and Y-cell axons from the lateral geniculate nucleus to cortical area 17 in the cat. *Journal of Comparative Neurology, 233,* 159–189.

Jenkins, W. M., Merzenich, M. M., Ochs, M. T., Allard, T., & Guic-Rocbles, E. (1990). Functional reorganization of primary somatosensory cortex in adult owl monkeys after behaviorally controlled tactile stimulation. *Journal of Neurophysiology, 63,* 82–104.

Kaas, J. H., Krubitzer, L. A., Chino, Y. M., Langston, A. L., Polley, E. H., & Blair, N. (1990). Reorganization of retinotopic cortical maps in adult mammals after lesions of the retina. *Science, 248,* 229–231.

Kapadia, M. K., Gilbert, C. D., & Westheimer, G. (1994). *A quantitative measure for short-term cortical plasticity in human vision.* Journal of Neuroscience, 14, 451–457.

Karni, A., & Sagi, D. (1991). Where practice makes perfect in texture discrimination: Evidence for primary visual cortex plasticity. *Proceedings of the National Academy of Sciences of the United States of America, 88,* 4966–4970.

Lee, C. J., & Whitsel, B. L. (1992). Mechanisms underlying somatosensory cortical dynamics: I. In vivo studies. *Cerebral Cortex, 2,* 81–106.

Martin, K. A. C., & Whitteridge, D. (1984). Form, function and intracortical projections of spin neurnes in the striate visual cortex of the cat. *Journal of Physiology, 353,* 463–504.

McKee, S. P., & Westheimer, G. (1978). Stereoscopic acuity for moving retinal images. *Journal of the Optical Society of America, 68,* 450–455.

Merzenich, M. M., Nelson, R. J., Stryker, M. P., Cynader, M. S., Schoppmann, A., & Zook, J. M. (1984). Somatosensory cortical map changes following digital amputation in adult monkeys. *Journal of Comparative Neurology, 224,* 591–605.

Merzenich, M. M., Recanzone, G., Jenkins, W. M., Allard, T. T., & Nudo, R. J. (1988). Cortical representational plasticity. In P. Rakic & W. Singer (Eds.), *Neurobiology of neocortex* (pp. 41–68). Chichester: Wiley.

Paradiso, M. A., & Nakayama, K. (1991). Brightness perception and filling-in. *Vision Research, 31,* 1221–1236.

Pettet, M. W., & Gilbert, C. D. (1992). Dynamic changes in receptive field size in cat primary visual cortex. *Proceedings of the National Academy of Sciences of the United States of America, 89,* 8366–8370.

Poggio, T., Fahle, M., & Edelman, S. (1992). Fast perceptual learning in visual hyperacuity. *Science, 256,* 1018–1021.

Pons, T. P., Garraghty, P. E., Ommaya, A. K., Kaas, J. H., Taub, E., & Mishkin, M. (1991). Massive cortical reorganization after sensory deafferentation in adult macaques. *Science, 252,* 1857–1860.

Ramachandran, V. S., & Gregory, T. L. (1991). Perceptual filling in of artificially induced scotomas in human vision. *Nature, 350,* 699–702.

Rasmusson, D. D. (1982). Reorganization of raccoon somatosensory cortex following removal of the fifth digit. *Journal of Comparative Neurology, 205,* 313–326.

Rasmusson, D. D., Turnbill, B. G., & Leech, C. K. (1985). Unexpected reorganization of somatosensory cortex in a raccoon with extensive forelimb loss. *Neuroscience Letters, 55,* 167–172.

Recanzone, G. H., Merzenich, M. M., Jenkins, W. M., Kamil, A. G., & Dinse, H. R. (1992). Topographic reorganization of the hand representation in cortical area 3b of owl monkeys trained in a frequency-discrimination task. *Journal of Neurophysiology, 67,* 1031–1056.

Rockland, K. S., & Lund, J. S. (1982). Widespread periodic intrinsic connections in the tree shew visual cortex. *Brain Research, 169,* 19–40.

Rockland, K. S., & Lund, J. S. (1983). Intrinsic laminar lattice connections in primate visual cortex. *Journal of Comparative Neurology, 216,* 303–318.

Sanes, J. N., Suner, S., Lando, J. F., & Donoghue, J. P. (1988). Rapid reorganization of adult rat motor cortex somatic representation patterns after motor nerve injury. *Proceedings of the National Academy of Sciences of the United States of America, 85,* 2003–2007.

Sanes, J. N., Wang, J., & Donoghue, J. P. (1992). Immediate and delayed changes of rat motor cortical output representation with new forelimb configurations. *Cerebral Cortex, 2,* 141–152.

Volchan, E., & Gilbert, C. D. (1992). Cortical mechanisms of receptive field expansion in the cat striate cortex. *Society for Neuroscience Abstracts, 18,* 209.

Wall, P. D., & Werman, R. (1976). The physiology and anatomy of long ranging afferent fibres within the spinal cord. *Journal of Physiology, 255,* 321–334.

Weinberger, N. M., Ashe, J., & Edeline, J. M. (in press). Learning-induced receptive field plasticity in the auditory cortex: Specificity of information storage. In J. Delacour (Ed.), *Neural bases of learning and memory.* Singapore: World Scientific Publishing.

Westheimer, G., & Truong, T. T. (1988). Target crowding in foveal and peripheral stereoacuity. *American Journal of Optometry and Physiology in Optics, 65,* 395–399.

12

The Plasticity of Sensory Representations in Adult Primates

JON H. KAAS

Functional circuits in the brain must be capable of change because we learn, acquire new or improved skills, compensate for hearing loss, glasses and other modifications of sensory inputs, and recover to varying extents from strokes and other types of brain damage. Yet, except for a few brain structures such as the hippocampus, it has been difficult to determine where and how changes in the mature brain take place. Thus, there has been only limited progress in understanding the mechanisms of brain plasticity, and in acquiring the means to promote and maximize this process. Nevertheless, there are reasons for optimism, and new understandings are starting to emerge. This is because brain changes can be effectively studied in the multiple representations of sensory surfaces that exist in sensory and motor systems. Sensory representations are often large, especially in cortex, and their normal and altered organizations can be determined by microelectrode mapping techniques. Moreover, reorganizations can be induced in these representations that are of magnitudes well beyond the level of detection with current procedures, so that the parameters of change can be studied.

The discovery of extensive plasticity in adult sensory and motor systems was somewhat unexpected. Until recently, it was commonly thought that the organization's sensory systems were stable in adults, and were only susceptible to alteration during development, where susceptibility was often confined to a narrow window of time, the critical period (see Hubel & Wiesel, 1970). Early reports of adult plasticity were treated with suspicion. A common response was "we know that this just can't happen." But reorganizations have now been described in a large number of studies from a number of laboratories and in all major systems, and the basic phenomenon now seems well accepted (for earlier reviews, see Kaas, 1991; Kaas, Merzenich, & Killackey, 1983). Thus, we can expect an even greater surge in experimental investigation. In view of this expectation, it seems appropriate to ask, "What have we learned, and what do we need to know?"

To help answer these questions, this chapter concentrates on aspects of adult plasticity in sensory maps. Our research has focused on sensory maps in the cortex of monkeys. Such maps are large relative to the scale of the microelectrode mapping procedures, are often highly accessible on the surface of the brain, and a number of such representations exist in cortex for each sensory modality. Much of our research has been on the representation of the hand in the somatosensory areas of the anterior parietal cortex. The glabrous hand is an important sensory surface for monkeys, and the hand occupies a large extent of somatosensory representations, some of which are exposed on the brain surface in New World primates such as owl and squirrel monkeys. Our research on the plasticity of visual cortex has been more limited, but it includes studies in monkeys and cats. Map reorganization in auditory cortex has not been extensively studied, in part because the normal organization of auditory cortex in primates is not well understood, but some of our preliminary findings are included in this chapter. Several conclusions based on experimental results follow.

CORTICAL REPRESENTATIONS IN THE SENSORY AND MOTOR SYSTEMS ARE CAPABLE OF REORGANIZATION AFTER PARTIAL DEACTIVATIONS

Much of neocortex of all mammals is occupied by systematic representations of sensory surfaces. The number of representations, however, varies from few in mammals with proportionately little neocortex to many in higher primates (see Kaas, 1987). Parts of these orderly representations can be deactivated by removing inputs from sectors of the sensory surfaces. For example, a sensory nerve can be blocked or cut, a region of retina can be lesioned, or hair cells in high- or low-tone portions of the cochlea can be damaged. Such procedures remove the normal source of activation for parts of sensory maps. A similar procedure of cutting nerves to muscles can deprive parts of motor cortex of its normal effector target. The questions we and others have asked are if these deprivations are effective in deactivating parts of sensory or motor maps, and, if so, is there any recovery over time.

Remarkably, cortical sensory and motor maps have the potential for major reorganizations and reactivations after such procedures. Our early research on the plasticity of sensory cortex showed that the large hand representation in primary somatosensory cortex (area 3b) of monkeys (Fig. 12.1A–12.1C) is capable of major change (Huerta, Wall, & Kaas, 1986; Merzenich et al., 1983a). When we cut and sutured (to prevent regeneration) the median nerve to the thumb (D1) side of the glabrous hand, the driving input, as relayed over brain stem and thalamic structures, was removed for nearly half of the large hand representation (Fig. 12.1D). If cortical maps were completely stable in adults, one would expect this procedure to deactivate the deprived half of the representation. Instead, when the cortex was mapped with microelectrodes several months after the deafferentation, the deprived portion of cortex was activated by other, normally innervated parts of

A. Location of Map

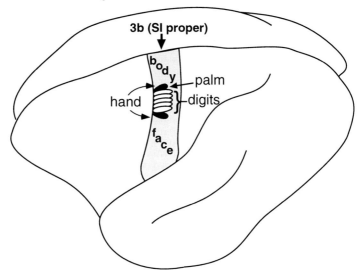

3b (SI proper)

body

palm

hand

digits

face

B. Representation Order

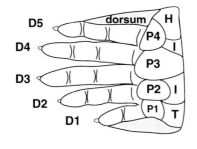

D5   dorsum   H
D4   P4
                I
D3   P3
D2   P2   I
        D1   P1   T

C. Normal Map

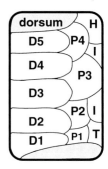

dorsum   H
D5   P4
          I
D4
          P3
D3
D2   P2   I
D1   P1   T

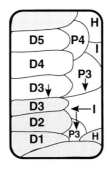

D5   P4
      I
D4
      P3
D3
Deprived

D. Portion deprived by nerve section

H
D5   P4
      I
D4
      P3
D3↓
D3   ←I
D2
D1   P3   H

E. Reorganization after nerve section

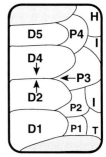

H
D5   P4
      I
D4↓
      ←P3
D2↑
      P2   I
D1   P1   T

F. Reorganization after D3 removed

the hand (Fig. 12.1E), largely the dorsal hairy surfaces of the same digits with glabrous skin denervated by section of the median nerve. Even more remarkably, after completely removing inputs from the glabrous skin of the hand by section of both the median nerve to the D1 side of the glabrous hand and the ulnar nerve to the D5 side of the glabrous hand, the map of the hand in area 3b became responsive throughout to the remaining inputs from the back of the hand (Garraghty & Kaas, 1991a). A more restricted sensory loss of all inputs from a single digit (Merzenich et al., 1984) resulted in cortex formerly devoted to that digit becoming responsive to inputs from adjoining digits (Fig. 12.1E), and a much larger denervation of all afferents from the complete forelimb, given a long recovery (years), resulted in complete reactivation of forelimb cortex by afferents from the face (Pons et al., 1991). Such recoveries are not limited to monkeys. Reactivations after nerve block or section or digit loss have been reported for rats (Wall & Cusick, 1984), cats (Kalaska & Pomeranz, 1979; Metzler & Marks, 1979), raccoons (Kelahan & Doetsch, 1984; Rasmusson, 1982), and bats (Calford & Tweedale, 1988, 1991a).

The reorganizations reported after peripheral nerve block or damage are not limited to primary somatosensory cortex (area 3b), and they probably occur in all other somatosensory fields. Reorganizations have been reported for area 1 of monkeys (Merzenich et al., 1983a), but other cortical fields have not yet been considered after such manipulations. However, given the essential role of area 3b in activating the second somatosensory area (S-II) in monkeys (Garraghty, Pons, & Kaas, 1990; Pons, Garraghty, Friedman, & Mishkin, 1987), S-II and other higher fields must reflect changes relayed from area 3b. Furthermore, lesions of cortex that deprive parts of S-II of activating input are followed by a recovery of responsiveness and a reorganized map in S-II (Pons, Garraghty & Mishkin, 1988).

Reorganizations also occur in visual and auditory cortex of adult mammals. In our own studies of plasticity in primary visual cortex of cats (VI), regions of cortex were binocularly deprived of normal activation by placing a small 5°–10°

FIGURE 12.1. Types of reorganization of primary somatosensory cortex (area 3b) of monkeys after nerve cut or digit removal. (A) Dorsolateral view of an owl monkey brain showing the location of the representation of the hand in area 3b. (B) The topography of the hand representation in area 3b; glabrous digits are presented in order, the glabrous palm is split so that digit pads reach the border, and representations of the dorsal digits and hand (shaded area) are medial and lateral. (C) The topography of the hand representation as compressed to fit area 3b. (D) The portion of the hand representation deprived of normal activation by cutting the median nerve to the thumb (D1) side of the glabrous hand. (E) The reorganization of the activation pattern determined months after nerve section. The deprived region is activated largely by the dorsal surfaces of digits 1–3 (based on Merzenich et al., 1983a). (F) The reorganization that occurs after removal of digit 3. The deprived cortex becomes activated by the glabrous surfaces of digits 2 and 4 (based on Merzenich et al., 1984). Digits and palm pads are numbered, and thenar, hypothenar, and insular pads are lettered.

laser lesion in the retina of one eye and removing the other eye. When recordings were made months later, the deprived region of cortex had become activated by inputs from regions of the retina around the lesion (Chino, Kaas, Smith, Langston, & Cheng, 1992; Kaas et al., 1990). Similar reorganizations have been reported for V1 of macaque monkeys after matched retinal lesions in both eyes (Gilbert & Wiesel, 1992; Heinen & Skavenski, 1991). In the auditory system, Robertson and Irvine (1989) deprived part of primary auditory cortex (A1) of rodents by lesioning the midfrequency portion of the cochlea. After a period of recovery, neurons in the deprived region of A1 responded to higher or lower frequencies at normal thresholds. Similarly, we have used drugs to damage hair cells and selectively deafen monkeys for high frequencies (Schwaber, Garraghty, & Kaas, 1993). Primary auditory cortex that was formerly activated by high frequencies in these monkeys became responsive to lower frequencies. Thus, rather extensive but partial deactivations of both primary visual cortex and primary auditory cortex are followed by map reorganization so that intact portions of the receptor sheets enlarge their cortical representations and fill the deprived zones.

Motor maps in cortex are also capable of reorganization after lesions that deactivate or remove muscle groups. In rats, forelimb amputation or section of the motor nerve to the musculature of facial vibrissae is followed by a reorganization of primary motor cortex (MI) so that electrical stimulation of sectors of MI formerly devoted to removed or inactivated muscles produced movements of normally innervated muscles of the body (Donoghue, Suner, & Sanes, 1990; Sanes, Suner, Lando, & Donoghue, 1988; Sanes, Suner, & Donoghue, 1990). It also appears that motor cortex of humans reorganizes after limb amputations so that cortex related to that limb represents movements of other parts of the body (Cohen, Bandinelli, Findley, & Hallett, 1991).

WHAT IS THE RATE OF REORGANIZATION?

Some types of reorganization emerge immediately after the experimental manipulation, while other changes take weeks or longer to develop. These differences in time courses suggest that a number of different mechanisms are involved.

In an early study of the time course of reorganization of area 3b of monkeys after median nerve cut, different monkeys were studied at various times after nerve section, and one monkey was sequentially recorded before and immediately after nerve section, and then 11, 22, and 144 days later (Merzenich et al., 1983b). Immediately after nerve section, nearly half of the deprived zone of cortex was already responsive to stimuli on the back of the hand, although the rest of the depressed zone was unresponsive. At 11 days, much of the deprived zone remained unresponsive. By 22 days, however, almost all of the cortex had recovered. A similar, but more rapid progressive recovery occurs after nerve cut in rats (Wall & Cusick, 1984). Thus, the recovery seems to depend on a mixture of rapid and slow changes.

Other studies have shown that under some conditions neurons in deprived cortex can acquire new receptive fields (within minutes or hours). New receptive fields have been found immediately after digit amputation in raccoons (Kelahan & Doetsch, 1984; also see Turnbull & Rasmasson, 1990, where only offset responses were noted), bats (Calford & Tweedale, 1988; 1991a), and rats (Byrne & Calford, 1991), and after anesthetic block in cats (Metzler & Marks, 1979) and monkeys (Calford & Tweedale, 1991b). In our studies of visual cortex reorganization in cats, we found that no map reorganization occurs after a lesion of only one retina, even after long periods of recovery, if the other eye is intact. Reorganization related to a long-standing lesion, however, immediately follows the removal of the intact eye (Chino et al., 1992).

Such changes in cortical organization suggest that any input can have a suppressive or inhibitory effect on other inputs, so they are not normally expressed. Thus, one mechanism of reorganization may be the reduction of "lateral" inhibition in the system, as a result of removing the input that activates the lateral inhibition (e.g., see Jacobs & Donoghue, 1991). Other immediate effects may be mediated by the short-term persistence of generalized activation produced by the burst of neural activity that can accompany injury. The activation of widespread excitatory pathways can potentiate the specific somatosensory relays. For example, neurons in the brainstem that release the neurotransmitter, acetylcholine, project broadly to cortex. The activation of this system could produce widespread increases in neural activity, including the emergence of previously subthreshold responses in deprived cortex (see Juliano, Ma, & Eslin, 1991; Webster, Hanisch, Dykes, & Biesold, 1991). The changes that persist or develop over longer times could also depend on this system and on a wide range of other modifications and regulations. Lower levels of neural activity can promote compensatory reductions in GABA expression (see Garraghty et al., 1990), synaptic effectiveness might increase (see Bear, Cooper, & Ebner, 1987; Brown, Chapman, Kairiss, Keenan, 1988; Kano, Iino, & Kano, 1991), and new synapses and local connections might form (e.g., Ganchrow & Bernstein, 1981).

THE EXTENT OF THE REORGANIZATION VARIES
WITH TIME OF RECOVERY AND TYPE OF DEPRIVATION

As already noted, the amount of deprived cortex reactivated after median nerve section in monkeys increases in time over a period of weeks (Merzenich et al., 1983b). An even greater amount of cortex is reactivated in monkeys studied years after deafferentation of the entire forearm (Pons et al., 1991), suggesting that further change may take place after months. Clearly, further investigation is needed.

The amount of reactivation also varies with type of deprivation. A large expanse of cortex including ~90% of the hand representation reorganizes to represent the back of the hand after median and ulnar nerve section in monkeys (Garraghty & Kaas, 1991a), while reactivation of a much smaller zone of deprived cortex in the same time period is incomplete after cutting the ulnar and radial nerves (Garraghty, Hanes, Florence, & Kaas, 1992) or removal of two digits (Merzenich et al., 1984). These puzzling differences, we believe, relate to structural features of the somatosensory system (see below) that may be species-variable.

SOME FEATURES OF CORTICAL REORGANIZATION ARE RELAYED FROM SUBCORTICAL STATIONS

There have long been reports of somatotopic reorganizations in the spinal cord (Devor & Wall, 1981; Lisney, 1983), dorsal column nuclei (Kalaska & Pomeranz, 1982; Miller, Basbaum, & Wall, 1976), and thalamus (Wall & Egger, 1971) after peripheral nerve damage. However, the validity of such reports has been questioned, in part because these structures, especially in rats, are small and difficult to map, and small measurement errors could produce the effects (see Wilson & Snow, 1987). Nevertheless, such reports raise the possibility that some or all of the changes seen in cortex are simply relayed from reorganized lower structures. We have recently obtained evidence for extensive reorganization of the ventroposterior (VP) nucleus after ulnar and median nerve section in squirrel monkeys. Squirrel monkeys provided several advantages in studying the possibility of reorganization in VP. In squirrel monkeys, a large, histologically distinct subnucleus represents the hand (Kaas, Nelson, Sur, Dykes, & Merzenich, 1984). As for the hand area of somatosensory cortex, cutting the median and ulnar nerves, thereby deafferenting all of the glabrous skin of the hand, would deprive 90% or more of the subnucleus in VP. Because of the large size of the subnucleus and its clear boundaries, 20–30 recording sites could be spaced across the nucleus in a single case. Such recordings obtained 2–5 months after the nerve sections revealed that all of the subnucleus was activated by inputs from the dorsal hand (Garraghty & Kaas, 1991a). About 90% of the nucleus was reactivated, and the reactivation was similar to that seen in area 3b of these same monkeys (Garraghty & Kaas, 1991b). Thus, the cortical reactivation could be largely or completely accounted for by the thalamic reorganization.

While some types of cortical reorganization may depend on the plasticity of subcortical structures, not all cortical changes can be explained this way. For instance, a more limited reactivation takes place in the lateral geniculate nucleus of cats after retinal lesions (Eysel, 1982; Gonzalez-Aquilar, & Mayer, 1980), and the extent of this geniculate reactivation cannot account for the extent of the cortical reactivation (Kass et al., 1990). Similarly, the amount of reactivation thought to occur in the lateral geniculate nucleus of monkeys would not account for the cortical reorganization (Gilbert & Wiesel, 1992). It is also difficult to account for cortical plasticity after cortical lesions in terms of subcortical mechanisms. For example, lesions of SI (3b) abolish the cutaneous driving of neurons in S-II of monkeys (Garraghty et al., 1990; Pons et al., 1987); but partial lesions of SI removing the hand representation are followed by reorganization of S-II so that all parts of S-II are activated and the foot representation is enlarged (Pons, Garraghty, & Mishkin, 1988). Since the deprivation in S-II depends on disrupting a cortical relay, recovery almost certainly depends on cortical mechanisms. In a similar manner, deprived parts of the middle temporal visual area may recover responsiveness to visual stimuli after lesions of parts of area 17 (Kaas & Krubitzer, 1992).

NERVE REGENERATION CAN RESTORE NORMAL ORGANIZATION

While a nerve cut or crush can abolish the central flow of sensory activity, deprive portions of central representations, and produce central reorganizations, cut or crushed nerves can regenerate, and this regeneration can take place after reorganization has occurred. Thus, an obvious question is how regeneration impacts on the reorganized maps.

The question is best addressed by crushing rather than cutting nerves, since crushed nerves can regenerate accurately, but cut nerves often regenerate only in part, and with many location errors (see Wall & Kaas, 1985). When the median nerve was crushed in the lower arm of monkeys, it took well over a month for the nerve to regenerate into the glabrous skin of the hand, during which time the cortex would completely reorganize as a result of deprivation (see Merzenich et al., 1983a). In fact, recordings made in such monkeys one month after nerve crush showed that most of the deprived cortex was abnormally activated by the back of digits 1–3, as in monkeys with a permanent loss of median nerve input (Wall et al., 1986). In contrast, monkeys recorded after 6 or more months of recovery had fully regenerated median nerves and completely normal maps of the hand in area 3b (Wall, Felleman, & Kaas, 1983). Moreover, in monkeys recorded both before crush and after regeneration, the individual maps specific to each monkey were reestablished. This suggests that the connectional framework established during development is not fully degraded during adult deprivation, and that the potency of this framework returns so that it displaces others when normal activity in peripheral nerves is restored.

REORGANIZATION CAN BE A RESULT OF STIMULATION AS WELL AS DEPRIVATION

Our general view is that reorganization is the result of dramatic changes in activity patterns in parts of representations (e.g., Kaas et al., 1983). Changes should result from overstimulation as well as deprivation. For example, when monkeys were trained to overstimulate the skin of part of the hand, increases in the representation of the stimulated skin were found in area 3b (Jenkins, Merzenich, Ochs, Allard, & Guic-Robles, 1990; Recanzone, Merzenich, Jenkins, Kamil, & Druse, 1992a). However, larger and more consistent map changes were produced by directly stimulating parts of the map in area 3b through microelectrodes, so that adjoining parts of the map came to represent the stimulated part (Recanzone, Merzenich, & Dinse, 1992b). Stimulating motor cortex also produces changes in map structure (Nudo, Jenkins, & Merzenich, 1990).

PLASTICITY MAY RESULT FROM THE REPLACEMENT OF DEACTIVATED INPUTS WITH POTENTIATED, PREVIOUSLY INEFFECTIVE INPUTS

The bulk of the results on adult plasticity support the hypothesis that more active inputs displace and substitute for less active inputs (Garraghty & Kaas, 1992; Kaas et al., 1983; Kaas, 1991; Merzenich, Reconzone, Jenkins, & Grajski, 1990). We propose that deactivated pathways relay greatly reduced levels of neural activity, and that these newly inactive connections can be effectively replaced by previously existing connections with subthreshold effects that become potentiated by being proportionately more active than the deactivated pathways. The mechanisms of displacement are uncertain, but they probably include an array of cellular adjustments, including an immediate rebalancing of inhibitory and excitatory circuits to formulate a new setpoint, as well as induced increases and decreases in the expression of neurotransmitters and modulators (see Garraghty, Lachica, & Kaas, 1991), and the generation and placement of synapses. Hebbian mechanisms of increasing and decreasing synaptic strength (see Brown, Kairiss, & Keenan, 1990) through synchronous and asynchronous activity in pre- and postsynaptic cells may be important in this framework of activity-dependent plasticity (see Kaas, 1991). The general magnitudes of changes and the reversibility of at least some of the changes are observations that are consistent with this possibility.

Substitutions could occur at several levels (Fig. 12.2). We have previously emphasized the possible role of overlapping thalamocortical arbors, so that previously ineffective fringes of highly active arbors become more potent and replace formerly effective but deactivated arbors. Since arbor widths of these axons are generally in the range of ~0.5 mm (e.g., Blasdel & Lund, 1983; Garraghty & Sur, 1990; Garraghty, Pons, Sur, & Kaas, 1989), such reorganizations would expectedly be on the order of 1 mm or less of cortical width. More extensive cortical reorganizations do occur, however, and they might depend on lateral, intrinsic connections within areas, as emphasized by Gilbert and Wiesel (1992), or on the overlap of converging corticocortical connections for higher order representations, depending on cortical inputs.

Other substitutions might occur at subcortical levels and be relayed to cortex. Only limited reorganization would be expected in thalamic nuclei such as the lateral geniculate nucleus because the arbors of input axons are restricted and would mediate little lateral spread. Consistent with this assumption, little reorganization occurs in the lateral geniculate nucleus, and thus the reorganization observed in visual cortex is largely mediated by cortical changes. Similar assumptions apply to the ventroposterior nucleus. Arbors from the medial lemniscus are limited in extent, and they would not mediate extensive reorganizations through

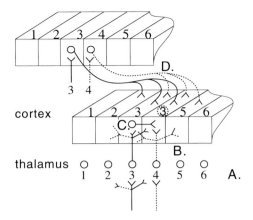

FIGURE 12.2. Possible substitutions that reorganize cortex. Modifications may depend on substitutions where neurons formerly activated by inactive arbors (dotted lines) become activated by the potentiated fringes of adjacent, normally activated arbors. (A) Subcortical substitutions of active for inactive overlapping arbors may occur in the thalamus, brain stem, and spinal cord. (B) Substitution often may be of one set of thalamocortical arbors for another. (C) Other substitutions may involve normally subthreshold, lateral intrinsic connections within a field that becomes potentiated. (D) Overlapping active corticocortical inputs may gain potency and substitute for inactive inputs.

overlap. Nevertheless, the complete hand subnucleus of the ventroposterior nucleus reorganizes after cutting the median and ulnar nerves. This reorganization cannot be a result of substitutions of medial lemniscus inputs through arbor overlap.

There are at least two ways of accounting for the reorganization in the ventroposterior nucleus. One possibility is that spinothalamic inputs to this nucleus distribute in a pattern that is somatotopically less precise than the medial lemniscus pattern. The spinothalamic pattern normally is not expressed, however, but it becomes potent after deactivations that remove competing medial lemniscus inputs. There is some experimental support for this hypothesis. In rats, lesions of the principal trigeminal nucleus remove the equivalent of the medial lemniscus input to the ventroposterior nucleus, and the equivalent of the spinothalamic inputs becomes effective and reactivates the nucleus (Rhoades, Belford, & Killackey, 1987). The neurons newly activated by these inputs have much larger than normal receptive fields. Something similar could happen in monkeys. An alternative explanation is that the switching in monkeys took place at an earlier level in the cuneate subnucleus of the dorsal column-trigeminal complex (Fig. 12.3). The cuneate nucleus is subdivided into clusters of cells that are isolated within a fiber-rich, cell-poor matrix. Different clusters of neurons receive inputs from different digits, but the same clusters receive inputs from both dorsal and ventral surfaces of the digits (Florence, Wall, & Kaas, 1991). This arrangement would make it unlikely that arbors related to different digits would overlap and could substitute for each other in the cuneate nucleus, but arbors related to the dorsal surface of a

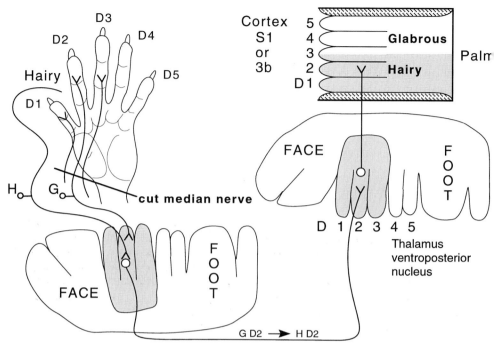

FIGURE 12.3.   Small-scale substitution in the cuneate nucleus may result in major reorganization in the cortex. Inputs from the dorsal surfaces and ventral surfaces of each finger converge on a single cell cluster in the cuneate nucleus (see Florence et al., 1991). Cutting the median nerve would deactivate much of these cell clusters, and allow inputs from dorsal skin via the radial nerve to gain effectiveness and activate entire clusters. The reactivated clusters would relay to the thalamus and then to the cortex. At both of these levels, massive reorganizations would be expressed. *H*, hairy skin; *G*, glabrous skin; *D1-5*, digits of the hand; *shading*, parts of the hand representation formerly devoted to the glabrous hand that come to represent the hairy skin of the hand; *crosshatching*, normal cortical representation of the hairy hand (see Fig. 12.1).

digit probably overlap and could substitute for those related to the ventral surface of the same digit. Thus, small local substitutions at the brainstem level could have a major reorganizing impact at the cortical level of the system. Much larger subcortical substitutions would be needed, however, to produce the more limited cortical reorganizations that follow digit amputations, and thus they most likely are limited by the framework for substitution in area 3b.

Other mechanisms appear to be necessary to explain the massive cortical reorganization that occurs following long-standing section of the dorsal roots to deafferent the entire forelimb of monkeys (Pons et al., 1991). In such monkeys, studied years after surgery, the large forelimb and hand sector of area 3b is responsive throughout to stimuli on the lower face. The extent of this reorganization is well beyond that made possible by overlaps in thalamocortical arbors, and no projections from the face subnucleus of the ventroposterior nucleus terminate in the hand and forelimb region of 3b. There are also no known intrinsic connections between face and forelimb regions of cortex. It also seems unlikely that higher order somatosensory areas such as S-II provide feedback connections capable of activating area 3b, and feedback connections from the face in S-II to 3b appear to be at least grossly somatotopic (e.g., Krubitzer & Kaas, 1990) so that they would not activate the hand region of area 3b. Although large-scale sprouting following injury is thought to occur only early in life, the results from these massively deprived monkeys support the possibility that new connections can form in adult monkeys, given sufficient time and substantial deprivation. The reorganization could be mediated by the new growth that occurs cortically or subcortically, but the distances involved would be shorter subcortically (see Florence, Garraghty, Carlson, & Kaas, 1993). For instance, medial lemniscus axons course past the hand subnucleus of VP to terminate in the face subnucleus, and these axons could be induced to sprout collaterals that would innervate the hand subnucleus. This activation would then be relayed to cortex. The exciting implication about this possibility is that regions of the brain with normal connections, but greatly reduced levels of neural activity, can compensate by releasing a growth factor that induces nearby axons to grow and form new connections. An understanding of the factors that promote and direct new growth clearly could be therapeutically significant. There is already indirect evidence that similar reorganizations occur in the brains of humans, since patients with forelimb amputations sometimes report stimuli on the lower face as colocalized on the missing limb (Ramachandran, Stewart, & Rogers-Ramachandran, 1992). Thus, new connections may form in the human brain as a result of deprivation.

CONCLUSIONS

Sensory and motor representations have the potential to express different maps of sensory surfaces and muscles after partial deactivation or increased stimulation. Most of the changes appear to be mediated by the potential of previously existing connections. A number of cellular mechanisms are likely to be involved, since reorganizations include rapid and slow components. Reorganizations occur in all sensory systems, and probably at all levels in each system. The types of substitutions that can occur at each level depend on the nature of the overlap in axon arbors so that an understanding of the potential for reorganization and the contribution made at each level depends on a detailed knowledge of the structural anatomy. This anatomy is so important that reorganization can be completely reversed by reactivating the deactivated pathways. Yet, some reorganization is of a magnitude that is difficult to explain by the substitution of one previously existing pathway for another, and the possibility of new growth in a deprived system needs to be considered.

REFERENCES

Bear, M. F., Cooper, L. N., & Ebner, F. F. (1987). A physiological basis for a theory of synapse modification. *Science, 237,* 42–48.

Blasdel, G. G., & Lund, J. S. (1983). Termination of afferent axons in macaque striate cortex. *Journal of Neuroscience, 3,* 1389–1413.

Brown, T. H., Chapman, P. F., Kairiss, E. W., and Keenan, C. L. (1988). Long-term synaptic potentiation. *Science, 243,* 724–728.

Brown, T. H., Kairiss, E. W., & Keenan, C. L. (1990). Hebbian synapses: Biophysical mechanisms and algorithms. *American Review of Neuroscience, 13,* 475–511.

Byrne, J. A., & Calford, M. B. (1991). Short-term expansion of receptive fields in rat primary somatosensory cortex after hindpaw digit denervation. *Brain Research, 565,* 218–224.

Calford, M. B., & Tweedale, R. (1988). Immediate and chronic changes in responses of somatosensory cortex in adult flying-fox after digit amputation. *Nature, 332,* 446–448.

Calford, M. B., & Tweedale, R. (1991a). Acute changes in cutaneous receptive fields in primary somatosensory cortex after digit denervation in adult flying foxes. *Journal of Neurophysiology, 65,* 178–187.

Calford, M. B., & Tweedale, R. (1991b). Immediate expansion of receptive fields of neurons in area 3b of macaque monkeys after digit denervation. *Somatosensory Motor Research, 8,* 249–260.

Chino, Y. M., Kaas, J. H., Smith, E. L., III, Langston, A.L., & Cheng, H. (1992). Rapid reorganization of cortical maps in adult cats following restricted deafferentation in retina. *Vision Research, 32,* 789–796.

Cohen, L. G., Bandinelli, S., Findley, T. W., & Hallett, M. (1991). Motor reorganization after upper limb amputation in man. A study with focal magnetic stimulation. *Brain, 114,* 615–627.

Devor, M., & Wall, P. D. (1981). Plasticity of spinal cord sensory map following peripheral nerve injury in rats. *Journal of Neuroscience, 1,* 679–684.

Donoghue, J. P., Suner, S., & Sanes, J. N. (1990). Dynamic organization of primary motor cortex output to target muscles in adult rats II. Rapid reorganization following motor nerve lesions. *Experimental Brain Research, 79,* 492–503.

Eysel, U. T. (1982). Functional reconnections without new axonal growth in a partially denervated visual relay nucleus. *Nature, 299,* 442–444.

Eysel, U. T., Gonzalez-Aquilar, F., & Mayer, U. (1981). Time-dependent decrease in the extent of visual deafferentation in the lateral geniculate nucleus of adult cats with small retinal lesions. *Experimental Brain Research, 41,* 256–263.

Florence, S. L., Wall, J. T., & Kaas, J. H. (1991). Central projections from the skin of the hand in squirrel monkeys. *Journal of Comparative Neurology, 311,* 563–578.

Florence, S. L., Garraghty, P. E., Carlson, M., & Kaas, J. H. (1993). Sprouting of peripheral nerve axons in the spinal cord of monkeys. *Brain Research, 601,* 343–348.

Ganchrow, D., & Bernstein, J. H. (1981). Bouton renewal patterns in rat hindlimb cortex after thoracic dorsal funicular lesions. *Journal of Neuroscience Research, 6,* 525–537.

Garraghty, P. E., & Kaas, J. H. (1991a). Large-scale functional reorganization in adult monkey cortex after peripheral nerve injury. *Proceedings of the National Academy of Sciences of the United States of America, 88,* 6976–6980.

Garraghty, P. E., & Kaas, J. H. (1991b). Functional reorganization in adult monkey thalamus after peripheral nerve injury. *NeuroReport, 2,* 747–750.

Garraghty, P. E., & Kaas, J. H. (1992). Dynamic features of sensory and motor maps. *Current Opinion in Neurobiology, 2,* 522–527.

Garraghty, P. E., & Sur, M. (1990). Morphology of single intracellularly stained axons terminating in area 3b of macaque monkeys. *Journal of Comparative Neurology, 294,* 583–593.

Garraghty, P. E., Lachica, E. A., & Kaas, J. H. (1991). Injury-induced reorganization of somatosensory cortex is accompanied by reductions in GABA staining. *Somatosensory Motor Research, 8,* 347–354.

Garraghty, P. E., Pons, T. P., & Kaas, J. H. (1990). Ablations of areas 3b (S1 Proper) and 3a of somatosensory cortex in marmosets deactivate the second and parietal ventral somatosensory areas. *Somatosensory and Motor Research, 7,* 125-135.

Garraghty, P. E., Hanes, D. P., Florence, S. L., & Kaas, J. H. (1992). The extent of cortical reorganization after nerve injury is limited by the content of the deprevation. *Society of Neuroscience Abstracts, 18,* 1548.

Garraghty, P. E., Pons, T. P., Sur, M., & Kaas, J. H. (1989). The arbors of axons terminating in middle cortical layers of somatosensory area 3b in owl monkeys. *Somatosensory Motor Research, 6,* 401-411.

Gilbert, C. D., & Wiesel, T. N. (1992). Receptive field dynamics in adult primary visual cortex. *Nature, 356,* 150-152.

Heinen, S. J., & Skavenski, A. A. (1991). Recovery of visual responses in foveal V1 neurons following bilateral foveal lesions in adult monkey. *Experimental Brain Research, 83,* 670-674.

Hubel, D. H., & Wiesel, T. N. (1970). The period of susceptibility to the physiological effects of unilateral eye closure in kittens. *Journal of Physiology, 206,* 419-436.

Huerta, M. F., Wall, J. T., & Kaas, J. H. (1986). Changes in topography of somatosensory cortex after nerve loss in adult and neonatal marmoset monkeys. *Society for Neuroscience Abstracts, 12,* 954.

Jacobs, K. M., & Donoghue, J. P. (1991). Reshaping the cortical motor map by unmasking latent intracortical connections. *Science, 251,* 944-947.

Jenkins, W. M., Merzenich, M. M., Ochs, M. T., Allard T., & Guic-Robles, E. (1990). Functional reorganization of primary somatosensory cortex in adult owl monkeys after behaviorally controlled tactile stimulation. *Journal of Neurophysiology, 63,* 82-104.

Juliano, S. L., Ma, W., & Eslin, D. (1991). Cholinergic depletion prevents expansion of topographic maps in somatosensory cortex. *Proceedings of the National Academy of Sciences of the United States of America, 88,* 780-784.

Kaas, J. H. (1987). The organization of neocortex in mammals: Implications for theories of brain function. *Annual Review of Psychiatry, 38,* 129-151.

Kaas, J. H. (1991). Plasticity of sensory and motor maps in adult mammals. *Annual Review of Neuroscience, 14,* 137-167.

Kaas, J. H., & Krubitzer, L. A. (1992). Area 17 lesions deactivate area MT in owl monkeys. *Visual Neuroscience, 9,* 399-407.

Kaas, J. H., Merzenich, M. M., & Killackey, H. P. (1983). The reorganization of somatosensory cortex following peripheral nerve damage in adult and developing mammals. *Annual Review of Neuroscience, 6,* 325-356.

Kaas, J. H., Krubitzer, L. A., Chino, Y. M., Langston, A. L., Polley, E. H., & Blair, N. (1990). Reorganization of retinotopic cortical maps in adult mammals after lesions of the retina. *Science, 248,* 229-231.

Kaas, J. H., Nelson, R. J., Sur, M., Dykes, R. W., & Merzenich, M. M. (1984). The somatopic organization of the ventroposterior thalamus of the squirrel monkey, *Saimiri sciureus, Journal of Comparative Neurology, 226,* 111-140.

Kalaska, J., & Pomeranz, B. (1979). Chronic paw denervation causes an age-dependent appearance of novel responses from forearm in "paw cortex" of kittens and adult cats. *Journal of Neurophysiology, 42,* 618-633.

Kalaska, J., & Pomeranz, B. (1982). Chronic peripheral nerve injuries after the somatotopic organization of the cuneate nucleus in kittens. *Brain Research, 236,* 35-47.

Kano, M., Iino, K., & Kano, M. (1991). Functional reorganization of adult cat somatosensory cortex is dependent on NMDA receptors. *NeuroReport, 2,* 77-80.

Kelahan, A. M., & Doetsch, G. S. (1984). Time-dependent changes in the functional organization of somatosensory cerebral cortex following digit amputation in adult raccoons. *Somatosensory Research, 2,* 49-81.

Krubitzer, L. A., & Kaas, J. H. (1990). The organization and connections of somatosensory cortex in marmosets. *Journal of Neuroscience, 10,* 952-974.

Lisney, S. J. W. (1983). Changes in the somatotopic organization of the cat lumbar spinal cord following peripheral nerve transection and regeneration. *Brain Research, 259,* 31-39.

Merzenich, M. M., Kaas, J. H., Wall, J., Nelson, R. J., Sur, M., & Felleman, D. (1983a). Topographic reorganization of somatosensory cortical areas 3b and 1 in adult monkeys following restricted deafferentation, *Neuroscience, 8,* 33-55.

Merzenich, M. M., Kaas, J. H. Wall, J. T., Sur, M., Nelson, R. J., & Felleman, D. J. (1983b). Progression of change following median nerve section in the cortical representation of the hand in areas 3b and 1 in adult owl and squirrel monkeys. *Neuroscience, 10,* 639-665.

Merzenich, M. M., Nelson, R. J., Stryker, M. P., Cynader, M. S., Schoppman, A., & Zook, J. M. (1984). Somatosensory cortical map changes following digit amputation in adult monkeys. *Journal of Comparative Neurology, 224,* 591-605.

Merzenich, M. M., Reconzone, G. H., Jenkins, W. M., & Grajski, K. A. (1990). Adaptive mechanisms in cortical networks underlying cortical contributions to learning and nondeclarative memory. *Cold Spring Harbor Symposium on Quantum Biology, 55,* 873-887.

Metzler, J., & Marks, P. S. (1979). Functional changes in cat somatic sensory-motor cortex during short-term reversible epidural blocks. *Brain Research, 177,* 379-383.

Miller, J., Basbaum, A. I., & Wall, P. D. (1976). Restructuring of the somatotopic map and appearance of abnormal activity in the gracile nucleus after partial deafferentation. *Experiments in Neurology, 50,* 658-672.

Nudo, R. J., Jenkins, W. M., & Merzenich, M. M. (1990). Repetitive microstimulation alters the cortical representation of movements in adult rats. *Somatosensory Motor Research, 7,* 463-483.

Pons, T. P., Garraghty, P. E., Friedman, D. P., & Mishkin, M. (1987). Physiological evidence for serial processing in somatosensory cortex. *Science, 237,* 417-420.

Pons, T. P., Garraghty, P. E., & Mishkin, M. (1988). Lesion-induced plasticity in the second somatosensory cortex of adult macaques. *Proceedings of the National Academy of Sciences of the United States of America, 85,* 5279-5281.

Pons, T. P., Garraghty, P. E., Ommaya, A. K., Kaas, J. H., Taub, E., & Mishkin, M. (1991). Massive cortical reorganization after sensory deafferentation in adult macaques. *Science, 252,* 1857-1860.

Ramachandran, V. S., Stewart, M., & Rogers-Ramachandran, D. C. (1992). Perceptual correlates of massive cortical reorganization. *NeuroReport, 3,* 583-587.

Rasmusson, D. D. (1982). Reorganization of raccoon somatosensory cortex following removal of the fifth digit. *Journal of Comparative Neurology, 205,* 313-326.

Reconzone, G. H., Merzenich, M. M., Jenkins, W. M., Kamil, A. G., & Dinse, H. R. (1992a). Topographic reorganization of the hand representation in cortical area 3b of owl monkeys trained in a frequency-discrimination task. *Journal of Neurophysiology, 67,* 1031-1056.

Reconzone, G. H., Merzenich, M. M., & Dinse, H. R. (1992b). Expansion of the cortical representation of a specific skin field in primary somatosensory cortex by intracortical microstimulation. *Cerebral Cortex, 2,* 181-196.

Rhoades, R. W., Belford, G. R., & Killackey, H. P. (1987). Receptive-field properties of rat ventral posterior medial neurons before and after selective kainic acid lesions of the trigeminal brain stem complex. *Journal of Neurophysiology, 57,* 1577-1600.

Robertson, D., & Irvine, D. R. F. (1989). Plasticity of frequency organization in auditory cortex of guinea pigs with partial unilateral deafness. *Journal of Comparative Neurology, 282,* 456-471.

Sanes, J. N., Suner, S., Lando, J. F., & Donoghue, J. P. (1988). Rapid reorganization of adult rat motor cortex somatic representation after motor nerve injury. *Proceedings of the National Academy of Sciences of the United States of America, 85,* 2003-2007.

Sanes, J. N., Suner, S., & Donoghue, J. P. (1990). Dynamic organization of primary motor cortex output to target muscles in adult rats. I. Long-term patterns of reorganization following motor or mixed nerve lesions. *Experimental Brain Research, 79,* 479-491.

Schwaber, M. K., Garraghty, P. E., and Kaas, J. H. (1993). Neuroplasticity of the adult primate auditory cortex following cochlear hearing loss. *Journal of Otology, 14,* 252-258.

Turnbull, B. G., & Rasmusson, D. D. (1990). Acute effects of total or partial digit denervation on raccoon somatosensory cortex. *Somatosensory Motor Research, 7,* 365–389.

Wall, J. T., & Cusick, C. G. (1984). Cutaneous responsiveness in primary somatosensory (S-I) hindpaw cortex before and after partial hindpaw deafferentation in adult rats. *Journal of Neuroscience, 4,* 1499–1515.

Wall, P. D., & Egger, M. D. (1971). Formation of new connections in adult rat brains after partial deafferentation. *Nature, 232,* 542–545.

Wall, J. T., Felleman, D. J., & Kaas, J. H. (1983). Recovery of normal topography in the somatosensory cortex of monkeys after nerve crush and regeneration. *Science, 221,* 771–773.

Wall, J. T., & Kaas, J. H. (1985). Cortical reorganization and sensory recovery following nerve damage and regeneration. In C. W. Cotman (Ed.), *Synaptic plasticity* (pp. 231–259). New York: Guilford.

Wall, J. T., Kaas, J. H., Sur, M., Nelson, R. J., Felleman, D. J., & Merzenich, M. M. (1986). Functional reorganization in somatosensory cortical areas 3b and 1 of adult monkeys after median nerve repair: Possible relationships to sensory recovery in humans. *Journal of Neuroscience, 6,* 218–233.

Webster, H. H., Hanisch, U.-K., Dykes, R. W., & Biesold, D. (1991). Basal forebrain lesions with or without reserpine injection inhibit cortical reorganization in rat hindpaw primary somatosensory cortex following sciatic nerve section. *Somatosensory Motor Research, 8,* 327–346.

Wilson, P., & Snow, P. J. (1987). Reorganization of the receptive fields of spinocervical tract neurons following denervation of a single digit in the cat. *Journal of Neurophysiology, 57,* 803–813.

13

In Vitro Studies of Visual Cortical Plasticity

K. TOYAMA
Y. KOMATSU
M. TANIFUJI

Studies of visual cortical (VC) plasticity for the last three decades (Blakemore & Cooper, 1970; Hebb, 1949; Wiesel & Hubel, 1965) have revealed that even the most elementary structures, such as retinotopy and columnar organization, including ocular dominance and orientation columns, depend on visual experience. For instance, the removal of retinal activity by injection of tetrodotoxin (Stryker & Harris, 1986) or the deprivation of visual experience by dark-rearing or by eyelid suture (Swindale, 1981; Wiesel & Hubel, 1965) impairs the proper development of these structures. The issue of VC plasticity has been mainly studied in in vivo preparations (Blakemore & Cooper, 1970; Stryker & Harris, 1986; Swindale, 1981; Wiesel & Hubel, 1965), and limited to the elucidation of modifiability in VC neuronal responsiveness.

NEURODYNAMICS IN VC CIRCUITRY STUDIED IN SLICE PREPARATIONS

In contrast to the abundance of knowledge about how neuronal responsiveness is modified by visual experience, very little is known about the changes in the VC neural circuitry underlying the VC plasticity. In order to solve this problem, we need to know the basic operation of VC circuitry. We investigated this question by using slice preparations and optical recording (Toyama & Tanifuji, 1991). Optical recording is a technique to stain neurons with a voltage-sensitive dye and to determine membrane potential changes as changes in light absorbance or fluorescence (Grinvald, 1985). Transverse slices were dissected from the VC of adult rats and stained with a voltage-sensitive dye (RH155). The neural events produced by white matter (WM) stimulation (asterisk and circle in Fig. 13.1A) were studied by time-lapse imaging of optical responses using a cooled charge-coupled device (CCD) digital video camera and using strobe illumination synchronized to WM stimulation.

The imaging of optical responses revealed a sequence of events: (1) impulses being propagated vertically from WM to the cortical surface along the geniculate axons as well as those propagated laterally along the axon collaterals of cortical efferent cells (Fig. 13.1B); (2) monosynaptic excitation produced in layer IV by the geniculate impulses, and that produced in layer VI by recurrent collateral impulses (Fig. 13.1C); (3) polysynaptic excitation transferred to layers II–III from layer IV (Fig. 13.1D); and finally (4) reverberation of the polysynaptic excitation in layers II–III back to layer V–VI, which peaked at several milliseconds after WM stimulation and continued for a few tens of milliseconds (Fig. 13.1E).

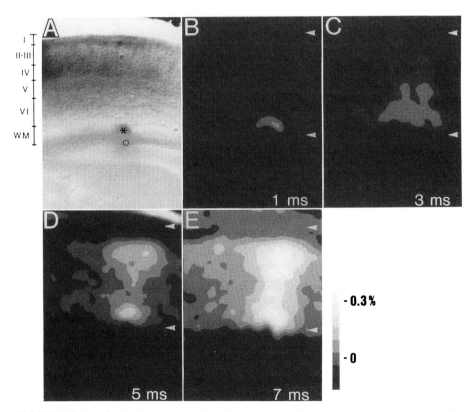

FIGURE 13.1.   Optical recording of excitation propagation in a visual cortical slice. (A) An image of visual cortical slice stained with a voltage-sensitive dye. Asterisk indicates the point (cathode) of WM stimulation (amplitude and duration of current pulses, 2 mA and 0.08 ms). (B)–(E) Time-lapse images of cortical excitation taken at different intervals after WM stimulation. Top and bottom arrows indicate cortical surface and border between VC and WM. (Toyama & Tanifuji, 1991.)

An interesting feature was that the excitation in layer VI produced by the recurrent collaterals was restricted to that layer, while the major component of the geniculate excitation produced in layer IV was transferred to the upper layers and further back to lower layers along a vertical column of roughly 500 μm width, although a weak component propagated laterally along layers II–III and V–VI, probably due to axon collaterals of efferent cells in these layers. This mode of excitation propagation was found in all slices studied ($n = 5$).

It was also found that partial removal of cortical inhibition by bicuculline (0.5 μM/l) very strongly enhanced the later stage of reverberation without practically affecting the early stages of excitation propagation, including monosynaptic and polysynaptic geniculate excitation. The excitation continued to increase for several hundred milliseconds and spread throughout the whole VC slice. These findings indicate that a reverberating pathway in which lateral geniculate nucleus (LGN) excitation is transferred through layers IV, II–III, V, and VI cells, and probably further back to layer IV cells, constructs the basic computational module in VC, and that studies of VC plasticity should reveal how neural elements in the modules are modified by visual signals.

LONG-TERM POTENTIATION
IN VISUAL CORTICAL SLICES

We have studied long-term potentiation (LTP) in VC slices to answer this question (Komatsu, Fujii, Maeda, Sakaguchi, & Toyama, 1988; Komatsu, Fujii, Nakajima, Umetani, & Toyama, 1985; Komatsu, Nakajima, & Toyama, 1991; Komatsu, Toyama, Maeda, & Sakaguchi, 1981; Toyama, Komatsu, Yamamoto, Kurotani, & Yamada, 1991). The experimental design was analogous to that used in hippocampal slices, where the investigation of LTP as a form of synaptic plasticity has been successfully used to demonstrate the power of slice preparations. Instead of natural visual experience, electrical stimulation of the WM was introduced to study the activity-dependent changes in synaptic transmission. These changes were assessed by analysis of the field potentials (FPs) and intracellular responses produced in VC by test stimulation.

Coronal sections (0.4–0.5 mm in thickness) were dissected from the VC (area 17) of infant kittens, and were perfused with Krebs-Ringer solution saturated with a mixture of 95% O_2 and 5% CO_2 (Fig. 13.2A). A pair of stimulating electrodes (s_1 and s_2 in Fig. 13.2A) were placed in the WM. A train of pulses was applied as conditioning stimuli through s_1, while single pulses were applied through s_2 as test stimuli to assess the changes in synaptic transmission that were caused by conditioning stimulation. A glass microelectrode (m_1) was inserted in the cortical slice to record the FPs extracellularly, and another microelectrode (m_2) was placed in the WM to monitor the effects of the conditioning and test stimulation (Fig. 13.2B).

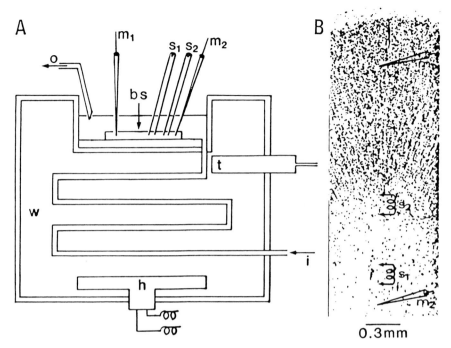

FIGURE 13.2. Experimental arrangement for slice experiments. (A) Schematic diagram illustrating a recording chamber. *bs*, visual cortical (VC) slice. m_1 and m_2, glass microelectrodes. S_1 and S_2, stimulating electrodes. (B) Arrangements of electrodes illustrated in a histological section of the slice. *i* and *o*, inlet and outlet of a perfusing system. *w*, water. *h*, a heater. *T*, a thermistor. (Komatsu et al., 1981.)

Dynamics of Long-Term Potentiation Induction and Expression

As expected, conditioning stimulation produced LTP of FPs evoked by test stimulation that lasted for more than 10 hours after full development (Fig. 13.3A). The LTP was basically similar to hippocampal LTP, but was different in many features. First of all, a short-term (order of seconds) high-frequency stimulation (50–100 Hz), which was most effective in inducing hippocampal LTP, was not effective in infant VC slices. Instead, long-term (30–60 min) low-frequency (2-Hz) stimulation was optimal for induction of LTP in VC slices. Second, development of LTP was much slower than that for hippocampal LTP. There was usually depression during conditioning stimulation, and LTP gradually developed for several hours after its termination (Fig. 13.3B and 13.4). This is in contrast to the very rapid onset of hippocampal LTP, which occurs immediately after posttetanic potentiation. These findings indicate that the induction and/or expression mechanisms for VC LTP have much slower dynamics than those for hippocampal LTP.

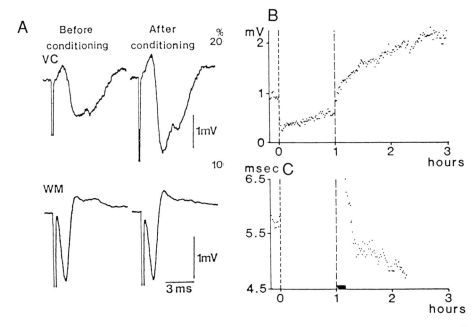

FIGURE 13.3.   LTP of FPs evoked in VC (area 17) of an infant kitten. (A) FPs produced in VC (upper row) and the WM by test stimulation (frequency, 0.02 Hz) of WM before and after conditioning (2 Hz) stimulation (bottom row). (B) and (C) Changes in amplitude of FPs evoked in VC and those in orthodromic latencies of extracellular responses in a VC cell during and after conditioning stimulation. Dotted and dashed lines represent the beginning and end of conditioning stimulation, respectively. (Komatsu et al., 1988.)

Age Dependency

A third difference exists in the age dependency of LTP. Systematic studies conducted in slices ($n = 76$) of kittens aged 7 to 49 days ($n = 59$) showed that induction of LTPs was critically age-dependent. Long-term potentiation occurred most frequently (>80%) around the fourth week (P21–34), moderately (50%) at earlier or later ages (P14–20 or P35–41), and never at even earlier or later ages (P7–13 or P42–49). The best age for induction of LTP in the VC corresponds to the critical period for modification of neuronal responsiveness in the VC (Blakemore & Van Sluyters, 1975; Hubel & Wiesel, 1970). No such rigid age dependency has been reported for hippocampal LTP.

Laminar Dependency

A fourth difference is the laminar dependency of LTP. The synapses responsible for LTP were investigated using current-source-density (CSD) analysis of the FPs, which is a technique to determine the distribution of local current densities underlying the LTP (Mitzdorf & Singer, 1978). The CSD analysis revealed that LTP occurred much more strongly in the second-order synapses compared with first order synapses. Figure 13.4 illustrates the results of the CSD analysis. Before the application of conditioning stimulation, the FPs represented small positive–negative waves near the cortical surface, and gradually changed into small positive-large–negative waves in deeper layers (traces FP in Fig. 13.4A).

The CSD analysis revealed the main components of current sinks (hatched areas in traces CD) for excitatory transmission were localized in the middle layers. The early currents (indicated by an upward arrow) probably represent the first-order excitatory transmission and were localized in the upper half of layer IV. Late currents (downward arrow) probably represented second- or higher order transmission and were localized in layers II and III as well as in the lower half of layer IV. The CSD analysis conducted 3 hours after conditioning stimulation indicated that LTP occurred in both early and late currents (Fig. 13.4B), but LTP was much larger in layers II and III, and rather small in the early currents in layer IV.

Figure 13.5 shows the laminar distribution of LTP by plotting the maximum amplitude of the early and late currents as a function of cortical depth. Before conditioning stimulation, the early currents (filled circles in Fig. 13.5A) are localized in layer IV, while the late currents are predominantly distributed in layers II and III (filled circles in Fig. 13.5B). Conditioning stimulation produced a 2-fold increase in the early currents in the superficial half of layer IV, and a 6-fold

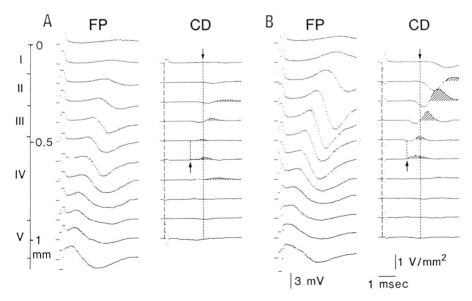

FIGURE 13.4. LTP studied by CSD analysis of FPs. (A) and (B) FPs (column FP) and local currents determined by CSD analysis (CD) evoked in kitten VC by test WM stimulation. (A) Before conditioning stimulation. (B) Three hours after termination of conditioning. Upward deflection represents a current sink, and shading indicates major current sinks. Upward and downward arrows indicate the onsets of early and late currents. (Komatsu et al., 1988.)

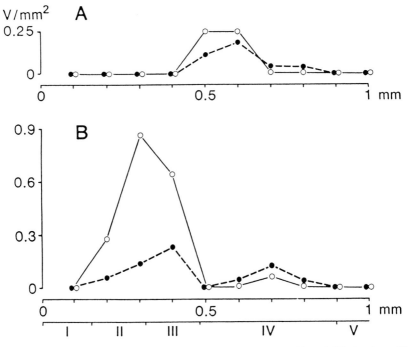

FIGURE 13.5.   Depth profile of early and late current LTPs. (A) and (B) depth profile of early and late currents before and 3 hours after conditioning stimulation (closed and open circles). (Komatsu et al., 1988.)

increase in the late currents throughout layers II and III (open circles in Fig. 13.5A and 13.5B).

An analysis of the time course of LTP, by plotting the maximal amplitudes of the early and late currents as functions of the time interval after conditioning stimulation, revealed that LTP of the early currents occurred even during the period of conditioning stimulation, reached a maximum one hour after conditioning stimulation, and declined gradually for the succeeding 11 hours (circles in Fig. 13.6). In contrast, the late currents, which were markedly depressed during conditioning stimulation, rapidly increased during the hour after conditioning stimulation, and continued to increase rather gradually for the succeeding 11 hours (triangles in Fig. 13.6).

A statistical analysis of the results for many slices ($n = 11$) dissected from kittens about 4 weeks old indicated that early current LTP was less remarkable in the amplitude as well as the probability of induction (Table 13.1). The amplitude of LTP was 1.8-fold for the early currents in layer IV and 2.8-fold for the late currents in layer II. LTP of the late currents was smaller in layer III. The probability of LTP induction was 80% for the early currents and 100% for the late currents.

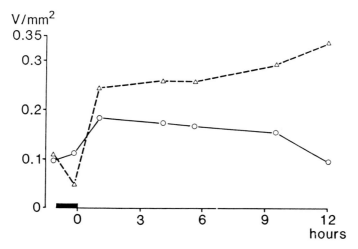

FIGURE 13.6. Time courses of early and late current LTP. The peak amplitudes of the early (circles) and late currents (triangles) are plotted as functions of time intervals after conditioning stimulation. (Komatsu et al., 1988.)

RECEPTOR MECHANISMS FOR LONG-TERM POTENTIATION

The molecular mechanisms underlying the difference between VC and hippocampal LTP were investigated by intracellular analysis of synaptic events in VC cells. One of the biggest difficulties in an intracellular study of LTP was the slow dynamics in induction and expression of VC LTP. In order to overcome this difficulty, we used a low concentration of bicuculline (0.5–1 μM) in the perfusing solution, in order to partially block cortical inhibition. With this technique, it is possible to shorten the period of conditioning stimulation (15 min) as well as the time for development (15 min). Intracellular study of the excitatory postsynaptic

TABLE 13.1 Age Dependency of Field LTP

	Field LTP	
Age of Kittens	Probability of Induction	Amplitude of Induced LTP
P7–13	0 (0/5)	—
P14–20	0.57 (4/7)	1.7 ± 0.5
P21–34	0.81 (43/53)	2.4 ± 0.6
P35–41	0.45 (5/11)	1.7 ± 0.4
P42–49	0 (0/5)	—

potentials (EPSPs) produced by WM stimulation revealed that they contained two components, one fast and one slow.

The fast EPSPs occurring before orthodromic spikes were resistant to DL-2-amino-5-phsophonovalerate (APV), which is a potent blocker of N-methyl-D-aspartate (NMDA) receptors, and depressed by 6,7-dinitro-quinoxaline-2,3-dione (DNQX), which blocks non-NMDA receptors. This indicates that the fast EPSPs represent non-NMDA transmission (Fig. 13.7A and 13.7B). In contrast, the slow EPSPs occurred after orthodromic spikes, and were completely abolished by a small dose (100 μM) of APV and enhanced in Mg-free solution (Fig. 13.7B and 13.7C). Therefore, they represent NMDA transmission.

Intracellular studies indicated the involvement of non-NMDA but not NMDA mechanisms in the induction of LTP. The amplitudes of the fast EPSPs as determined by the maximum rate of rise (MRR) were remarkably decreased during conditioning stimulation, and started to increase immediately after the termination of stimulation (Fig. 13.8A–13.8E). In contrast, the slow EPSPs were significantly potentiated during stimulation, transiently depressed after termination of stimulation, and then started to be potentiated (Fig. 13.8A–13.8D and 13.8F).

LTP of the fast EPSPs was still inducible in exactly the same way as in the control solution, even under complete blockade of the slow EPSPs by application of APV (Fig. 13.9). Therefore, LTP of non-NMDA transmission does not depend

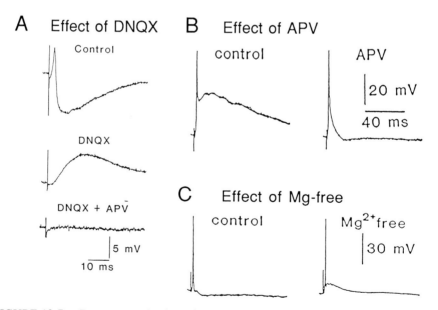

FIGURE 13.7. Receptor mechanisms for postsynaptic potentials in infant VC cells. (A) Effect of DNQX (20 μm) and APV (100 μm) on excitatory postsynaptic potentials (EPSPs) evoked in layer III cells of infant (P30) VC by WM stimulation. (B) Effect of APV on slow EPSPs. (C) Effect of Mg-free solution on slow EPSPs. (Komatsu et al., 1991.)

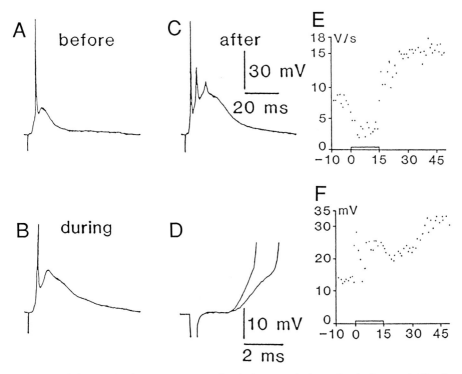

FIGURE 13.8.   LTP of EPSPs in control solution. (A) before, (B) during, and (C) after conditioning stimulation. (D) EPSP onsets for those before and after conditioning, shown in an expanded time scale. (E) and (F) Amplitude plots of fast and slow EPSPs. Zero time and blank bar represent the onset and the period of conditioning stimulation, respectively. All records were taken under partial blockade of GABA inhibition (1-μM bicuculline methiodide). (Komatsu et al., 1991.)

on NMDA transmission. Although LTP most commonly (roughly 80% of slices studied) occurred in both transmissions, occasionally LTP occurred in either only NMDA or non-NMDA transmissions, suggesting that the expression mechanisms of the two LTPs are independent. It was not quite clear, however, whether LTP of the slow EPSPs is inducible by activation of non-NMDA mechanisms.

CA CHANNELS FOR LONG-TERM POTENTIATION

If the LTP is not dependent on NMDA mechanisms that permeate Ca, then how does activation of non-NMDA-mediated ionic channels, which are not strongly permeable to Ca, induce LTP? The most plausible mechanism is the entrance of Ca through voltage-dependent Ca channels. Evidence for this has recently been provided by experiments using specific blockers for voltage-gated Ca channels (Komatsu & Iwakiri, 1992). The induction of fast EPSP LTP was prevented by a

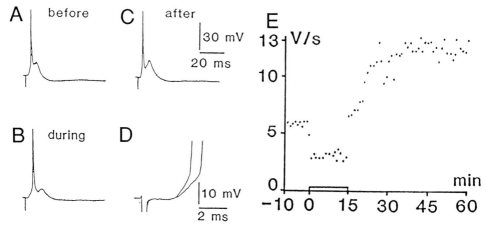

FIGURE 13.9.   LTP under blockade of NMDA transmission. (A)–(D) and (E) Similar to Figure 13.7A–13.7D and E, but under blockade of NMDA transmission (100 μM APV). (Komatsu et al., 1991.)

low concentration (100 μM) of Ni, which blocks the low-threshold voltage-gated Ca channels (cf. Fig. 13.10A and 13.10D with 13.10C). It is known that Ni also blocks Ca permeation through NMDA-mediated ionic channels. However, it was shown that the concentration of Ni used does not affect the slow EPSPs at all. In contrast, LTP induction was not affected by nifedipine (10 μM), which blocks high-threshold voltage-gated Ca channels (Fig. 13.10B).

A developmental study further showed that the Ca response mediated by low-threshold voltage-gated Ca channels exhibits a similar age dependency as that for LTP induction. An intracellular study of VC cells in kittens around the fifth postnatal week revealed a relatively large depolarizing response occurring on the withdrawal of a hyperpolarizing pulse in the presence of a sustained depolarization (specimen records of Fig. 13.11A). These responses were completely blocked by Ni, and therefore represent Ca permeation through low-threshold voltage-gated Ca channels. The Ca response was very weak in kittens around the first postnatal week, strongest around the fifth week, and gradually declined for the succeeding several weeks (Fig. 13.11B). This time course exactly corresponds to the age dependency of LTP induction and the time course of VC plasticity.

COMPARISON OF INFANT VISUAL CORTICAL LONG-TERM POTENTIATION WITH ADULT VC AND HIPPOCAMPAL LONG-TERM POTENTIATIONS

Table 13.2 summarizes the properties of LTP in the infant VC currently studied in comparison with those reported for LTP in the hippocampal (Anderson, Sundberg, Sveen, & Wigstrom, 1977; Bliss & Lomo, 1973; Collingridge & Bliss, 1988; Gustafsson & Wingstrom; Malenka, Kauer, Perkel, & Nicoll, 1989) and

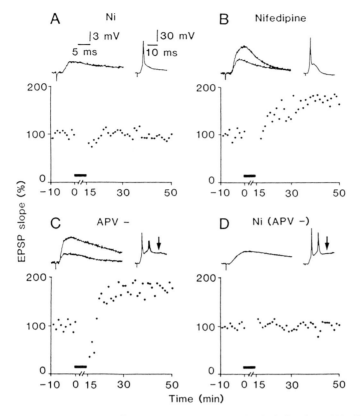

FIGURE 13.10. Effects of Ca^{2+} channel blockers on LTP induction. (A)–(D) These parts show the effects of conditioning stimulation (2 Hz) on the fast EPSPs in various perfusing solutions. (A) With Ni^{2+} (100 μM) and APV (100 μM). (B) With nipedipine (10 μM) and APV (100 μM). (C) In control solution containing only bicuculline (1 μM). (D) Only with Ni^{2+}. (Komatsu and Iwakiri, 1992.)

adult visual cortices (Artora & Singer, 1987, 1990; Kimura, Nishigori, Shiro-kawa, & Tsumoto, 1989). Long-term potentiation in the infant VC certainly shares a common basis with hippocampal and adult VC LTPs. Both represent glu-taminergic transmission, and are probably based on a Hebbian rule in which LTP is induced by conjoint activation of pre- and postsynaptic neuronal elements. Infant VC LTP, however, differs from hippocampal and adult VC LTPs in many aspects.

First of all, infant VC LTP is limited to infancy, while hippocampal and adult VC LTPs are rather remarkable in adulthood. The infant type of VC LTP is much slower in the stimulus parameters (optimal frequency and stimulus duration) for induction as well as the time course of induction, compared to adult VC or hippocampal LTPs. It is also different in the receptor mechanisms for induction and expression. In infant VC LTP, induction depends on Ca entry through low-

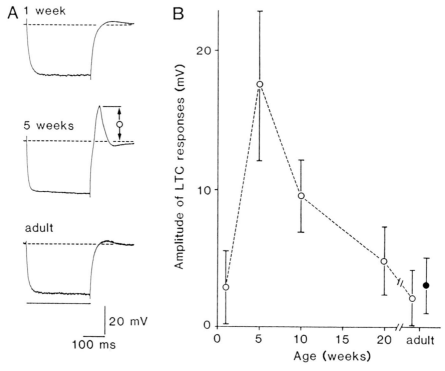

FIGURE 13.11.   Development of Ni^{2+}-sensitive low-threshold Ca responses. (A) Ni-sensitive Ca responses evoked in kitten VC cells at various stages of development. (B) Amplitude plots of Ca responses as a function of the animal age. (Komatsu and Iwakiri, 1992.)

threshold voltage-dependent Ca channels opened by activation of non-NMDA receptors, and the critical factor for age dependency for infant VC LTP is the development of the Ca channels rather than that of the receptors. In contrast, adult VC and hippocampal LTP depends on Ca entry through ionic channels of NMDA receptors.

These differences in the properties of LTPs could reflect a difference in the types of learning in which these two types of LTP are involved. The hippocampal LTP might provide a basis for acquisition of episodic memory, the dynamics of which should be fast enough to memorize the experienced events at each instance. The adult VC LTP could also be involved in relatively fast modification of photic responsiveness in VC cells, such as adaptation to sustained visual stimulation. In contrast, infant VC LTP might be the basis for procedural learning, which proceeds gradually by exposure to visual experience during postnatal life, and hence the learning dynamics can be much slower than those for episodic memory or transient memory of visual adaptation.

TABLE 13.2   Comparison of Infant VC LTP with Adult VC and Hippocampal LTPs

	Infant VC	Adult VC and Hippocampal Cortex (CA1)
Age dependency	P3–5W	Adult
Stimulus dependency		
Stimulus Frequency	2 Hz	100 Hz
Stimulus Period	15–60 min	<1 sec
Period of expression	1–15 hr	<5 min
Receptor mechanisms		
Expression	NMDA and non-NMDA	non-NMDA
Induction	Non-NMDA and low-threshold Ca channel	NMDA

POSTNATAL DEVELOPMENT IN VISUAL CORTICAL CIRCUITRY

In support of the earlier view, changes in synaptic transmission comparable with those in infant VC LTP were found to occur during normal development. In the VC immediately after birth (P2), WM stimulation produced only early currents that were broadly distributed through layers II–IV, and there was no trace of late currents. Very interestingly, the distribution of early currents corresponded with the termination area of geniculate axonal arborizations anterogradely labeled with horseradish peroxidase (Fig. 13.12A).

Both the early currents and the termination area of geniculate arborizations retracted down to halfway between layers II and III in the third week (P19), and completely restricted to layer IV at the end of the fourth week (P28). Correspondingly, the late currents appeared in the area of layers II–III, from which the early currents had retracted, and continued to increase during the period of infancy (P19–28), which exactly corresponds to the critical period for neuronal learning of response selectivity in the VC and suggests that the cortico–cortical transmission is the primary site of synaptic modification during cortical learning (Fig. 13.12B and 13.12C). This aspect of late current development is in perfect agreement with that for the LTPs induced by electrical stimulation of the visual pathway in infant kittens, and therefore it is likely that both cortical learning and LTP share common synaptic sites for modification of synaptic transmission.

The fact that LTP is greater in cortico–cortical synapses than in geniculo–cortical synapses suggests the possibility that synaptic plasticity is larger in the former synapses, and that neuronal response selectivity is learned via the cortico–cortical connectivity. Meanwhile, the geniculo–cortical connectivity, which works as a prenatal mechanism to control the learning process (Fig. 13.13), might impose constraints on the learning.

Layer II–III cells, which have more plastic cortico–cortical synapses but less matured response selectivity, may be like students who learn response selectivity, while layer IV cells, which have less plastic geniculo–cortical synapses but more

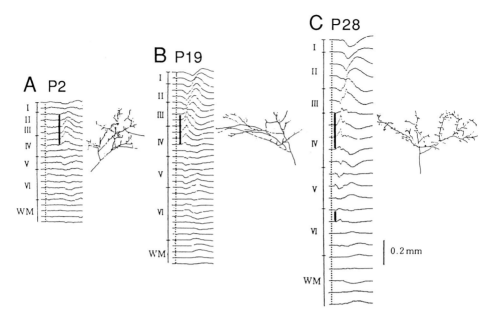

FIGURE 13.12. Development of visual cortical circuitry. (A)–(C) CSD analysis of FPs evoked in in vivo kitten VC at four different ages by LGN stimulation. Filled bars indicate the termination area of axonal arborizations of LGN axons visualized by anterograde labeling with horseradish peroxidase. (Komatsu et al., 1985.)

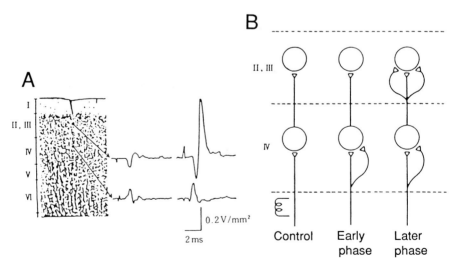

FIGURE 13.13. Schematic diagram illustrating synapses involved in LTP. (A) Primary sites of early and late current LTPs shown in a Nissl-stained section of VC. (B) Schematic diagram showing the synapses involved in the early and late current LTP and the time course of the LTPs.

matured selectivity, are like teachers who instruct the learning of layer II–III cells by selecting the incoming visual signals on the basis of their matured response selectivities and pass those signals onto the students. This could be a basic mechanism for prenatal control of cortical learning, which would provide a solution for the dispute between Nurture (Hubel & Wiesel, 1963, 1970; Wiesel & Hubel, 1963, 1965) versus Nature theories (Blakemore & Cooper, 1970; Blakemore & Van Sluyters, 1975; Hebb, 1949).

REFERENCES

Anderson, P., Sundberg, S. H., Sveen, O., & Wigstrom, H. (1977). Specific long-lasting potentiation of synaptic transmission in hippocampal slices. *Nature, 266,* 736–737.

Artola, A., & Singer, W. (1987). Long-term potentiation and NMDA receptors in rat visual cortex. *Nature, 330,* 649–652.

Artola, A., & Singer, W. (1990). The involvement of N-Methyl-D-aspartate receptors in induction and maintenance of long-term potentiation in rat visual cortex. *European Journal of Neuroscience, 2,* 254–270.

Blakemore, C., & Cooper, G. P. (1970). Development of the brain depends on the visual environment. *Nature, 228,* 477–478.

Blakemore, C., & Van Sluyters, R. C. (1975). Innate and environmental factors in the development of the kitten's visual cortex. *Journal of Physiology, London, 248,* 663–716.

Bliss, T. V. P., & Lomo, T. (1973). Long-lasting potentiation of synaptic transmission in the dentate area of the anesthetized rabbit following stimulation of the perforant path. *Journal of Physiology, 232,* 331–356.

Collingridge, G. L., & Bliss, T. V. P. (1987). NMDA receptors—Their role in long-term potentiation. *Trends in Neurosciences, 10,* 288–293.

Grinvald, A. (1985). Real-time optical mapping of neuronal activities: From style growth cones to the intact mammalian brain. *Annual Brain of Neuroscience, 8,* 263–305.

Gustafsson, B., & Wigstrom, H. (1988). Physiological mechanisms underlying long-term potentiation. *Trends in Neurosciences, 11,* 156–162.

Hebb, D. O. (1949). *The organization of behavior.* New York: Wiley.

Hubel, D. H., & Wiesel, T. N. (1963). Receptive fields of cells in striate cortex of very young, visually inexperienced kittens. *Journal of Neurophysiology, 26,* 994–1002.

Hubel, D. H., & Wiesel, T. N. (1970). The period of susceptibility to the physiological effects of unilateral eye closure in kittens. *Journal of Physiology, London, 206,* 419–436.

Kimura, F., Nishigori, A., Shirokawa, T., & Tsumoto, T. (1989). Long-term potentiation and N-methyl-D-aspartate receptors in the visual cortex of young rats. *Journal of Physiology, 414,* 125–144.

Komatsu, Y.; & Iwakiri, M. (1992). Low-threshold Ca^{2+} channels mediate induction of long-term potentiation in kitten visual cortex. *Journal of Neurophysiology, 67,* 401–410.

Komatsu, Y., Fujii, K., Maeda, J., Sakaguchi, H., & Toyama, K. (1988). Long-term potentiation of synaptic transmission in kitten visual cortex. *Journal of Neurophysiology, 59,* 124–141.

Komatsu, Y., Fujii, K., Nakajima, S., Umetani, K., & Toyama, K. (1985). Electrophysiological and morphological correlates in the development of visual cortical circuitry in infant kittens. *Developmental Brain Research, 22,* 305–309.

Komatsu, Y., Nakajima, S., & Toyama, K. (1991). Induction of long-term potentiation without participation of N-methyl-D-aspartate receptors in kitten visual cortex. *Journal of Neurophysiology, 65,* 20–32.

Komatsu, Y., Toyama, K., Maeda, J., & Sakaguchi, H. (1981). Long-term potentiation investigated in a slice preparation of striate cortex of young kittens. *Neuroscience Letters, 26,* 269–274.

Malenka, R. C., Kauer, J. A., Perkel, D. J., & Nicoll, R. A. (1989). The importance of postsynaptic calcium on synaptic transmission—Its role in long-term potentiation. *Trends in Neurosciences, 12,* 444-450.

Mitzdorf, U., & Singer, W. (1978). Prominent excitatory pathway in cat visual cortex (A17 and A18): A current source-density analysis of electrically evoked potentials. *Experimental Brain Research, 33,* 371-394.

Stryker, M. P., & Harris, A. H. (1986). Binocular impulse blockade prevents the formation of ocular dominance columns in cat visual cortex. *Journal of Neuroscience, 6,* 2117-2133.

Swindale, N. V. (1981). Absence of ocular dominance patches in dark-reared cats. *Nature, 290,* 332-333.

Toyama, K., Komatsu, Y., Yamamoto, N., Kurotani, T., & Yamada, K. (1991). In vitro approach to visual cortical development and plasticity. *Neuroscience Research, 12,* 57-71.

Toyama, K., Matsunami, K., Ohno, T., & Tokashiki, S. (1974). An intracellular study of neuronal organization in the visual cortex. *Experimental Brain Research, 21,* 45-66.

Toyama, K., & Tanifuji, M. (1991). Seeing excitation propagating in visual cortical slice. *Biomedical Research, 12,* 145-147.

Wiesel, T. N., & Hubel, D. H. (1963). Single cell responses in striate cortex of kittens deprived of vision in one eye. *Journal of Neurophysiology, 26,* 1003-1017.

Wiesel, T. N., & Hubel, D. H. (1965). Comparison of the effects of unilateral and bilateral eye closure on cortical unit responses in kittens. *Journal of Neurophysiology, 28,* 1029-1040.

14

Mechanisms of Learning, Memory, and Plasticity in Adult Sensory Cortex

MICHAEL B. CALFORD

The past decade has produced a number of studies showing examples of physiological plasticity in the adult mammalian brain. The first studies showing large-scale reorganization in topographic representations were in the somatosensory system, and these have been followed by studies of the motor system, auditory system, and most recently, the visual system (for review see Dykes, 1990; Kaas, 1991). Initially, there was some reluctance by the general neuroscience community to accept the implications of these findings. This was not because they demonstrated plasticity in the adult nervous system, for there was ample evidence of this in many experiments (e.g., in the cerebellum, Greenough & Anderson, 1991; in the superior colliculus, Jay & Sparks, 1984), but because topographic representation of the fundamental feature of a system (e.g., retinal place in vision; frequency in audition) was considered to be the result of neuronal wiring and therefore immutable in the adult. This view was particularly strong among vision researchers, who could dismiss the early work in the somatosensory system by stating that visual cortex is different. We now have ample evidence of both short-term unmasking and long-term reorganizational plasticity in visual cortex (Gilbert & Darian-Smith, this volume, Chapter 11; Chino, Kaas, Smith, Langston, & Cheng, 1992; Gilbert & Wiesel, 1992; Kaas et al., 1990). Ironically, it is the very precision of the topographic representations (maps) in the primary sensory cortices that allowed the investigation of cortical plasticity. For whereas a priori other cortical areas (frontal, parietal) would have been expected to show more plasticity, the maps provide the necessary scale against which change can be measured. It is also ironic that the anatomy *never* showed precise point-to-point connections in the projection of one topographic representation to another—say, from thalamus to cortex. Rather there is a divergent projection from a given place in thalamus to multiple places (often patches) in the corresponding representation in cortex (Merzenich & Kaas, 1980). Local connectivity, both inhibitory and excitatory, is then necessary to reestablish topography and precision in the cortical representation. At a simple level of analysis it can be shown that such divergence and convergence in a projection is a necessary condition for further feature extraction—for maintenance of precise topography would merely replicate the representation at the lower level. It should be remembered that the projections to cortex conveying encoded sensations are always excitatory. Hence, the necessary inhibition must be contributed by local intracortical neurons. Blocking of such inhibition by the iontophoresis of inhibitory antagonists has been shown to disrupt precision of topographic encoding (Alloway & Burton, 1991; Dykes, Landry, Metherate, & Hicks, 1984) and feature extraction (Sillito, 1977).

The plasticity described in Chapters 11 and 12 of this volume appears to reflect this underlying divergence or, in cortical place terms, *convergence* of multiple projections to each locus in cortex. That cortical neurons have the cellular ability to react to a changed set of effective inputs through synaptic plasticity and hence for previously ineffective inputs to be expressed is well demonstrated through the work of Toyama and colleagues (see Chapter 13 of this volume). Such neuronal plasticity can also be demonstrated in the intact animal. Clear examples come from Weinberger and colleagues' use of classical conditioning paradigms to alter the tuning specificity of single neurons in auditory cortex and thalamus of awake adult guinea pigs (Bakin & Weinberger, 1990; Weinberger et al., 1990; Weinberger & Diamond, 1987). One experiment involves obtaining a profile of the discharges evoked from a cortical neuron as the stimulus is altered in frequency (amplitude constant). A best frequency (BF) is defined as the frequency evoking the maximum discharge. Conditioning in which the conditioned stimulus (CS) is a frequency to which the neuron responds at less than BF level and where the unconditioned stimulus (UCS) is a nonauditory event (e.g. foot shock), alters the response profile toward the CS. In many cases the response at the CS exceeds that to the original BF. In the somatosensory system long-term training has been shown to increase the cortical representation of the specific area stimulated (Recanzone, Merzenich, & Jenkins, 1992; Recanzone, Merzenich, Jenkins, Grajski, & Dinse, 1992) and of the training stimulus (a 20–30 Hz vibration, Recanzone, Merzenich, & Schreiner, 1992). In neither system does repeated presentation of a stimulus, without a conditioning or other behaviorally relevant link, equivalently change the cortical representation. The implication of these findings is that some forms of learning and memory appear to produce changes in the fundamental representation of sensory stimuli in their primary cortical representations. Thus, the neural processes of feature extraction and stimulus encoding share some of the same neural machinery as processes of learning and memory.

The shift in tuning in Weinberger's experiment occurs within the limits of the responsive area (receptive field or RF) and therefore differs from the changes underlying the expression of new receptive fields when an original RF is removed, as with the work presented in Chapters 11 and 12 of this volume. But the difference may be in the definition of the receptive field, for there are some physiologically "normal" conditions demonstrating a larger array of inputs to a cortical locus than is normally represented in the RF. One of these is the use of a stimulus mask, centered on the RF, to demonstrate that where a classically defined visual

RF is 2°–3° across, large stimuli can be shown to produce responses (Chapter 11, this volume). The visual blind spot formed by the lack of receptors at the optic nerve insertion into the retina can be considered a natural mask. A recent intriguing demonstration of the interaction of a wide input to a locus in cortex is that interpolated receptive fields in visual cortex form a topographic progression across the blindspot "representation" (Fig. 14.1; Fiorani, Rosa, Gattass, & Rocha-Miranda, 1992). Attention is also drawn to the recent work of Kasamatsu and colleagues (Kasamatsu, Kitano, Sutter, & Norcia, 1991), who have used a pair of microelectrodes with a tip separation of 300 μm to sample the local evoked potential in striate cortex of cats. With appropriate stimulus conditions, a postsynaptic potential is generated for stimuli from over 30° of visual space—about 10 times the dimensions of the single-unit receptive fields recorded at the same sites.

These underlying inputs can be "unmasked" very rapidly to form large classically defined receptive fields following removal of drive in the area of the normal

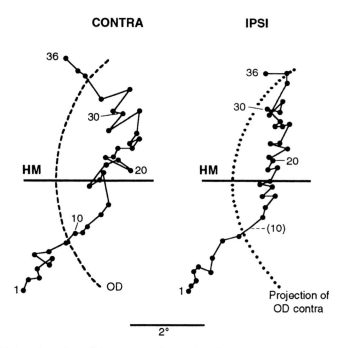

FIGURE 14.1. Location of the centers of receptive fields (right, ipsi) and of interpolated receptive fields (left, contra) recorded in a single tangential electrode penetration through primary visual cortex in a *Cebus* monkey. The dotted lines indicate the projected boundary of the optic disc (blind spot) for the contralateral eye; thus no responses were elicited for stimulation at the indicated centers when the ipsilateral eye was covered. However, large bars that straddled the optic disc were effective stimuli. Use of bars of various orientation allowed the calculation of an interpolated receptive field, at each recording site. The interpolated receptive fields showed a remarkable topographic progression. (From Fiorani et al., 1992.)

receptive field. This is demonstrated by the rapid effects of bilaterally matched small retinal scotomata (Gilbert & Wiesel, 1992). Work in my laboratory has shown similar rapid unmasking in the somatosensory cortex of flying foxes, macaque monkeys, rats, and cats following various manipulations of the peripheral innervation. Figure 14.2 presents an example of rapid expansion of the cutaneous RF of a unit cluster recorded in somatosensory area 3b of an anesthetized macaque monkey, when innervation of the original RF is blocked by local anesthetic. The original RF was confined to the glabrous skin of one digit, whereas, at maximal extent, the unmasked RF covered most of the hand (including hairy skin). A receptive field of this size is never seen in an intact animal, and around 25 mm^2 of cortex is normally devoted to the representation of this skin surface. In linear extent the limits of the expanded field are normally represented about 6 mm from the site of the recording. This is a dramatic example of the viability of a massive input to a cortical locus that is not apparent when the input from a normal RF is intact. That the input from the original RF normally masks the expression of the

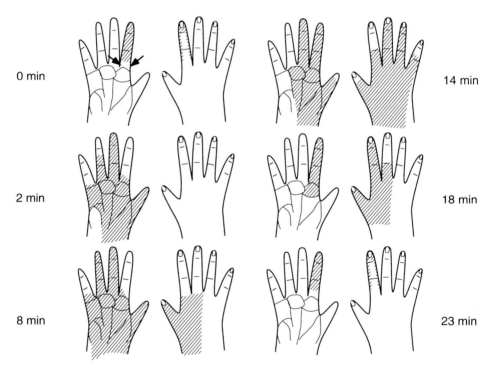

FIGURE 14.2.   Rapid expression of a new RF of cortical neurons following local anesthesia of a digit. The RF is defined as the area in which cutaneous stimulation produces activity in a small group of neurons (unit cluster) recorded through a microelectrode at a depth of 4000 μm down the caudal bank of the central sulcus (area 3b) in an adult macaque monkey (RM1). Arrows indicate the site of lignocaine injections (4 by 10 μl of 2%). Other experimental details in Calford & Tweedale (1991b).

wider responsiveness is as clearly demonstrated by the shrinkage back to the original RF when esthesia returns to the digit as it is by the initial unmasking.

A difference between the visual and somatosensory work is the need to infer a source of topographically appropriate tonic inhibition to explain the immediate unmasking in the somatosensory system (for full reasoning, see Calford & Tweedale, 1990; Calford & Tweedale, 1991c). Although lack of precise topography in projections of the somatosensory pathway and the need for local inhibition at each level provide a means of accounting for the sources of the unmasked sensitivity, there is no obvious link between a small peripheral denervation and a down regulation of cortical inhibition. The problem exists because most mechanosensitive primary afferent fibers (and all from glabrous skin) have no ongoing, or tonic, activity. Thus if it were loss of input from these afferents that reduced the activity of the cortical inhibitory interneurons, then a period of no stimulation should be as effective as a denervation in producing unmasking. There are, however, other primary afferent fibers innervating the skin. Low-threshold mechanoreceptor afferents have rapidly conducting myelinated axons (A-fibers). Slowly conducting, unmyelinated C-fibers, about half of which are associated with pain perception, are also blocked by a local anesthetic denervation. C-fibers can be rapidly and selectively blocked by direct application, to an exposed nerve, of the plant derivative capsaicin. Such application produces a rapid expansion of receptive fields in cortex (Fig. 14.3). The pathway by which some C-fibers innervate primary somatosensory cortex is well described (Gingold, Greenspan, & Apkarian, 1991). Which subclass of C-fibers is involved in providing an ongoing input to the inhibitory neurons of cortex is yet to be established. The finding also raises the possibility that receptive field size of cortical neurons may be under active modulation by varying levels of C-fiber activity.

Whereas the need for a source of peripheral tonic drive is a difference between the somatosensory and visual system experiments, there may indeed be a parallel. When a small retinal laser lesion is made, the photoreceptors and the outer nuclear layer are destroyed, removing the source of drive to the ganglion cells that remain intact. As Gilbert and Darion-Smith (chapter 11, this volume) have pointed out, a mask can produce similar effects. The effect of a mask is habituation of the ganglion cell output in that region. Such a drop in the basal level of stimulation in the corresponding area of cortex could be viewed as a reduction in the tonic drive compared to the viewing of any patterned stimulus, and would be expected to have a profound effect on local cortical inhibition. Thus, when integrated over a period of a few tens of seconds (or across sufficient cortical surface), the total activity reaching a locus in cortex after a small retinal lesion can be viewed as a reduction in tonic input.

Due to the nature of the sensory signals and of the neuronal pathways, the sensory representations differ in their appropriateness for particular questions. The retina to lateral geniculate to striate cortex projection is both simpler and better understood than the projections to auditory or somatosensory cortex. Thus the fact that long-term reorganization has a significant cortical involvement is best demonstrated in that system, where the extent of reorganization in thalamus does

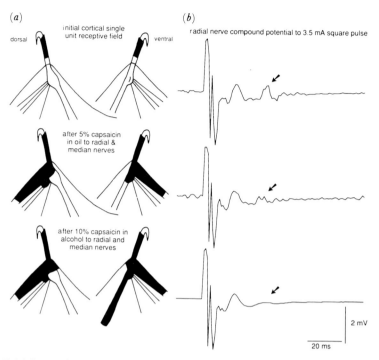

FIGURE 14.3.   Evidence that tonic activity in C-fibers provides a source of drive for central inhibitory circuits that mask some potential mechanoreceptor inputs to neurons in primary somatosensory cortex. The example comes from work with the flying fox. (a) The RF (on dorsal and ventral views of digit 1 and the wing) of a neuron in primary somatosensory cortex. (b) Potentials recorded from the radial nerve laid across two tungsten hook electrodes 87 mm above a pair of stimulating electrodes (100 μs pulse, 3.5 mA). Within a few minutes of adding one drop (25 μl) of 5% capsaicin in sunflower oil to the exposed radial and median nerves the C-fiber potential (arrowed) was diminished and the single unit RF expanded. Application of further capsaicin (10% dihydrocapsaicin in 70% ethanol) abolished the C-fiber potential and further expanded the RF.

not account for that in cortex (Darian-Smith, Gilbert, & Wiesel, 1992; Eysel, 1982; Gilbert & Darian-Smith, chapter 11, this volume; Gilbert & Wiesel, 1992). For reasons of ease of presentation of stimuli, study of the auditory representation is advantageous where quantitative questions are being asked. A finding in the demonstration of long-term reorganization of auditory cortex following restricted cochlear lesions by Robertson and Irvine (1989) was that thresholds in the expanded representations of frequencies at the edge of the lesions were normal. Thus, although there is some rapid unmasking of wider receptive fields in auditory cortex after peripheral damage (Rajan, Irvine, Calford, & Wise, 1992; Robertson & Irvine, 1989), the long-term effects must involve plasticity that both improves sensitivity and narrows the frequency range of responses.

Such multiple dimensions of stimulus representation are yet to be examined in the comparison of short- and long-term effects in the somatosensory and visual systems. Nevertheless, even from the simple response properties examined a central question arises concerning the comparison of immediate and long-term reorganization. In both visual (Gilbert & Wiesel, 1992) and somatosensory (Calford & Tweedale, 1988, 1991a, 1991b) systems some small peripheral denervations produce rapid unmasking of new or enlarged receptive fields, and there are no silent or unresponsive regions. Larger retinal lesions and larger peripheral lesions can leave temporarily (Cusick, Wall, Whiting, Wiley, 1990; Gilbert & Wiesel, 1992; Merzenich et al., 1984; Turnbull & Rasmusson, 1991) or permanently unresponsive regions in cortex (Heinen & Skaenski, 1991; Merzenich et al., 1984). As pointed out by Kaas in chapter 12 of this volume, the outcome of a particular lesion may also depend upon the details of the central representation being manipulated. A "cortically large" denervation, such as cutting the ulnar nerve, can lead to complete filling-in (Garraghty & Kaas, 1991), whereas the "cortically smaller" amputation of two digits does not (Merzenich et al., 1984). The interpretation is that although the ulnar nerve innervates a very large area of the glabrous surface of the hand, its central representation (at the dorsal column, thalamus, and cortex) is tightly linked to the radial nerve representation of the hairy skin of that part of the hand. The geometric proximity and probable overlap of a small number of fibers provides a possible basis for some observations of very large plasticity, and it is possible that such changes occur at precortical levels of the pathway (Dostrovsky, Millar, & Wall, 1976; Shin, Raymond, Strichartz, 1991). There is no evidence for new neuronal connections or for any observable afferent sprouting. Using a model of large-scale reorganization in raccoons where denervation of a single digit represents an equivalently large area of denervated cortex as an entire forelimb in a monkey, Rasmusson and Nance were unable to detect any anatomical changes in the ascending somatosensory pathway (Rasmusson, 1988; Rasmusson & Nance, 1986). In addition to overlap within the topographic projections at successive stations in a sensory pathway, other possible sources of input that can account for the reorganization are connections between the multiple representations that each sense has in cortex (Doetsch, Stoney & Hauge, 1992), as well as horizontally projecting neurons within a cortical field (Gilbert, 1992). Work with raccoons gives emphasis to the role of corticocortical connections. Zarzecki and colleagues (Smits, Gordon, Witte, Rasmusson, & Zarzecki, 1991; Witte, Zarzecki, & Rasmusson, 1990; Zarzecki et al., 1993) have shown through in vivo intracellular recording that relatively slow EPSPs evoked in primary somatosensory cortex by electrical stimulation of another cortical field—the heterogeneous zone—have faster rising phases a few months after amputation of the digit initially represented in this area of cortex. This change is not accompanied by changes in amplitude, but there is a dramatic increase in the proportion of EPSPs evoked from peripheral stimulation of off-focus digits. The former result suggests a mechanism of reorganization by strengthening of existing corticocortical connections, while the latter suggests formation of new synapses. There is an obvious need for similar work to be done in other species.

The very large-scale reorganization such that the chin representation expands to encompass the denervated forelimb representation in macaque monkeys (Kaas, chapter 12, this volume; Pons et al., 1991) may appear to be too large to be explained by existing connectivity. However, even here we must look for such connectivity since equivalent psychophysical changes have been demonstrated in human forearm amputees by Ramachandran (Ramachandran, Stewart, & Rogers-Ramachandran, 1992) soon after the surgery—too soon for any putative new neuronal projections to reach their targets. Also it is interesting to note that although the reorganization found by Pons et al. (1991) was in animals that carried their deafferentation for a decade, in terms of cortical extent (note that relatively little cortex is devoted to the representation of the arm compared to the hand) the expansion is only double that apparent within a few minutes of a single-digit denervation (Fig. 14.2).

A hypothesis that links the short-term unmasking with longer term reorganization and the demonstration of potentiation in cortical slices (Toyama et al., chapter 13, this volume) is that the initial unmasking is necessary to allow subsequent plasticity. Long-term potentiation (LTP) in adult visual cortex is known to involve N-methyl-D-aspartate (NMDA) receptors. To be activated NMDA receptors require a significant depolarization to remove a Mg^{2+} block on the Ca^{2+} channel. Experimentally this can be achieved by deactivating local inhibition with bicuculline (a GABA-receptor antagonist). It is possible that the local disinhibition seen after a peripheral restricted denervation (evidenced as an unmasking of large fields where the denervation is small, and immunohistochemically for larger denervations; Garraghty, LaChica, & Kaas, 1991; Hámori, Takács, Verley, Petrusz, & Farkas, 1990; Hendry & Jones, 1988) provides suitable depolarization and an environment whereby NMDA-receptor-based Hebbian-type plasticity can operate. This could provide an explanation for the shrinking (Calford & Tweedale, 1988) of the rapidly unmasked, large receptive fields in the week following a small denervation. Such a mechanism could also operate to allow very weak inputs to become effective, even where the limits of immediate unmasking are exceeded.

A similar hypothesis has been put forward for the role of the basal forebrain cholinergic projection to cortex. The cellular process whereby ACh-muscarinic-receptor-mediated depolarization is permissive for NMDA-receptor-based potentiation was hypothesized by Nicoll in 1988, and evidence supporting its involvement in somatosensory cortical reorganization comes from the work of Webster, Hanisch, Dykes, and Biesold (1991). Using a model of reorganization first developed by Wall and Cusick (1984), Webster et al. (1991) showed that the chronic invasion of sciatic nerve "territory" in cortex by the saphenous nerve after sciatic section is blocked by lesions depleting the cortex of ACh.

REFERENCES

Alloway, K. D., & Burton, H. (1991). Differential effects of GABA and bicuculline on rapidly- and slowly-adapting neurons in primary somatosensory cortex of primates. *Experimental Brain Research, 85,* 598–610.

Bakin, J. S., & Weinberger, N. M. (1990). Classical conditioning induces CS-specific receptive field plasticity in the auditory cortex of the guinea pig. *Brain Research, 536,* 271–286.

Calford, M. B., & Tweedale, R. (1988). Immediate and chronic changes in responses of somatosensory cortex in adult flying-fox after digit amputation. *Nature, 332*, 446–448.

Calford, M. B., & Tweedale, R. (1990). The capacity for reorganization in adult somatosensory cortex. In M. Rowe & L. Aitkin (Eds.), *Information processing in mammalian auditory and tactile systems* (pp. 221–236). New York: Alan R. Liss.

Calford, M. B., & Tweedale, R. (1991a). Acute changes in cutaneous receptive fields in primary somatosensory cortex after digit denervation in adult flying fox. *Journal of Neurophysiology, 65*, 178–187.

Calford, M. B., & Tweedale, R. (1991b). Immediate expansion of receptive fields of neurons in area 3b of macaque monkeys after digit denervation. *Somatosensory and Motor Research, 8*, 249–260.

Calford, M. B., & Tweedale, R. (1991c). C-fibres provide a source of masking inhibition to primary somatosensory cortex. *Proceedings of the Royal Society of London, Section B, 243*, 269–275.

Chino, Y. M., Kaas, J. H., Smith, E. I., Langston, A. L., & Cheng, H. (1992). Rapid reorganization of cortical maps in adult cats following restricted deafferentation in retina. *Vision Research, 32*, 789–796.

Cusick, C. G., Wall, J. T., Whiting, J. J., & Wiley, R. G. (1990). Temporal progression of cortical reorganization following nerve injury. *Brain Research, 537*, 355–358.

Darian-Smith, C. D., Gilbert, C. D., & Wiesel, T. D. (1992). Cortical reorganization following binocular focal retinal lesions in the adult cat and monkey. *Society for Neuroscience Abstracts, 18*, 11.

Doetsch, G. S., Stoney, S. J., & Hauge, D. H. (1992). Convergent inputs to single neurons in two different subdivisions of somatosensory forepaw digit cortex of the raccoon. *Experimental Neurology, 115*, 250–259.

Dostrovsky, J. O., Millar, J., & Wall, P. D. (1976). The immediate shift of afferent drive of dorsal column nucleus cells following deafferentation: A comparison of acute and chronic deafferentation in gracile nucleus and spinal cord. *Experimental Neurology, 52*, 480–495.

Dykes, R. W. (1990). Acetylcholine and neuronal plasticity in somatosensory cortex. In M. Steriade & D. Biesold (Eds.), *Brain cholinergic systems* (pp. 294–313). New York: Oxford University Press.

Dykes, R. W., Landry, P., Metherate, R., & Hicks, T. P. (1984). Functional role of GABA in cat primary somatosensory cortex: Shaping receptive fields of cortical neurons. *Journal of Neurophysiology, 52*, 1066–1093.

Eysel, U. T. (1982). Functional reconnections without new axonal growth in a partially denervated visual relay nucleus. *Nature, 299*, 442–444.

Fiorani, M., Rosa, M. G. P., Gattass, R., & Rocha-Miranda, C. E. (1992). Dynamic surrounds of receptive fields in primate striate cortex: A physiological basis for perceptual completion? *Proceedings of the National Academy of Sciences of the United States of America, 89*, 8547–8551.

Garraghty, P. E., & Kaas, J. H. (1991). Large-scale functional reorganization in adult monkey cortex after peripheral nerve injury. *Proceedings of the National Academy of Sciences of the United States of America, 88*, 6976–6980.

Garraghty, P. E., LaChica, E. A., & Kaas, J. H. (1991). Injury-induced reorganization of somatosensory cortex is accompanied by reductions in GABA staining. *Somatosensory and Motor Research, 8*, 347–354.

Gilbert, C. D., & Wiesel, T. N. (1992). Receptive field dynamics in adult primary visual cortex. *Nature, 356*, 150–152.

Gingold, S. I., Greenspan, J. D., & Apkarian, A. V. (1991). Anatomic evidence of nociceptive inputs to primary somatosensory cortex in squirrel monkeys. *Journal of Comparative Neurology, 308*, 467–490.

Greenough, W. T., & Anderson, B. J. (1991). Cerebellar synaptic plasticity. Relation to learning versus neural activity. *Annals of the New York Academy of Sciences, 627*, 231–247.

Hámori, J., Takács, J., Verley, R., Petrusz, P., & Farkas, B. E. (1990). Plasticity of GABA- and glutamate-containing terminals in the mouse thalamic ventrobasal complex deprived of vibrissal afferents: An immunogold-electron microscopic study. *Journal of Comparative Neurology, 302,* 739–748.

Heinen, S. J., & Skaenski, A. A. (1991). Recovery of visual responses in foveal V1 neurons following bilateral foveal lesions in adult monkey. *Experimental Brain Research, 83,* 670–674.

Hendry, S. H. C., & Jones, E. G. (1988). Activity-dependent regulation of GABA expression in the visual cortex of adult monkeys. *Neuron, 1,* 701–712.

Jay, M., & Sparks, D. L. (1984). Auditory receptive fields in primate superior colliculus shift with changes in eye position. *Nature, 309,* 345–347.

Kaas, J. H. (1991). Plasticity of sensory and motor maps in adult mammals. *Annual Review of Neuroscience, 14,* 137–167.

Kaas, J. H., Krubitzer, L. A., Chino, Y. M., Langston, A. L., Polley, E. H., & Blair, N. (1990). Reorganization of retinotopic cortical maps in adult mammals after lesions of the retina. *Science, 248,* 229–231.

Kasamatsu, T., Kitano, M., Sutter, E. E., & Norcia, A. M. (1991). Intracortical interaction in cat visual cortex: Evidence from postsynaptic field potentials. *Society for Neuroscience Abstracts, 17,* 1089.

Merzenich, M. M., & Kaas, J. (1980). Principles of organization of sensory-perceptual systems in mammals. In J. M. Sprague & A. N. Epstein (Eds.), *Progress in psychobiology and physiological psychology* (pp. 1–42). New York: Academic Press.

Merzenich, M. M., Nelson, R. J., Stryker, M. P., Cynader, M. S., Schoppmann, A., & Zook, J. M. (1984). Somatosensory cortical map changes following digit amputation in adult monkeys. *Journal of Comparative Neurology, 224,* 591–605.

Nicoll, R. A. (1988). The coupling of neurotransmitter receptors to ion channels in the brain. *Science, 241,* 545–551.

Pons, T. P., Garraghty, P. E., Ommaya, K., Kaas, J. H., Taub, E., & Mishkin, M. (1991). Massive cortical reorganization after sensory deafferentation in adult macaques. *Science, 252,* 1857–1860.

Rajan, R., Irvine, D. R. F., Calford, M. B., & Wise, L. Z. (1992). Effect of frequency-specific losses in cochlear neural sensitivity in the processing and representation of frequency in primary auditory cortex. In A. L. Dancer, D. Henderson, R. J. Salvi, & R. P. Hamernik (Eds.), *Noise-induced hearing loss* (pp. 119–129). St. Louis, MO: Mosby—Year Book.

Ramachandran, V. S., Stewart, M., & Rogers-Ramachandran, D. C. (1992). Perceptual correlates of massive cortical reorganization. *NeuroReport, 3,* 583–586.

Rasmusson, D. D. (1988). Projection patterns of digit afferents to the cuneate nucleus in the raccoon before and after partial deafferentation. *Journal of Comparative Neurology, 277,* 549–556.

Rasmusson, D. D., & Nance, D. M. (1986). Non-overlapping thalamocortical projections for separate forepaw digits before and after cortical reorganization in the raccoon. *Brain Research Bulletin, 16,* 399–406.

Recanzone, G. H., Merzenich, M. M., & Jenkins, W. M. (1992). Frequency discrimination training engaging a restricted skin surface results in an emergence of a cutaneous response zone in cortical area 3a. *Journal of Neurophysiology, 67,* 1057–1070.

Recanzone, G. H., Merzenich, M. M., Jenkins, W. M., Grajski, K. A., & Dinse, H. R. (1992). Topographic reorganization of the hand representation in cortical area 3b of owl monkeys trained in a frequency-discrimination task. *Journal of Neurophysiology, 67,* 1031–1056.

Recanzone, G. H., Merzenich, M. M., & Schreiner, C. E. (1992). Changes in the distributed temporal response properties of SI cortical neurons reflect improvements in performance on a temporally based tactile discrimination task. *Journal of Neurophysiology, 67,* 1071–1091.

Robertson, D., & Irvine, D. R. F. (1989). Plasticity of frequency organization in auditory cortex of guinea pigs with partial unilateral deafness. *Journal of Comparative Neurology, 282,* 456–471.

Shin, H.-C., Raymond, S. A., & Strichartz, G. R. (1991). Reversible changes of the receptive fields of DCN, VPL thalamic and SI cortical neurons following peripheral application of lidocaine. *Society for Neuroscience Abstracts, 17,* 841.

Sillito, A. M. (1977). Inhibitory processes underlying the directional specificity of simple, complex and hypercomplex cells in the cat's visual cortex. *Journal of Physiology (London), 271,* 699–720.

Smits, E., Gordon, D. C., Witte, S., Rasmusson, D. D., & Zarzecki, P. (1991). Synaptic potentials evoked by convergent somatosensory inputs in raccoon somatosensory cortex: Substrates for plasticity. *Journal of Neurophysiology, 66,* 688–695.

Turnbull, B. G., & Rasmusson, D. D. (1991). Chronic effects of total or partial digit denervation on raccoon somatosensory cortex. *Somatosensory and Motor Research, 8,* 201–213.

Wall, J. T., & Cusick, C. G. (1984). Cutaneous responsiveness in primary somatosensory (S-I) hindpaw cortex before and after partial hindpaw deafferentation in adult rats. *Journal of Neuroscience, 4,* 1499–1515.

Weinberger, N. M., Ashe, J. H., Metherate, R., McKenna, T. M., Diamond, D. M., & Bakin, J. (1990). Retuning auditory cortex by learning: A preliminary model of receptive field plasticity. *Concepts of Neuroscience, 1,* 91–132.

Weinberger, N. M., & Diamond, D. M. (1987). Physiological plasticity in auditory cortex: Rapid induction by learning. *Progress in Neurobiology, 29,* 1–55.

Webster, H. H., Hanisch, U. K., Dykes, R. W., & Biesold, D. (1991). Basal forebrain lesions with or without reserpine injection inhibit cortical reorganization in rat hindpaw primary somatosensory cortex following sciatic nerve section. *Somatosensory and Motor Research, 8,* 327–346.

Witte, S., Zarzecki, P., & Rasmusson, D. D. (1990). New somatosensory epsps in reorganized raccoon cortex without a change in the incidence of corticocortical epsps. *Society for Neuroscience Abstracts, 16,* 44.

Zarzecki, P., Witte, S., Smits, E., Gordon, D. C. Kirchberger, P., & Rasmusson, D. D. (1993). Synaptic mechanisms of cortical representational plasticity: Somatosensory and corticocortical EPSPs in reorganized raccoon SI cortex. *Journal of Neurophysiology, 69,* 1422–1432.

15

Gradients of Cortical Plasticity

JOAQUIN M. FUSTER

I begin by summarizing some conventional wisdom with regard to cortical plasticity. Then I challenge that wisdom even further than has been done in the chapters by Gilbert and Darian-Smith, Kaas, and Toyama, Komatsu, and Tanifuji, by bringing in a bit of my evidence of active memory in primary sensory cortex. And finally, I conclude by suggesting that conventional wisdom is still basically sound; it simply needs some qualifiers.

Figure 15.1 shows a peculiar, although time-honored picture of the human cortex: It is a cortical developmental map by Von Bonin, made basically in accord with the one proposed by Flechsig at the turn of the century. The numbers in it, of course, do not refer at all to cytoarchitectonic areas, but to the order of myelination of the various areas of the cortex in the course of ontogeny. Low numbers have been assigned to primary sensory and motor areas, which attain complete myelination around birth, whereas high numbers are placed on areas of association, whose intrinsic and extrinsic fibers myelinate later in life. Although the precise order of this developmental scheme can be questioned on technical grounds, modern studies (e.g., Gibson, 1991) have indicated that it is essentially correct. It does need, however, substantiation with data from use of other developmental indices, such as synaptic formation, cellular growth and density, dendritic arborization, and so forth. An obvious inference from this scheme, already drawn by Flechsig early on with an associationist frame of mind, is that primary cortex is preformed and functionally rigid, whereas the vast areas of cortex of association are amenable to change and constitute a suitable substrate for learning and memory.

Of course, as conventional wisdom also has it, these structural and functional concepts agree with phylogenetic evidence, because the associative areas of the frontal lobe and the temporoparietal regions are the last to evolve. And indeed, the picture that emerges from these considerations is that, whereas primary areas accommodate the experience of the species, which I call "phyletic memory," areas of association accommodate individual memory, the memory of the individual. Posterior (postcentral) areas would be largely the seat of perceptual memory,

250

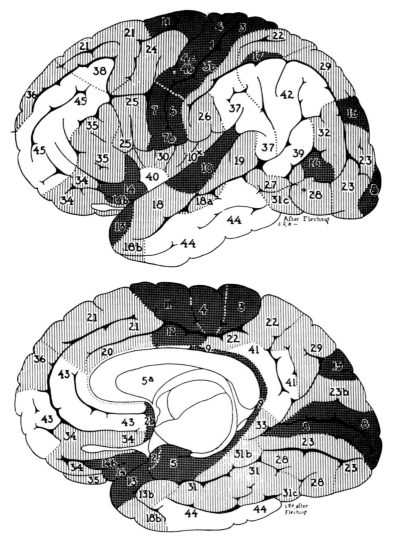

FIGURE 15.1. Order of myelination of cortical areas, according to Flechsig. (From Von Bonin & Bailey, 1950.)

while anterior (precentral) areas would serve motor memory, the memory of the action, whether it be speech, behavior, or perhaps even the thought process.

How is individual memory formed in the cortex? We do not know for sure, but other authors in this volume have offered extremely interesting ideas and data about it. In any case, I do not want to proceed without mentioning a few principles that in the past few years have become part of our thinking in this regard. High among these principles is the principle of *synchronous convergence*. This principle is what I consider Hebb's "second rule," as enunciated in the following words by him:

> . . . any two cells or systems of cells that are repeatedly active at the same time will
> tend to become 'associated', so that activity in one facilitates activity in the other . . .
> [W]hat I am proposing is a possible basis of association of two afferent fibers of the
> same order—in principle, a sensori-sensory association. (Hebb, 1949, p. 70).

Synchronous convergence is in fact probably more important for the formation of memory in the central nervous system (CNS) than Hebb's well-known cardinal rule. Invertebrate data certainly suggest that this is the case (Hawkins, Abrams, Carew, & Kandel, 1983).

Similarly, it would be simultaneous convergence of inputs on cortical neurons that would cause the structural changes to take place, which would reinforce synaptic efficacy and the self-organization of memory networks. Figure 15.2 depicts that process in highly schematic form. Note that the scheme embodies the principles of connectivity invoked by Gilbert and Darian-Smith and by Toyama et al.: convergence, divergence, and recurrence. It also features the lateral connectivity that Gilbert and Darian-Smith have emphasized. When two stimuli arrive simultaneously at their respective networks of representation (1), synaptic changes will be made (2), such that subsequently, one input will be sufficient to activate not only its network but that representing the other input as well, the two now actually forming a unified representational network (3). What's more, that memory network will stay activated for as long as the memory needs to be retained for subsequent action by the animal. That is what we call *active memory*. We prefer this term to that of "working memory" to emphasize that we refer here to one and the same substrate in a different state, in the *active state*. Active memory does not connote a special memory *system,* as working memory does (besides, it avoids an awkward translation to other languages).

How is a memory maintained in the active state? Delay tasks are the best operational definition of active memory. The evidence from lesion studies, includ-

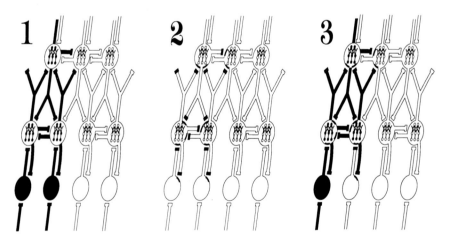

FIGURE 15.2.   Hypothetical enhancement of synapses from synchronous convergence in cortical memory formation (see text).

ing those from our laboratory by use of reversible—cryogenic—lesions (Bauer & Fuster, 1976; Fuster, 1989; Fuster, Bauer, & Jervey, 1981), clearly leads to the conclusion that cortical associative areas are involved in active memory. It is the study of *memory cells,* however, that has in my opinion opened the best possibility so far of delineating the topographic substrate and dynamics of active memory (Funahashi, Bruce, & Goldman-Rakic, 1989; Fuster, 1973; Fuster & Alexander, 1971; Fuster & Jervey, 1982; Niki, 1974; Quintana & Fuster, 1992). These are cells that show sustained elevated discharge during active memory.

Let us briefly examine two memory cells in visual cortex of the monkey (Fuster, 1990). Both seem to encode the color red. The first cell is in inferotemporal cortex (Fig. 15.3). It is inhibited during the stimulus, as if it were "gated," then it is activated, especially during the first few seconds of memorizing red. The second unit (Fig. 15.4) is also preferentially activated during memorization of the color red, but this one is V1, in primary visual cortex. To be sure, memory cells like this one are rare in V1. Besides, they are somewhat different from those of inferotemporal cortex, in that they tend to be more attuned to the sensory properties of the stimulus and less to its cognitive properties than those of inferotemporal cortex. Note that the second cell is protractedly reactivated by the matching stimulus at

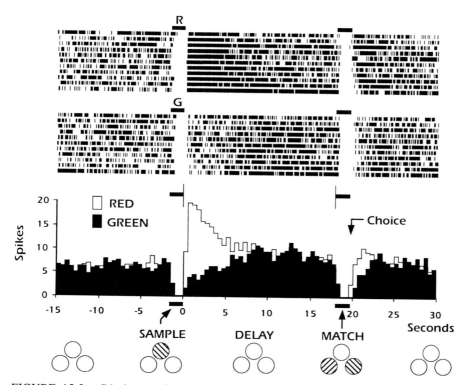

FIGURE 15.3. Discharge of an inferotemporal neuron during a visual memory task (delayed matching-to-sample, paradigm at bottom). The cell is activated during memorization of red; returns to baseline firing shortly after choice (which includes red).

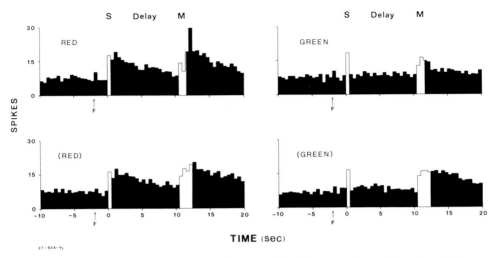

FIGURE 15.4.   Frequency histograms from a unit in V1 cortex during delayed matching. The sample or memorandum is a complex stimulus consisting of a combination of form and color. In top histograms the sample color is behaviorally relevant; in lower histograms it is not. The unit is persistently activated after red samples.

the end of the trial, whereas the cell in Figure 15.3 returns promptly to baseline firing at the end of the trial.

Memory cells can also be found in parietal cortex. We (Koch & Fuster, 1989; Zhou & Fuster, 1992) have analyzed over one thousand neurons in parietal cortex (areas 3, 1, 2, 5, and 7) during haptic memory tasks. Remarkably, we have found many cells with activated discharge during tactile memorization in primary (SI) somatosensory cortex (Figure 15.5). The unit in Figure 15.5, top, is in area 2; it is preferentially activated by the touch of vertical edges on a rod, and also shows some memory activity for the same stimulus. The unit at bottom, in area 3a, shows memory activity for a rough object, not for a smooth object of the same dimensions.

In conclusion, memory cells can be found, for the appropriate modality, in both primary visual and primary somatosensory cortex, although they seem more common in the latter than the former. We can only speculate about the reason for this intermodality difference. The fact remains, however, that a certain number of elements in both cortices show unmistakable signs of involvement in a state of memory that is context-dependent and behaviorally adaptive. Yet, overall, memory cells seem more common in associative than in primary cortex, certainly more common in prefrontal and inferotemporal areas than in V1. Wherever they are found, these cells imply the plasticity that is necessary to represent and to retain behaviorally relevant sensory information.

Thus, from the limited perspective of our data I finish by suggesting that there are probably gradients of plasticity from primary areas to areas of association. Primary areas exhibit plasticity mostly, but not exclusively, under two conditions:

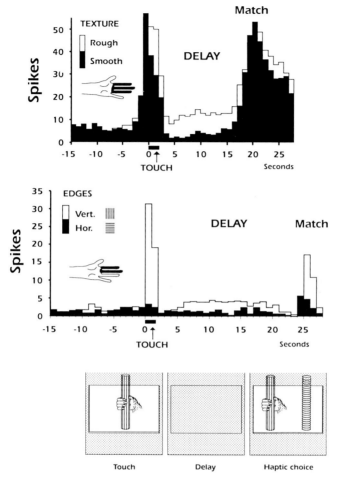

FIGURE 15.5.   Two units of somatosensory cortex in haptic delayed matching (paradigm below). Receptive fields in hand diagrams.

(1) one is in "critical periods," which in my view would be nothing but a necessary rehearsal of phyletic memory, a rehearsal of the memory of the species; this memory may well have been established there through millions of years and perhaps by the same principles, including synchronous convergence, by which individual memory is formed. (2) In the adult, the second condition is after accidental or experimental injury, as demonstrated by the experiments by Kaas, Gilbert, and their colleagues. As we proceed phylogenetically and ontogenetically toward higher areas, plasticity would increase, and the function of those areas would become progressively idiosyncratic and more subject to "top-down" control. Those areas would thus be shaped to accommodate the history of the individual and to interpret and to categorize the world.

REFERENCES

Bauer, R. H., & Fuster, J. M. (1976). Delayed-matching and delayed-response deficit from cooling dorsolateral prefrontal cortex in monkeys. *Journal of Comparative Physiology and Psychology, 90,* 293–302.

Funahashi, S., Bruce, C. J., & Goldman-Rakic, P. S. (1989). Mnemonic coding of visual space in the monkey's dorsolateral prefrontal cortex. *Journal of Neurophysiology, 61,* 331–349.

Fuster, J. M. (1973). Unit activity in the prefrontal cortex during delayed response performance: Neuronal correlates of transient memory. *Journal of Neurophysiology, 36,* 61–78.

Fuster, J. M. (1989). *The prefrontal cortex: Anatomy, physiology, and neuropsychology of the frontal lobe* (2nd ed.). New York: Raven Press.

Fuster, J. M. (1990). Inferotemporal units in selective visual attention and short-term memory. *Journal of Neurophysiology, 64,* 681–697.

Fuster, J. M., & Alexander, G. E. (1971). Neuron activity related to short-term memory. *Science, 173,* 652–654.

Fuster, J. M., Bauer, R. H., & Jervey, J. P. (1981). Effects of cooling inferotemporal cortex on performance of visual memory tasks. *Experimental Neurology, 71,* 398–409.

Fuster, J. M., & Jervey, J. P. (1982). Neuronal firing in the inferotemporal cortex of the monkey in a visual memory task. *Journal of Neuroscience, 2,* 361–375.

Gibson, K. R. (1991). Myelination and behavioral development: A comparative perspective on questions of neoteny, altriciality and intelligence in brain maturation and cognitive development. In K. R. Gibson & A. C. Petersen (Eds.), *Brain maturation and cognitive development* (pp. 29–63). New York: de Gruyter.

Hawkins, R. D., Abrams, T. W., Carew, T. J., & Kandel, E. R. (1983). A cellular mechanism of classical conditioning in Aplysia: Activity-dependent amplification of presynaptic facilitation. *Science, 219,* 400–405.

Hebb, D. O. (1949). *The Organization of Behavior.* New York: Wiley.

Koch, K. W., & Fuster, J. M. (1989). Unit activity in monkey parietal cortex related to haptic perception and temporary memory. *Experimental Brain Research, 76,* 292–306.

Niki, H. (1974). Prefrontal unit activity during delayed alternation in the monkey. II. Relation to absolute versus relative direction of response. *Brain Research, 68,* 197–204.

Quintana, J., & Fuster, J. M. (1992). Mnemonic and predictive functions of cortical neurons in a memory task. *NeuroReport, 3,* 721–724.

Von Bonin, G. F., & Bailey, P. (1950). *Essay on the Cerebral Cortex.* Springfield, IL: Thomas.

Zhou, Y. D., & Fuster, J. M. (1992). Unit discharge in monkey's parietal cortex during perception and mnemonic retention of tactile features. *Society for Neuroscience Abstracts, 18,* 706.

IV

Long-Term Potentiation and Memory

16

Hippocampal Synaptic Enhancement as a Basis for Learning and Memory: A Selected Review of Current Evidence from Behaving Animals

C. A. BARNES

C. A. ERICKSON

S. DAVIS

B. L. McNAUGHTON

Since the discovery of long-term synaptic enhancement (LTE/LTP) by Lømo, Bliss, and Gardner-Medwin (Bliss & Gardner-Medwin, 1973; Bliss & Lømo, 1973; Lømo, 1966), a substantial body of empirical support has accumulated for the theory that LTP of hippocampal synapses represents the experimental activation of processes that normally subserve distributed information storage. Although most experiments have yielded data that tend to support this hypothesis, recently some of this evidence has been called into question. The present overview is an examination of the current status of the suggestion that a process based on LTP underlies information storage. In addition to electrically induced LTP, another form of synaptic strengthening can be induced through behavioral means at some hippocampal synapses (Green, McNaughton, & Barnes, 1990; Sharp, McNaughton, & Barnes, 1989). The extent to which this latter process [short-term exploratory modulation (STEM)] may reflect information acquisition by the hippocampus is also discussed.

IN VITRO VERITAS?

The fact that it has been extremely difficult to build a case for a linkage between LTP and learning and memory in mammals should not discourage the pursuit of an answer to this critical question. It is all too easy to overlook the central assumption, underlying all work that examines LTE/LTP, that this process has some relevance to the way in which the brain normally acquires information. As our methods become more "sophisticated" (e.g., brain slices, minislices, cell culture) and removed from the awake, freely behaving preparation, it is tempting to believe that this increased experimental control will lead necessarily to a more accurate description of the process we believe underlies memory. A number of recent examples, however, illustrate the physiological differences that can arise when departures from the whole animal preparation are made.

For example, there may be important differences between the processes that can be observed with patch-electrodes at cold temperatures in vitro compared with extracellular electrodes in intact in vivo preparations. One illustration of this involves the recent controversy concerning which quantal parameters are altered following high-frequency stimulation of hippocampal afferents. Malinow and Tsien (1990) reported a change in both quantal size and content following LTP induction using patch-clamp methods with slices at room temperature. This method yields very stable membrane recordings; however, at more physiological temperatures (32–33°C), using conventional intracellular recording methods, Foster and McNaughton (1991) observed only a change in quantal size following the LTP-inducing stimulation. More recent evidence from this laboratory (McNaughton, Shen, Rao, Foster, & Barnes, 1994) has shown that the apparent changes in quantal content that can be observed at low temperature are due, at least in part, to a temperature-dependent alteration in the excitability of presynaptic fibers. This excitability change leads to more reliable electrical activation following the stimulation intended to induce LTP. Interestingly, this excitability change can be blocked both by the N-methyl-D-aspartate (NMDA) antagonist APV, and by the antagonist of nitric oxide synthase, L-nitroarginine. At present it is not clear the extent to which this change in axonal excitability causes an artifactual increase in quantal content or represents a secondary correlate of a presynaptic LTP expression mechanism. What is clear is that the same experiments conducted at two different temperatures lead to radically different results.

A second example of plasticity mechanisms that appear to be preparation-dependent is the blockade of synaptic enhancement by inhibitors of nitric oxide or its synthesis: nitric oxide synthase inhibition can block synaptic enhancement in the hippocampal slice preparation under certain conditions (Böhme, Bon, Stutzmann, Doble, & Blanchard, 1991; Haley, Wilcox, & Chapman, 1992; O'Dell, Hawkins, Kandel, & Arancio, 1991; Schuman & Madison, 1991); however, nitric oxide synthase inhibition does not affect LTP induction or maintenance in fascia dentata of awake freely behaving rats (Barnes, McNaughton, Bredt, Ferris, & Snyder, 1994). An interesting possibility arises in this case, in relation to nitric oxide's role in response to tissue injury (e.g., Beckman, 1991; Dawson, Dawson, London, Bredt, & Snyder, 1991; Izumi, Benz, Clifford, & Zorumski, 1992). It may be easier to observe effects of nitric oxide in situations where the tissue has recently been damaged. On the other hand, there may be additional complex temperature and region-specific effects that result in these apparently contradictory findings (Li, Errington, Williams, & Bliss, 1992).

Finally, although hippocampal cell cultures are ideally suited for controlled examination of connected cells, the size of the unitary responses obtained are orders of magnitude larger than those observed in brain slices. This suggests unusual connectivity or metabolic conditions in cultured cells compared with intact tissue. These illustrations simply serve to emphasize the necessity for caution against over interpreting results from preparations that are far removed from normal physiological conditions. This does not imply that the processes that are unmasked under unusual temperature or other conditions are uninteresting, or unused by the nervous system. Rather, the implication is that conditions closer to physiological may reveal those plastic properties of the system that are more readily expressed in vivo. At the very least it is clear that, when possible, results obtained from reduced preparations should be compared with known data from intact animals. The similarities and differences may be quite revealing.

THEORETICAL INDICATIONS THAT SYNAPTIC ENHANCEMENT MIGHT UNDERLIE DISTRIBUTED INFORMATION STORAGE

There are a number of aspects of the LTP process that are consistent with theoretical concepts of memory in neural networks, and thus fuel the belief that LTP at hippocampal synapses may underlie information storage. One of the most obvious of these is its *durability*. The synaptic alterations physiologists had been examining since the 1940s [e.g., posttetanic potentiation (PTP)] were clearly much too short-lasting to form the basis of memories that last days, weeks, or perhaps a lifetime. The fact that LTP-inducing stimulation produced synaptic changes in chronically prepared animals that could be observed over extended time periods (Bliss & Gardner-Medwin, 1973; Douglas & Goddard, 1975) was, in itself, a critical observation. Moreover, repetition of LTP-inducing stimuli can extend the decay time constant of enhancement at the perforant path–granule cell synapse (Barnes, 1979; Jeffery, Abraham, Dragunow, & Mason, 1990). Because repetition or practice also improves behavioral performance, this property of LTP makes it plausible that a similar process might underlie enduring memories. There has been at least one experiment, however, that has shown the opposite effect of repetition. Instead of extending the decay time constant, Huang and colleagues (Huang, Colino, Selig, & Malenka, 1992) found that repeated high-frequency stimulation of Schaffer collaterals led to a decrease in the decay time constant of enhancement in CA1 in hippocampal slices (29–31°C, 0.1-mM picrotoxin). It is not clear whether this reflects a region difference or a preparation difference.

Perhaps the most compelling evidence for the theory that LTP may underlie information storage is the observation that it is a *cooperative* or associative process (Kelso, Ganong, & Brown, 1986; Lee, 1983; Levy & Steward, 1979; Malinow & Miller, 1986; McNaughton, Douglas, & Goddard, 1978; Wigström & Gustafsson, 1986), essentially fulfilling one of the main principles of associative memory outlined by Hebb (1949). The primary assumption of the associative principle was that modification of a synaptic connection on a cell should only occur if that input was coactive with other inputs to the cell. It is now clear that the synaptic enhancement process is controlled by the postsynaptic cell, acting through the voltage-dependent NMDA channels (Collingridge, Kehl, & McLennan, 1983). If sufficient input convergence occurs on the postsynaptic neuron, calcium enters through these channels and initiates a series of processes that result in a persistent change in the synaptic response.

Another important requirement of an efficient information storage mechanism is the property of pre- and postsynaptic *specificity*. Changes that occur over the entire postsynaptic cell or presynaptic axonal arbor, rather than exclusively at the synapses involved in the convergent input event, would have rather low information content. Evidence for input specificity has been demonstrated in a number of different ways. For example, the entorhinal cortex projects from its medial and lateral aspects to the middle and outer dendrites, respectively, of the hippocampal granule cells (Hjorth-Simonsen, 1972; Hjorth-Simonsen & Jeune, 1972; Steward & Scoville, 1976). At least under certain conditions both pathways can be enhanced independently without interacting with the other, even when convergence onto the same subset of postsynaptic cells has been demonstrated (postsynaptic specificity; Andersen, Sundberg, Sveen, & Wigström, 1977; Lynch, Dunwiddie, & Gribkoff, 1977; McNaughton & Barnes, 1977). Furthermore, axon collaterals of this pathway that cross to the other hemisphere do not undergo synaptic change when the ipsilateral component is enhanced (presynaptic specificity; Levy & Steward, 1979; McNaughton & Miller, 1986). Some question, however, has been raised concerning the specificity issue in region CA1 in vitro. Using slice cultures, Bonhoeffer, Staiger, and Aertsen (1989) have shown that if an axon connected to two adjacent cells is stimulated, but only one cell receives simultaneous postsynaptic depolarization, both cells will show enhanced synaptic responses. Unstimulated terminals on the depolarized cell are not enhanced. This effect is restricted to cells within about 150 μm of one another, and implies that some diffusible product, synthesized within the depolarized pyramidal cell, can affect any nearby active axonal terminal. Schuman and Madison (1994) have obtained similar results in conventional hippocampal slices, and implicate nitric oxide in this spread of synaptic enhancement. Because the spread of enhancement among axon terminals appears to be mediated by nitric oxide, the extent to which this effect occurs in vivo remains an open question.

EMPIRICAL SUPPORT FOR A LINKAGE
BETWEEN SYNAPTIC ENHANCEMENT AND BEHAVIOR

Although the linkage between LTP and memory is both weak and indirect, the majority of data are consistent with this notion. The main lines of evidence to date that have supported this idea, as well as more recent contradictory data, are outlined below. The first evidence that LTP and memory were correlated came from a within-animal age comparison of these processes (Barnes, 1979; Barnes &

McNaughton, 1980). Although old rats showed equivalent induction of LTP, the decay of synaptic enhancement over subsequent days tended to be faster in old than in young rats. The persistence of LTP was significantly correlated with memory for a spatial location, both within and between age groups (Barnes, 1979; Barnes & McNaughton, 1980). These findings were later confirmed and extended by de Toledo-Morrell and Morrell (1985).

More direct manipulations of memory and LTP have also been performed; certain treatments that facilitate memory tend to improve LTP induction, whereas those that impair memory tend also to impair the LTP process. Laroche and Bloch (1982) demonstrated that posttrial stimulation of the midbrain reticular formation, which improves avoidance conditioning, also improves LTP induction. Morris and his colleagues (Davis, Butcher, & Morris, 1992; Morris, 1989; Morris, Anderson, Lynch, & Baudry, 1986; Morris, Halliwell, & Bowery, 1989) have demonstrated the converse of this using the NMDA receptor antagonist APV. Both spatial learning and LTP are blocked by this treatment, whether the APV was delivered intraventricularly or directly into the hippocampus.

At the root of the hypothesis that LTP reflects a memory mechanism is the assumption that information is stored as a specific distribution of synaptic weights. By inference, a disruption of this distribution should interfere with the corresponding memory. Two separate experiments lent support to this hypothesis. McNaughton, Barnes, Rao, Baldwin, and Rasmussen (1986) saturated LTP of perforant path–granule cell synapses bilaterally in chronically prepared rats. The most powerful effect observed in these experiments was a large deficit in the ability of these rats to reverse a previously learned spatial habit on the Barnes circular platform task. Interestingly, LTP saturation produced no effect on a well-learned radial 8-arm maze working memory task. In another experiment, the possible confound of uncontrolled effects of stimulation was controlled for by including a group that received high-frequency stimulation to saturation levels, but were not trained on the behavioral task until the enhancement had decayed back to baseline levels (Castro, Silbert, McNaughton, & Barnes, 1989). In this study the Morris water task was used for the behavioral test. This task is conceptually similar to the circular platform task, although the training can be carried out with multiple trials during a single day, whereas for the circular platform one trial per day is optimal, and training takes about two weeks. Again, in this experiment, only those rats whose synapses were bilaterally enhanced at the time of training exhibited a spatial learning deficit.

Recently several different laboratories (Cain, Hargreaves, Boon, & Dennison, 1993; Jeffery & Morris, 1993; Sutherland, Dringenberg, & Huesing, 1993), including our own (Korol, Abel, Church, Barnes, & McNaughton, 1993a), have reported difficulty in replicating the results of Castro et al. (1989) with respect to bilateral LTP-saturation producing a spatial learning deficit. This raised the question of whether the earlier LTP saturation results of McNaughton et al. (1986) might also be unreliable. A replication of the circular platform/LTP experiment was therefore undertaken (Stevenson et al., 1993). This experiment confirmed the earlier findings in which bilateral saturation of LTP in fascia dentata caused a disruption of spatial learning performance in the circular platform task. When a subset of rats tested on the circular platform were also tested in the water task, no behavioral differences were observed between the control rats and those with the saturation treatment. It is not completely clear why performance on these two tasks should be affected differently by the saturation treatment; however, the mnemonic and motivational aspects of the two tasks may make different demands on hippocampal resources.

It should be emphasized that the same theory predicting that saturation of the synaptic weight distribution should lead to a memory impairment also predicts a nonlinear relationship between the extent of synaptic saturation and the behavioral deficit. Specifically, at low levels of saturation there should be virtually no effect whereas, above a critical point, the behavioral effects should increase steeply. Thus, it is possible that "partial saturation" of hippocampal synapses may be the explanation for the different behavioral outcomes on the circular platform and water tasks, as well as for the variability of results on a single task. We thus undertook an assessment of just how much of the hippocampal synaptic population is actually "saturated" by the standard LTP induction protocol. In one study, using multiple stimulation sites, we observed that saturation is not complete with the stimulus parameters and single stimulation placements that have been used in most laboratories (Korol, Jung, Barnes, & McNaughton, 1993b). In addition, activation of the immediate early gene *zif*268, which is highly correlated with LTP induction, was used as an anatomical marker to assess the distribution of LTP in the hippocampus. We found that, with the standard stimulation placements used in these experiments, only dorsal hippocampal synapses were affected by the saturation treatment (Barnes, McNaughton, Andreasson, Church, & Worley, 1993). Thus, it is probable that ventral hippocampal synapses would not have been modified to any significant extent. These findings suggest that variable saturation levels in the hippocampus may provide an answer to the variable behavioral impairments observed following LTP "saturation." When we used a treatment that causes robust electrophysiological LTP and activates *zif*268 at all dorsal/ventral levels (maximal electroconvulsive shock), we were able to find reliable spatial learning performance deficits on the water task (Barnes et al., 1993). Thus, we conclude that one necessary condition for the hypothesis that attempts to relate LTP to learning remains on reasonably strong ground.

CAN LASTING SYNAPTIC ENHANCEMENT BE INDUCED BEHAVIORALLY?

Conspicuously lacking from the list of empirical support for a role of LTP in memory has been a convincing demonstration for the spontaneous induction of LTP during learning. A number of experiments have reported experience-dependent, persistent changes in evoked hippocampal field potentials or intracellular records (Coulter et al., 1989; Ruthrich, Matthies, & Ott, 1982; Sharp, Barnes, & McNaughton, 1987; Sharp, McNaughton, & Barnes, 1985; Skelton, Scarth,

Wilkie, Miller, & Philips, 1987; Weisz, Clark, & Thompson, 1984). The problem is that the effects observed were robust only in the population spike or afterhyperpolarizing potentials, with no reliable effect on the synaptic response (with one exception; see Green & Greenough, 1986). As discussed in detail by Bliss and Lynch (1988), a change in the population spike alone probably reflects a nonspecific excitability mechanism that is not necessarily related to synaptic enhancement. This is not to imply that enduring changes in excitability are not of fundamental importance to information processing in the system. For example, in the Sharp et al. (1987) experiment, young and old rats were given exposure to a large room with complex objects, as well as other rats. Over several days, this led to an increase in the population spike that was equivalent between age groups. This increase persisted for about two weeks after return of the animals to their normal housing conditions; however, the old rats exhibited a more rapid decay of the population spike increase than did the young rats. This is very reminiscent of the faster decay of the synaptic response observed in old rats following LTP-inducing stimulation (Barnes, 1979). It is possible, therefore, that certain mechanisms may be shared between these sorts of behavioral treatments and LTP.

Although no studies have demonstrated physiological alterations in synaptic efficacy with the persistence of LTP, less enduring, but nevertheless large and reliable changes in the field EPSP can be observed following episodes of exploratory behavior in either novel or relatively familiar environments (Green et al., 1990; Sharp, McNaughton, & Barnes, 1989; and see McNaughton & Barnes, 1990). We call this phenomenon short-term exploratory modulation, or STEM (Fig. 16.1). The most obvious differences between STEM and LTP at the perforant path–granule cell synapse is that LTP can last for much longer than STEM, whose maximum persistence is not more than about an hour. Furthermore, although the EPSP is significantly increased during STEM, and the latency of the population spike shifts leftward (as in LTP), the population spike amplitude is reduced (Figs. 16.1 and 16.2). The independence of STEM and LTP is also suggested by the failure to detect occlusion between the two processes. When STEM was compared before and after the bilateral induction of LTP, they had an additive relationship (Erickson, McNaughton, & Barnes, 1993a). This suggests that they do not share a common mechanism, or may be expressed at different populations of synapses. The difference between LTP and STEM is reinforced by observations that these phenomenon affect the waveshape of the EPSP differently. LTP results in a uniform increase over the whole time course (hence is reflected in an increased EPSP slope), whereas STEM involves a distinct leftward shift in the apparent onset of the EPSP (Fig. 16.3) with much less of a change in slope (Erickson et al., 1993a). The EPSP increases in STEM are blocked, however, by systemic injections of the NMDA receptor antagonist MK-801 (Fig. 16.4; Croll, Sharp, & Bostock, 1992; Erickson, McNaughton, & Barnes, 1990). Following DSP4 treatment, which depletes norepinephrine throughout the brain (Jaim-Etcheverry & Zieher, 1980; Jonsson, Hallman, Ponsjo, & Ross, 1981; Ross, 1976), STEM was also found to be significantly attenuated (Fig. 16.5A; Davis, Wenk, Sage, Barnes, & McNaughton, 1992). Furthermore, antagonism of nore-

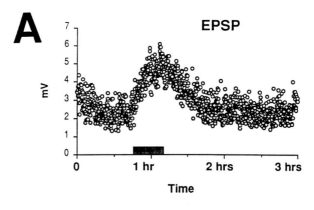

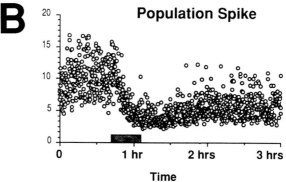

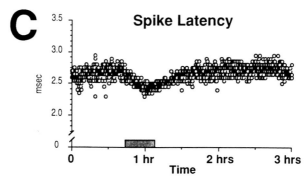

FIGURE 16.1. Example of short-term exploratory modulation (STEM) during a 3-hour experiment conducted on one individual rat. Each point represents the extracted values of the amplitude of the EPSP (AS), population spike area (B), and population spike latency (C) (see Fig. 16.2 for explanation of parameter extraction). The shaded bar on each graph denotes the time period during which the rat engaged in exploratory behavior on an elevated triangular platform. Both before and after the shaded bar, recordings were obtained from the rat while it sat in its home cage. Note that the EPSP increased and the population spike latency decreased gradually during the bout of exploratory behavior, but returned to baseline levels following cessation of exploration. On the other hand, the population spike area decreased during exploration and, in this example, did not return to baseline levels during the recording session.

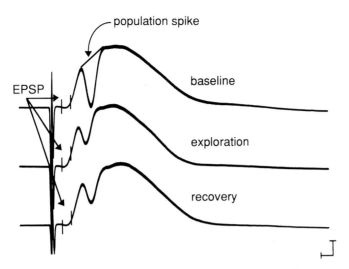

FIGURE 16.2. Perforant path–granule cell evoked response waveform averages: mean and standard error of the mean response from one rat. For the point plots constructed in Figures 16.1 and 16.4, the EPSP amplitude was measured as the voltage difference between two constant time points (see vertical lines), the population spike onset latency as the time at which the slope of the response turned from positive to negative polarity, and the size of the population spike was taken as the area of the response under the tangent line joining spike onset and offset. The top waveform is the average of the responses obtained during the baseline period before exploration; the middle average was collected during exploration; and the bottom waveform average was taken near the end of the 3-hour recording session (see Figure 16.1.). Calibration bar 3 mV, 1 msec.

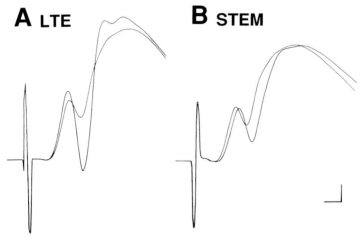

FIGURE 16.3. Examples of the change in the perforant path–granule cell field potential following LTE induction (A) compared with the change following exploratory behavior that leads to STEM (B). The points to note concern the differences in how the responses change: the slope of the synaptic wave is altered in LTE, but shifts leftward in STEM, whereas the amplitude of the population spike increases with LTE, and is reduced during STEM. Calibration: 1 ms, 0.25 mV.

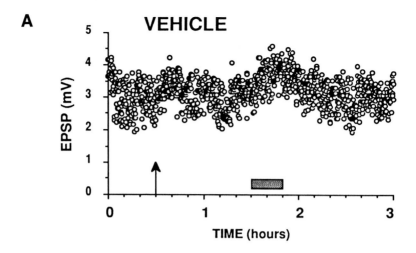

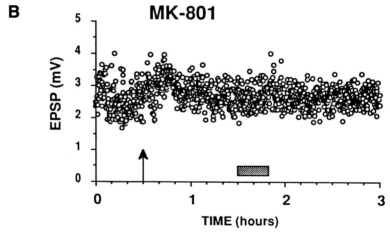

FIGURE 16.4. Example of the effect of the NMDA antagonist MK-801 on STEM. These data were obtained from the same rat on two separate days one week apart. (A) On the first day the rat was injected intraperitoneally with saline at the arrow, and returned to its home cage. During the 20-minute period indicated by the shaded bar the rat was allowed to explore on the triangular platform, following which it was placed back into its home cage for the remainder of the 3-hour recording period. (B) The identical procedure was used one week later, except that 0.3 mg/kg MK-801 was injected instead of saline. Normal STEM was observed during the exploratory period following the saline injection (A); however, STEM was abolished following the MK-801 injection (B). The EPSP increase observed in B following the injection was due to a bout of exploratory behavior by the rat in its home cage, which presumably occurred before the MK-801 reached the central nervous system.

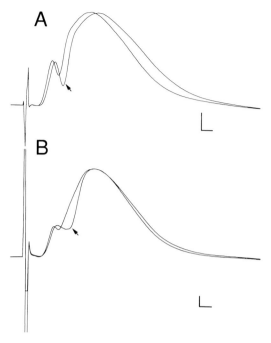

FIGURE 16.5.   Individual examples of the effects on STEM of interfering with the noradrenergic system either by treatment with the antagonist propranolol (A), or with DSP4,
which destroys noradrenergic terminals (B). The responses indicated by the arrows represent averages of the drug conditions compared with their corresponding vehicle controls
following 25 minutes of forced-choice behavior on the radial 8-arm maze. There were no
effects of the drug treatments on baseline responses or maze performance. Notice that the
EPSPs are larger and population spikes are smaller in the control STEM condition. Calibration bars: 1 mV, 2 msec.

pinephrine with injections of propranalol also attenuates STEM (Fig. 16.5B),
suggesting that norepinephrine may be normally involved in the full expression of
STEM.

Given the data concerning the behavioral induction of STEM, it was natural to
propose that these changes might reflect a mechanism for storage of specific
information that would be learned when the animal was engaged in attentive or
exploratory behaviors. This hypothesis appears now to be untenable, however, in
view of the recent findings of Moser, Mathiesen, and Andersen, (1993), who
showed that STEM results largely from an elevation in brain temperature resulting
from exploratory activity. We have also conducted experiments in which temperature was manipulated in intact, anesthetized rats via radiant heat lamps, and
confirm that relatively small changes in body temperature produce changes that
essentially duplicate those observed in the same animals when they were awake
and engaged in exploration. This includes both a reduction in the population spike
amplitude and a left shift of the EPSP (Fig. 16.6A). Therefore it appears that the
major component of the change in the EPSP and population spike that occurs

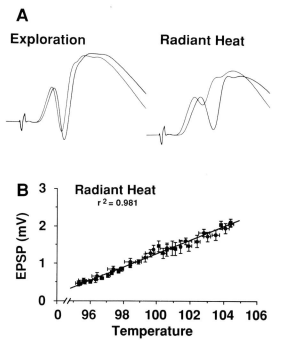

FIGURE 16.6. (A) Examples from an individual rat of the effects of exploratory behavior on the field potential in fascia dentata, and the effects of radiant heat while this same rat was anesthetized. (B) The size of the EPSP is shown plotted against the change in body temperature (the same rat as in (A), anesthetized with sodium pentobarbital). Such heating resulted in approximately a 10°F range of body temperature change, and waveform changes very similar to those observed during STEM.

during exploration may be due to brain temperature changes, possibly as a result of alterations in local blood flow (Fig. 16.6B), in which monoamines may play some direct role (Beckman, 1970; Feldberg & Myers, 1964; Poole & Stevensons, 1979). Furthermore, it is likely that the blockade of STEM by MK-801 can be explained by the brain temperature-reducing effects of MK-801 (Buchan & Pulsinelli, 1990; Corbett, Evans, Thomas, Wang, & Jonas, 1990) rather than its blockade of the NMDA receptor per se.

There are a number of important issues that remain to be resolved concerning the STEM phenomenon. Among these are whether brain temperature itself has an effect on hippocampal function, and whether any of the changes observed in the population spike or EPSP are independent of brain temperature. It has been suggested, for example, that temperature-dependent changes in the population spike may not reflect a reduction in granule cell output, but a reduction in the size of individual spikes. Although there are temperature-dependent alterations of individual, extracellular action, potential waveforms (single units), the changes in the individual spikes are not great enough to account for all of the changes in the population spike (unpublished observations). Furthermore, indirect evidence suggests that overall granule cell output is reduced by about 10% following either exploration or passive heating-induced temperature increases (Erickson et al., 1993b). The evidence for this comes from the observation that the disynaptic commissural response from the granule cells (corrected for peak shifts resulting from temperature) is always slightly smaller at relatively higher brain temperatures. This observation suggests that there are small *temperature-dependent* changes in the number of granule cells that fire to a given perforant path stimulus, and thus that brain temperature may play some modulatory role in general cell excitability.

Moser, Moser, & Andersen (1993) have recently observed a reliable short-lasting increase in the EPSP amplitude during exploration, which cannot easily be accounted for by changes in brain temperature. They found that when brain temperature increases are produced by exploratory behavior, the synaptic field potentials are approximately 8% greater than when the same brain temperatures are produced by whole body heating. The durability of this *temperature-independent* EPSP increase is about 15 minutes. As with any study involving the use of extracellular field potentials, which do not directly reflect either transmembrane potentials or their underlying conductances, a number of controls will be required before it can safely be concluded that the observed changes reflect synaptic potentiation. These include the tests for specificity, possible changes in extracellular conductivity or resting membrane potentials, and constancy of the presynaptic volley. Even with such controls, it will remain to be demonstrated whether the changes are distributed within the population in a manner reflecting actual information storage, or indicating merely a global modulation from some extrinsic source such as any one of the subcortical or hormonal systems known to affect hippocampal field potentials.

Although the temperature-independent effect of exploratory behavior is not durable enough to account for longer-lasting memories, the time course is interesting with respect to recent multiple single-cell recording experiments conducted while rats were engaging in exploratory activity. Significant increases in the strength of cross-correlations develop between individual hippocampal cells that have place fields that overlap in the environment (Wilson & McNaughton, 1993). These strengthened cross-correlations also persist after removal of the rat from the environment for a period of about 20 minutes. Although a similar time course does not necessarily imply a similar mechanism, it is possible that the short-lasting synaptic strength changes observed by Moser, Moser, & Andersen, (1993) may underlie the dynamic changes in population firing characteristics observed by Wilson and McNaughton (1993).

CONCLUSIONS

At this point LTP continues to be a viable candidate for the process used by the nervous system for the purpose of information storage. It is clear, however, that we remain in the early stages of the search for the elusive direct relationship we seek between biophysical phenomena in the nervous system and information storage in behaving animals. In the final analysis, the only way in which this search can be accomplished is through the use of intact, freely behaving animals. Although these preparations pose difficult challenges, we are learning more about the necessary controls and the sorts of data that will be required to develop strong arguments that will either allow us to discover convincing direct links between LTP, behavior and associative memory, or to convincingly refute the possibility that the brain uses an LTP-like process to store information.

ACKNOWLEDGMENTS

We thank Geeta Rao for assistance with figure preparation. This work was supported by grants from MH00897, MH48824, and the Office of Naval Research.

REFERENCES

Andersen, P., Sundberg, S. H., Sveen, O., & Wigström, H. (1977). Specific long-lasting potentiation of synaptic transmission in hippocampal slices. *Nature, 266,* 736–737.

Barnes, C. A. (1979). Memory deficits associated with senescence: A neurophysiological and behavior study in the rat. *Journal of Comparative Physiology and Psychology, 931,* 74–104.

Barnes, C. A., & McNaughton, B. L. (1980). Spatial memory and hippocampal synaptic plasticity in middle-aged and senescent rats. In D. Stein (Ed.), *Psychobiology of aging: Problems and perspectives* (pp. 253–272). New York: Elsevier/North-Holland.

Barnes, C. A., McNaughton, B. L., Andreasson, K., Church, L., & Worley, P. F. (1993). Comparison of LTE-inducing stimulation and electroconvulsive shock on the rostral-caudal extent of hippocampal *zif*268 mRNA activation, synaptic enhancement, and spatial memory disruption. *Society for Neuroscience Abstracts, 19,* 794.

Barnes, C. A., McNaughton, B. L., Bredt, D. S., Ferris, C. D., & Snyder, S. H. (1994). Nitric oxide synthase inhibition in vivo: Lack of effect on hippocampal synaptic enhancement or spatial memory. In M. Baudry & J. L. Davis (Eds.), *Long-term potentiation* (Vol. 2, pages 37–43).

Beckman, A. L. (1970). Effect of intrahypothalamic norephinephrine on thermoregulatory responses in the rat. *American Journal of Physiology, 218,* 1596–1604.

Beckman, J. S. (1991). The double-edged role of nitric oxide in brain function and superoxide-mediated injury. *Journal of Developmental Physiology, 15,* 53–59.

Bliss, T. V. P., & Gardner-Medwin, A. R. (1973). Long-lasting potentiation of synaptic transmission in the dentate area of the anaesthetised rabbit following stimulating of perforant path. *Journal of Physiology, 232,* 357–374.

Bliss, T. V. P., & Lømo, T. (1973). Long-lasting potentiation of synaptic transmission in the dentate area of the anaesthetised rabbit following stimulation of perforant path. *Journal of Physiology, 232,* 331–356.

Bliss, T. V. P., & Lynch, M. A. (1988). Long-term potentiation of synaptic transmission in the hippocampus; Properties and mechanisms. In P. Landfield & S. Deadwyler (Eds.), *Long-term potentiation: From biophysics to behavior* (pp. 3–72). New York: Alan R. Liss.

Bonhoeffer, T., Staiger, V., & Aertsen, A. (1989). Synaptic plasticity in rat hippocampal slice cultures: Local "Hebbian" conjunction of pre- and postsynaptic stimulation leads to distributed synaptic enhancement. *Proceedings of the National Academy of Sciences of the United States of America, 86,* 8113–8117.

Böhme, G. A., Bon, C., Stutzmann, J.-M., Doble, A., & Blanchard, J.-C. (1991). Possible involvement of nitric oxide in long-term potentation. *European Journal of Pharmacology, 199,* 379–381.

Buchan, A. & Pulsinelli, Wa. A. (1990). Hypothermia but not the N-methyl-D-aspartate, MK-801, attenuates neuronal damage in gerbils subjected to transient global ischemia. *The Journal of Neuroscience, 10,* 311–316.

Cain, D. P., Hargreaves, E. L., Boon, F., & Dennison, Z. (1993). An examination of the relations between hippocampal long-term potentiation, kindling, afterdischarge, and place learning in the water maze. *Hippocampus, 3,* 153–164.

Castro, C. A., Silbert, L. H., McNaughton, B. L., & Garnes, C. A. (1989). Recovery of spatial learning deficits following decay of electrically-induced synaptic enhancement in the hippocampus. *Nature, 342,* 545–548.

Collingridge, G., Kehl, S., & McLennan, H. (1983). Excitatory amino acids in synaptic transmission in the Schaffer collateral-commissural pathway of the rat hippocampus. *Journal of Physiology (London), 334,* 3–46.

Corbett D., Evans S., Thomas C., Wang D., & Jonas, R. A. (1990). MK-801 reduced cerebral ischemic injury by inducing hypothermia. *Brain Research, 514,* 300–304.

Coulter, D. A., LoTurco, J. J., Kubota, M., Disterhoft, J. F., Moore, J. W., & Alkon, D. L. (1989). Classical conditioning reduces amplitude and duration of calcium-dependent after hyperpolarization in rabbit hippocampal pyramidal cells. *Journal of Neurophysiology, 61(5),* 971–981.

Croll, S. D., Sharp, P. E., & Bostock, E. (1992). Evidence for NMDA receptor involvement in environmentally induced dentate gyrus plasticity. *Hippocampus, 2,* 23–28.

Davis, S., Butcher, S. P., & Morris, R. G. M. (1992). The NMDA receptor antagonist D-2-amino-5-phosphonopentanoate (D-AP5) impairs spatial learning and LTP *in vivo* at intracerebral concentrations comparable to those that block LTP *in vitro. Journal of Neuroscience, 12(1),* 21–34.

Davis, S., Wenk, G. L., Sage, A., Barnes, C. A., & McNaughton, B. L. (1992). The role of noradrenergic input in the generation of short-term synaptic plasticity in the dentate gyrus. *Society for Neuroscience Abstracts, 18,* 1217.

Dawson, V. L., Dawson, T. M., London, E. D., Bredt, D. S., & Snyder, S. H. (1991). Nitric oxide mediates glutamate neurotoxicity in primary cortical cultures. *Proceedings of the national Academy of Sciences of the United States of America, 88,* 6368–6371.

de Toledo-Morrell, L., & Morrell, F. (1985). Electrophysiological markers of aging and memory loss in rats. *Annals of the New York Academy of Sciences, 444,* 296–311.

Douglas, R. M., & Goddard, G. V. (1975). Long-term potentiation of the perforant path-granule cell synapse in the rat hippocampus. *Brain Research, 86,* 205–215.

Erickson, C. A., McNaughton, B. L., & Barnes, C. A. (1990). Exploration-dependent enhancement of synaptic responses in rat fascia dentata is blocked by MK801. *Society for Neuroscience Abstracts, 16,* 442.

Erickson, C. A., McNaughton, B. L., & Barnes, C. A. (1993a). Comparison of long-term enhancement and short-term exploratory modulation of perforant path synaptic transmission. *Brain Research, 615,* 275–280.

Erickson, C. A., McNaughton, B. L., & Barnes, C. A. (1993b). Temperature-dependent reduction in population spike area does not alter functional output of the fascia dentata in rat hippocampus. *Society for Neuroscience Abstracts, 19,* 793.

Feldberg, W., & Myers, R. D. (1964). Effects on temperature of amnines injected into the cerebral ventricles. A new concept of temperature regulation. *Journal of Physiology, 173,* 226–237.

Foster, T. C., & McNaughton, B. L. (1991). Long-term synaptic enhancement in hippocampal field CA1 is due to increased quantal size, not quantal content. *Hippocampus, 1,* 79–91.

Green, E. J., & Greenough, W. T. (1986). Altered synaptic transmission in dentate gyrus of rats reared in complex environments: Evidence from hippocampal slices miantained in vitro. *Journal of Neurophysiology, 55,* 739–749.

Green, E. J., McNaughton, B. L., & Barnes, C. A. (1990). Exploration-dependent modulation of evoked responses in fascia dentata: Dissociation of motor, EEG and sensory factors, and evidence for a synaptic efficacy change. *Journal of Neuroscience, 10,* 1455–1471.

Haley, J. E., Wilcox, G. L., & Chapman, P. F. (1992). The role of nitric oxide in hippocampal long-term potentiation. *Neuron, 8,* 211–216.

Hebb, D. O. (1949). *The organization of behavior.* New York: Wiley.

Hjorth-Simonsen, A. (1972). Projection of the lateral part of the entorhinal area to the hippocampus and fascia dentata. *The Journal of Comparative Neurology, 146,* 219–232.

Hjorth-Simonsen, A., & Jeune, B. (1972). Origin and termination of the hippocampal perforant path in the rat studied by silver impregnation. *Journal of Comparative Neurology, 144,* 215–232.

Huang, Y.-Y., Colino, A., Selig, D. K., & Malenka, R. C. (1992). The influence of prior synaptic activity on the induction of long-term potentiation. *Science, 255,* 730–733.

Izumi, Y., Benz, A. M., Clifford, D. B., & Zorumski, C. F. (1992). Nitric oxide inhibitors attenuate *N*-methyl-D-aspartate excitotoxicity in rat hippocampal slices. *Neuroscience Letters, 135,* 227–230.

Jaim-Etcheverry, G., & Zieher, L. M. (1980). DSP4: A novel compound with neurotoxic effects on noradrenergic neurons of adult and developing rats. *Brain Research, 188,* 513–523.

Jeffery, K. J., Abraham, W. C., Dragunow, M., & Mason, S. E. (1990). Induction of Fos-like immunoreactivity and the maintenance of long-term potentiation in the dentate gyrus of unanesthetized rats. *Molecular Brain Research, 8,* 267–274.

Jeffery, K. J., & Morris, R. G. M. (1993). Cumulative long-term potentiation in the rat dentate gyrus correlates with, but does not modify, performance in the water maze. *Hippocampus, 3,* 133–140.

Jonsson, G., Hallman, H., Ponsjo, F., & Ross, S. (1981). DSP4 N-(2-chloroethyl)-N-ethyl-2-bromo-benylamine)—A useful denervation tool for central and peripheral noradrenergic neurons. *European Journal of Pharmacology, 72,* 173–188.

Kelso, S. R., Ganong, A. H., & Brown, T. H. (1986). Hebbian synapses in hippocampus. *Proceedings of the National Academy of Sciences of the United States of America, 83,* 5326–5330.

Korol, D. L., Abel, T. W., Church, L. T., Barnes, C. A., & McNaughton, B. L. (1993a). Hippocampal synaptic enhancement and spatial learning in the Morris swim task. *Hippocampus, 3,* 127–132.

Korol, D. L., Jung, M. W., Barnes, C. A., & McNaughton, B. L. (1993b). How widespread is LTE "saturation" at perforant path-granule cell synapses? *Society for Neuroscience Abstracts, 19,* 794.

Laroche, S., & Bloch, V. (1982). Conditioning of hippocampal cells and long-term potentiation: An approach to mechanisms of post-trial memory facilitation. In C. Ajmone-Marsen & H. Matthies (Eds.) *Neuronal plasticity and memory formation* (pp. 575–587). New York: Raven Press.

Lee, K. S. (1983). Cooperativity among afferents for the induction of long-term potentiation in the CA1 region of the hippocampus. *Journal of Neuroscience, 7,* 1369–1372.

Levy, W. B., & Steward, O. (1979). Synapses as associative memory elements in the hippocampal formation. *Brain Research, 175,* 233–245.

Li, Y.-G., Errington, M. L., Williams, J. H., & Bliss, T. V. P. (1992). Temperature-dependent block of LTP by the NO synthase inhibitor L-NARG. *Society for Neuroscience Abstracts, 18,* 343.

Lynch, G. S., Dunwiddie, T., & Gribkoff, V. (1977). Heterosynaptic depression: A postsynaptic correlate of long-term potentiation. *Nature, 266,* 734–735.

Lømo, T. (1966). Frequency potentiation of excitatory synaptic activity in the dentate area of the hippocampal formation. *Acta Physiological Scandinavica, 68,* 28.

Malinow, R., & Miller, J. P. (1986). Postsynaptic hyperpolarization during conditioning reversibly blocks induction of long-term potentiation. *Nature, 321,* 529–530.

Malinow, R., & Tsien, R. W. (1990). Presynaptic changes revealed by whole-cell recordings of long-term potentiation in rat hippocampal slices. *Nature, 346,* 177–180.

McNaughton, B. L., & Barnes, C. A. (1977). Physiological identification and analysis of dentate granule cell response to stimulation of the medial and lateral perforant pathways in the rat. *Journal of Comparative Neurology, 175,* 439–454.

McNaughton, B. L., & Barnes, C. A. (1990). From cooperative synaptic enhancement to associative memory: Bridging the abyss. *Seminars in the Neurosciences, 2,* 403–416.

McNaughton, B. L., Barnes, C. A., Rao, G., Baldwin, J., & Rasmussen, M. (1986). Long-term enhancement of hippocampal synaptic transmission and the acquisition of spatial informa-tion. *Journal of Neuroscience, 6*(2), 563–571.

McNaughton, B. L., Douglas, R. M., & Goddard, G. V. (1978). Synaptic enhancement in fascia dentata: Cooperativity among coactive afferents. *Brain Research, 157,* 277–293.

McNaughton, N., & Miller, J. J. (1986). Collateral specific long-term potentiation of the output of field CA3 of the hippocampus of the rat. *Experimental Brain Research, 62,* 250–258.

McNaughton, B. L., Shen, J., Rao, G., Foster, T. C., and Barnes, C. A. (1994). Increased CA1 axon terminal excitability following repetitive electrical stimulation: Dependence on NMDA receptor activity, nitric oxide synthase, and temperature. *Proceedings of the National Academy of Sciences of the United States of America, 91,* 4830–4834.

Morris, R. G. M. (1989). Synaptic plasticity and learning: Selective impairment of learning in rats and blockade of long-term potentiation *in vivo* by the *N*-methyl-D-aspartate receptor antago-nist AP5. *Journal of Neuroscience, 9*(9), 3040–3057.

Morris, R. G. M., Anderson, E., Lynch, G. S., & Baudry, M. (1986). Selective impairment of learning and blockade of long-term potentiation by an *N*-methyl-D-aspartate receptor antag-onist, AP5. *Nature, 319*(6056), 774–776.

Morris, R. G. M., Halliwell, R. F., & Bowery, N. (1989). Synaptic plasticity and learning II: Do different kinds of plasticity underlie different kinds of learning? *Neuropsychologia, 27*(1), 41–59.

Moser, E., Mathiesen, I., & Andersen, P. (1993). Association between brain temperature and dentate field potentials in exploration and swimming rats. *Science, 259,* 1324–1326.

Moser, E., Moser, M.-B., & Andersen, P. (1993). Synaptic potentiation in the rat dentate gyrus during exploratory learning. *NeuroReport, 5,* 317–320.

O'Dell, T. J., Hawkins, R., Kandel, E. R., & Arancio, O. (1991). Tests of the roles of two diffusible substances in long-term potentiation: Evidence for nitric oxide as a possible early retro-grade messenger. *Proceedings of the National Academy Sciences of the United States of America, 88,* 11285–11289.

Poole, S., & Stevenson, J. D. (1979). Effects of noradrenaline and carbachol on temperature regula-tion of rats. *British Journal of Pharmacology, 65,* 43–51.

Ross, S. B. (1976). Long term effects of N-2-chloroethyl-N-ethyl-2-bromobenylamine hydrochloride on noradrenergic neurons in the rat brain and heart. *British Journal of Pharmacology, 58,* 521–527.

Ruthrich, H., Matthies, H., & Ott, T. (1982). Long-term changes in synaptic excitability of hippo-campal cell populations as a result of training. In A. Marsan & H. Matthies (Eds.), *Neuronal plasticity and memory formation* (pp. 589–594). New York: Raven Press.

Schuman, E. M., & Madison, D. V. (1991). A requirement for the intercellular messenger nitric oxide in long-term potentiation. *Science, 254,* 1503–1506.

Schuman, E. M., & Madison, D. V. (1994). Locally distributed synaptic potentiation in the hippo-campus. *Science, 263,* 532–536.

Sharp, P. E., Barnes, C. A., & McNaughton, B. L. (1987). Effects of aging on environmental modulation of hippocampal evoked responses. *Behaviorial Neuroscience, 101,* 170–178.

Sharp, P. E., McNaughton, B. L., & Barnes, C. A. (1985). Enhancement of hippocampal field potentials in rats exposed to a novel, complex environment. *Brain Research, 339,* 361–365.

Sharp, P. E., McNaughton, B. L., & Barnes, C. A. (1989). Exploration dependent modulation of evoked responses in fascia dentata: Fundamental observations and time course. *Psycho-biology, 17,* 257–269.

Skelton, R. W., Scarth, A. S., Wilkie, D. M., Miller, J. J., & Philips, G. (1987). Long-term increases in dentate granule cell responsivity accompany operant conditioning. *Journal of Neuro-science, 7,* 3081–3087.

Stevenson, G. D., Korol, D. L., Galganski, M. E., Abel, T. L., McNaughton, B. L., & Barnes, C. A. (1993). "Saturation" of perforant path granule cell LTE/LTP does disrupt some spatial tasks. *Society for Neuroscience Abstracts, 19,* 794.

Steward, O., & Scoville, S. A. (1976). Cells of origin of entorhinal cortical afferents to the hippocampus and fascia dentata of the rat. *Journal of Comparative Neurology, 169,* 347–370.

Sutherland, R. J., Dringenberg, H. C., & Hoesing, J. M. (1993). Induction of long-term potentiation at perforant path dentate synapses does not affect place learning or memory. *Hippocampus, 3,* 141–148.

Weisz, D. G., Clark, G. A., & Thompson, R. F. (1984). Increased responsivity of dentate granule cells during nictitating membrane response conditioning in rabbit. *Behavioral Brain Research, 12,* 145–154.

Wigström, H., & Gustafsson, B. (1986). Postsynaptic control of hippocampal long-term potentiation. *Journal of Physiology Paris, 81,* 228–236.

Wilson, M. A., & McNaughton, B. L. (1993). Persistence of behaviorally induced correlation in place cell activity during sleep. *Society for Neuroscience Abstracts, 19,* 795.

17

Neural Mechanisms of Associative Memory: Role of Long-Term Potentiation

SERGE LAROCHE
VALÉRIE DOYÈRE
CATHERINE RÉDINI-DEL NEGRO
FRANÇOIS BURETTE

Long-term potentiation (LTP) is a paradigm example of activity-dependent strengthening of synaptic connections of the kind that has long been invoked as a potential substrate for information storage. Since the original description by Bliss and Lømo (1973) of long-lasting changes in synaptic efficacy following tetanic stimulation of afferent fibers in the adult mammalian hippocampus, tremendous advances have been made in the characterization of the properties, mechanisms of induction, maintenance, and expression of LTP at certain pathways within the hippocampus (see Bliss & Collingridge, 1993; Bliss & Lynch, 1988; Kuba & Kumamoto, 1990; Wallace, Hawrylak, & Greenough, 1991, for reviews). Uncertainties and controversies still exist, but from current research, it can be advocated that none of the data available so far contradict the predictions that can be formulated if LTP is to be viewed as a neural model for synaptic changes in learning. For example, the associative property of LTP (Brown, Kairiss, & Keenan, 1990; Gustafsson & Wigström, 1986; Kelso, Ganong, & Brown, 1986; McNaughton, Douglas, & Goddard, 1978; White, Levy, & Steward, 1988), together with, at another level, the description of the voltage-dependent characteristics of the N-methyl-D-aspartate (NMDA) subtype of glutamate receptor that may provide a membranal device for associativity (see Collingridge & Bliss, 1987; Wigström & Gustafsson, 1988, for reviews) have provided powerful explanatory notions for elementary spatiotemporal rules for network remodeling. As remarkable as these similarities are, they by no means provide the kind of evidence required for accepting the idea that the brain does in fact exploit this property for the purpose of learning and memory formation. If LTP can indeed be viewed as one of the most popular preparations to evoke biochemical and structural substrates of network plasticity, synaptic plasticity cannot be taken as a global model of memory without an obvious semantic shift (trap). Asking whether or not a physiological mechanism like LTP *is* a model of memory, as it is often phrased, is not likely to be meaningful from a psychological standpoint because a mechanistic ability is implicitly converted into a global description in a way that overshadows a number of fundamental theoretical tenets drawn from behavioral analyses of memory.

Memory is a psychological construct. It refers to an organized collection of representations of events and of the relationships between events. And when cognitive psychologists began to dominate learning and memory research in the late 1960s, these concepts of sensory or mnemonic representations became key concepts in both psychological and physiological models of memory. In the common sense of the word, a representation refers to something that allows reflexively to present to oneself a piece of the world. Its formation is the result of a process of internalization of the properties of the world in an open functional space that uses its own systems of coordinates, its own referential. The major issue is to understand the neural code that serves this process, and is therefore used to create representations in a form that are not passive projections onto a mental screen— the simple copies of stimuli that were refered to during the area of naive realism— but are self-organizational constructions that create information.

Within this context, the search for the elementary mechanisms of memory focuses on two major questions: How is information represented and organized permanently in the brain? and What are the processes that control the construction, storage, retrieval, and utilization of these representations? From a neurobiological point of view, it is widely accepted that memory is an emergent property of the collective behavior of systems of neurons organized transiently or permanently into functional networks by preferential coupling. According to traditional views, events from the environment are transformed into sets of sensory messages and encoded as spatiotemporal patterns of activity that propagate in vast and complex circuits to constitute a collection of distributed representations at different levels of abstraction. The physical state produced by transient autoorganization of neural noise into specific activity patterns in a large population of distributed neurons can be identified with what Lewis (1979) called *active memory*, which, we believe, is the actual support of information.

Experimental studies over the past 50 years have, however, provided ample evidence that specific activity patterns cannot persist for periods of time sufficient to account for memory lasting more than a few minutes. So there should exist a second form of memory, a static or *inactive* form of memory leading to what is often called a *dormant engram*. The conceptual scheme elaborated by Hebb (1949), according to which changes take place at the cellular level to store these representations, is still prevalent. He proposed that "repeated stimulation of particular receptors" leads slowly to the growth of an "assembly of association-area cells which can act briefly as a closed system after stimulation has ceased," delivering facilitation to other such systems to constitute a "phase sequence—the thought process." From his well-known neurophysiological postulate, permanence of memory is accounted for by "some structural change that make the synapse more readily traversed." The only departure is that active and inactive memory, regarded as states of memory, do not necessarily result from serial operations. If it is a reasonable assumption to consider the encoding of inactive memory as a specific distribution of changes in strength or weights of modifiable synapses, inactive memory will then be characterized by the absence of specific activity in the network, and therefore it cannot be taken as the support of information per se. As discussed elsewhere, the dormant engram only provides the potential for reactivating the memory trace in its active form whenever a subset of the original information, or related information, is available (Bloch & Laroche, 1984). Inactive to active memory shifting can therefore be regarded as a necessary requirement for retrieval, recognition, rehearsal, or any operation performed on the memory store.

What must be deciphered therefore is both the syntax and semantics of neural representations, understanding how information in the brain is created, organized, and retrieved being a major challenge. If we seek to define the neural mechanisms exploited by the brain for the purpose of learning and memory formation, then the first questions about the possible biological significance of LTP that can at best be posed are: Is LTP one of the necessary, or at least useful, elementary mechanisms involved? and if so, What are the processes of the global function implemented by this mode of local interaction?

In this chapter, we consider different angles of attack that have been pursued in testing the LTP hypothesis in the context of associative learning and memory. First, several electrophysiological studies are introduced since they provide valuable information as to the nature of the hippocampal component of a representational system that encodes newly learned information in classical conditioning tasks. Experimental evidence is then presented that suggests that some of the mechanisms underlying enduring changes in synaptic strength in LTP are activated in hippocampal networks during encoding of associative information in classical conditioning. In addition, recent experiments suggest that these changes are necessary for the formation of the hippocampal component of the neural representation. Finally, studies indicate that continuous readjustment of synaptic weights plays an important role in the control of the strength of the memory trace, in both acquisition and long-term retention or forgetting. The possibility that changes also occur in cortical areas, and in particular at hippocampal outputs to the prefrontal cortex, is discussed. The results provide a working framework within which the dynamics of information storage in hippocampal and cortical networks is profiled.

CLASSICAL CONDITIONING AND THE NATURE
OF THE HIPPOCAMPAL COMPONENT
OF AN ASSOCIATIVE MEMORY TRACE

Throughout this chapter we are primarily concerned with associative learning by which an animal acquires knowledge about the relationships or associations between events of its environment. In our studies, we used a classical conditioning task in which animals learn an association between two sensory stimuli: a tone, for example, acting as a conditioned stimulus (CS); and a footshock acting as an unconditioned stimulus (US). Acquisition and retention are measured by suppression of lever-pressing for food reward to the behaviorally significant CS in a standard conditioned suppression paradigm. We chose this paradigm because the extensive literature based on well-defined behavioral procedures enables the control of the sequence of events that engage the learning process and allows analysis of the learning processes underlying response change within a well-defined conceptual framework (e.g., Dickinson, 1980; Mackintosh, 1974).

From a number of recording experiments performed in various behavioral conditions in many laboratories, it is well documented that hippocampal neurons present consistent changes in activity in correlation with stimulus relationships during classical conditioning tasks (e.g., Berger, Alger, & Thompson, 1976; Olds, Disterhoft, Segal, Kornblith, & Hirsh, 1972). During the learning of a tone–shock association, neurons in the dentate gyrus and hippocampus, but not in entorhinal cortex, show a marked increase in activity in response to the behaviorally significant CS (Bloch & Laroche, 1981; Laroche, Falcou, & Bloch, 1983). Importantly, this associative cell response develops very rapidly, within a few learning trials. Its development parallels behavioral conditioning and the neurons sustain stimulus-evoked responses for periods of several months. From many behavioral experiments investigating discrimination learning and reversal, extinction, sensory preconditioning, latent inhibition, transfer-of-control tasks, or blocking procedures (Berger & Thompson, 1982; Best & Best, 1976; Deadwyler, West, & Lynch, 1979; Laroche, Neuenschwander-El Massioui, Edeline, & Dutrieux, 1987b; Neuenschwander-El Massioui, Dutrieux, & Edeline, 1991; Port, Beggs, & Patterson, 1987), it is clear that the response of these neurons reflects an active state of a neural representation of the learned association. Its development, therefore, is involved in or reflects the rapid formation of a *hippocampal component* of the acquired CS–US representation (Laroche, Bloch, Doyère, & Rédini-Del Negro, 1991a).

Although the existence of a conditioned cell response in the hippocampus and dentate gyrus is sufficient to provide a rationale for studying possible synaptic mechanisms underlying its formation, the evidence that rats with bilateral hippocampal lesions perform almost normally in simple classical conditioning tasks (Garrud et al., 1984; Rickert, Lorden, Dawson, & Smyly, 1981; see also Gallistel, Chapter 20, this volume) raises questions as to the role the hippocampus may play in learning and/or retention in this task. The most straightforward conclusion from these data is that the hippocampus is not necessary for the *expression* of the behavioral response in a simple version of the task. However, several other experiments have shown severe learning deficits after hippocampal lesions in more complex conditioning tasks (Rudy & Sutherland, 1989; Schmajuk, 1984; Solomon, 1977; Thompson et al., 1984). The apparent contradiction between electrophysiological data attesting that hippocampal circuits form a representation of a CS–US association on the one hand, and lesion experiments in various forms of conditioning task on the other, can be resolved however, if the hippocampus is implicated in the formation of a representation of the CS–US association that is only used upon certain demands of the task. The important issue then is to understand the nature of the associative representation encoded within these circuits, and of which the associative cell response is an index. In other words, how does one interpret this index of network activation in terms of information content? In classical conditioning, one element of learning is that the tone predicts shock, and learning consists of the formation of a novel knowledge structure that is only indirectly manifest in behavior. This knowledge structure, however, is not unitary in nature. It involves multimodal representations of environmental events and of their relationships, including information about the external and internal contexts. Moreover, the memory architecture consists of the formation of multiple internal representations encoding the learned experience under different informational domains. For example, in considering the simple CS–US relationship, a distinction has been drawn between a declarative form of the representation describing the relationship between the events in a way that enables integration of disparate, but relevant, items of information, and a procedural form allowing translation of knowledge into action, that is, reflecting the use through which the knowledge will control behavior (Dickinson, 1980). The former can be related to a CS–US link through which the representation of the CS will activate the representation of the US, whereas the latter reflects activation of a representation of the conditioned response (CR) through a CS–CR link. The electrophysiological approach has provided important clues in regard to this distinction. First, in a transfer-of-control task, hippocampal cell responses to the behaviorally significant CS have been shown to correlate with the association being learned between environmental events, whatever actual behavior or response tendency is exhibited as a direct consequence of this knowledge (Laroche et al., 1987b). In tone–shock conditioning, the cell response to the CS can therefore be dissociated from the behavioral response it elicits. Second, in a blocking paradigm, hippocampal cells do respond to the "blocked" stimulus that is paired with shock, but nonetheless behaviorally silent (Neuenschwander-El Massioui et al., 1991). These data, in line with the growing belief that the hippocampus is predominantly implicated in declarative or explicit aspects of memories (see Squire, 1992, for a recent review), suggest that the hippocampal cell response is a neural index of the declarative form of the CS–US representation, a conclusion that has also been reached from the cellular correlates observed in delayed nonmatching to sample tasks (Otto & Eichenbaum, 1992). This does not exclude contributions of other structures or systems, some of which being presumably involved in encoding the same associative event under different contents and dimensions. For example, a role for the cerebellum in more procedural aspects of conditioning tasks has been suggested (Thompson et al., 1984), whereas information about the affective valence of the representation may implicate the amygdala and its multiple routes of interaction with limbic structures (Iwata, LeDoux, Meeley, Arneric, & Reis, 1986; LeDoux, 1991; see also Davis, Campeau, Kim, & Falls, Chapter 1, this volume).

Although the specialized functions that different structures and systems serve is still a matter of debate, the possibility should not be underestimated that the brain forms representations that are not *necessary* for the expression of a given behavioral response. As far as the hippocampus is concerned, the argument as a whole suggests that, even in the absence of an *explicit* demand, as in simple classical conditioning, hippocampal circuits are part of a network probably involved in the formation of a "declarative" aspect of the CS–US representation for which the CS-specific neural response is an index. In the simplest version of the task, mediation of the behavioral response would probably not depend critically on the activation of this representation. On a broader perspective, however, this will obviously provide a primary adaptive value from the malleability and predisposition that will be confered to the representational system.

SYNAPTIC EFFICACY CHANGES IN LEARNING

In the past few years, a number of authors have investigated whether learning is accompanied by a change in the amplitude of field potentials, since this measure is the usual test for LTP (Buzsáki, Grastyán, Czopf, Kellényi, & Prohaska, 1981; Jaffard & Jeantet, 1981; Laroche, 1985; Rüthrich, Matthies, & Ott, 1982; Weisz, Solomon, & Thompson, 1984). However, no coherent picture has yet emerged, and there has been no convincing demonstration for any hippocampal subfields that classical conditioning produces an increase in the amplitude of synaptic potentials. The difficulty in detecting changes in synaptic potentials during learning has generally been attributed to two possible sources. First, learning may induce synaptic changes over a limited set of active afferents, and sparse changes might be difficult to detect with the field potential recording technique. Second, potentiation of one set of synapses may be accompanied by depression at other synapses, so that the averaged synaptic strength would remain constant. In an ex vivo study, an increase in synaptic potentials has been found several days after exposure to an enriched environment (Green & Greenough, 1986), and a resurgence in the interest in using the field potential recording technique in behaving animals has been prompted by a report of increases in synaptic potentials during exploration of a novel environment (Green, McNaughton, & Barnes, 1990). Although the increase in the excitatory postsynaptic potential (EPSP) in the dentate gyrus during exploration suggests a form of synaptic plasticity that may reflect a similar mechanism as LTP, it is not immediately obvious in exploration how to isolate what is due to learning per se, and how to quantify exactly what is learned and when learning takes place. Moreover, the interpretation that enhanced synaptic strength in the dentate gyrus reflects an information storage process has been challenged on the basis of experiments suggesting that the increase in synaptic potentials during exploration may be attributed to a concomitant increase in brain temperature associated with motor activity (Moser, Mathiesen, & Andersen, 1993).

Despite these caveats we have attempted to investigate potential learning-induced changes in synaptic efficacy in our conditioning paradigm that requires little movement and enables the use of control animals subjected to the same behavioral context and sensory experience, and we have monitored changes in the perforant path-evoked potential in the dentate gyrus and temperature changes during the course of learning (Laroche, Doyère, & Rédini-Del Negro, 1991b). As in our previous experiments, we used a classical conditioning paradigm in which a tone acting as a CS was paired with a footshock as a US, whereas pseudoconditioned rats experienced unpaired tone and shock presentations. Variations in the efficacy of synaptic transmission was quantified by measuring the maximal slope of EPSP. The main outcome of this experiment is that learning the CS–US relationship is accompanied by a rapid increase in the slope of the EPSP that persists for a period of time that lasts longer than the learning session by 15 to 20 minutes (Fig. 17.1). In contrast, synaptic transmission in pseudoconditioned rats show no significant changes during unpaired tone and shock presentations, but decreases abruptly (within a time period of about 2 intertrial intervals) and persistently (for more than one hour) after pseudoconditioning sessions. Detailed analysis of the dynamics of the EPSP growth early in conditioning indicated that the increase in EPSP slope occurred after five CS–US paired trials, that is, at about the same time at which both behavioral conditioning and the dentate cell response to the CS are normally seen. In subsequent sessions, presentation of the trials again produced an enduring increase in synaptic efficacy. There was, however, a clear tendency for the effect to attenuate in amplitude and duration with overtraining when the association is well learned. Temperature measured in the dentate gyrus of rats undergoing an identical procedure was found to increase slightly and transiently during training, but these changes had no obvious relationship with the observed changes in the field EPSP. First, temperature was found to increase with an identical amplitude time course in both conditioned and pseudoconditioned rats. This finding is at variance with the differential effect that conditioning and pseudoconditioning have on changes in EPSP slope. Second, the rapid increase in EPSP slope in conditioning was in contrast to the much more progressive increase in temperature in the dentate gyrus. Third, the lack in correlation between temperature and EPSP changes was even more pronounced across sessions, since the increase in temperature was closely similar in amplitude and time course on every conditioning and pseudoconditioning session, while changes in EPSP slope clearly differed across sessions. Thus, these results reveal several dissociations between changes in synaptic efficacy and variations in brain temperature in this learning paradigm. Although further experiments are needed to estimate the consequences of the increase in brain temperature in both conditioning and pseudoconditioning, it seems unlikely that this increase can be entirely responsible for the differential changes in synaptic efficacy that were found to accompany conditioning and pseudoconditioning. We are therefore led to conclude that most of the changes in field EPSPs observed in conditioned and pseudoconditioned animals reflect training-related modifications in synaptic efficacy at the perforant path-dentate granule cell synapses. In summary, changes in the efficacy of synaptic transmission can

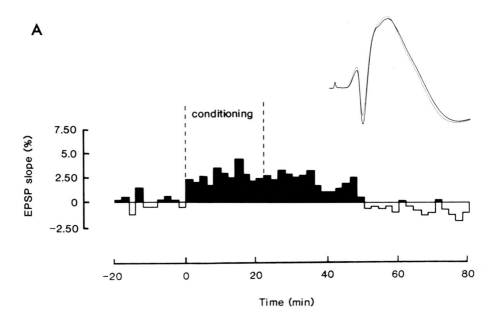

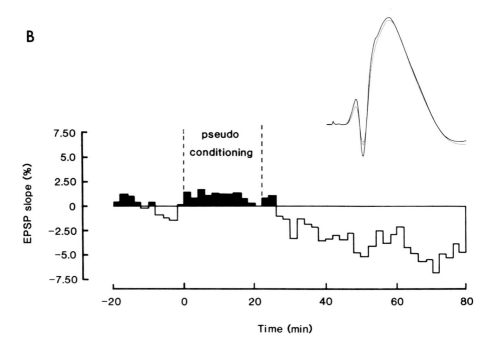

be produced in the gentate gyrus during learning of an associative relationship between sensory events in classical conditioning. In addition, synaptic potentiation or synaptic depression can both be produced, and the direction of the change seems to be determined by the temporal relationships between environmental events. The parallels between variations in synaptic efficacy, the responsiveness of hippocampal cells to significant events of the task, and behavioral conditioning are consistent with the involvement of synaptic potentiation in the initial learning process, as well as in the improvement of learning over repeated distributed training until the task is mastered.

The mechanisms underlying these potentiation and depression effects controlled by environmental events remain to be investigated. In any case, however, CS–US associative learning is presumably accompanied by a substantial potentiation of a set of perforant path afferents. If we speculate that information about the CS and US are conveyed to hippocampal circuits by distinct sets of perforant path afferents converging onto dentate granule cells (see Witter, Groenewegen, Lopes da Silva, & Lohman, 1989), then the inverse changes that occur when paired or unpaired trials are given can be interpreted as reflecting the temporal constraint of synchronous or asynchronous activation of these afferents in establishing synaptic potentiation or depression. Possible functional consequences are discussed more fully later.

LONG-LASTING CHANGES IN SYNAPSE PHYSIOLOGY AND CHEMISTRY AFTER LEARNING

Obviously, however, the changes described so far are not of the long-term type one might expect if an enduring LTP-like change underlies a stable memory trace. However, there is also evidence for longer lasting changes in synapse physiology and chemistry after conditioning. For example, electrophysiological evidence has

FIGURE 17.1.   Amplitude–time course of the changes in synaptic efficacy in the dentate gyrus in classical conditioning (A) and pseudoconditioning (B). Perforant path single shocks were applied at a rate of one per 30 seconds prior to, during, and for one hour after training sessions. Each bar represents the group mean average of the EPSP slope values taken from four consecutive field potentials, and expressed as a percentage of mean value obtained prior to training. The data are averaged across four consecutive training sessions of eight trials. Dashed lines on each graph indicate the period during which CS–US paired [in (A)] or unpaired [in (B)] trials were given. On top of graphs are representative waveforms of the responses obtained in individual rats of each group. Responses obtained during conditioning [dotted line in (A)] and after pseudoconditioning [dotted line in (B)] are superimposed on a control response in each case (solid line). Conditioning was accompanied by an increase in EPSP slope that lasted longer than the period during which the CS–US trials were presented, whereas the EPSP slope decreased abruptly after the period of unpaired trials presentation. Note on the waveforms that the amplitude of the population spike decreased equally in the two groups.

shown that synaptic responsiveness during tetanic stimulation measured in in vitro slices is increased in CA1 one day after classical conditioning in the rabbit (Lo-Turco, Coulter, Alkon, 1988), as is tetanus-induced LTP in the dentate gyrus in vivo after classical conditioning in the rat (Bergis, Bloch, & Laroche, 1990). The increase in the ability of the synapses in the dentate gyrus to display LTP is illustrated in Fig. 17.2: a tetanus applied 5 days after training produced a greater LTP in conditioned rats than in pseudoconditioned rats. These data are evidence for long-lasting changes in synaptic function after learning, and the LTP-strengthening effect suggests that both artificially induced LTP and learning-induced changes may share, at least in part, common underlying mechanisms.

To test this hypothesis more directly, and as another approach for studying synaptic changes in learning, we have undertaken a series of experiments to investigate whether synaptic changes induced by learning involve biochemical mechanisms similar to those associated with LTP. That the expression of LTP in certain hippocampal pathways is at least in part due to persistent presynaptic increases in neurotransmitter release has been largely discussed on the basis of biochemical and, more recently, quantal analyses (see Bekkers & Stevens, 1991; Bliss & Collingridge, 1993; Larkman, Hannay, Stratford, & Jack, 1992; Malinow & Tsien, 1990; McNaughton, 1991; Voronin, Kuhnt, & Gusev, 1991). At the origin of the proposed presynaptic mechanism is the demonstration that LTP at the perforant path–dentate granule cell synapses is correlated with a sustained in-

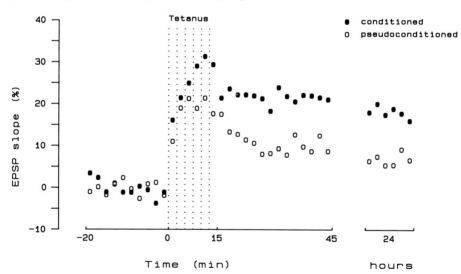

FIGURE 17.2.   Increase in tetanus-induced LTP in the dentate gyrus 5 days after conditioning. Six high-frequency trains (400 Hz–20 msec) given at 2-minute intervals (dotted lines) were applied 5 days after four training sessions in conditioned (filled circles) and pseudoconditioned (open circles) rats. Each point is the group mean of the EPSP slope values of the average of four evoked responses to perforant path single shocks. The values are expressed as a percentage of the pretetanus baseline. LTP was significantly enhanced in conditioned compared to pseudoconditioned rats.

crease in the release of glutamate, the putative transmitter for this pathway (see Bliss & Lynch, 1988). In learning experiments, we used an ex vivo technique, successfully applied to investigate neurotransmitter release in LTP (Bliss, Errington, Laroche, & Lynch, 1987; Feasey, Lynch, & Bliss, 1986), in which the dentate gyrus is removed at various times after learning to examine on slices or synaptosomes the release of radiolabelled glutamate. Release is stimulated by depolarization in elevated potassium in the presence and absence of calcium. Three different sets of experiments lend support to the hypothesis that learning is associated with a rapid and sustained increase in the capacity of the synapses in the dentate gyrus to release glutamate. In these experiments, the calcium-dependent component of potassium-stimulated release, a measure of the ability of terminals to release glutamate, was found to be increased one hour and one day after learning (Laroche, Errington, Lynch, & Bliss, 1987a; Laroche, Rédini-Del Negro, Clements, & Lynch, 1990b). In another experiment, an increase in the capacity of the synases to release glutamate was found 50 days after a single learning session (Laroche, Doyère, & Rédini-Del Negro, 1991c). The details of the mechanisms by which tone–shock associative learning induces this rapid and persistent change in neurotransmitter release are unknown. But the argument that synaptic changes induced by learning involves mechanisms similar to those activated in LTP is greatly strengthened by the demonstration that the increase in glutamate release associated with learning is, as is LTP at medial perforant path synapses, blocked by infusion within the dentate gyrus of the NMDA receptor antagonist AP5 during learning (Rédini-Del Negro & Laroche, 1993). Moreover, at the presynaptic site, learning is associated with an enduring increase in the production of inositol phosphates and diacylglycerol (Laroche et al., 1990b), both of which function as second messengers in a cascade for signal transduction that involve activation of protein kinase C. This cascade has been implicated in LTP (Akers, Lovinger, Colley, Linden, & Routtenberg, 1986; Bär, Wregant, Lopes da Silva, & Gispen, 1984; Clements, Errington, Bliss, & Lynch, 1990; Tsien & Malinow, 1990), and translocation of protein kinase C from the cytosol to its active site in the membrane has been observed in area CA1 following eyelid conditioning in the rabbit (Bank, DeWeer, Kuzirian, Rasmussen, & Alkon, 1988).

In summary, the evidence to date strongly supports the hypothesis that synaptic changes do occur in hippocampal circuits as a result of associative learning. Biochemical data indicate a considerable degree of similarity in the changes associated with classical conditioning and LTP, although this should obviously not be regarded as exclusive, since many other parallel neurochemical cascades could be involved as well. Learning-dependent synaptic changes can be regarded as an elementary mechanism for the marking of the topological structure of the network that would serve to produce a latent engram (inactive memory). The persistence of neurochemical changes as described earlier, possibly coupled with alteration in synapse morphology (Wallace et al., 1991) and in receptor sensitivity (Tocco et al., 1991), would then contribute to the increased probability of the stabilized network to be reactivated when spatiotemporally patterned depolarizations are produced in the network as a result of bombardment by pertinent input signals.

Long-lasting changes in synapse physiology and chemistry are therefore presumed to serve a process of specification and consolidation of hippocampal networks initially activated during the formation of memory.

ARE LTP-LIKE CHANGES NECESSARY OR AT LEAST USEFUL FOR LEARNING AND MEMORY?

While the argument as a whole that synaptic changes of an LTP form do occur during learning is an important step in itself, it provides no direct evidence for or against the next major issue as to whether these changes in hippocampal circuits are necessary, or at least useful, for the building up of the hippocampal component of the memory trace, as would be predicted from the general marking hypothesis discussed earlier. Many experimental efforts in recent years have been directed at addressing this issue, using in behavioral experiments maneuvers that specifically block or reduce LTP. Stimulated by the early observation by Morris and his collaborators that intraventricular infusion of the NMDA receptor antagonist AP5 impairs spatial learning in rats (Morris, Anderson, Lynch, Baudry, 1986), a number of authors have reported that pharmacological blockade of NMDA-dependent forms of LTP produces severe learning deficits in tasks that are known to be affected by hippocampal lesions (see Morris, Davis, & Butcher, 1990; Staubli, Thibault, DiLorenzo, & Lynch, 1989, and Staubli, Chapter 18, in this volume, for reviews). In our own attempts to address this issue, we have shown that chronic infusion of AP5 into the dentate gyrus through implanted cannulaes prevents the acquisition of a CS–US association in a classical conditioning paradigm in which high-frequency stimulation of the perforant path served as a cue signal (Laroche, Doyère, & Bloch, 1989). The approach is currently being pursued in several laboratories using a variety of pharmacological manipulations (see Chapter 18 by Staubli in this volume), or the more recently developed gene knocking out technique, as examplified by studies of genetically altered mice that do not express the α subunit of Ca^{2+}/calmodulin-dependent protein kinase II, and which display spatial learning deficits and a reduced ability for LTP (Silva, Paylor, Wehner, & Tonegawa, 1992a; Silva, Stevens, Tonegawa, & Wang, 1992b).

Despite the success of this approach as a whole, little information is gained as to whether or not a blockade of LTP-like synaptic changes in a given circuit during training actually affects the neural representation that is presumably encoded within the circuit under study. To address this question, we recently conducted an experiment designed at investigating whether blockade of synaptic changes of an LTP form would affect the development of neuronal responses to the significant CS during conditioning. In this experiment (Rédini-Del Negro & Laroche, 1992), AP5 was perfused through osmotic minipumps into the dentate gyrus during conditioning while recording cell discharges to the CS near the infusion site. As illustrated in Figure 17.3, AP5 infusion produced nearly complete abolishment of the sustained CS-evoked cell response that is normally seen in control rats or in rats receiving saline infusion. Not all components of the response were completely

A **Controls**

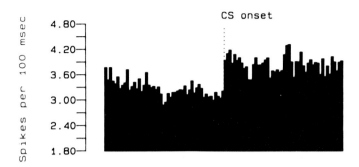

B **AP5 infusion within the dentate gyrus**

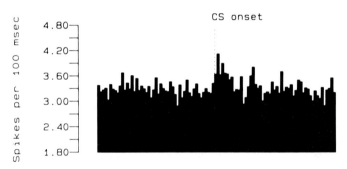

FIGURE 17.3.   Suppression of the CS-evoked conditioned cell response by infusion of AP5 into the dentate gyrus during conditioning. The graphs are peristimulus time histograms (100-msec bin width) of dentate multiunit activity recorded during the last of three conditioning sessions in rats with no infusion or vehicle infusion (A) and in rats receiving AP5 infusion (B). Each histogram is based on a group mean and averages of ten CS–US paired trials for the 5 sec just prior to the CS and the 5 sec of the CS. Dotted line indicates CS onset. AP5 infusion into the dentate gyrus prevented the development of the sustained associative cell response that is normally seen to the CS during classical conditioning.

abolished, however, and an early component can still be detected, although its amplitude and stability were significantly reduced. Interestingly, Foster, Hampson, West, and Deadwyler (1988) showed that lesion of the medial septum affects preferentially this early component of the neural response. The early, NMDA-independent, burst response could therefore be mediated by afferent excitation from other sources. However, contribution of other mechanisms such as an increased excitability, or NMDA-independent forms of LTP, such as that described at lateral perforant path (Bramham, Milgram, & Srebro, 1991), cannot be ruled out at present. In any event, the most striking effect in rats treated with AP5 is the absence of the sustained component of the response that demonstrates CS selectivity in classical conditioning (Deadwyler et al., 1979; Edeline, Dutrieux, & Neuenschwander-El Massioui, 1988; Foster et al., 1988; Laroche et al., 1987b). Importantly, spontaneous spiking activity, the reactivity of these cells to a loud and novel tone, as well as a previously established conditioned cell response, all remained intact under AP5. Since blocking NMDA-dependent synaptic plasticity during learning is almost sufficient to produce a critical suppression of sustained conditioned cell response, the findings strongly support the hypothesis that an NMDA-dependent form of synaptic plasticity is necessary for the full development of the hippocampal component of the CS–US associative representation.

MAGNITUDE OF SYNAPTIC POTENTIATION: ITS ROLE IN THE CONTROL OF LEARNING STRENGTH

Several predictions relating the magnitude of synaptic changes to the strength of learning can be derived from physiological and theoretical models of memory based on elementary synaptic weighing rules. If LTP-like mechanisms serve a process of synapse strengthening and network stabilization that is critical for the formation of a neural representation in an inactive form during learning, then a first prediction is that the strength of learning should be at least in part determined by the magnitude of synaptic changes within the activated network.

A first indication that this might indeed be the case was provided by experiments showing learning facilitation by a maneuver that amplifies LTP. Specifically, it was shown that electrical stimulation of the midbrain reticular formation (MRF), which facilitates LTP at perforant path synapses and prolongs its duration (Bloch & Laroche, 1985), facilitates in parallel behavioral conditioning, the development of the associative responses of dentate and hippocampal cells to the significant CS and learning-induced synaptic changes as expressed by the LTP-strengthening effect described earlier (Bergis et al., 1990; Bloch & Laroche, 1981). Interestingly, these experiments revealed a temporal gradient of efficacy of MRF stimulation, both in learning and in LTP experiments, which is indicative of a critical time window during which the development of synaptic changes is open to modulatory control affecting their stabilization.

What would be required, however, for a more direct test of the preceding prediction is an experimental design that will allow correlative studies of both physiological and behavioral variables in the same animals. The difficulty here relies in the multidimensional and distributed nature of memory that makes very unlikely the possibility for the amplitude of synaptic changes at a single locus in the brain to be directly correlated with performance. However, using a task in which direct activation of the perforant path serves as a cue signal should in principle alleviate this problem since the procedure would allow direct estimation of synaptic strength within a set of perforant path fibers primarily and necessarily involved in the learning task. Adopting this procedure, we trained rats to learn an association between a high-frequency stimulation of the perforant path (the CS) and a footshock (the US). The amount the animals learned and remembered about the CS–US relationship was quantified by measuring conditioned suppression of lever-pressing for food reward. In this task, animals were able to learn the CS–US association when stimulation parameters were set to produce reliable LTP in the dentate gyrus during learning. Interestingly, animals reaching nearly maximal performance displayed much greater LTP than those that did learn the task, but to a lesser extent (see Laroche et al., 1991c), suggesting a direct relation between the amount of learning and the magnitude of potentiation at the activated synapses. This relationship was further established in other experiments in which three different methods were used to block or reduce the amount of LTP during learning (infusion of AP5 into the dentate gyrus, stimulation parameters below the threshold for LTP induction, inhibitory activation of commissural inputs to the dentate gyrus). The prediction that learning deficits would be proportional to LTP reduction was confirmed in this study, and most importantly, a linear correlation emerged between the magnitude of synaptic potentiation and performance at the end of training (Laroche et al., 1989). We can therefore conclude that the more synaptic potentiation is produced in the network activated during memory formation, the more the animals learn. In addition, the pharmacological approach followed by Davis, Butcher, & Morris, (1992) leads to a similar conclusion, since the authors found, after intraventricular infusion of AP5, an inverse correlation between the content of AP5 in hippocampal tissue and both the magnitude of hippocampal LTP and spatial learning performance.

DECAY OF SYNAPTIC POTENTIATION: ITS ROLE IN LONG-TERM MEMORY AND FORGETTING

The second prediction relates the maintenance or fading over time of learning-induced synaptic changes to long-term memory or forgetting. Efficient retrieval from long-term memory store has been hypothesized to rely on the probability for the network to be selectively reactivated upon excitation from a sufficient subset of the original information (Bloch & Laroche, 1984). The assumption is implicit that the maintenance or decay of the memory trace at any given time will be determined by the residual strength of the synapses that were originally strengthened by learning, so that forgetting might occur on condition of regression of synaptic changes to prelearning values. On a long-term basis, the idea was supported by the very long-lasting change in glutamate release observed 50 days after learning a CS–US association that is perfectly remembered.

Different approaches provided indirect experimental support for this hypothesis. First, Barnes and McNaughton (1985) observed a striking parallel between the decay rate of LTP in the dentate gyrus and the forgetting rate of spatial information in old and young rats. Second, MRF stimulation was shown to prolong LTP and to promote the long-term maintenance of the associative cell response to a CS after classical conditioning (Bloch & Laroche, 1981, 1985). Third, the converse was found using protein synthesis inhibitors that prevent the formation of long-term memory and suppress the late phases of LTP in the dentate gyrus (Krug, Lössner, & Ott, 1984; Otani, Marshall, Tate, Goddard, & Abraham, 1989). In a recent experiment, we specifically addressed the issue of the relationship between the residual fraction of synaptic changes a long time after learning and long-term retention of associative memory, using the task in which direct activation of a set of perforant path fibers serves as a cue signal. The decay of LTP was followed for a month after learning in rats having equivalent levels of performance and of LTP magnitude by the end of training, and then retention was assessed behaviorally. It was found that rats with a slowly decaying function of LTP, and for which most of the LTP induced during learning was therefore preserved at the time of retention, displayed high levels of retention of the CS–US association, whereas forgetting was observed in cases for which LTP had decayed to very low levels. Here again, a correlation was found between the magnitude of LTP preserved just prior to the retention test and performance displayed at this test (Doyère & Laroche, 1992), suggesting that long-term associative memory depends, at least in part, on the maintenance of synaptic changes induced during learning.

THREE CONSIDERATIONS

On the Duration of Long-Term Potentiation

The experiments reported earlier strongly support the hypothesis that the strength of the memory trace, both during learning and in long-term memory, depends on the magnitude of synaptic changes within the relevant network. The demonstration that the decay of LTP is associated with apparent forgetting suggests that forgetting itself may involve an actual deterioration of synaptic weights at neural connections originally strengthened by learning. In principle, this could lead to information loss, retrieval failure, or both. In any case, the decay of synaptic weights may well be correlated with decrease in speed, efficacy, or completeness of recall. If, as the present data suggest, the maintenance of the hippocampal component of the memory trace is a function of the residual strength of the synapses involved, it remains to be investigated how this simple rule can apply to widespread distributed networks through which neural representations are encoded. On the one hand, learning leads presumably to multiple, distributed storage sites, and the general view holds that the memory trace is multidimensional in nature (Spear, 1978; Underwood, 1969). Multidimensionality, as well as multiple encoding, were admittedly reduced to a large extent in the artificial situation we have used in which the CS is an electrical stimulation of the perforant path. From the results of the correlation experiments, it can be suggested that in more natural conditions the apparent strength of the memory trace would rely on a function of all synaptic weights allocated along the relevant networks, each point having its own history of consolidation, decay, and possibly refreshment.

A relevant issue that is often debated concerns the duration of LTP (see Gallistel, Chapter 20, this volume). In particular, the view that LTP in most brain areas usually decays at a faster rate than what is expected for memories seems to compromise the hypothesis that LTP-like mechanisms subserve long-term information storage. In our opinion, it seems premature to conclude that the hypothesis is false on the basis of the rather meager data currently available. First, the similarity argument is not in itself particularly compelling, and even if almost nondecremental forms of LTP have been described in CA1 (Staubli & Lynch, 1987) and in the dentate gyrus (Doyère & Laroche, 1992) under certain conditions, the duration of tetanus-induced LTP in various conditions and, most importantly, of learning-induced synaptic changes must be further investigated. Second, the issue is complicated by the fact that memory architecture is not exempt from reorganization over time. For example, behavioral experiments have demonstrated differential efficacy of various retrieval cues in promoting retrieval after learning (Gisquet-Verrier, Dekeyne, & Alexinsky, 1989). As another example, there is evidence in certain tasks that the influence of the hippocampus in long-term retention fades over time, while other, possibly cortical, structures become prevalent (Zola-Morgan, Squire, & Amaral, 1986; and see Squire, 1992, for review). As a tentative hypothesis derived from the correlation reported earlier between LTP decay and forgetting when the cue signal is a stimulation of hippocampal inputs, it is tempting to propose that the decay of learning-induced synaptic changes originally established during acquisition may be paralleled by the decreasing prevalence of the hippocampus over time. The important need to test this hypothesis, and possibly extend it to other structures, is for correlative studies investigating the decay of synaptic changes in a given circuit in parallel with the *status* of the representation that is encoded throughout this circuit, and it should not be overlooked by the few long-term experiments that have been performed to date, that learning-induced synaptic changes could be sufficiently stable in the hippocampus for maintaining, for the time it lasts, the hippocampal component of the memory trace, or its ability to be reactivated.

On Synaptic Mechanisms of Network Specification: A Trace Refinement Hypothesis

The experiments reported here offer striking support for the view that associative learning is accompanied by long-lasting changes of an LTP form at hippocampal inputs. Among the most important questions about the biological significance of LTP for learning and memory is the issue of whether associative LTP is the actual mechanism by which associative representations are formed at the synaptic level. Although still unanswered experimentally, some clues as to the hypothetized function can be derived from a closer comparison of the numerous data accumulated. First is the issue of the apparent dissociation between long-term changes in synapse physiology and chemistry and the suggested role for these changes in long-term memory, on the one hand, and the much shorter lasting effect on the EPSP component of the evoked response as described in the first experiment, on the other. As already discussed, learning can induce synaptic changes, as examplified by the increased capacity of the synapses to release glutamate, that are only realized in conditions of sufficiently strong depolarization (see Lynch et al., 1990). This may well be realized during learning when the information is available and for a relatively short postlearning consolidation period when spatiotemporally patterned depolarizations are produced in the network as a result of bombardement by input signals. The hypothesis predicts that a similar effect would be produced during memory retrieval, a prediction that should be possible to examine experimentally. Whatever the underlying mechanism(s), however, the functional outcome for the network would be that fewer synapses will remain strengthened, so that learning would result in progressive specification and refinement of the hippocampal associative trace. This hypothesis finds support in the attenuation of the increase in dentate gyrus field EPSPs observed both with time after learning sessions and in overtraining when the association is well learned, as described earlier. Interestingly, it has also been reported that the number of hippocampal neurons activated by a behaviorally significant cue at the time of learning decreases in overtraining (Cahusac, Rolls, Miyashita, & Niki, 1993; Rolls, 1990), again suggesting refinement of memory trace as learning proceeds. We can then speculate that the number of synapses involved during initial learning progressively decreases so that a smaller population of possibly more finely tuned neurons will fire in response to a given event. This process of network specification will lead after learning to what may be small individual changes in synaptic weights widely distributed over the relevant hippocampal network, changes that would not be easily detected by the field potential recording technique. Among the possible mechanisms, trace refinement can be accounted for by simple signal processing operations in autoassociator or longer reentrant loop devices, such as those proposed on the basis of anatomical and physiological considerations (Buzsáki, Chen, & Gage, 1990; Lynch, 1986; Miller, 1991; Rolls, 1990). Synaptic depression as observed in pseudoconditioning could also contribute to selective network specification. We have speculated earlier that information about the CS and US might activate different sets of input fibers that could undergo synaptic potentiation if temporal synchrony and spatial convergence criteria are met. The mirror image supposes that either insufficient convergence or asynchrony will lead to depression of active synapses. Pseudoconditioning itself would then be considered as a procedure that maximizes synaptic depression. If this is the case, then depression of a subset of activated synapses could occur in conditioning as well at synapses where a conjunction threshold is not reached, thereby enhancing the contrast between strengthened and unstrengthened (or depressed) synapses in a manner that will direct flow of activation toward a small population of recipient neurons. The main advantage provided by the trace refinement model is of increasing the computational properties of the network as a whole and of confering to hippocampal circuits a greater capacity for the temporary storage of discrete events. The hypothesis should in principle be testable using various behavioral paradigms, such as discrimination, reversal, and extinction.

On Long-Term Potentiation in Multiple Brain Areas

The discovery of forms of LTP, or LTD, in a number of nonhippocampal brain areas, such as the sensory and motor areas of the cortex (Artola & Singer, 1987; Baranyi, Szente, & Woody, 1991; Bindman, Christofi, Murphy, Nowicky, 1991; Bindman, Murphy, & Pockett, 1988; Iriki, Pavlides, Keller, & Asanuma, 1989), prefrontal cortex (Hirsh & Crépel, 1990; Laroche, Jay, & Thierry, 1990a), thalamic nuclei (Gerren & Weinberger, 1983), amygdala (Clugnet & LeDoux, 1990), nucleus accumbens (Pennartz, Ameerun, & Lopes da Silva, 1992), and cerebellum (Ito, 1984; Racine, Wilson, Gingell, & Sunderland, 1986), among others, raises the question of whether LTP-like weighing rules are properties that are exploited to strengthen connections at multiple sites in learning. The evidence from recording experiments is fragmentary but encouraging. For example, increases in field potentials have been observed in piriform cortex in an olfactory discrimination task in which the odor serving as a cue signal is replaced by patterned stimulation of the lateral olfactory tract (Roman, Staubli, & Lynch, 1987; Roman, Chaillan, & Soumireu-Mourat, 1993). In a recent series of experiments, we examined a direct projection from CA1 and subiculum to the prelimbic area of the prefrontal cortex that has been characterized with anatomical techniques in the rat (Jay, Glowinski, & Thierry, 1989; Jay & Witter, 1991). This pathway supports LTP (Laroche et al., 1990a) and probably uses glutamate as a transmitter (Jay, Thierry, Wiklund, & Glowinski, 1992). Interestingly, LTP on this pathway can last for several days, and series of short trains mimicking the theta-bursting pattern displayed by CA1 pyramidal cells during certain learning tasks (Otto, Eichenbaum, Wiener, & Wible, 1991), are efficient parameters for LTP induction in the unanesthetized rat (Doyère, Burette, Rédini-Del Negro, & Laroche, 1993). To investigate the possible significance of LTP on this pathway in learning, we monitored field potentials in the prefrontal cortex induced by CA1-subicular stimulation in a tone–shock classical conditioning paradigm. The results indicate that while pseudoconditioning is accompanied by a decrease in the amplitude of the field potentials in a manner similar to what was found at perforant path inputs to the dentate gyrus, conditioning results in a delayed increase, occurring on average 30 minutes after the period during which CS–US paired trials were given, and the postlearning increase in postsynaptic potentials was mostly visible in overtraining when the task is mastered (Doyère et al., 1993). The mechanisms involved remain to be investigated. However, the electrophysiological data suggest an important role for this pathway in hippocampo–cortical communication in learning and memory. In line with many theories that postulate a critical role for the hippocampus in directing and organizing cortical representations (Goldman-Rakic, 1987; Mishkin, 1990; Rolls, 1989; Squire, 1992; Teyler & DiScenna, 1986; Wickelgren, 1979), the delayed onset and time-course of enhanced transmission at the hippocampal–prefrontal pathway after conditioning is compatible with the idea that an LTP-like mechanism on this pathway may serve a process of late consolidation by which the hippocampus can help stabilize a cortical representation of the learned association.

In parallel with the growing evidence derived from neuropsychological data for multiple memory systems (e.g., Squire, 1992; Tulving, 1987; Tulving & Schacter, 1990), much emphasis has recently been placed on a nonmonolytic view of memory in behavioral neuroscience. Specifically, the point at issue is not simply whether LTP is involved in all or only some forms of learning because LTP-like mechanisms in any particular circuit can only be involved in forms of learning that are *realized* within this circuit, but whether or not the same mechanisms operate in multiple brain areas and systems to construct and stabilize forms of representation for which these areas and their multiple routes of interaction have a role to play. The strategies that have been mostly employed for studying the possible biological significance of LTP in the hippocampus are still to be developed at the system level in a behavioral context. This will undoubtedly be a most exciting line of research in the future.

ACKNOWLEDGMENTS

The work of the authors was supported in part by grants from the Human Frontier Science Program and the European Community (SC1-CT910685).

REFERENCES

Akers, R. F., Lovinger, D. M., Colley, P. A., Linden, D. J., & Routtenberg, A. (1986). Translocation of protein kinase C activity may mediate hippocampal long-term potentiation. *Science, 231,* 587–589.

Artola, A., & Singer, W. (1987). Long-term potentiation and NMDA receptors in rat visual cortex. *Nature, 330,* 649–652.

Bank, B., DeWeer, A., Kuzirian, A. M., Rasmussen, H., & Alkon, D. L. (1988). Classical conditioning induces long-term translocation of protein kinase C in rabbit hippocampal CA1 cells. *Proceedings of the National Academy of Sciences of the United States of America, 85,* 1988–1992.

Baranyi, A., Szente, M. B., & Woody, C. D. (1991). Properties of associative long-lasting potentiation induced by cellular conditioning in the motor cortex of conscious cats. *Neuroscience, 42,* 321–334.

Barnes, C. A., & McNaughton, B. L. (1985). An age comparison of the rates of acquisition and forgetting of spatial information in relation to long-term enhancement of hippocampal synapses. *Behavioral Neuroscience, 99,* 1040–1048.

Bär, P. R., Wiegant, F., Lopes da Silva, F. H., & Gispen, W. H. (1984). Tetanic stimulation affects the metabolism of phosphoinositides in hippocampal slices. *Brain Research, 321,* 381–385.

Bekkers, J. M., & Stevens, C. F. (1991). Application of quantal analysis to the study of long-term potentiation: Errors, assumptions, and precautions. In M. Baudry & J. L. Davis (Eds.), *Long-term potentiation: A debate of current issues* (pp. 63–76). Cambridge: MIT Press.

Berger, T. W., Alger, B., & Thompson, R. F. (1976). Neuronal substrate of classical conditioning in the hippocampus. *Science, 192,* 483–485.

Berger, T. W., & Thompson, R. F. (1982). Hippocampal cellular plasticity during extinction of classically conditioned nictitating membrane behavior. *Behavioral Brain Research, 4*, 63–76.

Bergis, O. E., Bloch, V., & Laroche, S. (1990). Enhancement of long-term potentiation in the dentate gyrus two days after associative learning in the rat. *Neuroscience Research Communications, 6*, 119–128.

Best, M. R., & Best, P. J. (1976). The effects of latent inhibition on hippocampal unit activity in the rat. *Experimental Neurology, 51*, 546–573.

Bindman, L. J., Christofi, G., Murphy, K., & Nowicky, A. (1991). Long-term potentiation (LTP) and depression (LTD) in the neocortex and hippocampus: An overview. In T. W. Stone (Ed.), *Aspects of synaptic transmission, Vol. 1* (pp. 3–25). London: Taylor & Francis.

Bindman, L. J., Murphy, K. P. S. J., & Pockett, S. (1988). Postsynaptic control of the induction of long-term changes in efficacy of transmission at neocortical synapses in slices of rat brain. *Journal of Neurophysiology, 60*, 1053–1065.

Bliss, T. V. P., & Collingridge, G. L. (1993). A synaptic model of memory: Long-term potentiation in the hippocampus. *Nature, 361*, 31–39.

Bliss, T. V. P., Errington, M. L., Laroche, S., & Lynch, M. A. (1987). Increase in K^+-stimulated, Ca^{2+}-dependent release of (^{3}H)glutamate from rate dentate gyrus three days after induction of long-term potentiation. *Neuroscience Letters, 83*, 107–112.

Bliss, T. V. P., & Lømo, T. (1973). Long-lasting potentiation of synaptic transmission in the dentate area of the anaesthetized rabbit following stimulation of the perforant path. *Journal of Physiology (London), 232*, 331–356.

Bliss, T. V. P., & Lynch, M. A. (1988). Long-term potentiation of synaptic transmission in the hippocampus: Properties and mechanisms. In P. W. Landfield & S. A. Deadwyler (Eds.), *Long-term potentiation: From biophysics to behavior* (pp. 3–72). New York: Alan R. Liss.

Bloch, V., & Laroche, S. (1981). Conditioning of hippocampal cells: Its acceleration and long-term facilitation by post-trial reticular stimulation. *Behavioral Brain Research, 3*, 23–42.

Bloch, V., & Laroche, S. (1984). Facts and hypotheses related to the search for the engram. In G. Lynch, J. L. McGaugh, & N. M. Weinberger (Eds.), *Neurobiology of learning and memory* (pp. 249–260). New York: Guilford Press.

Bloch, V., & Laroche, S. (1985). Enhancement of long-term potentiation in the rat dentate gyrus by post-trial stimulation of the reticular formation. *Journal of Physiology (London), 360*, 215–231.

Bramham, C. R., Milgram, N. W., & Srebro, B. (1991). Activation of AP5-sensitive NMDA receptors is not required to induce LTP of synaptic transmission in the lateral perforant path. *European Journal of Neuroscience, 3*, 1300–1308.

Brown, T. H., Kairiss, E. W., & Keenan, C. L. (1990). Hebbian synapses: Biophysical mechanisms and algorithms. *Annual Review of Neuroscience, 13*, 475–511.

Buzsáki, G., Chen, L. S., & Gage, F. H. (1990). Spatial organization of physiological activity in the hippocampal region: Relevance to memory formation. In J. Storm-Mathisen, J. Zimmer, & O. P. Ottersen (Eds.), *Progress in brain research: Understanding the brain through the hippocampus, Vol. 83* (pp. 257–268). Amsterdam: Elsevier.

Buzsáki, G., Grastyán, E., Czopf, J., Kellényi, J., & Prohaska, O. (1981). Changes in neuronal transmission in the rat hippocampus during behavior. *Brain Research, 225*, 235–247.

Cahusac, P. M. B., Rolls, E. T., Miyashita, Y., & Niki, H. (1993). Modification of the response of hippocampal neurons in the monkey during the learning of a conditional spatial response task. *Hippocampus, 3*, 29–42.

Clements, M. P., Errington, M. L., Bliss, T. V. P., & Lynch, M. A. (1990). Time-related changes in basal phosphoinositide turnover after induction of long-term potentiation in the dentate gyrus are blocked by commissural stimulation. *European Journal of Neuroscience, 2*, 383–387.

Clugnet, M. C., & LeDoux, J. E. (1990). Synaptic plasticity in fear conditioning circuits: Induction of LTP in the lateral nucleus of the amygdala by stimulation of the medial geniculate body. *Journal of Neuroscience, 10*, 2818–2824.

Collingridge, G. L., & Bliss, T. V. P. (1987). NMDA receptors—Their role in long-term potentiation. *Trends in Neuroscience, 10*, 288–293.

Davis, S., Butcher, S. P., & Morris, R. G. M. (1992). The NMDA receptor antagonist D-2-amino-5-phosphonopentanoate (D-AP5) impairs spatial learning and LTP in vivo at intracerebral concentrations comparable to those that block LTP in vitro. *Journal of Neuroscience, 12,* 21–34.

Deadwyler, D. A., West, M., & Lynch, G. (1979). Activity of dentate granule cells during learning: Differentiation of perforant path input. *Brain Research, 169,* 29–43.

Dickinson, A. (1980). *Contemporary animal learning theory.* Cambridge: Cambridge University Press.

Doyère, V., Burette, F., Rédini-Del Negro, C., & Laroche, S. (1993). Long-term potentiation of hippocampal afferents and efferents to prefrontal cortex: Implications for associative learning. *Neuropsychologia, 31,* 1031–1053.

Doyère, V., & Laroche, S. (1992). Linear relationship between the maintenance of hippocampal long-term potentiation and retention of an associative memory. *Hippocampus, 2,* 39–48.

Edeline, J. M., Dutrieux, G., & Neuenschwander-El Massioui, N. (1988). Multiunit changes in hippocampus and medial geniculate body in free-behaving rats during acquisition and retention of a conditioned response to a tone. *Behavioral and Neural Biology, 50,* 61–79.

Feasey, K. J., Lynch, M. A., & Bliss, T. V. P. (1986). Long-term potentiation is associated with an increase in calcium-dependent, potassium-stimulated release of (^{14}C)-glutamate from hippocampal slices: An ex vivo study in the rat. *Brain Research, 364,* 39–44.

Foster, T. C., Hampson, R. E., West, M. O., & Deadwyler, S. A. (1988). Control of sensory activation of granule cells in the fascia dentate by extrinsic afferents: Septal and entorhinal inputs. *Journal of Neuroscience, 8,* 3869–3878.

Garrud, P., Rawlins, J. N. P., Mackintosh, N. J., Goodall, G., Cotton, N. M., & Feldon, J. (1984). Successful overshadowing and blocking in hippocampectomized in rats. *Behavioral Brain Research, 12,* 39–53.

Gerren, R. A., & Weinberger, N. M. (1983). Long-term potentiation in the magnocellular medial geniculate nucleaus of the anaesthetized cat. *Brain Research, 265,* 138–142.

Gisquet-Verrier, P., Dekeyne, A., & Alexinsky, T. (1989). Differential effects of several retrieval cues over time: Evidence for time-dependent reorganization of memory. *Animal Learning and Behavior, 17,* 394–408.

Goldman-Rakic, P. S. (1987). Circuitry of primate prefrontal cortex and regulation of behavior by representational memory. In S. Plum (Ed.), *Handbook of physiology, Vol. IV: The nervous system* (pp. 373–417). Bethesda, MD: American Physiological Society.

Green, E. J., & Greenough, W. T. (1986). Altered synaptic transmission in dentate gyrus of rats reared in complex environments: Evidence from hippocampal slices maintained in vitro. *Journal of Neurophysiology, 55,* 739.

Green, E. J., McNaughton, B. L., & Barnes, C. A. (1990). Exploration-dependent modulation of evoked responses in fascia dentata: Dissociation of motor, EEG, and sensory factors and evidence for a synaptic efficacy change. *Journal of Neuroscience, 10,* 1455–1471.

Gustafsson, B., & Wigström, H. (1986). Hippocampal long-lasting potentiation produced by pairing single volleys and brief conditioning tetani evoked in separate afferents. *Journal of Neuroscience, 6,* 1575–1582.

Hebb, D. O. (1949). *The organization of behavior.* New York: Wiley.

Hirsch, J. C., & Crépel, F. (1990). Use-dependent changes in synaptic efficacy in rat prefrontal neurons in vitro. *Journal of Physiology (London), 427,* 31–49.

Iriki, A., Pavlides, C., Keller, A., & Asanuma, H. (1989). Long-term potentiation in the motor cortex. *Science, 245,* 1385–1387.

Ito, M. (1984). *The cerebellum and neural control.* New York: Raven Press.

Iwata, J., LeDoux, J. E., Meeley, M. P., Arneric, S., & Reis, D. J. (1986). Intrinsic neurons in the amygdaloid field projected to by the medial geniculate body mediate emotional responses conditioned to acoustic stimuli. *Brain Research, 371,* 395–399.

Jaffard, R., & Jeantet, Y. (1981). Posttraining changes in excitability of the commissural path-CA1 pyramidal cell synapse in the hippocampus of mice. *Brain Research, 220,* 167–172.

Jay, T. M., Glowinski, J., & Thierry, A. M. (1989). Selectivity of the hippocampal projection to the prelimbic area of the prefrontal cortex in the rat. *Brain Research, 505,* 337–340.

Jay, T. M., Thierry, A. M., Wiklund, L., & Glowinski, J. (1992). Excitatory amino acid pathway from the hippocampus to the prefrontal cortex. Contribution of AMPA receptors in hippocampo-prefrontal cortex transmission. *European Journal of Neuroscience, 4,* 1285–1295.

Jay, T. M., & Witter, M. P. (1991). Distribution of hippocampal CA1 and subicular efferents in the prefrontal cortex of the rat studies by means of anterograde transport of Phaseolus vulgaris-leucoagglutinin. *Journal of Comparative Neurology, 313,* 574–586.

Kelso, S. R., Ganong, A. H., & Brown, T. H. (1986). Hebbian synapses in hippocampus. *Proceedings of the National Academy of Sciences of the United States of America, 83,* 5326–5330.

Krug, M., Lössner, B., & Ott, T. (1984). Anisomycin blocks the late phase of long-term potentiation in the dentate gyrus of freely moving rats. *Brain Research Bulletin, 13,* 39–42.

Kuba, K., & Kumamoto, I. (1990). Long-term potentiations in vertebrate synapses: A variety of cascades with common subprocesses. *Progress in Neurobiology, 34,* 197–269.

Larkman, A., Hannay, T., Stratford, K., & Jack, J. (1992). Presynaptic release probability influences the locus of long-term potentiation. *Nature, 360,* 70–73.

Laroche, S. (1985). What can the long-term potentiation procedure tell us about the neural mechanisms of learning and memory? In B. E. Will, P. Schmitt, & J. C. Dalrymple-Alford (Eds.), *Brain plasticity, learning, and memory, Advances in behavioral biology, Vol. 28* (pp. 139–155). New York: Alan R. Liss.

Laroche, S., Bloch, V., Doyère, V., & Rédini-Del Negro, C. (1991a). Significance of long-term potentiation for learning and memory. In F. Morell (Ed.) *Kindling and synaptic plasticity: The legacy of Graham Goddard* (pp. 12–37). Boston: Birkhäuser.

Laroche, S., Doyère, V., & Bloch, V. (1989). Linear relation between the magnitude of long-term potentiation in the dentate gyrus and associative learning in the rat. A demonstration using commissural inhibition and local infusion of an N-methyl-D-aspartate antagonist. *Neuroscience, 28,* 375–386.

Laroche, S., Doyère, V., & Rédini-Del Negro, C. (1991b). Short and long term changes in synaptic physiology in the dentate gyrus during associative learning in the rat. *Society for Neuroscience Abstracts, 17,* 1399.

Laroche, S., Doyère, V., & Rédini-Del Negro, C. (1991c). What role for long-term potentiation in learning and the maintenance of memories? In M. Baudry & J. L. Davis (Eds.), *Long-term potentiation: A debate of current issues* (pp. 301–316). Cambridge: MIT Press.

Laroche, S., Errington, M. L., Lynch, M. A., & Bliss, T. V. P. (1987a). Increase in (^{3}H)glutamate release from slices of dentate gyrus and hippocampus following classical conditioning in the rat. *Behavioral Brain Research, 25,* 23–29.

Laroche, S., Falcou, R., & Bloch, V. (1983). Post-trial reticular facilitation of associative changes in multiunit activity: Comparison between dentate gyrus and entorhinal cortex. *Behavioral Brain Research, 9,* 381–387.

Laroche, S., Jay, T. M., & Thierry, A. M. (199a). Long-term potentiation in the prefrontal cortex following stimulation of the hippocampal CA1 subicular region. *Neuroscience Letters, 114,* 184–190.

Laroche, S., Neuenschwander-El Massioui, N., Edeline, J. M., & Dutrieux, G. (1987b). Hippocampal associative cellular responses: Dissociation with behavioral responses revealed by a transfer-of-control technique. *Behavioral and Neural Biology, 47,* 356–368.

Laroche, S., Rédini-Del Negro, C., Clements, M. P., & Lynch, M. A. (1990b). Long-term activation of phosphoinositide turnover associated with increased release of amino acids in the dentate gyrus and hippocampus following classical conditioning in the rat. *European Journal of Neuroscience, 2,* 534–543.

LeDoux, J. E. (1991). Emotion and the limbic system concept. *Concepts in Neuroscience, 2,* 169–199.

Lewis, D. J. (1979). Psychobiology of active and inactive memory. *Psychological Bulletin, 86,* 1054–1083.

LoTurco, J. J., Coulter, D. A., & Alkon, D. L. (1988). Enhancement of synaptic potentials in rabbit CA1 pyramidal neurons following classical conditioning. *Proceedings National Academy of Sciences of the United States of America, 85,* 1672–1676.

Lynch, G. (1986). *Synapses, circuits, and the beginnings of memory.* Cambridge: MIT Press.

Lynch, M. A., Errington, M. L., Clements, M. P., Bliss, T. V. P., Rédini-Del Negro, C., & Laroche, S. (1990). Increases in glutamate release and phosphoinositide metabolism associated with long-term potentiation and classical conditioning. In J. Storm-Mathisen, J. Zimmer, & O. P. Ottersen (Eds.), *Progress in brain research: Understanding the brain through the hippocampus, Vol. 83* (pp. 257–268). Amsterdam: Elsevier.

Mackintosh, N. J. (1974). *The psychology of animal learning.* Longon: Academic Press.

Malinow, R., & Tsien, R. W. (1990). Presynaptic enhancement shown by whole-cell recordings of long-term potentiation in hippocampal slices. *Nature, 346,* 177–180.

McNaughton, B. L. (1991). The mechanisms of expression of long-term synaptic enhancement: Thesis, antithesis, synthesis. In M. Baudry & J. L. Davis (Eds.), *Long-term potentiation: A debate of current issues* (pp. 77–92). Cambridge: MIT Press.

McNaughton, B. L., Douglas, R. M., & Goddard, G. V. (1978). Synaptic enhancement in fascia dentata: Cooperativity among coactive afferents. *Brain Research, 157,* 277–293.

Miller, R. (1991). *Cortico-hippocampal interplay and the representation of contexts in the brain.* Berlin: Springer-Verlag.

Mishkin, M. (1990). Vision, memory, and the temporal lobe: Summary and perspective. In *Vision, memory, and the temporal lobe* (pp. 427–436). Amsterdam: Elsevier.

Morris, R. G. M., Anderson, E., Lynch, G. S., & Baudry, M. (1986). Selective impairment of learning and blockade of long-term potentiation by an N-methyl-D-aspartate receptor antagonist, AP5. *Nature, 319,* 774–776.

Morris, R. G. M., Davis, S., & Butcher, S. P. (1990). Hippocampal synaptic plasticity and NMDA receptors: A role in information storage? *Philosophical Transactions of the Royal Society of London, Series B, 329,* 187–204.

Moser, E., Mathiesen, I., & Andersen, P. (1993). Association between brain temperature and dentate field potentials in exploring and swimming rats. *Science, 259,* 1324–1326.

Neuenschwander-El Massioui, N., Dutrieux, G., & Edeline, J. M. (1991). Conditioned hippocampal cellular response to a behaviorally silent conditioned stimulus. *Behavioral Neuroscience, 105,* 91–103.

Olds, J., Disterhoft, J. F., Segal, M., Kornblith, C. L., & Hirsh, R. (1972). Learning centers of rat brain mapped by measuring latencies of conditioned unit responses. *Journal of Neurophysiology, 35,* 202–219.

Otani, S., Marshall, C. J., Tate, W. P., Goddard, G. V., & Abraham, W. C. (1989). Maintenance of long-term potentiation in rat dentate gyrus requires protein synthesis but not messenger RNA synthesis immediately post-tetanization. *Neuroscience, 28,* 519–526.

Otto, T., & Eichenbaum, H. (1992). Neuronal activity in the hippocampus during delayed non-match to sample performance in rats: Evidence for hippocampal processing in recognition memory. *Hippocampus, 2,* 323–334.

Otto, T., Eichenbaum, H., Wiener, S. I., & Wible, C. G. (1991). Learning-related patterns of CA1 spike trains parallel stimulation parameters optimal for inducing hippocampal long-term potentiation. *Hippocampus, 1,* 181–192.

Pennartz, C. M. A., Ameerun, R. F., & Lopes da Silva, F. H. (1992). Synaptic plasticity in the rat prefrontal-accumbens pathway studied in vitro. *Society for Neuroscience Abstracts, 18,* 1347.

Port, R. L., Beggs, A. L., & Patterson, M. M. (1987). Hippocampal substrate of sensory association. *Physiology and Behavior, 39,* 643–647.

Racine, R. J., Wilson, D. A., Gingell, R., & Sunderland, D. (1986). Long-term potentiation in the interpositus and vestibular nuclei in the rat. *Experimental Brain Research, 63,* 158–162.

Rédini-Del Negro, C., & Laroche, S. (1992). Learning-induced changes in dentate neuronal activity and in glutamate release are blocked by the NMDA receptor antagonist AP5. *Society for Neuroscience Abstracts, 18,* 522.

Rédini-Del Negro, C., & Laroche, S. (1993). Learning-induced increase in glutamate release in the dentate gyrus is blocked by the NMDA receptor antagonist AP5. *Neuroscience Research Communications, 13,* 157–165.

Rickert, E. J., Lorden, J. F., Dawson, R., & Smyly, E. (1981). Limbic lesions and the blocking effect. *Physiology and Behavior, 26,* 601–606.

Rolls, E. T. (1989). The representation and storage of information in neuronal networks in the primate cerebral cortex and hippocampus. In R. Durbin, C. Miall, & G. Mitchison (Eds.), *The computing neuron* (pp. 125–159). Workingham, England: Addison-Wesley.

Rolls, E. T. (1990). Functions of the primate hippocampus in spatial processing and memory. In D S. Olton & R. P. Kesner (Eds.), *Neurobiology of comparative cognition, Vol. 2* (pp. 339–362). Hillsdale, NJ: Erlbaum.

Roman, F., Staubli, U., & Lynch, G. (1987). Evidence for synaptic potentiation in a cortical network during learning. *Brain Research, 418,* 221–226.

Roman, F., Chaillan, F. H., & Soumireu-Mourat, B. (1993). Long-term potentiation in rat piriform cortex following discrimination learning. *Brain Research, 601,* 265–272.

Rudy, J. W., & Sutherland, R. J. (1989). The hippocampus is necessary for rats to learn and remember configural discriminations. *Behavioural Brain Research, 34,* 97–109.

Rüthrich, H., Matthies, H., & Ott, T. (1982). Long-term changes in synaptic excitability of hippocampal cell populations as a result of training. In C. Ajmone Marsan & H. Matthies (Eds.), *Neuronal plasticity and memory formation, IBRO Monograph Series, Vol. 9* (pp. 589–594). New York: Raven Press.

Schmajuk, N. A. (1984). Psychological theories of hippocampal function. *Physiological Psychology, 12,* 166–183.

Silva, A. J., Paylor, R., Wehner, J. M., & Tonegawa, S. (1992a). Impaired spatial learning in α-calcium-calmodulin kinase II mutant mice. *Science, 257,* 206–211.

Silva, A. J., Stevens, C. F., Tonegawa, S., & Wang, Y. (1992b). Deficient hippocampal long-term potentiation in α-calcium-calmodulin kinase II mutant mice. *Science, 257,* 201–206.

Solomon, P. R. (1977). Role of the hippocampus in blocking and conditioned inhibition of the rabbit's nictitating membrane response. *Journal of Comparative Physiology and Psychology, 91,* 407–417.

Spear, N. E. (1978). *The processing of memories: Forgetting and retention.* Hillsdale, NJ: Erlbaum.

Squire, L. R. (1992). Memory and the hippocampus: A synthesis from findings with rats, monkeys, and humans. *Psychological Review, 99,* 195–231.

Staubli, U., & Lynch, G. (1987). Stable hippocampal long-term potentiation elicited by "theta" pattern stimulation. *Brain Research, 435,* 227–234.

Staubli, U., Thibault, O., DiLorenzo, M., & Lynch, G. (1989). Antagonism of NMDA reptors impairs acquisition but not retention of olfactory memory. *Behavioral Neuroscience, 103,* 54–60.

Teyler, T. J., & DiScenna, P. (1986). The hippocampal memory indexing theory. *Behavioral Neuroscience, 100,* 147–154.

Thompson, R. F., Clark, G. A., Donegan, N. H., Lavond, D. G., Lincoln, J. S., Madden J., IV, Mamounas, L. A., Mauk, M. D., McCormick, D. A., & Thompson, J. K. (1984). Neuronal substrates of learning and memory: A "multiple-trace" view. In G. Lynch, J. L. McGaugh, & N. M. Weinberger (Eds.) *Neurobiology of learning and memory* (pp. 137–164). New York: Guilford.

Tocco, G., Devgan, K. K., Hauge, S. A., Weiss, C., Baudry, M., & Thompson, R. F. (1991). Classical conditioning selectivity increases AMPA/quisqualate receptor binding in rabbit hippocampus. *Brain Research, 559,* 331–336.

Tsien, R. W., & Malinow, R. (1990). Long-term potentiation: Presynaptic enhancement following postsynaptic activation of Ca^{++}-dependent protein kinases. *Cold Spring Harbor Symposia on Quantitative Biology, Vol. LV,* 147–159.

Tulving, E. (1987). Multiple memory systems and consciousness. *Human Neurobiology, 6,* 67–80.

Tulving, E., & Schacter, D. L. (1990). Priming and human memory systems. *Science, 247,* 301–306.

Underwood, B. J. (1969). Attributes of memory. *Psychobiological Review, 76,* 559–573.

Voronin, L. L., Kuhnt, U., & Gusev, A. G. (1991). Analysis of EPSP fluctuations indicates increased presynaptic release during long-term potentiation in area CA1 of hippocampal slices. *Neuroscience Research Communications, 8,* 87–94.

Wallace, C. S., Hawrylak, N., & Greenough, W. T. (1991). Studies of synaptic structural modifications after long-term potentiation and kindling: Context for a molecular morphology. In M. Baudry & J. L. Davis (Eds.), *Long-term potentiation: A debate of current issues* (pp. 189–232). Cambridge: MIT Press.

Weisz, D., Solomon, P. R., & Thompson, R. F. (1984). Increased responsivity of dentate granule cells during nictitating membrane response conditioning in rabbit. *Behavioral Brain Research, 12,* 145–154.

White, G., Levy, W. B., & Steward, O. (1988). Evidence that associative interactions between synapses during the induction of long-term potentiation occur within local dendritic domains. *Proceedings of the National Academy of Sciences of the United States of America, 85,* 2368–2372.

Wickelgren, W. A. (1979). Chunking and consolidation: A theoretical synthesis of semantic networks configuring in conditioning, S-R versus cognitive learning, normal forgetting, the amnesic syndrome, and the hippocampal arousal system. *Psychological Review, 86,* 44–60.

Wigström, H., & Gustafsson, B. (1988). Presynaptic and postsynaptic interactions in the control of hippocampal long-term potentiation. In P. W. landfield & S. A. Deadwyler (Eds.), *Long-term potentiation: From biophysics to behavior.* New York: Alan R. Liss.

Witter, M. P., Groenewegen, H. J., Lopes da Silva, F. H., & Lohman, A. H. M. (1989). Functional organization of the extrinsic and intrinsic circuitry of the parahippocampal region. *Progress in Neurobiology, 33,* 161–253.

Zola-Morgan, S., Squire, L. R., & Amaral, D. G. (1986). Human amnesia and the medial temporal region: Enduring memory impairment following a bilateral lesion limited to field CA1 of the hippocampus. *Journal of Neuroscience, 6,* 2950–2967.

18

Parallel Properties of Long-Term
Potentiation and Memory

URSULA V. STAUBLI

The discovery of the long-term potentiation effect (Bliss & Lomo, 1973) is generally held to have been a major step forward in the search for the mechanisms of memory. Long-term potentiation (LTP) develops within seconds (Gustafsson, Asztely, Hanse, & Wigstrom, 1989), is specific to the activated synapses (e.g., Dunwiddie & Lynch, 1978; McNaughton, Douglas, & Goddard, 1978), passes through a "consolidation" period lasting for at least several minutes (Arai, Larson, & Lynch, 1990; Barrionuevo, Schottler, & Lynch, 1980; Fujii, Saito, Miyakawa, Ito, & Kato, 1991; Larson, Xiao, & Lynch, 1993; Staubli & Lynch, 1990), and can last for a very long time (Barnes, 1979; Bliss & Lomo, 1973; Staubli & Lynch, 1987). These properties provided the starting material for the hypothesis that LTP is the variant of synaptic plasticity underlying the encoding of certain forms of memory. Simple recognition memories in humans, for example, are formed quickly, incorporated into a high-capacity storage system (Standing, 1973), susceptible to disruption during a limited time after formation (e.g., McGaugh, 1966), and can persist for years. Thus, critical attributes of an everyday recognition memory system used by humans have their analogues within the phenomenon of LTP.

The hypothesis that LTP is involved in memory makes several predictions, among which are the following:

1. Physiological activity patterns that occur in the brain during learning should be related to the chemistries that trigger LTP;
2. LTP should form concurrently with memory in those brain areas in which information is being encoded;
3. Drugs that interfere with LTP should interfere with the encoding of memory but leave already stored information intact;
4. Experimental manipulations that facilitate LTP should facilitate the encoding of memory;
5. The properties of LTP should be reflected in the properties of memory— predictions between memory and LTP should go in both directions.

The following sections review evidence pertinent to these predictions.

BRAIN RHYTHMS ASSOCIATED WITH LEARNING ARE ALSO RELATED TO THE INDUCTION OF LONG-TERM POTENTIATION

Theta is a commonly observed EEG rhythm in the hippocampus of small mammals during exploration and learning (for reviews, see Landfield, 1976; Vanderwolf, 1969; Vertes, 1989). As shown by Hill (1978), individual pyramidal neurons fire in short bursts synchronized with the peaks of theta while rats are engaged in exploring spatial mazes. Work conducted using hippocampal slices revealed that the theta bursting is an excellent stimulation pattern for inducing LTP (Diamond, Dunwiddie, & Rose, 1988; Larson, Wong, & Lynch, 1986). The cellular mechanisms linking theta activity to potentiation have been identified. Intracellular recording studies showed that stimulation at theta frequency optimally exploits a refractory period associated with inhibitory postsynaptic potentials (IPSPs) in field CA1 and thereby creates conditions needed for activating the N-methyl-D-aspartate (NMDA) receptor currents that trigger LTP (Larson & Lynch, 1986; 1988). Single theta bursts do not elicit NMDA receptor-mediated synaptic currents, presumably because the duration and degree of depolarization associated with them are not sufficient to remove the magnesium block of the receptor ionophore. A second burst occurring 200 msec later (the period of the theta wave) causes a substantially greater depolarization, and with it a reasonable NMDA receptor response, because at this time point the IPSPs are maximally refractory. Work by Mott and Lewis (1991) indicates that the refractory period is caused by GABAb receptors leading to the idea that autoreceptors on inhibitory terminals cause a transient suppression of GABA release. In any event, theta can be seen as a mechanism for momentarily suspending hyperpolarizing responses that under most circumstances prevent activation of NMDA receptors.

If NMDA-receptor-mediated LTP plays a role in memory, then, from the preceding results, we would expect the learning of specific cues to be associated with the onset of afferent activity spaced at theta frequency in order to circumvent the normally present blockade of the NMDA receptor ionophore. That this is indeed the case is nicely shown in experiments on the acquisition of odor discriminations, a circumstance in which cue sampling and cell activity can be measured at the same time. Odor sampling during learning involves stereotyped sniffing at 5–8 Hz (Youngentob, Mozell, Sheebe, & Hornung, 1987) and the theta rhythm throughout the olfactory–hippocampal pathway is phase locked with this sampling activity (Eichenbaum, Kuperstein, Fagan, & Nagode, 1987; Komisaruk, 1977). Eichenbaum and coworkers have shown that hippocampal pyramidal cells during olfactory learning tend to fire in brief high-frequency bursts riding on the peaks of theta waves, and thus in synchrony with individual sniffs (Otto, Eichenbaum, Wiener, & Wible, 1991). In sum, physiological activity patterns coupled by known mechanisms to LTP induction are present in the very brief time period during which specific environmental stimuli are available to the animal for encoding into memory.

Correlation Between Synaptic LTP and Behavioral Learning

Evidence that LTP *does* occur in a learning animal in synapses participating in the encoding of information is of fundamental importance to the hypothesis that LTP-like mechanisms are critical for memory. Only a few studies have attempted to establish a direct link of this kind. For instance, using stimulation of the perforant path as a conditioned stimulus, Laroche, Doyère, and Bloch (1989) observed a correlation between the magnitude of LTP and performance in a classical conditioning task. Another example is provided by an experiment by Barnes and her colleagues (McNaughton, Barnes, Rao, Baldwin, & Rasmussen, 1986) in which they showed that previous induction of LTP in the perforant path impaired the ability of trained rats to learn new spatial information but left old memories intact. Interestingly, the learning impairment was found to be transient as shown by a regained capacity to learn new spatial configurations following the decay of perforant path LTP over a period of several days (Castro, Silbert, McNaughton, & Barnes, 1989). However, these findings have become the subject of considerable controversy (Korol, Abel, Church, Barnes, & McNaughton, 1993; Sutherland, Dringenberg, & Hoesing, 1993; Barnes, Erickson, Davis, & McNaughton, Chapter 16, this volume).

A quite different approach to testing for a direct correlation between the encoding of memory and the occurrence of LTP was conducted using an "electric odor" paradigm that allows the investigator to measure synaptic strength in those pathways processing the to-be-learned cue. The paradigm is based on the observation that stimulation bursts delivered at theta frequency (which, as noted, is the frequency at which rats sniff) to the lateral olfactory tract (LOT) can be used as behaviorally relevant discriminative cue (i.e., an electric odor) in place of a natural odor in a two-odor olfactory discrimination task (Staubli, Roman, & Lynch, 1985). Specifically, rats were fitted with 2–3 stimulating electrodes at different positions in the LOT and with a recording electrode in the dendritic zone of layer II/III cells of the piriform (olfactory) cortex, such that monosynaptically evoked field potentials to each of the stimulating electrodes could be monitored. The animals were then trained on a series of two-odor discriminations until they solved new problems rapidly. At this point, theta burst stimulation of the LOT was used as a cue in a novel problem and was assigned positive or negative reward valence in place of a natural odor. The animals learned quickly to distinguish the electric odor from the actual odor and performed correctly after a few trials. Subsequent experiments were successful in training animals on problems in which both odors were replaced with electric odors. As a result of learning, the LOT connections activated by the electric odor were found to exhibit a substantial ($\sim$20–40%) and lasting increment in synaptic strength that was absent in synapses activated by control electrodes (Roman, Staubli, & Lynch, 1987). Naive animals, and animals that had been trained with natural odors but were stimulated outside the context of the discrimination task, did not exhibit LTP in response to theta burst stimulation. Work from other laboratories indicates that LTP does not occur in the piriform cortex of intact (naive) animals following high-frequency stimulation (Racine, Milgram, & Hafner, 1983; Stripling, Patneau, & Gramlich, 1988). Apparently, the learning situation in some way exerts an influence on the olfactory cortex, such that afferent activity patterns are able to impress a lasting potentiation on synapses. Long-term potentiation once induced in the olfactory cortex of animals, is extremely stable (Roman, Chaillan, Staubli, & Soumireu-Mourat, 1992; Roman, Staubli, & Lynch, 1987); this is noteworthy because olfactory memories in rats are very stable, lasting in some cases for more than one year (Staubli & Granger, unpublished observations).

In all, the previously described electric odor studies established that LTP develops in synapses that are processing a discriminative cue, as that cue is being encoded into memory. This finding, combined with the evidence that theta patterns of physiological activity optimally effective in activating NMDA receptors appear during olfactory learning, provide strong support for the hypothesis that NMDA receptor activation and LTP play a role in learning.

The electric odor experiments also revealed that, at least in the inputs to olfactory cortex, LTP induction is dependent upon behavioral variables associated with experience. That is, stimulation of the LOT does not induce potentiation unless it is used as a cue that has significance based on past learning episodes. Work using in vitro slices confirmed that LTP with properties very similar to those described for hippocampus can be elicited in piriform cortex, and made the further point that the effect is more difficult to elicit in LOT versus associational synapses (Jung, Larson, & Lynch, 1990; Kanter & Haberly, 1990). Identifying the origin of this difference may provide clues as to how variables such as selective attention might interact with the machinery that alters synaptic strength. Work in progress has confirmed the behavioral dependency of LTP in the lateral olfactory tract synapses, and provided preliminary evidence pointing to the horizontal limb of the diagonal band of Broca as the extrinsic source controlling whether LTP and learning will occur (Roman et al., 1992).

COMPARING THE EFFECTS OF DRUGS ON LONG-TERM POTENTIATION VS. LEARNING

The discovery, made several years ago, that antagonists of the NMDA receptor selectively prevent LTP induction (Collingridge, Kehl, & McLennan, 1983) seemingly opened the way for pharmacological testing of the hypothesis that LTP is the neurobiological variable that underlies encoding of information. One of the unique features of the NMDA receptor is that, at least in some areas of the forebrain, it plays a minimal role in baseline synaptic transmission and instead becomes only activated under conditions of repetitive synaptic stimulation (Collingridge et al., 1983; Larson & Lynch, 1988). This suggests that NMDA receptor antagonists can be applied in concentrations that block the neuronal plasticity triggered by unusual physiological activity related to learning while leaving intact behaviors not dependent on such physiological activities.

The use of drugs that block the NMDA receptor in memory studies entails several difficulties, however, among which are the following: (1) memory is not a single phenomenon, and it is reasonable to assume that the plasticities involved in encoding one type of memory are different from the plasticities subserving other types of memory (e.g., Squire, 1986; Staubli, Faraday, & Lynch, 1985; for a review see Lynch, Larson, Staubli, & Granger, 1991). Moreover, the concentration of NMDA receptors varies greatly among different regions of the brain, with some areas in the forebrain displaying high concentrations, while regions in the cerebellum and brainstem almost completely lack the receptor (Monaghan & Cotman, 1985). It can be expected, therefore, that blockade of the NMDA receptor will interrupt some types of memory and leave others untouched. When testing the effects on learning of NMDA receptor antagonists (or other drugs that block LTP), it is necessary to select a learning task subserved by brain areas likely to exhibit LTP mediated by the NMDA receptor. (2) In addition to its role in producing synaptic plasticity, the NMDA receptor is known to be involved in brain functions that do not produce synaptic plasticity, at least in nonmammalian vertebrates (e.g., Grillner & Wallen, 1985; Wallen & Grillner, 1987), and thus may contribute to unknown behaviors in mammals. In cases in which antagonists are found to block memory, a further challenge lies in showing that the learning impairment is due to suppression of synaptic plasticity as opposed to side effects of various kinds (e.g., NMDA receptor involvement in performance variables or drug effects unrelated to the receptor.

Over the past few years a considerable body of evidence has accumulated concerning the effects of NMDA receptor antagonists on learning. Several of these experiments have attempted to establish correspondences between the effects of NMDA receptor antagonists and of lesions to specific brain regions rich in NMDA receptors. The most notable examples are comparisons between hippocampal lesions and NMDA antagonists: assuming that plasticity in the hippocampus plays a role in the encoding of specific types of memory, then it would follow that administration of NMDA blockers should reproduce some of the effects found in animals with hippocampal ablations. In accord with this prediction, NMDA receptor antagonists were found to disrupt the encoding of spatial cues (e.g., Morris, Anderson, Lynch, & Baudry, 1986; Robinson, Crooks, Shinkman, & Gallagher, 1989), and, as is well established, lesions of the hippocampus produce pronounced effects on behavior of this type (O'Keefe & Nadel, 1978; Olton, Becker, & Handelmann, 1979).

The approach of predicting the forms of memory that should, and should not, be affected by antagonists of the NMDA receptor has also been tested by comparing the action of NMDA receptor blockers and hippocampal system damage on 2-odor olfactory discrimination learning. Lesions that disconnect the olfactory input from the hippocampus produce a syndrome in which rats are impaired in the acquisition of simultaneous two-odor discriminations, but eventually do learn the two cues (Staubli, Fraser, Kessler & Lynch, 1986; Staubli, Ivy & Lynch, 1984). Comparable effects are observed after intraventricular infusion of the NMDA receptor antagonist AP5: the animals lose the ability to learn simultaneous discriminations rapidly, but with sufficient trials eventually will acquire the task (Staubli, Thibault, DiLorenzo, & Lynch, 1989). Furthermore, denervation of the hippocampus does not cause retrograde amnesia for olfactory cues (Staubli et al., 1986), and, in a similar manner, AP5 has no detectable effect on animal's ability to utilize odors learned before drug administration. It should be noted that the effective dose shown in the preceding study to impair acquisition, but not retention, of olfactory information corresponds to that reported to block induction of hippocampal LTP in vivo (Morris, Anderson, Lynch, & Baudry, 1986).

As expected from arguments presented above, NMDA receptor antagonists do not block all forms of learning. Visual discriminations are still acquired in the presence of drug concentrations sufficient to disrupt spatial learning (Morris et al., 1986). Active avoidance is also left unimpaired by infusions of AP5 adequate to disturb olfactory learning (Staubli et al., 1989). Neither of these AP5 insensitive tasks is detectably impaired by lesions of the hippocampus.

N-methyl-D-aspartate receptor antagonists are by no means the only drugs that block LTP; to the contrary, a very large array of drugs are reported to have this effect. Most of these are not suitable for behavioral experiments because the cellular targets of the compounds are known to (or are likely to) play important roles in the moment-to-moment operation of the nervous system. An important exception to this is calpain, a neutral thiol protease activated by concentrations of calcium well above those needed for most cellular functions. Calpain inhibitors were found to block the stabilization of LTP in chronic rats (Staubli, Larson, Thibault, Baudry, & Lynch, 1988), a result that was replicated and extended in slices of hippocampus (del Cerro, Larson, Oliver, & Lynch, 1990; Denny, Polan-Curtain, Ghuman, Wayner, & Armstrong, 1990; Oliver, Baudry, & Lynch, 1990). Infusions of calpain inhibitors, in concentrations that block LTP, had little effect on ingestive behavior or spontaneous activity, but did cause a pronounced impairment of olfactory learning (Staubli, Baudry, & Lynch, 1984, 1985). As was the case with AP5, the calpain inhibitor had no detectable effect on avoidance conditioning (Staubli et al., 1985). These differential behavioral effects are suggestive of fundamental differences in the chemistries of memory; that is, the existence of both LTP- and non-LTP-based forms of memory. To the extent that this is true, it should be possible to block avoidance conditioning without disrupting olfactory or spatial memory. This prediction was confirmed using protein synthesis inhibitors which, at dosages that blocked the consolidation of avoidance learning, were found to have no obvious effects on acquisition or retention of an olfactory discrimination (Staubli et al., 1985). The pharmacological double dissociation (protein synthesis inhibitors versus suppression of LTP; avoidance conditioning versus olfactory learning) resulting from the preceding collection of results indicates that the brain uses multiple chemical as well as multiple anatomical systems to encode different types of memory.

In summary, two drugs that interfere with very different steps in the sequence that produces LTP, impair spatial and/or olfactory learning. Various controls for nonspecific actions of the drugs on performance or motivational factors have been used, including the following:

1. The dosages used were shown to block LTP induction in intact animals;
2. The concentrations of drugs needed to produce visible side effects were higher than those needed to interfere with learning;
3. Forms of learning not affected by hippocampal lesions were not impaired by the drugs;
4. In a few cases it was shown that the drug affected the acquisition of new information, without impairing the utilization of previously acquired memories (e.g., Robinson et al., 1989; Staubli et al., 1989).

This last control seems particularly compelling since it holds performance and motivational levels constant, while varying the demands on learning. A reasonable strategy will be to test old and novel information in the *same* animal, the *same* session, and the *same* situation. Antagonists that interfere with the behavior when novel information is presented, but have no effect when familiar information is being processed, are good candidates for agents that affect the encoding process.

Testing if compounds that block LTP also block learning is not the only strategy for asking if the potentiation effect is a substrate of memory. The reverse approach is also possible: do manipulations, which produce reasonably selective anterograde amnesia in humans and/or animals, disrupt the formation of LTP? Benzodiazepines, widely used as anxiolytics, do not product gross disturbances of human behavior, yet are reported to have amnestic effects (e.g., Brown & Dundee, 1968; Lister, 1985). Infusion of either of two of these drugs into slices of hippocampus was found to produce a partial suppression of LTP without reliably changing baseline physiological measures (del Cerro, Jung, & Lynch, 1992). How the drugs do this has not been established, but it is likely that their known effects on GABA receptors are involved. As noted above, GABA-mediated hyperpolarizing responses modulate the depolarizing effects of theta bursts and hence the degree and duration of NMDA receptor activation. While the previous results raise the possibility that benzodiazepine-induced amnesia is related to a suppression of LTP, more work is needed before this idea can be treated as a formal hypothesis. Chronic recording studies could test if dosages of peripherally administered benzodiazepine, which interfere with learning in rats, are also sufficient to block the potentiation effect. Several of the controls cited for the studies using inhibitors of LTP would be applicable to analysis of the behavioral and physiological effects of the benzodiazepines.

A second and perhaps more challenging strategy for testing the links between LTP and memory is to ask if drugs that facilitate the potentiation effect also enhance memory. One that promises to be useful in this regard is aniracetam, a drug classified as a member of the family of nootropics. Work by Ito and coworkers (Ito, Tanabe, Khoda, & Sugiyama, 1990), using the frog oocyte expression system, established that aniracetam selectively facilitates the current mediated by the AMPA, but not NMDA or GABA receptors. Moreover, studies using hippocampal slices showed that aniracetam, but not other nootropics, increases synaptic responses mediated by the AMPA receptor (Ito et al., 1990; Staubli, Kessler, & Lynch, 1990; Xiao, Staubli, Kessler, & Lynch, 1991). Experiments with excised patches from hippocampal neurons indicate that aniracetam prolongs the mean open time of the channel associated with the AMPA receptor, probably by reducing the rate of desensitization (Tang, Shi, Katchman, & Lynch, 1991). The AMPA subtype of glutamate receptor is the likely site of LTP expression (Kauer, Malenka, & Nicoll, 1988; Muller, Joly, & Lynch, 1988; Staubli, Ambros-Ingerson, & Lynch, 1992); it is also the receptor that dominates in cortical areas and hence can be assumed to play a crucial role in cognition. Independent of hypotheses about mechanisms for LTP, however, the selective facilitatory action of aniracetam on currents mediated by the AMPA receptor should cause the drug to be effective in promoting LTP. Specifically, the following predictions can be made for cases when the drug is present: (1) less activation should be needed to reach the threshold for the activation of the voltage-dependent NMDA receptor, and thus to induce LTP, and (2) a given amount of stimulation will lead to more pronounced activation of NMDA currents, causing greater increments of LTP to be produced. These predictions have been partially confirmed in studies of the hippocampal slice, in which it was shown that aniracetam reduces the number of stimulation bursts needed to produce a maximal degree of LTP (Arai & Lynch, 1992). Aniracetam, however, did not change the ceiling on LTP. These authors also found that forskolin, which blocks GABAb receptor-mediated hyperpolarizations (Madison & Nicoll, 1986), nearly doubles the maximum degree of potentiation. These results indicate that the amount of depolarization occurring during a single theta burst affects the LTP increment produced per burst, while the size of the hyperpolarization occurring between bursts governs the LTP ceiling (Arai & Lynch, 1992).

The arguments just outlined can be carried even further: if LTP-like processes provide the substrate for memory encoding, then subjects given aniracetam should exhibit faster learning with fewer than normal training trials, and perhaps longer retention following partial training compared to untreated controls. Similarly, compounds that reduce the slow IPSP in postsynaptic neurons should enhance the absolute strength of memory. The first point is currently being addressed in a series of behavioral studies conducted in the author's laboratory. Tests of the hypothesis are complicated by the fact that aniracetam is rapidly metabolized in the blood; accordingly, potentially more stable variants of aniracetam developed by G. Lynch and G. Rogers are being examined for their effects on learning and retention following intraperitoneal injections in rats. The preliminary findings have been encouraging in that animals, treated with the analogs before receiving partial training in an olfactory discrimination task, showed significantly better retention than matched controls when tested 2 to 4 days later (Staubli, Rogers, & Lynch, 1994).

As indicated, the use of drugs that facilitate LTP to test the hypothesis that the potentiation effect is the substrate of certain forms of memory is still in its earliest stages. It is nonetheless interesting to consider the control problems that go with this approach. A primary concern will be to determine that the drugs of interest affect LTP and memory at comparable dosages. Nonspecific disturbances of performance and motivational variables, the great problem with experiments using the suppression of LTP strategy, presumably would not enhance memory formation. But there is an analogous difficulty. A host of drugs are known to facilitate learning and memory consolidation in rats and mice (though not in humans), and many of these act in a generalized fashion or on a system projecting diffusely throughout the brain. These results suggest that "state" variables (arousal, motivation, stress) are readily influenced by a number of transmitter and hormonal systems. This, coupled with the likelihood that cell activity patterns are also readily changed and are also influential factors during learning, provide formidable challenges to linking any specific neurobiological phenomenon to memory enhancement. Previously cited evidence indicates, however, that LTP is restricted in terms of the pathways in which it is likely to occur and, in accord with this, is not likely to be involved in many forms of learning in rodents. Therefore, drugs intended to facilitate LTP, like those that suppress it, should have selective effects on memory, presumably enhancing memory in tasks such as odor discrimination and spatial learning, while leaving unchanged acquisition and retention in other paradigms. This criterion, coupled with experiments comparing drug effects on behavior involving previously learned versus novel material, may allow for a determination of whether memory enhancement was achieved by an action on the chemistry of plasticity.

LONG-TERM POTENTIATION AS A COMPONENT OF NEUROBIOLOGICALLY BASED THEORIES OF MEMORY

Traditionally, the neurobiological study of memory has been concerned with understanding (1) physiological and chemical mechanisms responsible for memory storage and (2) the contributions of different brain regions to specific aspects of behavioral memory. One strategy that combines elements of both approaches is to characterize the types of plasticity in different brain regions, and then relate these to one or more classes of memory. It is clear that LTP is not the only form of long-lasting (hours or longer) synatic plasticity in the brain; that is, long-term depression in the cerebellum (Ito, 1987) and mossy fiber potentiation in the hippocampus are examples of this. It is further not unlikely that there may be various other brain regions that exhibit forms of plasticity unrelated to the NMDA receptor or to the induction of LTP. Thus, the question arises as to whether different types of memory might be subserved by regional variants of plasticity, and if so, what kind of memories emerge from the combination of different plasticities, different internal wiring arrangements, and different input–output connections.

Analysis of possible contributions by regional variants of plasticity to different forms of memory are facilitated by focusing on a well-defined series of brain regions processing the same environmental stimuli. The olfactory hippocampal system constitutes such a series. Work by the author and others has resulted in a description of synaptic potentiation in several components, beginning with the olfactory cortex and extending through hippocampus. The results can be summarized as follows:

- *Olfactory cortex:* LTP is found in the afferents of the cortex (Roman et al., 1992; Roman et al., 1987; Staubli, et al., 1985) and in its intrinsic associational system (Jung et al., 1990; Kanter & Haberly, 1990). The first is unique in that it is dependent upon prior learning.
- *Cortex to dentate gyrus:* LTP was discovered in perforant path synapses (Bliss & Lomo, 1973); subsequent work with chronic rats showed that the potentiation decays steadily, reaching baseline within 2 to 4 weeks (Barnes, 1979; Castro et al., 1989; Sutherland et al., 1993). This distinguishes it from LTP in olfactory cortex (Roman et al., 1987) and field CA1 of hippocampus (Staubli & Lynch, 1987).
- *Cortex to CA3/CA1:* LTP is present in these connections (Doller & Weight, 1985; Xiao, personal communication, 1992), but there are no data on persistence.
- *Dentate gyrus to field CA3:* Mossy fiber potentiation is a peculiarly long-lasting variant of presynaptic facilitation processes that has little in common with LTP (Staubli, 1992; Staubli, Larson, & Lynch, 1990; Zalutsky and Nicoll, 1990, 1992).
- *CA3 associational:* LTP exists in these synapses (Bradler & Barrionuevo, 1990; Zalutsky & Nicoll, 1990, 1992), but again, chronic recording data on persistence are lacking.
- *CA3 to CA1:* LTP is easily induced and shows no evident decay over 2 to 4 weeks (Staubli & Lynch, 1987).

These results led to the working hypothesis that the successive stages of olfactory–hippocampal circuitry add different features to the memory for odors (Lynch et al., 1991; Lynch & Staubli, 1991; Staubli, 1992). The specific links between stages and memory were proposed to be as follows:

- Olfactory cortex: Classification/recognition memory;
- Cortex/dentate gyrus: Sense of how long since last encounter with odor ("recency" memory);
- Dentate gyrus/CA3: Transient memory of last response to odor ("working memory");
- CA3/CA1: Serial linkage between odor and object. This reflects the work of Ranck (1973) and may relate to general hypotheses about the role of hippocampus in encoding cue relationships (see Eichenbaum, Otto, & Cohen, 1992).

In sum, LTP is found at several sites in hippocampus and olfactory cortex; it is known to be stable in two areas and to decay over a period of days at a third site. Potentiation in the mossy fibers involves induction and expression mechanisms different from those responsible for LTP. Several forms of memory have been identified and there is considerable evidence linking LTP to certain of these. It is possible that regional variations in synaptic plasticity are in part responsible for the existence of memory subtypes. The sequence of connections running from olfactory cortex through hippocampus contains variants of LTP as well as mossy fiber potentiation.

It remains for future work to determine precisely what aspects of memory arise from operations of each step in the circuit. This is likely to be a very challenging endeavor. At present our understanding of learning and memory is quite incomplete and fragmentary; there seems to be no consensus on the taxonomy of memory nor an estimate of the number or types of memory that are continuously used by mammals, a central point overlooked by most arguments in the literature. It is not clear, for example, that motor skill learning and classical conditioning share common substrates or features, nor can we assume that the memory systems that are involved in rapid encoding of sensory cues are in any way related to those involved in repeated practice. This being the situation, we look to neurobiological studies of potential encoding devices to provide us with explanations of features of memory as well as with novel insights into how memories are acquired, organized, and utilized.

SUMMARY AND COMMENT

The conclusion that LTP is the substrate of one or more types of memory does not arise from any single experiment or line of research. It follows instead from the experimental testing of a demanding set of predictions arising from a hypothesis positing this relationship. Memory as manifested in the recognition of cues, to take a simple example, involves a rapid but stable modification of communication between brain cells. It must be discrete (i.e., changing only a few synapses without affecting the remainder) in order to accommodate the evident capacity of recognition memory. These are strong constraints, but as shown by physiological experiments in slices and animals, they are met by LTP. To be a memory substrate, a given mechanism would have to have a deep relationship to patterns of brain activity occurring during learning. The remarkable agreement between at least one cell firing pattern found during learning and the conditions that trigger LTP satisfy this prediction. Evidence that LTP appears in the appropriate synapses as memory appears at the behavioral level, and that induction of LTP affects the subsequent course of learning, confirms another prediction of the hypothesis. Finally, results showing that pharmacological manipulations of LTP produce corresponding changes in memory encoding satisfies the last obvious demand imposed by the hypothesis. These findings, individually or together, do not "prove" the hypothesis that LTP is the substrate of memory, but they give ample reason to accept it.

Viewed from this perspective, LTP research has provided a satisfactory answer to one of the most difficult and fundamental questions encountered in the neurobiological study of behavior. But the value of hypotheses is gauged not only in terms of how well they account for disparate phenomena, but also in terms of their "utility." What do we gain by accepting LTP as the substrate of a class of memories: Three recent developments are pertinent here. First, it appears that different types of learning involve different chemistries—it may now become possible to categorize these variants in terms orthogonal to earlier behavioral and neurological criteria. Second, the LTP work may help explain certain amnestic phenomena and suggest novel approaches to memory enhancement. The discovery of relationships between patterns of activity and the chemistry of LTP induction, for example, leads inevitably to the idea that drugs that disrupt these patterns will block memory formation. This would explain the amnestic effects of anticholinergic compounds in rats and humans. Similarly, the interactions between GABA and NMDA receptors provide one route through which benzodiazepines might disturb LTP and learning. Recent findings, that manipulation of various aspects of theta burst responses affects the rate at which maximal LTP is reached, point to ways in which the strength of memory might be improved. As noted, only fragmentary results on these issues are available, but future work should test the exploratory power of the "LTP as memory substrate" hypothesis. Third, descriptions of LTP have become sufficiently detailed that they can be used as critical components of neurobiologically based predictions regarding behavioral phenomenology. That is, in addition to providing potential explanations for aspects of memory, LTP can be combined with various neurophysiological and neuroanatomical features of brain circuitries to suggest novel or underappreciated features of memory. It is perhaps in this area that LTP research has its greatest potential for helping us to understand the nature of memory.

REFERENCES

Arai, A., Larson, J., & Lynch, G. (1990). Anoxia reveals a vulnerable period in the development of long-term potentiation. *Brain Research, 511,* 353–357.

Arai, A., & Lynch, G. (1992). Factors regulating the magnitude of LTP induced by theta pattern stimulation. *Brain Research, 598,* 173–184.

Barnes, C. A. (1979). Memory deficits associated with senescence: A neurophysiological and behavioral study in the rat. *Journal of Comparative Physiology and Psychology, 93,* 74–104.

Barrionuevo, G., Schottler, F., Lynch, G. (1980). The effects of repetitive low frequency stimulation on control and 'potentiated' synaptic responses in the hippocampus. *Life Sciences, 27,* 2385–2391.

Bliss, T. V. P., & Lomo, T. (1973). Long-lasting potentiation of synaptic transmission in the dentate area of the anesthetized rabbit following stimulation of the perforant path. *Journal of Physiology (London), 232,* 334–356.

Bradler, J. E. & Barrionuevo, G. (1990). Heterosynaptic correlates of long-term potentiation induction in hippocampal CA3 neurons. *Neuroscience, 35,* 265–271.

Brown, S. S., & Dundee, J. W. (1968). Clinical studies of induction agents XXV: Diazepam. *British Journal of Anaesthesiology, 40,* 108–112.

Castro, C. A., Silbert, L. H., McNaughton, B. L., & Barnes, C. A. (1989). Recovery of spatial learning deficits after decay of electrically induced synaptic enhancement in the hippocampus. *Nature, 342,* 545–548.

Collingridge, G. L., Kehl, S. J., & McLennan, H. (1983). Excitatory amino acids in synaptic transmission in the Schaffer-commissural pathway of the rat hippocampus. *Journal of Physiology (London), 334,* 33–46.

del Cerro, S., Jung, M., & Lynch, G. (1992). Benzodiazepines block long-term potentiation in rat hippocampal and piriform cortex slices. *Neuroscience, 49*, 1–6.

del Cerro, S., Larson, J., Oliver, M., & Lynch, G. (1990). Development of hippocampal long-term potentiation is reduced by recently introduced calpain inhibitors. *Brain Research, 530*, 91–95.

Denny, J. B., Polan-Curtain, J., Ghuman, A., Wayner, M. J., & Armstrong, D. L. (1990). Calpain inhibitors block long-term potentiation. *Brain Research, 534*, 317–320.

Diamond, D., Dunwiddie, T., & Rose, G. (1988). Characteristics of hippocampal primed burst potentiation in vitro and in the awake rat. *Journal of Neuroscience, 8*, 4079–4088.

Doller, H. J., & Weight, F. F. (1985). Perforant path-evoked long-term potentiation of CA1 neurons in the hippocampal slice preparation. *Brain Research, 333*, 305–310.

Dunwiddie, T., & Lynch, G. (1978). Long-term potentiation and depression of synaptic responses in the hippocampus: Localization and frequency dependency. *Journal of Physiology (London), 276*, 353–367.

Eichenbaum, H., Kuperstein, M., Fagan, A., & Nagode, J. (1987) Cue-sampling and goal-approach correlates of hippocampal unit activity in rats performing an odor-discrimination task. *Journal of Neuroscience, 7*, 716–732.

Eichenbaum, H. M., Otto, T., & Cohen, N. (1992). The hippocampus—What does it do? *Behavioral and Neural Biology, 57*, 2–36.

Fujii, S., Saito, K., Miyakawa, H., Ito, K., & Kato, H. (1991). Reversal of long-term potentiation (depotentiation) induced by tetanus stimulation of the input to CA1 neurons of guinea pig hippocampal slices. *Brain Research, 555*, 112–122.

Grillner, S., & Wallen, P. (1985). The ionic mechanisms underlying N-methyl-D-aspartate receptor-induced, tetrodotoxin-resistant membrane potential oscillations in lamprey neurons active during locomotion. *Neuroscience Letters, 60*, 289–294.

Gustafsson, B., Asztely, F., Hanse, E., & Wigstrom, H. (1989). Onset characteristics of long-term potentiation in the guinea-pig hippocampal CA1 region *in vitro*. *European Journal of Neuroscience, 1*, 382–394.

Hill, A. J. (1978). First occurrence of hippocampal spatial firing in a new environment. *Experimental Neurology, 62*, 282–297.

Ito, M. (1987). Characterization of synaptic plasticity in the cerebellar and cerebral neocortex. In J.-P. Changeux & M. Konishi (Eds.,) *The neural and molecular basis of learning* (pp. 263–280). New York: Wiley.

Ito, I., Tanabe, S., Khoda, A., & Sugiyama, H. (1990). Allosteric potentiation of quisqualate receptors by a nootropic drug aniracetam. *Journal of Physiology (London), 424*, 533–543.

Jung, M., Larson, J., & Lynch, G. (1990). Role of NMDA and non-NMDA receptors in synaptic transmission in rat piriform cortex. *Experimental Brain Research, 82*, 451–455.

Kanter, E. D., & Haberly, L. B. (1990). NMDA-dependent induction of long-term potentiation in afferent and association fiber systems of piriform cortex in vitro. *Brain Research, 525*, 175–179.

Kauer, J. A., Malenka, R. C., & Nicoll, R. A. (1988). A persistent postsynaptic modification mediates long-term potentiation in the hippocampus. *Neuron, 1*, 911–917.

Komisaruk, B. R. (1977). The role of rhythmical brain activity in sensorimotor integration. *Progress in Psychobiology, Physiology, and Psychology, 7*, 55–90.

Korol, D. L., Abel, T. W., Church, L. T., Barnes, C. A., & McNaughton, B. L. (1993). Hippocampal synaptic enhancement and spatial learning in the Morris swim task. *Hippocampus, 3*, 127–132.

Landfield, P. W. (1976). Synchronous EEG rhythms: Their nature and their possible functions in memory. In W. H. Gispen (Ed.), *Molecular and functional neurobiology* (pp. 389–424). Amsterdam: Elsevier.

Laroche, S., Doyère, V., & Bloch, V. (1989). Linear relationship between the magnitude of long-term potentiation in the dentate gyrus and associative learning in the rat. A demonstration using commissural inhibition and local infusion of an N-methyl-D-aspartate receptor antagonist. *Neuroscience, 28*, 375–386.

Larson, J., & Lynch, G. (1986). Induction of synaptic potentiation in hippocampus by patterned stimulation involves two events. *Science, 232,* 985–988.

Larson, J., & Lynch, G. (1988). Role of N-Methyl-D-Aspartate receptors in the induction of synaptic potentiation by burst stimulation patterned after the hippocampal theta rhythm. *Brain Research, 441,* 111–118.

Larson, J., Wong, D., & Lynch, G. (1986). Patterned stimulation at the theta frequency is optimal for induction of hippocampal long-term potentiation. *Brain Research, 368,* 347–350.

Larson, J., Xiao, P., & Lynch, G. (1993). Reversal of LTP by theta frequency stimulation. *Brain Research, 600,* 97–102.

Lister, R. G. (1985). The amnesic action of benzodiazepines in man. *Neuroscience and Biobehavioral Review, 9,* 87–94.

Lynch, G., Larson, J., Staubli, U., & Granger, R. (1991). Variants of synaptic potentiation and different types of memory operations in hippocampus and related structures. In L. R. Squire, N. M. Weinberger, G. Lynch, & J. L. McGaugh (Eds.), *Memory: Organization and Locus of Change* (pp. 330–363). New York: Oxford University Press.

Lynch, G., & Staubli, U. (1991). Possible contributions of long-term potentiation to the encoding and organization of memory. *Brain Research Review, 16,* 204–206.

Madison, D. V., & Nicoll, R. A. (1986). Cyclic-adenosine 3',5'-monophosphate mediates beta-receptor actions of noradrenaline in rat hippocampal pyramidal cells. *Journal of Physiology, 372,* 245–259.

McGaugh, J. L. (1966). Time-dependent processes in memory storage. *Science, 153,* 1351–1358.

McNaughton, B. L., Barnes, C. A., Rao, G., Baldwin, J., & Rasmussen, M. (1986). Long-term enhancement of hippocampal synaptic transmission and the acquisition of spatial information. *Journal of Neuroscience, 6,* 563–571.

McNaughton, B. L., Douglas, R. M., & Goddard, G. V. (1978). Synaptic enhancement in fascia dentata: Co-operativity among coactive afferents. *Brain Research, 157,* 277–293.

Monaghan, D. T., & Cotman, C. W. (1985). Distribution of N-methyl-D-aspartate-sensitive L-[3H]glutamate-binding sites in rat brain. *Journal of Neuroscience, 5,* 2909–2919.

Morris, R. G. M., Anderson, E., Lynch, G. S., & Baudry, M. (1986). Selective impairment of learning and blockade of long-term potentiation by an N-methyl-D-aspartate receptor antagonist, APV. *Nature, 319,* 774–776.

Mott, D. D., & Lewis, D. V. (1991). Facilitation of the induction of long-term potentiation by GABAb receptors. *Science, 252,* 1718–1720.

Muller, D., Joly, M., & Lynch, G. (1988). Contributions of quisqualate and NMDA receptors to the induction and expression of LTP. *Science, 242,* 1694–1697.

O'Keefe, J., & Nadel, L. (1978). *The hippocampus as a cognitive map.* Oxford: Oxford University Press.

Oliver, M., Baudry, M., & Lynch, G. (1990). The protease inhibitor leupeptin interferes with the development of LTP in hippocampal slices. *Brain Research, 505,* 233–238.

Olton, D. S., Becker, J. T., & Handelmann, G. E. (1979). Hippocampus, space and memory. *Behavioral and Brain Sciences, 2,* 313–365.

Otto, T., Eichenbaum, H., Wiener, S. I., & Wible, C. (1991). Learning related patterns of CA1 spike trains parallel stimulation parameters optimal for inducing hippocampal long-term potentiation. *Hippocampus, 1,* 181–192.

Racine, R. J., Milgram, N. W., & Hafner, S. (1983). Long-term potentiation phenomena in the rat limbic forebrain. *Brain Research, 260,* 217–231.

Ranck, J. B., Jr. (1973). Studies on single neurons in dorsal hippocampal formation and septum in unrestrained rats. *Experimental Neurology, 41,* 461–555.

Robinson, G. S., Jr., Crooks, G. B., Jr., Shinkman, P. B., & Gallagher, M. (1989). Behavioral effects of MK-801 mimic deficits associated with hippocampal damage. *Psychobiology, 17,* 156–164.

Roman, F. S., Chaillan, F. A., Staubli, U., & Soumireu-Mourat, B. (1992). Modulation of LTP in piriform cortex. *Abstract Proceedings of the Fifth Conference on the Neurobiology of Learning and Memory.* Irvine, California.

Roman, F., Staubli, U., & Lynch, G. (1987). Evidence for synaptic potentiation in a cortical network during learning. *Brain Research, 418,* 221-226.

Squire, L. (1986) Mechanisms of memory. *Science, 232,* 1612-1619.

Standing, L. (1973). Learning 10,000 pictures. *Quarterly Journal of Experimental Psychology, 25,* 207-222.

Staubli, U. (1992). A peculiar form of potentiation in mossy fiber synapses. In C. E. Ribak, C. M., Gall, & I. Mody (Eds.), *The dentate gyrus and its role in seizures* (pp. 151-157). New York: Elsevier.

Staubli, U., Ambros-Ingerson, J., & Lynch, G. (1992). Receptor changes and LTP: An analysis using aniracetam, a drug that reversibly modifies glutamate (AMPA) receptors. *Hippocampus, 2,* 49-58.

Staubli, U., Baudry, M., & Lynch, G. (1984). Leupeptin, a thiol-proteinase inhibitor, causes a selective impairment of maze performance in rats. *Behavioral and Neural Biology, 40,* 58-69.

Staubli, U., Baudry, M., & Lynch, G. (1985). Olfactory discrimination learning is blocked by leupeptin, a thiol protease inhibitor. *Brain Research, 337,* 333-336.

Staubli, U., Faraday, R., & Lynch, G. (1985). Pharmacological dissociation of memory: Anisomycin, a protein synthesis inhibitor, and leupeptin, a protease inhibitor, block different learning tasks. *Behavioral and Neural Biology, 43,* 287-297.

Staubli, U., Fraser, D., Kessler, M., & Lynch, G. (1986). Studies on retrograde and anterograde amnesia of olfactory memory after denervation of the hippocampus by entorhinal cortex lesions. *Behavioral and Neural Biology, 46,* 432-444.

Staubli, U., Ivy, G., & Lynch, G. (1984). Hippocampal denervation causes rapid forgetting of olfactory information in rats. *Proceedings of the National Academy of Science of the United States of America, 81,* 5885-5887.

Staubli, U., Kessler, M., & Lynch, G. (1990). Aniracetam has proportionally smaller effects on synapses expressing long-term potentiation: Evidence that receptor changes subserve LTP. *Psychobiology, 18,* 377-381.

Staubli, U., Larson, J., Thibault, O., Baudry, M., and Lynch, G. (1988). Chronic administration of a thiol-proteinase inhibitor blocks long-term potentiation of synaptic responses. *Brain Research, 444:*153-158.

Staubli, U., Larson, J., & Lynch, G. (1990). Mossy fiber potentiation and long-term potentiation involve different expression mechanisms. *Synapse, 5,* 333-335.

Staubli, U., & Lynch, G. (1987). Stable hippocampal long-term potentiation elicited by 'theta' pattern stimulation. *Brain Research, 435,* 227-234.

Staubli, U., & Lynch, G. (1990). Stable depression of potentiated synaptic responses in the hippocampus induced by low frequency stimulation. *Brain Research, 513,* 113-118.

Staubli, U., Rogers, G., & Lynch, G. (1994). Facilitation of glutamate receptors enhances memory. *Proceedings of the National Academy of Science of the United States of America, 91,* 777-781.

Staubli, U., Roman, F., & Lynch, G. (1985). Selective changes of synaptic responses in a cortical network by behaviorally relevant electrical stimulation. *Society for Neuroscience Abstracts, 11,* 837.

Staubli, U., Thibault, O., DiLorenzo, M., & Lynch, G. (1989). Antagonism of NMDA receptors impairs acquisition but not retention of olfactory memory. *Behavioral Neuroscience, 103,* 54-60.

Stripling, J. S., Patneau, D. K., & Gramlich, C. A. (1988). Selective long-term potentiation in the pyriform cortex. *Brain Research, 441,* 281-291.

Sutherland, R. J., Dringenberg, H. C., & Hoesing, J. M. (1993). Induction of long-term potentiation at perforant path dentate synapses does not affect place learning or memory. *Hippocampus, 3,* 141-147.

Tang, C.-M., Shi, Q.-Y., Katchman, A., & Lynch, G. (1991). Modulation of the time course of fast EPSCs and glutamate channel kinetics by aniracetam. *Science, 254,* 288-290.

Vanderwolf, C. H. (1969). Hippocampal electrical activity and voluntary movement in the rat. *Electroencephalography and Clinical Neurophysiology, 26,* 407–418.

Vertes, R. P. (1989). Brainstem modulation of the hippocampus: Anatomy, physiology, and significance. In R. L. Isaacson & K. H. Pribram (Eds.), *The Hippocampus, Vol. 3.* New York: Plenum.

Wallen, P., & Grillner, S. (1987). N-methyl-D-aspartate receptor-induced oscillatory activity in neurons active during fictive locomotion in the lamprey. *Journal of Neuroscience, 7,* 2745–2755.

Xiao, P., Staubli, U., Kessler, M., & Lynch, G. (1991). Selective effects of aniracetam across receptor types and forms of synaptic facilitation in hippocampus. *Hippocampus, 1,* 373–380.

Youngentob, S. L., Mozell, M.M., Sheebe, P. R. & Hornung, D. E. (1987). A quantitative analysis of sniffing strategies in rats performing odor detection tasks. *Physiology and Behavior, 41,* 59–69.

Zalutsky, R. A., & Nicoll, R.A. (1990). Comparison of two forms of long-term potentiation in single hippocampal neurons. *Science, 248,* 1619–1624.

Zalutsky, R. A., & Nicoll, R. A. (1992). Mossy fiber long-term potentiation shows specificity but no apparent cooperativity. *Neuroscience Letters, 138,* 193–197.

19

On the Relevance of Long-Term
Potentiation to Learning and Memory

YADIN DUDAI

Long-term potentiation (LTP), no doubt, is a highly interesting experimental phenomenon. Its analysis unveils intricate, sometimes surprising cascades of molecular events that operate in and between neurons (for a recent review, see Bliss & Collingridge, 1993). But for investigators of learning and memory, *relevancy,* rather than interest, is the critical criterion. What is the relevance of LTP to in vivo mechanisms of learning and memory? Following the chapters by Barnes, Erickson, Davis, and McNaughton (Chapter 16), Laroche, Doyère, Rédini-Del Negro, and Burette (Chapter 17), and Staubli (Chapter 18), I have rephrased the problem in a set of questions: (1) Is LTP a candidate *memory* mechanism, or is it a candidate *cellular information storage* mechanism, and what is the difference between the two? (2) Is LTP a natural phenomenon? (3) Does LTP play an in vivo role in memory? (4) Which experimental methodologies can be used to support or refute (2) and (3)? And (5) What criteria should we use to determine whether we have been successful?

IS LONG-TERM POTENTIATION
A CANDIDATE MEMORY MECHANISM?

Memories are experience-dependent internal representations, that is, neuronally encoded versions of the world capable of guiding behavior (Dudai, 1989, 1992). Memory is thus a semantic token in the neuronal language of the brain. Neuronal alterations that instantiate memory are hence those that alter the representational properties of the nervous system. In most cases we don't yet know what these representational properties are. The reason for that is anchored in the level of analysis in which neuronal semantics is expected to emerge.

"Level" denotes a position on a complexity scale. In brain research an acceptable parsimonious division into levels is molecular, cellular, circuit (or network), brain, behavior. A critical issue is the delineation of functions performed in each level. It is the circuit level that is expected to encode specific representations and to perform molar computations on these representations. The ability of individual neurons within a network to independently encode meaningful chunks of information is still a matter of dispute, but most authorities propose that the representational information encoded in a single node of a neuronal network must be weighed only in the context of that network.[1] Accordingly, the investigation of a few or single neurons out of their in vivo context, and clearly that of individual synapses and molecular complexes, cannot disclose neuronal semantics. It can disclose only "universal" cellular information storage mechanisms that participate in the realization of memory. Long-term potentiation is a cellular and synaptic process. It follows, therefore, that LTP cannot be a *memory* mechanism; it is a candidate *cellular information storage* mechanism.

IS LONG-TERM POTENTIATION A NATURAL PHENOMENON?

The term LTP is conventionally assigned to phenomena in which brief trains of high-frequency stimulation to monosynaptic excitatory pathways cause an abrupt and sustained increase in the efficiency of synaptic transmission (Bliss & Collingridge, 1993). Simultaneous activation of thousands of fibers can occur in epilepsy; it is most unlikely to occur in situ under normal conditions. There are reports of the occurrence of population discharge of a large number of pyramidal cells in the hippocampus, resembling the conditions required to produce LTP ("sharp waves"; Buzsaki, Haas, & Anderson, 1987), but the physiological meaning of this observation is not clear. Therefore I would rather regard LTP as a paradigm that unveils cascades of molecular events capable of inducing neuronal plasticity; some or all of these events are recruited in vivo at some permutational arrangements and weights in response to natural neuronal input in a stimulated pathway. I thus regard *macroscopic* LTP in a given experimental preparation as an artificial phenomenon, but *microscopic* LTP as a potential natural kind of information storage device. Microscopic LTP consists of activation of N-methyl-D-aspartate (NMDA) receptors as well as other types of glutamatergic receptors, intracellular Ca^{2+} and lipid cascades, retrograde messages, and so forth, in an interlocked net of events that result in metabolic and morphologic alterations in the synaptic partners.

DOES LONG-TERM POTENTIATION PLAY AN IN VIVO ROLE IN MEMORY?

In their chapters, Barnes et al., Laroche et al., and Staubli have provided us with intriguing data and analysis. In terms of my estimate of the strength of their self-conviction that LTP is involved in experience-dependent modifications in the brain, as reflected in their chapters, Staubli and Laroche et al. are more decisive,

Barnes et al. more reserved, but all of them are cautious, and aptly so. I do not analyze their arguments one by one, but rather first classify the experimental tools employed by them and by other leading experts on LTP, and then weigh the types of arguments and conclusions in view of a set of criteria that should, so I think, be used in evaluating the outcome of the experiments.

THE METHODOLOGIES

Research on LTP employs experimental methodologies similar to those used in other facets of neurobiology:

1. *Observation.* This is the most straightforward approach; a biological phenomenon is observed to emerge, or its properties are outlined from observations. The latter might be incidental or focused on the suspected mechanism. For example, observations led to the suggestion that properties of LTP parallel those of learning and memory (Barnes et al. and Staubli, Chapters 16 and 18, this volume).
2. *Correlation.* The relevance of two or more mechanisms or phenomena to each other is here assessed by correlating their occurrence in time, space, or magnitude. Correlation might be of the first order, that is, of x with z, or of a higher order, for example, of x with y where y was previously correlated with z. Attempts to correlate LTP with the rate or magnitude of learning are examples of first-order correlation (Barnes, 1979; Skelton, Scarth, Wilkie, Miller, & Philips, 1987). Correlation of LTP with ageing is of a second order with regard to memory, as advanced age is itself correlated with a decrease in memory (Barnes, 1979).
3. *Inference of function from alteration of function.* Here we can distinguish two types of approaches. The prevalent one is inference of function from dysfunction: a system is lesioned, either anatomically or metabolically, and the effect of lesion on the phenomena in question is then assessed. A well-cited example is provided by studies that use NMDA receptor antagonists to determine whether NMDA receptors, and hence possibly LTP, are involved in learning (Morris, 1989). Another type of inference of function from alteration of function is to induce hyperfunction rather than dysfunction, for example, to use nootropic drugs that facilitate LTP to enhance learning, in an attempt to conclude that LTP is involved in learning (Staubli, Chapter 18, this volume).
4. *Mimicry.* Here LTP is used to mimic a physiological stimulus in the process of learning and to determine the outcome on learning. Examples are the use of LTP-like stimulation of the lateral olfactory tract to the piriform cortex as an "electric odor" in odor discrimination training (Staubli, Chapter 18, this volume), or the use of LTP in the perforant path as a conditioned stimulus in hippocampal-dependent conditioning paradigms (Skelton, Miller, & Philips, 1985; Laroche, Doyère, & Rédini-De Negro, 1991 and Chapter 17, this volume).

CRITERIA FOR RELEVANCE

The role of LTP in learning and memory, investigated by a combination of the aforementioned methodologies, can be assessed by several criteria.

Is Long-Term Potentiation Correlated with Learning and Memory?

The first evidence offered for a direct in vivo link between LTP and learning was that of Barnes (1979) demonstrating correlation of LTP with spatial memory within and between age groups in behaving rats. In addition, a converse correlation was reported between saturation of perforant path with LTP and a learning deficit in hippocampally dependent spatial learning; this type of experiment could also be construed as inference of necessity of function from dysfunction (see below; McNaughton, Barnes, Rao, Baldwin, & Rasmussen, 1986). However, as Barnes et al. detail in their chapter (this volume), several groups, including McNaughton et al. (1986), have been unable to replicate the saturation effects. Jeffrey and Morris (in press) recently found no effect of LTP saturation on the rate of learning of a water-maze task in rats, but did find a correlation between the rate of learning and the extent of LTP.

A short-term exploration-linked modulation of field potentials (STEM), which bears similarity to macroscopic LTP, though is clearly not identical with it, has been described in the hippocampal formation of behaving rats (Green, McNaughton, & Barnes, 1990; Barnes et al., Chapter 16, this volume). However, Andersen and his colleagues (personal communication, 1993) found that this enhancement in synaptic efficacy might be largely due to an increase of forebrain temperature that accompanies exercise. The latter report emphasizes a pitfall of correlation: the behavior is correlated with altered synaptic efficacy, but in this case there is no causal relation between behavior and synaptic efficacy, as both are linked via body temperature.

Several studies have reported a correlation between identified molecular and cellular facets of LTP and learning. For example, enduring alterations in neuronal excitability were reported following training in various learning paradigms (e.g., Coulter et al., 1989; Ruthrich, Matthies, & Oh, 1982; Weisz, Clark, Yang, Thompson & Solomon, 1982), though the role of locomotion versus learning (Hargreaves, Cain, & Vanderwolf, 1990) and of temperature changes (Anderson, personal communication, 1993) must yet be established. On the molecular level, an associative learning task has been correlated with increase in glutamate release and with phosphoinositides turnover in the dentate gyrus (Laroche et al., 1991); these two metabolic changes have been implicated in LTP (reviewed in Bliss & Collingridge, 1993). The latter is thus a second-order correlation.

In addition, the correlation between occurrence of LTP and the brain location in which it is revealed has been noted by many authors. Specifically, LTP is prominent in the hippocampal formation, a brain structure implicated in learning and memory. It was also detected in neocortex, which is also regarded as critical for some forms of learning.

All in all, the correlative data are consistent with the hypothesis that microcomponents of LTP participate in synaptic plasticity that subserves learning, but do not prove that macroscopic LTP is involved in learning and memory.

Does Long-Term Potentiation Bear Similarity *to Properties of Learning and Memory?*

Staubli (Chapter 18, this volume) as well as other authors substantiate the claim that LTP plays a role in memory by stating that it displays properties expected from memory, such as persistence following brief stimuli, associativity, order-dependency in associativity, and occurrence in brain regions critical for some types of memory (reviewed in Dudai, 1989). Such similarity is appealing, but may be misleading. One can detect, for example, persistent alterations following brief stimuli, and associativity of cellular events, in nonneuronal tissues in response to hormones and growth factors. Furthermore, there is no reason to expect that parts should display the properties of the whole and vice versa, hence that molecular and cellular devices should display the phenomenology of behavior (e.g., Bechtel, 1982).

Is Long-Term Potentiation Useful *for Generation and Retention of Memory?*

There are two versions to this criterion. The first is empirical usefulness, that is, is the process experimentally useful in inducing learning-related alterations. This can be tested in experiments that also aim at establishing correlation (above) or sufficiency (below). Thus, stimulation protocols similar to those eliciting LTP appear useful in conditioning rat piriform cortex and hippocampus in experiments in which electrical stimulation substitutes a conditioned stimulus (Laroche, et al. and Staubli, Chapters 17 and 18, this volume).

The second version of this criterion is conceptual usefulness, that is, can the implicated mechanism be integrated into models of learning and memory, thus forming a coherent picture of available data, capable of generating a testable hypothesis. Here LTP fits well into candidate molecular and cellular models of short- or intermediate-term plasticity. It is capable of modifying synapses following brief input stimulation, in an associative or context-dependent manner and for days or even weeks. Clearly, it cannot per se subserve long-term memory that endures for years. The conclusion is thus that even if LTP does subserve memory, it functions only as part of a more complex set of events.

Is Long-Term Potentiation Necessary *for Memory?*

Anatomical lesions, so widely employed in inference of function from dysfunction in brain research, are not applicable in the case of LTP that is a cellular phenomenon. Molecular lesions are widely employed. The most popular ones are those that block glutamatergic receptors and especially NMDA receptors. The classical study, since replicated by many other groups, is that of Morris (1989), demonstrating impairment of LTP as well as spatial learning in rats by the NMDA receptor antagonist APV. Recently, the same group has used an inhibitor of the NO (nitric oxide) pathway, implicated in LTP, to block both LTP and spatial learning in vivo. Learning was impaired but LTP was not (Bannerman, Kelly, Butcher, & Morris, 1993).

The use of metabolic inhibitors suggest that molecular entities like the NMDA receptor are important in learning. Unless an inhibitor is found that specifically blocks LTP as a unique, global entity (which is unlikely), metabolic inhibitors would not prove that LTP is necessary for learning.

A similar approach is to use mutations. This approach was first successfully employed in neurogenetic dissection of learning in *Drosophila* (Dudai, 1989), and recently applied to mice, LTP, and learning. Silva, Paylor, Wehner, and Tonegawa (1992) used knockout in the gene encoding Ca^{2+}/calmodulin-dependent protein kinase II (CAM-kinase II) to demonstrate impairment in both LTP and spatial learning. Grant et al. (1992) got similar results with a knockout in *fyn,* a tyrosine kinase gene. Genetic dissection is technologically intriguing, but conceptually does not much differ, at the current state of the art, from metabolic lesions. The effect of the mutation is not tissue or time specific; effects on other systems, and developmental effects, cannot be excluded. Moreover, the specificity of the effect on both LTP and learning must be scrutinized. It is especially important to verify that there are no developmental effects, and no physiological and behavioral impairment that might affect learning but are not due to lesions in the learning machinery per se. Neurogenetic dissection will become much more discriminative and powerful when methods are devised to generate tissue-specific mutations that can be activated at specific time windows in situ.

Thus again (and see "Is Long-term Potentiation *Correlated* with Learning and Memory?" earlier in this section), the current evidence suggests that some molecular components that subserve LTP are necessary for normal learning.

Does Long-Term Potentiation Suffice *for Memory Formation?*

This criterion is far more difficult to fulfill. The methodology is similar to that employed in attempts to fulfill criterion 3, "Is Long-term Potentiation *Useful* for Generation and Retention of Memory?", namely mimicry experiments, only that the claim and interpretation are more pretentious and in vivo causality is assumed. Experiments demonstrating that LTP-like stimulation in identified pathways can substitute for an associated stimulus in conditioning, can be interpreted as showing that LTP in a given pathway is sufficient to encode behaviorally relevant information in that pathway in vivo (Laroche et al., and Staubli, Chapters 17 and 18, this volume). But the observation that an artificial stimulus brings about a physical change does not prove that an identical stimulus functions in vivo.

Experiments that infer function from hyperfunction might also be construed as contributing to the notion that LTP is sufficient to realize a necessary step in memory formation. Such experiments use ligands that stimulate glutamatergic receptors implicated in LTP. Examples are the studies of Staubli (Chapter 18, this volume) using nootropics that facilitate AMPA receptors and enhance learning, and the report by Thompson, Moskal, and Disterhoft (1992) that activation of the glycine site on NMDA receptors enhances hippocampal-dependent learning. The most far-reaching conclusion that might be derived from these results is that activation of glutamatergic receptors of a certain type contributes to learning. No convincing evidence emerges on the contribution of macroscopic LTP and learning.

Is Long-Term Potentiation Exclusive?

This is the most demanding criterion. A claim for exclusiveness cannot be currently made for any candidate mechanism in learning. The question can be raised whether exclusiveness can at all be expected, since multiplicity of mechanisms and parallel pathways appear to be the rule in learning (Dudai, 1989), and operate in LTP itself at the cellular level (Bliss & Collingridge, 1993). Clearly, in the case of LTP the question must relate to specific steps in the process and to a specific case and site of learning.

CONCLUSIONS

In conclusion, my position is the following: (1) Mechanisms that are recruited in LTP may operate in certain types of learning. (2) Most current research on LTP epitomizes the problematics of a bottom-up strategy: to a large degree, LTP is a mechanism in search of a role, a process in search of a context. Research restricted to the molecular or cellular level cannot provide us with an answer to the question whether LTP plays a role in learning; the nature of the representation in the circuit and the effect of LTP on this representation must be addressed. (3) Similarities exist between properties of LTP and learning and memory, that is, rapid induction, stimulus specificity, associativity, and endurance. Such similarities may be also detected in nonneuronal systems (e.g., the immune system). Furthermore, there is no reason to assume that properties displayed by the molar activity of a system (i.e., behavior) will be displayed by the individual components of that system. Therefore I don't agree with Staubli's assumption (Chapter 18, this volume) that properties of LTP should be reflected in learning and vice versa. For the same reason, I do not see any problem in the observation that the time course of LTP is limited; this simply implies that if LTP indeed subserves memory, it plays a role only in initial events in the process.

Finally, the question can be posed: What do we need to have in order to be able to determine the role of LTP in in vivo learning? Following the aforementioned argumentation, I propose that we need a neuronal circuit that encodes a specific, identified internal representation. That neuronal circuit should also sustain LTP. Demonstration that an alteration in the representation encoded in the system is subserved by LTP, assessed by the criteria outlined in the last section, would be convincing indeed. In the meantime LTP remains an intriguing model capable of unveiling molecular components of neuronal plasticity.

ACKNOWLEDGMENTS
I am grateful to Rina Schul and Menachem Segal for comments, and to the Whitehall Foundation, Florida, and the Grodesky Center for Brain Research, The Weizmann Institute of Science, for support.

Note

[1] The crux of the argument is the criticality of the context rather than the number of units that represent the token. This argument does not contradict the ability to correlate the activity of a single or a few neurons with discrete stimuli or behavior, or to activate behavior by stimulation of a few neurons; for example, Gross, 1992.

REFERENCES

Bannerman, D., Kelly, P. Butcher, S. P., & Morris, R. G. M. (1993). *Inhibition of nitric oxide synthesis in vivo impairs spatial learning but does not block LTP or alter glucose uptake in hippocampus.* Manuscript in preparation.

Barnes, C. A. (1979). Memory deficits associated with senescence: A neurophysiological and behavioral study in the rat. *Journal of Physiology and Psychology, 93,* 74–104.

Bechtel, W. (1982). Two common errors in explaining biological and psychological phenomena. *Philosophy of Science, 49,* 549–574.

Bliss, T. V. P., & Collingridge, G. L. (1993). A synaptic model of memory: Long-term potentiation in the hippocampus. *Nature, 361,* 31–39.

Buzsaki, G., Haas, H. L., & Anderson, E. G. (1987). Long-term potentiation induced by physiologically relevant stimulus patterns. *Brain Research, 435,* 331–333.

Coulter, D. A., LoTurco, J. J., Kubota, M., Disterhoft, J. F., Moore, J. W., & Alkon, D. (1989). Classical conditioning reduces amplitude and duration of calcium-dependent after hyperpolarization in rabbit hippocampal pyramidal cells. *Journal of Neurophysiology, 61,* 971–981.

Dudai, Y. (1989). *The neurobiology of memory.* Oxford: Oxford University Press.

Dudai, Y. (1992). Why 'learning' and 'memory' should be redefined (or, an agenda for focused reductionism). *Concepts in Neuroscience, 3,* 99–121.

Grant, S. G. N., O'Dell, T. J., Karl, K. A., Stein, P. L., Soriano, P., & Kandel, E. R. (1992). Impaired long-term potentiation, spatial learning and hippocampal development in *fyn* mutant mice. *Science, 258,* 1903–1910.

Green, E. J., McNaughton, B. L., & Barnes, C. A. (1990). Exploration-dependent modulation of evoked responses in fascia dentata: Dissociation of motor, EEG and sensory factors, and evidence for a synaptic efficacy change. *Journal of Neuroscience, 10,* 1455–1471.

Gross, C. G. (1992). Representation of visual stimuli in inferior temporal cortex. *Philosophical Transactions of the Royal Society of London [Biology], 335,* 3–10.

Hargreaves, E. L., Cain, D. P., & Vanderwolf, C. H. (1990). Learning and behavioral long-term potentiation: Importance of controlling for motor activity. *Journal of Neuroscience, 10,* 1472–1478.

Jeffrey, K. J., & Morris, R. G. M. (in press). Asymptotic long-term potentiation in the rat dentate gyrus correlates, but does not modify, performance in the watermaze. *Hippocampus.*

Laroche, S., Doyère, V., & Rédini-Del Negro, C. (1991). What role for long-term potentiation in learning and in the maintenance of memories? In M. Baudry & J. L. Davis (Eds.), *Long-term potentiation, a debate of current issues* (pp. 301–316). Cambridge: MIT Press.

McNaughton, B. L., Barnes, C. A., Rao, G., Baldwin, J., & Rasmussen, M. (1986). Long-term enhancement of hippocampal synaptic transmission and the acquisition of spatial information. *Journal of Neuroscience, 6,* 563–571.

Morris, R. G. M. (1989). Synaptic plasticity and learning: Selective impairment of learning in rats and blockade of long-term potentiation in vivo by the N-methyl-D-aspartate agonist AP5. *Journal of Neuroscience, 9,* 3040–3057.

Ruthlich, H., Matthies, H., & Ott, T. (1982). Long-term changes in synaptic excitability of hippocampal cell populations. In C. Marsan & H. Mathies (Eds.), *Neuronal plasticity and memory formation* (pp. 589–594). New York: Raven Press.

Silva, A. J., Paylor, R., Wehner, J. M., & Tonegawa, S. (1992). Impaired spatial learning in alpha-calcium-calmodulin kinase II mutant mice. *Science, 257,* 206–211.

Skelton, R. W., Miller, J. J., & Philips, A. G. (1985). Long-term potentiation facilitates behavioral responding to single-pulse potentiation of the perforant path. *Behavioral Neuroscience, 99,* 603–620.

Skelton, R. W., Scarth, A. S., Wilkie, D. M., Miller, J. J., & Philips, A. G. (1987). Long-term increases in dentate granule cell responsivity accompany operant conditioning. *Journal of Neuroscience, 7,* 3081–3087.

Thompson, L. T., Moskal, J. R., & Disterhoft, J. F. (1992). Hippocampus-dependent learning facilitated by a monoclonal antibody or D-cycloserine. *Nature, 359,* 638–641.

Weisz, D., Clark, G., Yang, B., Thompson, R., & Solomon, P. (1982). Activity of the dentate gyrus during NM conditioning in rabbit. *Advances in Behavioral Biology, 26,* 131–145.

Whyte, L. L., Wilson, A. G., & Wilson, D. (Eds.). (1969). *Hierarchical Structures.* New York: American Elsevier.

20

Is Long-Term Potentiation
a Plausible Basis for Memory?

C. R. GALLISTEL

The discovery of the cellular and molecular bases of memory is among the most important quests in neuroscience. Long-term potentiation (LTP) is generally considered to be the most plausible candidate for the cellular-level change by which at least some kinds of behaviorally important information derived from experience are preserved in the nervous system. How good is the evidence we now have for this hypothesis and what kinds of evidence do we need to strengthen the case?

In their chapters, Barnes, Erickson, Davis, and McNaughton (Chapter 16), Laroche, Doyère, Rédini-Del Negro, and Burette (Chapter 17), and Staubli (Chapter 18) give two kinds of arguments: (1) A list of properties that LTP and memory have in common, and (2) experiments seeming to show that manipulating LTP manipulates memory formation (Castro, Silbert, McNaughton, & Barnes, 1989) and vice versa (Roman, Staubli, & Lynch, 1987). There is not much of the latter kind of evidence, and one of the more impressive results of this kind (Castro et al., 1989) has proved difficult to replicate. Since my space is limited, I focus my discussion on the evidence of the first kind, the properties that LTP and memories are said to have in common.

ARE THE PROPERTIES OF LONG-TERM POTENTIATION
AND MEMORY FORMATION SIMILAR?

Durability: Do They Endure for Similar Intervals?

LTP and memory are said to have durability in common, but do they? Barnes et al., Laroche et al., and Staubli (Chapters 16, 17, 18, this volume) all avoid specifying how long LTP lasts, with good reason: If you look in the literature for explicit or implicit answers to this question, you find answers ranging from minutes to months. Laroche, Doyère, and Rédini-Del Négro (1991) report a result that seems to indicate that a presumed mediator of LTP, elevated glutamate release in slice preparations of the rat dentate gyrus, is still present 50 days after classical conditioning. On the other hand, Castro et al. (1989) induced saturating levels of LTP and showed that they decayed to baseline levels in 15 days. There is no consensus about how long LTP lasts, and how long it lasts may depend on the strength of the inducing stimulation, yet the assumption that its durability is comparable to the durability of memories is among the first properties of LTP that most authors list when arguing that it is a plausible cellular basis for memory. Clearly, one kind of evidence we need are measurements in different labs by different methods that converge on an estimate of the decay constant of LTP.

How long do memories last? The common wisdom, supported by a number of mostly incidental experimental results, is that the memories formed in classical conditioning and in instrumental discrimination learning last indefinitely, that is, for years (Gleitman, 1971, pp. 12–19; Kimble, 1961, p. 281). However, there are other findings that, taken at face value, imply a much shorter duration (see the reviews just cited). In truth, psychologists can offer no clear answer to this fundamental question. In the average textbook on animal learning, the question is not even raised. The reasons for this neglect are not hard to see: (1) It's hard to build a career on experiments you must wait years to complete; (2) even if you are willing to wait out retention intervals measured in years, you must solve the formidable methodological problem of distinguishing between the effects of the retention interval on the memory per se and the effects of that interval on an array of other processes that determine the extent to which a memory will be manifest in what the animal does on a given test.

Barnes et al., Latcoche et al., and Staubli (Chapters 16, 17, 18, this volume), in common with most behavioral neuroscientists, favor a memory architecture involving changes in connectivity in distributed networks. Such an architecture, in contrast to the architecture of a conventional computer, does not readily support a distinction between storage failure and retrieval failure, because there is no clearly identifiable retrieval process; changes in connectivity simply alter signal flow the next time the net gets an input. Nonetheless, it is clear that in discussing human and animal memory, just as in discussing memory in a conventional computer, we must distinguish between storage failures and retrieval failures. A memory may not be manifest in what the animal does on a long delayed retest either because it has become illegible (storage failure) or because the retrieval process can no longer locate it. In a conventional computer, retrieval failures are much more common than storage failures. The same appears to be true for biological memories.

One compelling example of retrieval failure in biological memory is the retrograde amnesia that is present to varying extent following most concussive accidents. In concussive retrograde amnesia, the memories laid down during the amnestic interval are unretrievable but not gone. In the great majority of cases, most of the memories that were inaccessible for some while after the concussion eventually become accessible (Barbizet, 1970; Russell, 1959; Whitty & Zangwill, 1977). Transient retrograde amnesias of unknown etiology are also common (e.g.,

Kritchevsky, Squire & Zouzounis, 1988; see Gallistel, 1990, chap. 15, for a review of several other cases).

In accounts of both human and animal forgetting, interference theories dominate trace-decay theories (Gleitman, 1971; Underwood, 1957) There is much evidence that many memory failures are produced by interference, that is, that the memories remain potentially retrievable (because still stored). If we are going to try to answer the question how long memories last through behavioral experiments (and, in the absence of knowledge of the physical basis of memory, how else could you answer this question?), then we must devise methods for distinguishing between an increasing tendency to be unretrievable after a long interval since the last retrieval and an increasing tendency to be unreadable. It is presumably the latter property of memories that should be compared to the time course of LTP decay.

In short, durability comparisons provide very weak support for the claim that LTP is the physiological basis of memory, because there is no consensus on how long LTP lasts and no consensus on how long memories last. All we can say with confidence is that both last more than a few minutes.

Associability: Do They Both Depend on Temporal Pairing?

Barnes et al. (Chapter 16, this volume) and Laroche et al. (Chapter 17, this volume), in common with many other behavioral neuroscientists, argue that LTP and memory formation share a similar dependence on the temporal pairing of two activations. LTP only occurs when the activation of transmitter release from the presynaptic ending coincides with the depolarization of the postsynaptic cell. While it is true that Hebb (1949) proposed such a cellular mechanism and argued that it could explain many behavioral phenomena, it must not be thought that there is strong experimental evidence in support of the hypothesis that memory formation depends on the temporal coincidence or near coincidence of two stimuli. What many take to be a source of abundant evidence of this nature—the study of classical conditioning—has in fact shown that "the pairing or contiguity of two events . . . [is] neither necessary nor sufficient" for the establishment of an association (Rescorla, 1988, p. 152).

Behavioral neuroscientists have yet to come to terms with the realization that

> the facts [uncovered in experiments on classical conditioning done during the last three decades] have forced a change in the conceptualization of basic conditioning compatible with the general view that what is learned is not immutable reflexes but, rather, representations of events and relationships—memories—that are subject to substantial variance in their expression." (Spear, Miller, & Jagielo, 1990, p. 171).

Classical conditioning is now conceived of by the leading practitioners in the field as "the learning that results from exposure to relations among events in the environment." . . . [It provides] "a primary means by which the organism represents the structure of its world" (Rescorla, 1988, p. 152, quoted approvingly by Spear et al., 1990, p. 171).

Gallistel (1990, chap. 12) reviews the experimental findings that led to this revolution in the interpretation of classical conditioning. Among the more important findings are those showing that what the animal learns in a classical conditioning experiment is the temporal interval separating the conditioned stimulus (CS) from the unconditioned stimulus (US) (Church, 1984; Davis, Schlesinger, & Sorenson, 1989; Gibbon & Church, 1981; Gibbon, Church, & Meck, 1984; Hoehler & Leonard, 1976; Kehoe, Graham-Clarke, & Schreurs, 1989; Matzel, Held, & Miller, 1988). In other words, the brain of the animal undergoing classical conditioning does not form an excitatory or an inhibitory connection between the CS and the US representative; what it forms is a representation of the duration and sign of the temporal interval that separates CS onset and offset from the occurrence of the US. It also forms a representation of the temporal interval that separates one US from the next. What the animal does in consequence of what it has learned—the behavioral expression of the temporal intervals stored in memory—is determined by many different factors. One important factor is the ratio between the remembered CS–US interval and the remembered US–US interval. Another important factor is the sign of the remembered CS–US interval, whether positive (in which case the CS *pre*dicts the US) or negative (in which case the CS *retro*dicts the US).

Gibbon, Baldock, Locurto, Gold, and Terrace (1977) showed that the rate at which the pigeon develops an excitatory response to a CS that predicts food is determined not by the CS–US interval but by the ratio between the CS–US interval and the average US–US interval. Kaplan (1984) showed that when the CS–US interval is fixed, whether the pigeon develops an excitatory or an inhibitory response to the CS depends on the US–US interval. Both of these results show that it is not the CS–US interval per se that determines the response produced by conditioning, it is the ratio of the CS–US interval to the US–US interval. In other words, both show that learning these two intervals and computing arithmetic relations between them is what determines the conditioned response.

Matzel et al. (1988) first taught rats that clicking onset predicted tone onset with a lag of 5 seconds. Then, without giving any more training with clicking, they taught different groups of rats that the onset of footshock either followed the onset of the tone by 5 seconds (forward pairing group), or coincided with tone onset (simultaneous pairing group), or preceded tone onset by 5 seconds (backward pairing group). They then tested the rats for fearful reactions to the tone and the clicking, presented separately on different trials. The rats in the group given forward pairing of tone and shock, of course, reacted fearfully to the tone, but the rats in the other two groups (simultaneous and backward pairing of tone and shock) did not. This replicates the findings that have enshrined in textbooks the claim that associative conditioning depends on forward pairing. However, when Matzel et al. tested for the reaction to the clicking, they found that all three groups feared it equally strongly. The implication is that in the second phase of conditioning, all three groups (forward, simultaneous, and backward) learned the temporal relation between tone onset and shock onset, but only the group for which this interval was positive (that is, for whom tone onset *pre*dicted shock onset) responded fearfully to the tone.

In the Matzel et al. (1988) experiment, the learned relation between the shock and first-order CS (the tone) in the simultaneous and backwardly conditioned groups was not manifest in the conditioned response to the tone itself; it was manifest only in the conditioned response to the second-order CS (the clicking), which predicted the tone (and hence the shock). Findings like these are what lead Spear et al. (1990, see earlier) and most other students of classical conditioning to the conclusion that the "memories [formed during classical conditioning] . . . are subject to substantial variance in their expression." In different tests, the animal brings different behavioral strategies to bear in determining what response to make given the information in its memory about CS–US and US–US intervals. Hence, there is no simple relation between what the animal has learned and what it does.

Part of the attraction of the now outdated conditioned reflex conception was that it implied a simple relation between what was learned (the unobserved associations) and their behaviorally observable consequences (the conditioned response). There was no need to worry about decision processes that retrieved what had been learned from memory and determined what response to make. Associations determined what was done by virtue of their effect on the flow of signals from sensors to effectors, not by virtue of their role in decision processes. By contrast, memories that specify CS–US intervals and US–US intervals affect responding only when they are retrieved and used in decision processes.

In short, the findings of modern experiments on classical conditioning do not support the hypothesis that the memories formed during classical conditioning involve a change in synaptic connectivity (or in activation-conducting connections of any kind) based on the temporal pairing of CS and US activation. Rather, they support the hypothesis that the memories formed during classical conditioning specify the durations of the temporal intervals that separate CS's and US's. They also indicate that the brain can retrieve these duration values from memory and compute their sums, differences, and ratios in the course of deciding on the behavioral output (Church & Deluty, 1977; Gibbon & Church, 1990; Gibbon, Church, & Meck, 1984; Roberts & Church, 1978). Thus, the associative property of LTP does not serve to link it to the memories that form during classical conditioning. It is not clear that any form of commonly studied animal learning involves a change in connectivity based on the temporal pairing of stimuli; certainly spatial learning is difficult to conceptualize in these terms (see Gallistel, 1990, chaps. 3–6). The associative property of LTP is without readily apparent parallel in behaviorally identified memory formation processes.

Locality: Do They Both Occur in the Hippocampus?

Another property that memory formation and LTP are said to share is that both occur in the hippocampus. LTP in response to tetanic electrical stimulation of the perforant path clearly occurs in the hippocampus. It is much less clear that memories are stored in the hippocampus. The lesion data from animals and humans suggest, to me at least, that they are not. What the lesion data seem to show is that the hippocampus plays an important (but poorly understood) role in the data processing that culminates in memory storage and/or in the decision processes that retrieve stored memories and use them to determine behavior. But it is far from clear that the hippocampus is a site of memory storage. H.M.—the most famous human case in which the effects of hippocampectomy on memory have been experimentally studied—has both short-term (working) memories and long-term memories (Milner, Corkin, & Teuber, 1968). He remembers what you have just told him and he remembers what he learned prior to the hippocampectomy. His problem is that he cannot transfer what he has just been told from working memory to long-term memory. This implies that hippocampal circuitry is crucial to this transfer process. It does not imply that either short-term (working) or long-term memories are stored in the hippocampus. On the contrary, it implies that they are not.

In animals, lesions to the hippocampus do not abolish de novo classical conditioning (Berger & Orr, 1983; Solomon & Moore, 1975; see Schmajuk & Di Carlo, 1992, and Squire, 1992, for recent review). Nor do they destroy the memories produced by previous conditioning. For those memory-dependent tasks where these lesions do have an effect, the lesions produce anterograde amnesias not retrograde amnesias (Olton, Becker, & Handelmann, 1979), that is, they block the capacity to make new long-term memories; they do not wipe out memories already established. Even decerebration does not block classical conditioning of the eyeblink in the rabbit (Yeo, 1991) nor abolish a previously conditioned eyeblink response (Mauk & Thompson, 1987) A report from the laboratory of my colleague, Michael Fanselow (Kim & Fanselow, 1992), requires me to qualify this well-established generalization slightly. Kim and Fanselow found that hippocampal lesions did not interfere with the fear response to a tone that predicted shock during the prelesion training, but it did interfere with the fear response to the context (chamber) in which that conditioning had occurred, provided the conditioning had occurred no more than two weeks prior to the lesion. Note that this report supports the generalization that hippocampal lesions do not impair the memories produced by previous classical conditioning with a temporally discrete CS. Given this well-established finding, it is hard to know what to make of the impressive correlations reported by Laroche and his colleagues between the strength of LTP in the hippocampus and the strength of the conditioned response to a temporally discrete CS (e.g., Doyère & Laroche, 1992).

The puzzle about how to integrate the correlations demonstrated by Laroche and his collaborators with what we know from experiments on the effects of hippocampal lesions is made more acute when we bear in mind that lesions in the interpositus nucleus of the cerebellum do abolish previously learned conditioned responses (CRs) and permanently prevent future learning of simple CRs (Thompson, 1988), as would be expected of a lesion that destroyed the site where memories were stored. Lesions to the interpositus abolish classical conditioning, past and future, in animals with an intact hippocampus. Thus, an intact hippocampus is neither necessary nor sufficient for the expression of a previously learned conditioned response.

In short, the preponderance of the evidence is that the memories from previous conditioning are not stored in the hippocampus. Therefore, LTP and memory storage do not both occur in the hippocampus.

Pharmacology: Do They Have Similar Pharmacological Profiles?

N-Methyl-D-aspartate (NMDA) antagonists block LTP and they block some forms of learning. However, one drug does not a pharmacological profile make. As Staubli observes, "NMDA receptor antagonists are by no means the only drugs that block LTP; to the contrary, a very large array of drugs are reported to have this effect." The same may be said of memory (Gold, Chapter 2, this volume). The pharmacology of memory is a topic with a long and complex history. Many drugs, conspicuous among them the anticholinergic drugs (Deutsch, 1971; Deutsch & Falk, 1973; Fibiger, 1991), block learning (memory formation). In order to build a strong pharmacological case linking LTP to memory formation, we need data showing that over a broad spectrum of drugs, you can predict the (relative) dose required to block learning from the (relative) dose required to block LTP. In short, we need comparable pharmacological profiles for the behaviorally defined process and the cellular process.

I doubt that anyone is going to undertake to compare the pharmacological properties of LTP and memory formation any time soon, because such an effort must overcome methodological problems similar to those that deter research on how long memories last. In all the commonly studied learning tasks, memory formation is the final stage in a sequence of data-processing operations, most of which we do not understand at the psychological level, let alone at the pharmacological level of analysis. And, our behavioral tests of whether memories have formed or not invariably involve a sequence of poorly understood decision processes by which the memories are translated into an observable behavior. To do the behavioral pharmacology of storage, you must develop a behavioral assay that convincingly discriminates pharmacological blockade of the storage operation itself from pharmacological blockade of the data-processing operations that culminate in storage and from pharmacological blockade of the decision processes that make what has been stored manifest in behavior. Such an assay is not currently in sight (although, see Meck, 1983).

CONCLUSION

Clearly, it is not currently possible to make a strong case that LTP is the cellular change by which any behaviorally defined memory is stored. What this mostly proves is that behavioral neuroscience is difficult. Behavioral neuroscience attempts to identify the cellular level processes that mediate important processes, like memory formation, whose existence we infer from behavioral evidence. How hard is it to build compelling support for a linkage hypothesis that identifies a cellular process like LTP with a behaviorally defined process like memory? Well, Du Bois-Reymond discovered the action potential in the middle of the previous century (Du Bois-Reymond, 1852). He immediately conjectured that it was the physical realization of the nerve impulse, which was at that time a purely behavioral concept. (In fact, many scientists at that time thought that the nerve impulse was inherently nonphysical, that it was an elementary manifestation of the vital principle, the nonphysical essence of living things.) He spent the rest of his long life trying to prove this linkage hypothesis. He died near the end of the century. Forty years later, a leading figure in the physiology of nerve and muscle, in the introduction to one of the last major treatises on nerve excitation based purely on behavioral data (the twitch of the innervated muscle), stated that the physical identity of the nerve excitation process remained an unsolved problem (Hill, 1936).

That's how hard behavioral neuroscience is. On the other hand, we can take heart from the long history of attempts to establish the physical basis of nerve conduction because we did eventually establish it to everyone's satisfaction. We did it by a long, careful, and eventually compelling comparison of the properties of nerve excitation, as determined through its behavioral manifestations, and the electrophysiologically determined properties of the axonal membrane.

Thus, behavioral neuroscience is difficult but not impossible. To succeed, however, we must pay careful attention to both the behavioral data and the cellular data. Contemporary discussions of the cellular basis of learning, particularly those that focus on LTP, give the behavioral data short shrift. This will not do. Our linkage hypothesis cannot be stronger than the behavioral data on which it rests. The behavioral data form the buttress at one end of the bridge that links the behavioral phenomenon to its cellular substrate. A bridge is only as strong as its weakest buttress.

REFERENCES

Barbizet, J. (1970). *Human memory and its pathology.* San Francisco: Freeman.

Berger, T. W., & Orr, W. B. (1983). Hippocampectomy selectively disrupts discrimination reversal conditioning of the rabbit nictitating membrane response. *Behavioural Brain Research, 8,* 49–68.

Castro, C. A., Silbert, L. H., McNaughton, B. L., & Barnes, C. (1989). Recovery of spatial learning deficits following decay of electrically-induced synaptic enhancement in the hipoocampus. *Nature, 342,* 545–548.

Church, R. M. (1984). Properties of the internal clock. In J. Gibbon & L. Allan (Eds.), *Timing and time perception* (pp. 567–582). New York: New York Academy of Sciences.

Church, R. M. & Deluty, M. Z. (1977). Bisection of temporal intervals. *Journal of Experimental Psychology: Animal Behavior Processes, 3,* 216–228.

Davis, M., Schlesinger, L. S., & Sorenson, C. A. (1989). Temporal specificity of fear conditioning: Effects of different conditioned stimulus-unconditioned stimulus intervals on the fear-potentiated startle effect. *Journal of Experimental Psychology: Animal Behavior Processes, 15,* 295–310.

Deutsch, J. A. (1971). The cholinergic synapse and the site of memory. *Science, 174*, 788–794.

Deutsch, J. A., & Falk, J. L. (1973). Retrograde state-dependent learning. *Science, 180*, 878–880.

Doyère, V., & Laroche, S. (1992). Linear relationship between the maintenance of hippocampal long-term potentiation and the retention of an associative memory. *Hippocampus, 2*, 39–48.

Du Bois-Reymond, E. (1852). *Animal electricity.* London: Churchill.

Fibiger, H. C. (1991). Cholinergic mechanisms in learning, memory and dementia: A review of recent evidence. *Trends in Neurosciences, 14*(6), 220–223.

Gallistel, C. R. (1990). *The organization of learning.* Cambridge, MA: Bradford Books/MIT Press.

Gibbon, J., Baldock, M. D., Locurto, C. M., Gold, L., & Terrace, H. S. (1977). Trial and intertrial durations in autoshaping. *Journal of Experimental Psychology: Animal Behavior Processes, 3*, 264–284.

Gibbon, J., & Church, R. M. (1981). Time left: Linear versus logarithmic subjective time. *Journal of Experimental Psychology: Animal Behavior Processes, 7*(2), 87–107.

Gibbon, J., & Church, R. M. (1990). Representation of time. *Cognition, 37*(1 & 2), 23–54.

Gibbon, J., Church, R. M., & Meck, W. H. (1984). Scalar timing in memory. In J. Gibbon & L. Allan (Eds.), *Timing and time perception* (pp. 52–77). New York: New York Academy of Sciences.

Gleitman, H. (1971). Forgetting of long term memories in animals. In W. K. Honig & P. H. R. James (Eds.), *Animal memory* New York: Academic.

Hebb, D. O. (1949). *The organization of behavior: A neuropsychological theory.* New York: Wiley.

Hill, A. V. (1936). Excitation and accommodation in nerve. *Proceedings of the Royal Society of London. Series B, 119*, 305–355.

Hoehler, F. K., & Leonard, D. W. (1976). Double responding in classical nictitating membrane conditioning with single-CS, dual ISI pairing. *Pavlovian Journal of Biological Science, 11*, 180–190.

Kaplan, P. (1984). Importance of relative temporal parameters in trace autoshaping: From excitation to inhibition. *Journal of Experimental Psychology: Animal Behavior Processes, 10*, 113–126.

Kehoe, E. J., Graham-Clarke, P., & Schreurs, B. G. (1989). Temporal patterns of the rabbit's nictitating membrane response to compound and component stimuli under mixed CS–US intervals. *Behavioral Neuroscience, 103*, 283–295.

Kim, J., & Fanselow, M. (1992). Modality specific retrograde amnesia of fear. *Science, 256*, 675–677.

Kimble, G. A. (1961). *Hilgard and Marquis' conditioning and learning.* New York: Appleton-Century-Crofts.

Kritchevsky, M., Squire, L. R., & Zouzounis, J. A. (1988). Transient global amnesia: Characterization of anterograde and retrograde amnesia. *Neurology, 38*, 213–219.

Laroche, S., Doyère, V., & Rédini-Del Négro, C. (1991). What role for long-term potentiation in learning and the maintenance of memories? In M. Baudry & J. L. Davis (Eds.), *Long-term potentiation: A debate of current issues* (pp. 301–316). Cambridge, MA: MIT Press.

Matzel, L. D., Held, F. P., & Miller, R. R. (1988). Information and expression of simultaneous and backward associations: Implications for contiguity theory. *Learning and Motivation, 19*, 317–344.

Mauk, M. D., & Thompson, R. F. (1987). Retention of classically conditioned eyelid responses following acute decerebration. *Brain Research, 403*, 89–95.

Meck, W. H. (1983). Selective adjustment of the speed of internal clock and memory processes. *Journal of Experimental Psychology: Animal Behavior Processes, 9*, 171–201.

Milner, B., Corkin, S., & Teuber, H. (1968). Further analysis of the hippocampal amnesic syndrome: 14-year follow-up. *Neuropsychologia, 6*, 215–234.

Olton, D. S., Becker, J. T., & Handelmann, G. E. (1979). Hippocampus, space, and memory. *Behavioral and Brain Sciences, 2*, 313–365.

Rescorla, R. A. (1988). Pavlovian conditioning: It's not what you think it is. *American Psychologist, 43*, 151–160.

Roberts, S., & Church, R. M. (1978). Control of an internal clock. *Journal of Experimental Psychology: Animal Behavior Processes, 4,* 318–337.

Roman, F., Staubli, U., & Lynch, G. (1987). Evidence of synaptic potentiation in a cortical network during learning. *Brain Research, 418,* 221–226.

Russell, W. R. (1959). *Brain, memory, learning: A neurologist's view.* Oxford: Oxford University Press.

Schmajuk, N. A., & DiCarlo, J. J. (1992). Stimulus configuration, classical conditioning, and hippocampal function. *Psychological Review, 99,* 268–305.

Solomon, P. R., & Moore, J. W. (1975). Latent inhibition and stimulus generalization of the classically conditioned nictitating membrane response in rabbits (*Oryctolagus cuniculus*) following dorsal hippocampal ablation. *Journal of Comparative and Physiological Psychology, 89,* 1192–1203.

Spear, N. E., Miller, J. S., & Jagielo, J. A. (1990). Animal memory and learning. *Annual Review of Psychology, 41,* 169–212.

Squire, L. R. (1992). Memory and the hippocampus: A synthesis from findings with rats, monkeys, and humans. *Psychological Review, 99,* 195–231.

Thompson, R. F. (1988). The neural basis of basic associative learning of discrete behavioral responses. *Trends in Neurosciences, 11*(4), 152–155.

Underwood, B. J. (1957). Interference and forgetting. *Psychological Review, 64,* 49–60.

Whitty, C. W. M., & Zangwill, O. L. (1977). *Amnesia* (2nd ed.). New York: Appleton-Century-Crofts.

Yeo, C. H. (1991). Cerebellum and classical conditioning of motor responses. *Annals of the New York Academy of Sciences, 627,* 292–304.

Index

BRAIN AND MEMORY